The Adventist Home

Ellen G. White

1952

Foreword

The Adventist home is a home where Seventh-day Adventist standards and practices are lived and taught, a place to which Seventh-day Adventist fathers and mothers are commissioned by Christ to go and make Christians of the members of their own households. And in order to perform that task well, Seventh-day Adventist parents are looking for all the help they can possibly find.

Ellen G. White has written much and very valuable counsel for parents. She has touched upon every phase of the home, and offers specific instruction on many of the problems which give so much concern to thoughtful and often anxious parents today. Some years before her death, she indicated her desire to get out "a book for Christian parents" that would define "the mother's duty and influence over her children." In the present work an endeavor has been made to fulfill this expectation.

This book, *The Adventist Home,* is at once a sort of handbook or manual for busy parents, and a pattern or ideal of what the home can and should become. Here are the answers to your many questions, the words of wisdom from the heavenly Father.

In compiling this work, excerpts have been drawn from the Ellen G. White writings penned through seven decades, but especially from the thousands of E. G. White articles which were prepared for the journals of the denomination. The current published works, special testimonies issued in pamphlet form, and the E. G. White manuscript files have also enriched the Volume. Appropriate source credits are given in connection with each chapter. As the excerpts [6] drawn from different sources written at different times are linked together in their logical sequence, there may be occasionally a slight unavoidable break in thought or manner of address, for the compilers are limited in their work to selecting and arranging the subject matter and supplying the headings.

This document has been prepared in the office of the Ellen G. White Publications. The work has been done in harmony with Mrs.

White's instruction to her trustees in providing "for the printing of compilations" from her manuscripts, for they contain, she said, "instruction that the Lord has given me for his people."

Never in the history of the world has a book like this been needed more urgently than it is right now. Never have parents and children been more anxious for the right answer to the things which trouble them. Never have homes been in such jeopardy as they are today.

Every one of us knows that conditions in society are but a reflection of conditions in the homes of the nation. We likewise know that a change in the home will be mirrored in a changed society. To this end this Volume—*The Adventist Home*—has been prepared and, as a part of the Christian home library, is now sent forth on its important mission by the publishers and

The Trustees of the

Ellen G. White Publications

Washington, D.C.,

May 8, 1952.

[7]

Contents

Section 1—The Home Beautiful

Chapter 1—Atmosphere of the Home

Home Is the Heart of All Activity—Society is composed of families, and is what the heads of families make it. Out of the heart are "the issues of life"; and the heart of the community, of the church, and of the nation is the household. The well-being of society, the success of the church, the prosperity of the nation, depend upon home influences.[1]

The elevation or deterioration of the future of society will be determined by the manners and morals of the youth growing up around us. As the youth are educated, and as their characters are molded in their childhood to virtuous habits, self-control, and temperance, so will their influence be upon society. If they are left unenlightened and uncontrolled, and as the result become self-willed, intemperate in appetite and passion, so will be their future influence in molding society. The company which the young now keep, the habits they now form, and the principles they now adopt are the index to the state of society for years to come.[2]

The Sweetest Type of Heaven—Home should be made all that the word implies. It should be a little heaven upon earth, a place where the affections are cultivated instead of being studiously repressed. Our happiness depends upon this cultivation of love, sympathy, and true courtesy to one another.[3]

The sweetest type of heaven is a home where the Spirit of the Lord presides. If the will of God is fulfilled, the husband and wife [16] will respect each other and cultivate love and confidence.[4]

Importance of the Home Atmosphere—The atmosphere surrounding the souls of fathers and mothers fills the whole house, and is felt in every department of the home.[5]

To a large extent parents create the atmosphere of the home circle, and when there is disagreement between father and mother, the children partake of the same spirit. Make your home atmosphere fragrant with tender thoughtfulness. If you have become estranged and have failed to be Bible Christians, be converted; for the character you bear in probationary time will be the character you will have at the coming of Christ. If you would be a saint in heaven, you must first be a saint on earth. The traits of character you cherish in life will not be changed by death or by the resurrection. You will come up from the grave with the same disposition you manifested in your home and in society. Jesus does not change the character at His coming. The work of transformation must be done now. Our daily lives are determining our destiny.[6]

Creating a Pure Atmosphere—Every Christian home should have rules; and parents should, in their words and deportment toward each other, give to the children a precious, living example of what they desire them to be. Purity in speech and true Christian courtesy should be constantly practiced. Teach the children and youth to respect themselves, to be true to God, true to principle; teach them to respect and obey the law of God. These principles will control their lives and will be carried out in their associations with others. They will create a pure atmosphere—one that will have an influence that will encourage weak souls in the upward path that leads to holiness and heaven. Let every lesson be of an elevating and ennobling character, and the records made in the books of heaven will be such as you will not be ashamed to meet in the judgment.

[17]

Children who receive this kind of instruction will ... be prepared to fill places of responsibility and, by precept and example, will be constantly aiding others to do right. Those whose moral sensibilities have not been blunted will appreciate right principles; they will put a just estimate upon their natural endowments and will make the best use of their physical, mental, and moral powers. Such souls are strongly fortified against temptation; they are surrounded by a wall not easily broken down.[7]

God would have our families symbols of the family in heaven. Let parents and children bear this in mind every day, relating themselves to one another as members of the family of God. Then their lives will be of such a character as to give to the world an object lesson of what families who love God and keep His commandments may be. Christ will be glorified; His peace and grace and love will pervade the family circle like a precious perfume.[8]

Much depends on the father and mother. They are to be firm and kind in their discipline, and they are to work most earnestly to have an orderly, correct household, that the heavenly angels may be attracted to it to impart peace and a fragrant influence.[9]

Make Home Bright and Happy—Never forget that you are to make the home bright and happy for yourselves and your children by cherishing the Saviour's attributes. If you bring Christ into the home, you will know good from evil. You will be able to help your children to be trees of righteousness, bearing the fruit of the Spirit.[10]

[18]

Troubles may invade, but these are the lot of humanity. Let patience, gratitude, and love keep sunshine in the heart though the day may be ever so cloudy.[11]

The home may be plain, but it can always be a place where cheerful words are spoken and kindly deeds are done, where courtesy and love are abiding guests.[12]

Administer the rules of the home in wisdom and love, not with a rod of iron. Children will respond with willing obedience to the rule of love. Commend your children whenever you can. Make their lives as happy as possible.... Keep the soil of the heart mellow by the manifestation of love and affection, thus preparing it for the seed of truth. Remember that the Lord gives the earth not only clouds and rain, but the beautiful, smiling sunshine, causing the seed to germinate and the blossom to appear. Remember that children need not only reproof and correction, but encouragement and commendation, the pleasant sunshine of kind words.[13]

You must not have strife in your household. "But the wisdom that is from above is first pure, then peaceable, gentle, and easy to be intreated, full of mercy and good fruits, without partiality, and without hypocrisy. And the fruit of righteousness is sown in peace of them that make peace." It is gentleness and peace that we want in our homes.[14]

Tender Ties That Bind—The family tie is the closest, the most tender and sacred, of any on earth. It was designed to be a blessing to mankind. And it is a blessing wherever the marriage covenant is entered into intelligently, in the fear of God, and with due consideration for its responsibilities.[15]

[19]

Every home should be a place of love, a place where the angels of God abide, working with softening, subduing influence upon the hearts of parents and children.[16]

Our homes must be made a Bethel, our hearts a shrine. Wherever the love of God is cherished in the soul, there will be peace, there will be light and joy. Spread out the word of God before your families in love, and ask, "What hath God spoken?"[17]

Christ's Presence Makes a Home Christian—The home that is beautified by love, sympathy, and tenderness is a place that angels love to visit, and where God is glorified. The influence of a carefully guarded Christian home in the years of childhood and youth is the surest safeguard against the corruptions of the world. In the atmosphere of such a home the children will learn to love both their earthly parents and their heavenly Father.[18]

From their infancy the youth need to have a firm barrier built up between them and the world, that its corrupting influence may not affect them.[19]

Every Christian family should illustrate to the world the power and excellence of Christian influence.... Parents should realize their accountability to keep their homes free from every taint of moral evil.[20]

Holiness to God is to pervade the home.... Parents and children are to educate themselves to co-operate with God. They are to bring their habits and practices into harmony with God's plans.[21]

The family relationship should be sanctifying in its influence. Christian homes, established and conducted in accordance with God's plan, are a wonderful help in forming Christian character.... Parents and children should unite in offering loving service to Him who alone can keep human love pure and noble.[22] [20]

The first work to be done in a Christian home is to see that the Spirit of Christ abides there, that every member of the household may be able to take his cross and follow where Jesus leads the way.[23] [21]

---

[1] The Ministry of Healing, 349.

[2] Pacific Health Journal, June, 1890.

[3] Testimonies for the Church, Volume 3:539.

[4] The Signs of the Times, June 20, 1911.

[5] Manuscript 49, 1896.

[6] Letter 18b, 1891.

[7] Special Selections from the Testimonies for Students and Workers of our Sanitariums (1911) 4, 5.

[8] The Review and Herald, November 17, 1896.

[9]Manuscript 14, 1905.

[10]Letter 29, 1902.

[11]The Ministry of Healing, 393.

[12]The Review and Herald, July 9, 1901.

[13]Counsels to Teachers, Parents, and Students, 114.

[14]Manuscript 9, 1903.

[15]The Ministry of Healing, 356, 357.

[16]Letter 25, 1904.

[17]Letter 24a, 1896.

[18]Manuscript 126, 1903.

[19]Counsels to Teachers, Parents, and Students, 119.

[20]The Review and Herald, October 9, 1900.

[21]Letter 9, 1904.

[22]Manuscript 16, 1899.

[23]Manuscript 17, 1891.

Chapter 2—Fundamentals of True Homemaking

The Most Attractive Place in the World—While there are weighty responsibilities devolving upon the parents to guard carefully the future happiness and interests of their children, it is also their duty to make home as attractive as possible. This is of far greater consequence than to acquire estates and money. Home must not lack sunshine. The home feeling should be kept alive in the hearts of the children, that they may look back upon the home of their childhood as a place of peace and happiness next to heaven. Then as they come to maturity, they should in their turn try to be a comfort and blessing to their parents.[1]

The home should be to the children the most attractive place in the world, and the mother's presence should be its greatest attraction. Children have sensitive, loving natures. They are easily pleased, and easily made unhappy. By gentle discipline, in loving words and acts, mothers may bind their children to their hearts.[2]

Clean, Neat, Orderly—Cleanliness, neatness, and order are indispensable to the proper management of the household. But when the mother makes these the all-important duties of her life, and devotes herself to them, to the neglect of the physical development and the mental and moral training of her children, she makes a sad mistake.[3]

Believers should be taught that even though they may be poor, they need not be unclean or untidy in their persons or in their homes. [22] Help must be given in this line to those who seem to have no sense of the meaning and importance of cleanliness. They are to be taught that those who are to represent the high and holy God must keep their souls pure and clean, and that this purity must extend to their dress and to everything in the home, so that the ministering angels will have evidence that the truth has wrought a change in the life, purifying the soul and refining the tastes. Those who, after receiving the truth, make no change in word or deportment, in dress or

13

surroundings, are living to themselves, not to Christ. They have not been created anew in Christ Jesus, unto purification and holiness....

While we are to guard against needless adornment and display, we are in no case to be careless and indifferent in regard to outward appearance. All about our persons and our homes is to be neat and attractive. The youth are to be taught the importance of presenting an appearance above criticism, an appearance that honors God and the truth.[4]

A neglect of cleanliness will induce disease. Sickness does not come without a cause. Violent epidemics of fevers have occurred in villages and cities that were considered perfectly healthful, and these have resulted in death or broken constitutions. In many instances the premises of the very ones who fell victims to these epidemics contained the agents of destruction which sent forth deadly poison into the atmosphere, to be inhaled by the family and the neighborhood. It is astonishing to witness the prevailing ignorance relative to the effects which slackness and recklessness produce upon health.[5]

[23]

Order Necessary for a Happy Home—God is displeased with disorder, slackness, and a lack of thoroughness in anyone. These deficiencies are serious evils, and tend to wean the affections of the husband from the wife when the husband loves order, well-disciplined children, and a well-regulated house. A wife and mother cannot make home agreeable and happy unless she possesses a love for order, preserves her dignity, and has good government; therefore all who fail on these points should begin at once to educate themselves in this direction, and cultivate the very things wherein is their greatest lack.[6]

Vigilance and Diligence to Be Blended—When we give ourselves unreservedly to the Lord, the simple, commonplace duties of home life will be seen in their true importance, and we shall perform them in accordance with the will of God. We are to be vigilant, watching for the coming of the Son of man; and we must also be diligent; working as well as waiting is required; there must be a union of the two. This will balance the Christian character, making it well developed, symmetrical. We should not feel that we are to neglect everything else, and give ourselves up to meditation, study, or prayer; neither are we to be full of bustle and hurry and work, to the neglect of personal piety. Waiting and watching and working are to be blended. "Not slothful in business; fervent in spirit; serving the Lord."[7]

Provide Laborsaving Facilities—In many a home the wife and mother has no time to read, to keep herself well informed, no time to be a companion to her husband, no time to keep in touch with the developing minds of her children. There is no time or place for the precious Saviour to be a close, dear companion. Little by little she sinks into a mere household drudge, her strength and time and interest absorbed in the things that perish with the using. Too late she awakes to find herself almost a stranger in her own home. The precious opportunities once hers to influence her dear ones for the higher life, unimproved, have passed away forever. [24]

Let the homemakers resolve to live on a wiser plan. Let it be your first aim to make a pleasant home. Be sure to provide the facilities that will lighten labor and promote health.[8]

Even the Humblest Tasks Are the Work of God—All the work we do that is necessary to be done, be it washing dishes, setting tables, waiting upon the sick, cooking, or washing, is of moral importance.... The humble tasks before us are to be taken up by someone; and those who do them should feel that they are doing a necessary and honorable work, and that in their mission, humble though it may be, they are doing the work of God just as surely as was Gabriel when sent to the prophets. All are working in their order in their respective spheres. Woman in her home, doing the simple duties of life that must be done, can and should exhibit faithfulness, obedience, and love, as sincere as angels in their sphere. Conformity to the will of God makes any work honorable that must be done.[9] [25]

---

[1] The Review and Herald, February 2, 1886.

[2] The Ministry of Healing, 388.

[3] The Signs of the Times, August 5, 1875.

[4] The Review and Herald, June 10, 1902.

[5] Christian Temperance and Bible Hygiene, 105, 106.

[6] Testimonies For The Church 2:298, 299.

[7] The Review and Herald, September 15, 1891.

[8] The Ministry of Healing, 368, 369.

[9] Testimonies For The Church 3:79, 80.

Chapter 3—The Eden Home a Pattern

God Prepared Man's First Home—The Eden home of our first parents was prepared for them by God Himself. When He had furnished it with everything that man could desire, He said: "Let Us make man in Our image, after Our likeness." ...

The Lord was pleased with this last and noblest of all His creatures, and designed that he should be the perfect inhabitant of a perfect world. But it was not His purpose that man should live in solitude. He said: "It is not good that the man should be alone; I will make him an help meet for him."[1]

God Himself gave Adam a companion. He provided "an help meet for him"—a helper corresponding to him—one who was fitted to be his companion, and who could be one with him in love and sympathy. Eve was created from a rib taken from the side of Adam, signifying that she was not to control him as the head, nor to be trampled under his feet as an inferior, but to stand by his side as an equal, to be loved and protected by him. A part of man, bone of his bone, and flesh of his flesh, she was his second self; showing the close union and the affectionate attachment that should exist in this relation. "For no man ever yet hated his own flesh; but nourisheth and cherisheth it." "Therefore shall a man leave his father and his mother, and shall cleave unto his wife: and they shall be one."[2]

First Marriage Performed by God—God celebrated the first [26] marriage. Thus the institution has for its originator the Creator of the universe. "Marriage is honourable"; it was one of the first gifts of God to man, and it is one of the two institutions that, after the fall, Adam brought with him beyond the gates of Paradise. When the divine principles are recognized and obeyed in this relation, marriage is a blessing; it guards the purity and happiness of the race, it provides for man's social needs, it elevates the physical, the intellectual, and the moral nature.[3]

He who gave Eve to Adam as a helpmeet performed His first miracle at a marriage festival. In the festal hall where friends and

16

kindred rejoiced together, Christ began His public ministry. Thus He sanctioned marriage, recognizing it as an institution that He Himself had established....

Christ honored the marriage relation by making it also a symbol of the union between Him and His redeemed ones. He Himself is the Bridegroom; the bride is the church, of which, as His chosen one, He says, "Thou art all fair, My love; there is no spot in thee."[4]

Every Want Was Supplied—Adam was surrounded with everything his heart could wish. Every want was supplied. There were no sin and no signs of decay in glorious Eden. Angels of God conversed freely and lovingly with the holy pair. The happy songsters caroled forth their free, joyous songs of praise to their Creator. The peaceful beasts in happy innocence played about Adam and Eve, obedient to their word. Adam was in the perfection of manhood, the noblest of the Creator's work.[5]

Not a shadow interposed between them and their Creator. They knew God as their beneficent Father, and in all things their will was conformed to the will of God. And God's character was reflected in the character of Adam. His glory was revealed in every object of nature.[6]

[27]

Labor Was Appointed for Man's Happiness—God is a lover of the beautiful. He has given us unmistakable evidence of this in the work of His hands. He planted for our first parents a beautiful garden in Eden. Stately trees were caused to grow out of the ground, of every description, for usefulness and ornament. The beautiful flowers were formed, of rare loveliness, of every tint and hue, perfuming the air.... It was the design of God that man should find happiness in the employment of tending the things He had created, and that his wants should be met with the fruits of the trees of the garden[7]

To Adam was given the work of caring for the garden. The Creator knew that Adam could not be happy without employment. The beauty of the garden delighted him, but this was not enough. He must have labor to call into exercise the wonderful organs of the body. Had happiness consisted in doing nothing, man, in his state of holy innocence, would have been left unemployed. But He who created man knew what would be for his happiness; and no sooner had He created him than He gave him his appointed work.

The promise of future glory, and the decree that man must toil for his daily bread, came from the same throne.[8]

God Is Honored by a Christian Home—Fathers and mothers who make God first in their households, who teach their children that the fear of the Lord is the beginning of wisdom, glorify God before angels and before men by presenting to the world a well-ordered, well-disciplined family—a family that love and obey God instead of rebelling against Him. Christ is not a stranger in their homes; His name is a household name, revered and glorified. Angels delight in a home where God reigns supreme and the children are taught to reverence religion, the Bible, and their Creator. Such families can claim the promise, "Them that honour Me I will honour." As from such a home the father goes forth to his daily duties, it is with a spirit softened and subdued by converse with God.[9]

The presence of Christ alone can make men and women happy. All the common waters of life Christ can turn into the wine of heaven. The home then becomes as an Eden of bliss; the family, a beautiful symbol of the family in heaven.[10]

[28]

[29]

[30]

[1]The Youth's Instructor, August 10, 1899.
[2]Patriarchs and Prophets, 46.
[3]Ibid., 46.
[4]The Ministry of Healing, 356.
[5]The Signs of the Times, June 11, 1874.
[6]The Youth's Instructor, June 2, 1898.
[7]The Health Reformer, July, 1871.
[8]The Youth's Instructor, February 27, 1902.
[9]Testimonies For The Church 5:424.
[10]Manuscript 43, 1900.

Section 2—A Light in the Community

Chapter 4—Far-Reaching Influence of the Home

The Christian Home Is an Object Lesson—The mission of the home extends beyond its own members. The Christian home is to be an object lesson, illustrating the excellence of the true principles of life. Such an illustration will be a power for good in the world.... As the youth go out from such a home, the lessons they have learned are imparted. Nobler principles of life are introduced into other households, and an uplifting influence works in the community.[1]

The home in which the members are polite, courteous Christians exerts a far-reaching influence for good. Other families will mark the results attained by such a home, and will follow the example set, in their turn guarding the home against Satanic influences. The angels of God will often visit the home in which the will of God bears sway. Under the power of divine grace such a home becomes a place of refreshing to worn, weary pilgrims. By watchful guarding, self is kept from asserting itself. Correct habits are formed. There is a careful recognition of the rights of others. The faith that works by love and purifies the soul stands at the helm, presiding over the whole household. Under the hallowed influence of such a home, the principle of brotherhood laid down in the word of God is more widely recognized and obeyed.[2]

Influence of a Well-ordered Family—It is no small matter for a family to stand as representatives of Jesus, keeping God's law in an
[32] unbelieving community. We are required to be living epistles known and read of all men. This position involves fearful responsibilities.[3]

One well-ordered, well-disciplined family tells more in behalf of Christianity than all the sermons that can be preached. Such a family gives evidence that the parents have been successful in following God's directions, and that their children will serve Him in the church. Their influence grows; for as they impart, they receive to impart again. The father and mother find helpers in their children, who give to others the instruction received in the home. The neighborhood in which they live is helped, for in it they have become enriched for

20

time and for eternity. The whole family is engaged in the service of the Master; and by their godly example, others are inspired to be faithful and true to God in dealing with His flock, His beautiful flock.[4]

The greatest evidence of the power of Christianity that can be presented to the world is a well-ordered, well-disciplined family. This will recommend the truth as nothing else can, for it is a living witness of its practical power upon the heart.[5]

The best test of the Christianity of a home is the type of character begotten by its influence. Actions speak louder than the most positive profession of godliness.[6]

Our business in this world ... is to see what virtues we can teach our children and our families to possess, that they shall have an influence upon other families, and thus we can be an educating power although we never enter into the desk. A well-ordered, a well-disciplined family in the sight of God is more precious than fine gold, even than the golden wedge of Ophir.[7]

Wonderful Possibilities Are Ours—Our time here is short. We can pass through this world but once; as we pass along, let us make [33] the most of life. The work to which we are called does not require wealth or social position or great ability. It requires a kindly, self-sacrificing spirit and a steadfast purpose. A lamp, however small, if kept steadily burning, may be the means of lighting many other lamps. Our sphere of influence may seem narrow, our ability small, our opportunities few, our acquirements limited; yet wonderful possibilities are ours through a faithful use of the opportunities of our own homes. If we will open our hearts and homes to the divine principles of life, we shall become channels for currents of life-giving power. From our homes will flow streams of healing, bringing life, and beauty, and fruitfulness where now are barrenness and dearth.[8]

God-fearing parents will diffuse an influence from their own home circle to that of others that will act as did the leaven that was hid in three measures of meal.[9]

Faithful work done in the home educates others to do the same class of work. The spirit of fidelity to God is like leaven and, when manifested in the church, will have an effect upon others, and will be a recommendation to Christianity everywhere. The work of whole-souled soldiers of Christ is as far-reaching as eternity. Then why is it that there is such a lack of the missionary spirit in our churches? It is because there is a neglect of home piety.[10]

Influence of an Ill-regulated Family—The influence of an ill-regulated family is widespread, and disastrous to all society. It accumulates in a tide of evil that affects families, communities, and governments.[11]

[34] It is impossible for any of us to live in such a way that we shall not cast an influence in the world. No member of the family can enclose himself within himself, where other members of the family shall not feel his influence and spirit. The very expression of the countenance has an influence for good or evil. His spirit, his words, his actions, his attitude toward others, are unmistakable. If he is living in selfishness, he surrounds his soul with a malarious atmosphere; while if he is filled with the love of Christ, he will manifest courtesy, kindness, tender regard for the feelings of others and will communicate to his associates, by his acts of love, a tender, grateful, happy feeling. It will be made manifest that he is living for Jesus and daily learning lessons at His feet, receiving His light and His peace. He will be able to say to the Lord, "Thy gentleness hath [35] made me great."[12]

[1]The Ministry of Healing, 352.

[2]Letter 272, 1903.

[3]Testimonies For The Church 4:106.

[4]The Review and Herald, June 6, 1899.

[5]Testimonies For The Church 4:304.

[6]Patriarchs and Prophets, 579.

[7]Manuscript 12, 1895.

[8]The Ministry of Healing, 355.

[9]The Signs of the Times, September 17, 1894.

[10]The Review and Herald, February 19, 1895.

[11]Patriarchs and Prophets, 579.

[12]The Youth's Instructor, June 22, 1893.

Chapter 5—A Powerful Christian Witness

Best Missionaries Come From Christian Homes—Missionaries for the Master are best prepared for work abroad in the Christian household, where God is feared, where God is loved, where God is worshiped, where faithfulness has become second nature, where haphazard, careless inattention to home duties is not permitted, where quiet communion with God is looked upon as essential to the faithful performance of daily duties.[1]

Home duties should be performed with the consciousness that if they are done in the right spirit, they give an experience that will enable us to work for Christ in the most permanent and thorough manner. Oh, what might not a living Christian do in missionary lines by performing faithfully the daily duties, cheerfully lifting the cross, not neglecting any work, however disagreeable to the natural feelings![2]

Our work for Christ is to begin with the family, in the home.... There is no missionary field more important than this....

By many this home field has been shamefully neglected, and it is time that divine resources and remedies were presented, that this state of evil may be corrected.[3]

The highest duty that devolves upon youth is in their own homes, blessing father and mother, brothers and sisters, by affection and true interest. Here they can show self-denial and self-forgetfulness in caring and doing for others.... What an influence a sister may have over brothers! If she is right, she may determine the character of her brothers. Her prayers, her gentleness, and her affection may do much in a household.[3]

[36]

In the home those who have received Christ are to show what grace has done for them. "As many as received Him, to them gave He power to become the sons of God, even to them that believe on His name." A conscious authority pervades the true believer in Christ, that makes its influence felt throughout the home. This is favorable for the perfection of the characters of all in the home.[5]

An Argument That the Infidel Cannot Gainsay—A well-ordered Christian household is a powerful argument in favor of the reality of the Christian religion—an argument that the infidel cannot gainsay. All can see that there is an influence at work in the family that affects the children, and that the God of Abraham is with them. If the homes of professed Christians had a right religious mold, they would exert a mighty influence for good. They would indeed be the "light of the world."[6]

Children to Extend Knowledge of Bible Principles—Children who have been properly educated, who love to be useful, to help father and mother, will extend a knowledge of correct ideas and Bible principles to all with whom they associate.[7]

When our own homes are what they should be, our children will not be allowed to grow up in idleness and indifference to the claims of God in behalf of the needy all about them. As the Lord's heritage, they will be qualified to take up the work where they are. A light will shine from such homes which will reveal itself in behalf of the ignorant, leading them to the source of all knowledge. An influence will be exerted that will be a power for God and for His truth.[8]

[37] Parents who can be approached in no other way are frequently reached through their children.[9]

Cheerful Homes Will Be a Light to Neighbors—We need more sunshiny parents and more sunshiny Christians. We are too much shut up within ourselves. Too often the kindly, encouraging word, the cheery smile, are withheld from our children and from the oppressed and discouraged.

Parents, upon you rests the responsibility of being light-bearers and light-givers. Shine as lights in the home, brightening the path that your children must travel. As you do this, your light will shine to those without.[10]

From every Christian home a holy light should shine forth. Love should be revealed in action. It should flow out in all home intercourse, showing itself in thoughtful kindness, in gentle, unselfish courtesy. There are homes where this principle is carried out— homes where God is worshiped and truest love reigns. From these homes morning and evening prayer ascends to God as sweet incense, and His mercies and blessings descend upon the suppliants like the morning dew.[11]

Results of Family Unity—The first work of Christians is to be united in the family. Then the work is to extend to their neighbors nigh and afar off. Those who have received light are to let the light shine forth in clear rays. Their words, fragrant with the love of Christ, are to be a savor of life unto life.[12]

The more closely the members of a family are united in their work in the home, the more uplifting and helpful will be the influence that father and mother and sons and daughters will exert outside the home.[13]

Good Men Needed More Than Great Minds—The happiness of families and churches depends upon home influences. Eternal [38] interests depend upon the proper discharge of the duties of this life. The world is not so much in need of great minds as of good men who will be a blessing in their homes.[14]

Avoid Mistakes That May Close Doors—When religion is manifested in the home, its influence will be felt in the church and in the neighborhood. But some who profess to be Christians talk with their neighbors concerning their home difficulties. They relate their grievances in such a way as to call forth sympathy for themselves; but it is a great mistake to pour our trouble into the ears of others, especially when many of our grievances are manufactured and exist because of our irreligious life and defective character. Those who go forth to lay their private grievances before others might better remain at home to pray, to surrender their perverse will to God, to fall on the Rock and be broken, to die to self that Jesus may make them vessels unto honor.[15]

A lack of courtesy, a moment of petulance, a single rough, thoughtless word, will mar your reputation, and may close the door to hearts so that you can never reach them.[16]

Christianity in the Home Shines Abroad—The effort to make the home what it should be—a symbol of the home in heaven— prepares us for work in a larger sphere. The education received by showing a tender regard for each other enables us to know how to reach hearts that need to be taught the principles of true religion. The church needs all the cultivated spiritual force which can be obtained, that all, and especially the younger members of the Lord's family, may be carefully guarded. The truth lived at home makes itself felt in disinterested labor abroad. He who lives Christianity in the home [39]

[40]   will be a bright and shining light everywhere.[17]

[41]

[42]

[1]Manuscript 140, 1897.

[2]The Signs of the Times, September 1, 1898.

[3]Testimonies For The Church 6: 429, 430.

[3]Testimonies For The Church 3:80, 81.

[5]Manuscript 140, 1897.

[6]Patriarchs and Prophets, 144.

[7]Letter 28, 1890.

[8]Testimonies For The Church 6:430.

[9]Ibid., 4:70.

[10]The Review and Herald, January 29, 1901.

[11]Patriarchs and Prophets, 144.

[12]Manuscript 11, 1901.

[13]Letter 189, 1903.

[14]Testimonies For The Church 4, 522.

[15]The Signs of the Times, November 14, 1892.

[16]Testimonies For The Church 5, 335.1.

[17]The Signs of the Times, September 1, 1898.

Section 3—Choosing the Life Partner

Chapter 6—The Great Decision

A Happy or Unhappy Marriage?—If those who are contemplating marriage would not have miserable, unhappy reflections after marriage, they must make it a subject of serious, earnest reflection now. This step taken unwisely is one of the most effective means of ruining the usefulness of young men and women. Life becomes a burden, a curse. No one can so effectually ruin a woman's happiness and usefulness, and make life a heartsickening burden, as her own husband; and no one can do one hundredth part as much to chill the hopes and aspirations of a man, to paralyze his energies and ruin his influence and prospects, as his own wife. It is from the marriage hour that many men and women date their success or failure in this life, and their hopes of the future life.[1]

I wish I could make the youth see and feel their danger, especially the danger of making unhappy marriages.[2]

Marriage is something that will influence and affect your life both in this world and in the world to come. A sincere Christian will not advance his plans in this direction without the knowledge that God approves his course. He will not want to choose for himself, but will feel that God must choose for him. We are not to please ourselves, for Christ pleased not Himself. I would not be understood to mean that anyone is to marry one whom he does not love. This would be sin. But fancy and the emotional nature must not be allowed to lead

on to ruin. God requires the whole heart, the supreme affections.[3]

Make Haste Slowly—Few have correct views of the marriage relation. Many seem to think that it is the attainment of perfect bliss; but if they could know one quarter of the heartaches of men and women that are bound by the marriage vow in chains that they cannot and dare not break, they would not be surprised that I trace these lines. Marriage, in a majority of cases, is a most galling yoke. There are thousands that are mated but not matched. The books of heaven are burdened with the woes, the wickedness, and the abuse that lie hidden under the marriage mantle. This is why I would warn the young who are of a marriageable age to make haste slowly in the choice of a companion. The path of married life may appear beautiful and full of happiness; but why may not you be disappointed as thousands of others have been?[4]

Those who are contemplating marriage should consider what will be the character and influence of the home they are founding. As they become parents, a sacred trust is committed to them. Upon them depends in a great measure the well-being of their children in this world, and their happiness in the world to come. To a great extent they determine both the physical and the moral stamp that the little ones receive. And upon the character of the home depends the condition of society; the weight of each family's influence will tell in the upward or the downward scale.[5]

Vital Factors in the Choice—Great care should be taken by Christian youth in the formation of friendships and in the choice of companions. Take heed, lest what you now think to be pure gold turns out to be base metal. Worldly associations tend to place obstructions in the way of your service to God, and many souls are ruined by unhappy unions, either business or matrimonial, with those who can never elevate or ennoble.[6]

[45]

Weigh every sentiment, and watch every development of character in the one with whom you think to link your life destiny. The step you are about to take is one of the most important in your life, and should not be taken hastily. While you may love, do not love blindly.

Examine carefully to see if your married life would be happy or inharmonious and wretched. Let the questions be raised, Will this union help me heavenward? Will it increase my love for God? And will it enlarge my sphere of usefulness in this life? If these reflections present no drawback, then in the fear of God move forward.[7]

Most men and women have acted in entering the marriage relation as though the only question for them to settle was whether they loved each other. But they should realize that a responsibility rests upon them in the marriage relation farther than this. They should consider whether their offspring will possess physical health and mental and moral strength. But few have moved with high motives and with elevated considerations which they could not lightly throw off—that society had claims upon them, that the weight of their family's influence would tell in the upward or downward scale.[8]

The choice of a life companion should be such as best to secure physical, mental, and spiritual well-being for parents and for their children—such as will enable both parents and children to bless their fellow men and to honor their Creator.[9]

Qualities to Be Sought in a Prospective Wife—Let a young man seek one to stand by his side who is fitted to bear her share of life's burdens, one whose influence will ennoble and refine him, and who will make him happy in her love.

[46]

"A prudent wife is from the Lord." "The heart of her husband doth safely trust in her.... She will do him good and not evil all the days of her life." "She openeth her mouth with wisdom; and in her tongue is the law of kindness. She looketh well to the ways of her household, and eateth not the bread of idleness. Her children arise up, and call her blessed; her husband also, and he praiseth her," saying, "Many daughters have done virtuously, but thou excellest them all." He who gains such a wife "findeth a good thing, and obtaineth favor of the Lord."[10]

Here are things which should be considered: Will the one you marry bring happiness to your home? Is [she] an economist, or will she, if married, not only use all her own earnings, but all of yours to gratify a vanity, a love of appearance? Are her principles correct in this direction? Has she anything now to depend upon? ... I know that to the mind of a man infatuated with love and thoughts of marriage these questions will be brushed away as though they were of no consequence. But these things should be duly considered, for they have a bearing upon your future life....

In your choice of a wife study her character. Will she be one who will be patient and painstaking? Or will she cease to care for your mother and father at the very time when they need a strong son to lean upon? And will she withdraw him from their society to carry out her plans and to suit her own pleasure, and leave the father and mother who, instead of gaining an affectionate daughter, will have lost a son?[11]

[47]

Qualities to Be Sought in a Prospective Husband—Before giving her hand in marriage, every woman should inquire whether he with whom she is about to unite her destiny is worthy. What has been his past record? Is his life pure? Is the love which he expresses of a noble, elevated character, or is it a mere emotional fondness? Has he the traits of character that will make her happy? Can she find true peace and joy in his affection? Will she be allowed to preserve her individuality, or must her judgment and conscience be surrendered to the control of her husband? ... Can she honor the Saviour's claims as supreme? Will body and soul, thoughts and purposes, be preserved pure and holy? These questions have a vital bearing upon the well-being of every woman who enters the marriage relation.[12]

Let the woman who desires a peaceful, happy union, who would escape future misery and sorrow, inquire before she yields her affections, Has my lover a mother? What is the stamp of her character? Does he recognize his obligations to her? Is he mindful of her wishes and happiness? If he does not respect and honor his mother, will he manifest respect and love, kindness and attention, toward his wife? When the novelty of marriage is over, will he love me still? Will he be patient with my mistakes, or will he be critical, overbearing, and dictatorial? True affection will overlook many mistakes; love will not discern them.[13]

Accept Only Pure, Manly Traits—Let a young woman accept as a life companion only one who possesses pure, manly traits of character, one who is diligent, aspiring, and honest, one who loves and fears God.[14]

Shun those who are irreverent. Shun one who is a lover of idleness; shun the one who is a scoffer of hallowed things. Avoid the society of one who uses profane language, or is addicted to the use of even one glass of liquor. Listen not to the proposals of a man who has no realization of his responsibility to God. The pure truth which sanctifies the soul will give you courage to cut yourself loose from the most pleasing acquaintance whom you know does not love and fear God, and knows nothing of the principles of true righteousness. We may always bear with a friend's infirmities and with his ignorance, but never with his vices.[15]

Easier to Make a Mistake Than to Correct It—Marriages that are impulsive and selfishly planned generally do not result well, but often turn out miserable failures. Both parties find themselves deceived, and gladly would they undo that which they did under an

[48]

infatuation. It is easier, far easier, to make a mistake in this matter than to correct the error after it is made.[16]

Better to Break Unwise Engagement—Even if an engagement has been entered into without a full understanding of the character of the one with whom you intend to unite, do not think that the engagement makes it a positive necessity for you to take upon yourself the marriage vow and link yourself for life to one whom you cannot love and respect. Be very careful how you enter into conditional engagements; but better, far better, break the engagement before marriage than separate afterward, as many do.[17]

You may say, "But I have given my promise, and shall I now retract it?" I answer, If you have made a promise contrary to the Scriptures, by all means retract it without delay, and in humility before God repent of the infatuation that led you to make so rash a pledge. Far better take back such a promise, in the fear of God, than keep it, and thereby dishonor your Maker.[18]

[49]

Let every step toward a marriage alliance be characterized by modesty, simplicity, sincerity, and an earnest purpose to please and honor God. Marriage affects the afterlife both in this world and in the world to come. A sincere Christian will make no plans that God cannot approve.[19]

[50]

---

[1]The Review and Herald, February 2, 1886.

[2]Testimonies For The Church 4, 622.

[3]The Review and Herald, September 25, 1888.

[4]The Review and Herald, February 2, 1886.

[5]The Ministry of Healing, 357.

[6]Fundamentals of Christian Education, 500.

[7]Ibid., 104, 105.

[8]Messages to Young People, 461.

[9]The Ministry of Healing, 357, 358.

[10]Ibid., 359.

[11]Letter 23, 1886.

[12]Testimonies For The Church 5:362.

[13]Fundamentals of Christian Education, 105.

[14]The Ministry of Healing, 359.

[15]Letter 51, 1894.

[16]Letter 23, 1886.

[17]Fundamentals of Christian Education, 105.

[18]Testimonies For The Church 5, 365.

[19]The Ministry of Healing, 359.

Chapter 7—True Love or Infatuation

Love Is a Precious Gift From Jesus—Love is a precious gift, which we receive from Jesus. Pure and holy affection is not a feeling, but a principle. Those who are actuated by true love are neither unreasonable nor blind.[1]

There is but little real, genuine, devoted, pure love. This precious article is very rare. Passion is termed love.[2]

True love is a high and holy principle, altogether different in character from that love which is awakened by impulse, and which suddenly dies when severely tested.[3]

Love is a plant of heavenly growth, and it must be fostered and nourished. Affectionate hearts, truthful, loving words, will make happy families and exert an elevating influence upon all who come within the sphere of their influence.[4]

True Love Versus Passion—Love ... is not unreasonable; it is not blind. It is pure and holy. But the passion of the natural heart is another thing altogether. While pure love will take God into all its plans, and will be in perfect harmony with the Spirit of God, passion will be headstrong, rash, unreasonable, defiant of all restraint, and will make the object of its choice an idol. In all the deportment of one who possesses true love, the grace of God will be shown. Modesty, simplicity, sincerity, morality, and religion will characterize every step toward an alliance in marriage. Those who are thus controlled will not be absorbed in each other's society, at a loss of interest in the prayer meeting and the religious service. [51] Their fervor for the truth will not die on account of the neglect of the opportunities and privileges that God has graciously given to them.[5]

That love which has no better foundation than mere sensual gratification will be headstrong, blind, and uncontrollable. Honor, truth, and every noble, elevated power of the mind are brought under the slavery of passions. The man who is bound in the chains of this infatuation is too often deaf to the voice of reason and conscience;

33

neither argument nor entreaty can lead him to see the folly of his course.[6]

True love is not a strong, fiery, impetuous passion. On the contrary, it is calm and deep in its nature. It looks beyond mere externals, and is attracted by qualities alone. It is wise and discriminating, and its devotion is real and abiding.[7]

Love, lifted out of the realm of passion and impulse, becomes spiritualized, and is revealed in words and acts. A Christian must have a sanctified tenderness and love in which there is no impatience or fretfulness; the rude, harsh manners must be softened by the grace of Christ.[8]

Sentimentalism to Be Shunned as Leprosy—Imagination, lovesick sentimentalism, should be guarded against as would be the leprosy. Very many of the young men and women in this age of the world are lacking in virtue; therefore great caution is needed.... Those who have preserved a virtuous character, although they may lack in other desirable qualities, may be of real moral worth.[9]

There are persons who have for some time made a profession of religion who are, to all intents and purposes, without God and without a sensitive conscience. They are vain and trifling; their conversation is of a low order. Courtship and marriage occupy the mind, to the exclusion of higher and nobler thoughts.[10]

[52]

The young are bewitched with the mania for courtship and marriage. Lovesick sentimentalism prevails. Great vigilance and tact are needed to guard the youth from these wrong influences.[11]

Daughters are not taught self-denial and self-control. They are petted, and their pride is fostered. They are allowed to have their own way, until they become headstrong and self-willed, and you are put to your wits' end to know what course to pursue to save them from ruin. Satan is leading them on to be a proverb in the mouth of unbelievers because of their boldness, their lack of reserve and womanly modesty. The young boys are likewise left to have their own way. They have scarcely entered their teens before they are by the side of little girls of their own age, accompanying them home and making love to them. And the parents are so completely in bondage through their own indulgence and mistaken love for their children that they dare not pursue a decided course to make a change and restrain their too-fast children in this fast age.[12]

Counsel to a Romantic, Lovesick Girl—You have fallen into the sad error which is so prevalent in this degenerate age, especially with women. You are too fond of the other sex. You love their society; your attention to them is flattering, and you encourage, or permit, a familiarity which does not always accord with the exhortation of the apostle, to "abstain from all appearance of evil." ...

Turn your mind away from romantic projects. You mingle with your religion a romantic, lovesick sentimentalism, which does not elevate, but only lowers. It is not yourself alone who is affected; others are injured by your example and influence.... Daydreaming and romantic castle building have unfitted you for usefulness. You have lived in an imaginary world; you have been an imaginary martyr and an imaginary Christian. [53]

There is much of this low sentimentalism mingled with the religious experience of the young in this age of the world. My sister, God requires you to be transformed. Elevate your affections, I implore you. Devote your mental and physical powers to the service of your Redeemer, who has bought you. Sanctify your thoughts and feelings that all your works may be wrought in God.[13]

Caution to a Youthful Student—You are now in your student's life; let your mind dwell upon spiritual subjects. Keep all sentimentalism apart from your life. Give to yourself vigilant self-instruction, and bring yourself under self-control. You are now in the formative period of character; nothing with you is to be considered trivial or unimportant which will detract from your highest, holiest interest, your efficiency in the preparation to do the work God has assigned you.[14]

Results of Unwise Courtship and Marriage.—We can see that innumerable difficulties meet us at every step. The iniquity that is cherished by young as well as old; the unwise, unsanctified courtship and marriages cannot fail to result in bickerings, in strife, in alienations, in indulgence of unbridled passions, in unfaithfulness of husbands and wives, unwillingness to restrain the self-willed, inordinate desires, and in indifference to the things of eternal interest.... [54]

The holiness of the oracles of God is not loved by very many who claim to be Bible Christians. They show by their free, loose conduct that they prefer a wider scope. They do not want their selfish indulgences limited.[15]

Guard the Affections—Gird up the loins of your mind, says the apostle; then control your thoughts, not allowing them to have full scope. The thoughts may be guarded and controlled by your own determined efforts. Think right thoughts, and you will perform right actions. You have, then, to guard the affections, not letting them go out and fasten upon improper objects. Jesus has purchased you with His own life; you belong to Him; therefore He is to be consulted in all things, as to how the powers of your mind and the affections of

[55]   your heart shall be employed.[16]

[1] The Ministry of Healing, 358, 359.

[2] Testimonies For The Church 2, 381.

[3] Patriarchs and Prophets, 176.

[4] Testimonies For The Church 4, 548.

[5] The Review and Herald, September 25, 1888.

[6] The Signs of the Times, July 1, 1903.

[7] Testimonies For The Church 2, 133.

[8] Testimonies For The Church 5, 335.

[9] Testimonies For The Church 5, 123.

[10] Testimonies For The Church 4, 589.

[11] Ibid., 5:59.

[12] Ibid., 2:460.

[13] Ibid., 248-251.

[14] Letter 23, 1893.

[15] Manuscript 14, 1888.

[16] The Youth's Instructor, April 21, 1886.

Chapter 8—Common Courtship Practices

Wrong Ideas of Courtship and Marriage—The ideas of courtship have their foundation in erroneous ideas concerning marriage. They follow impulse and blind passion. The courtship is carried on in a spirit of flirtation. The parties frequently violate the rules of modesty and reserve and are guilty of indiscretion, if they do not break the law of God. The high, noble, lofty design of God in the institution of marriage is not discerned; therefore the purest affections of the heart, the noblest traits of character are not developed.

Not one word should be spoken, not one action performed, that you would not be willing the holy angels should look upon and register in the books above. You should have an eye single to the glory of God. The heart should have only pure, sanctified affection, worthy of the followers of Jesus Christ, exalted in its nature, and more heavenly than earthly. Anything different from this is debasing, degrading in courtship; and marriage cannot be holy and honorable in the sight of a pure and holy God, unless it is after the exalted Scriptural principle.[1]

The youth trust altogether too much to impulse. They should not give themselves away too easily, nor be captivated too readily by the winning exterior of the lover. Courtship as carried on in this age is a scheme of deception and hypocrisy, with which the enemy of souls has far more to do than the Lord. Good common sense is needed here if anywhere; but the fact is, it has little to do in the matter.[2] [56]

Keeping Late Hours—The habit of sitting up late at night is customary; but it is not pleasing to God, even if you are both Christians. These untimely hours injure health, unfit the mind for the next day's duties, and have an appearance of evil. My brother, I hope you will have self-respect enough to shun this form of courtship. If you have an eye single to the glory of God, you will move with deliberate caution. You will not suffer lovesick sentimentalism to so

37

blind your vision that you cannot discern the high claims that God has upon you as a Christian.[3]

Satan's angels are keeping watch with those who devote a large share of the night to courting. Could they have their eyes opened, they would see an angel making a record of their words and acts. The laws of health and modesty are violated. It would be more appropriate to let some of the hours of courtship before marriage run through the married life. But as a general thing, marriage ends all the devotion manifested during the days of courtship.

These hours of midnight dissipation, in this age of depravity, frequently lead to the ruin of both parties thus engaged. Satan exults and God is dishonored when men and women dishonor themselves. The good name of honor is sacrificed under the spell of this infatuation, and the marriage of such persons cannot be solemnized under the approval of God. They are married because passion moved them, and when the novelty of the affair is over, they will begin to realize what they have done.[4]

Satan knows just what elements he has to deal with, and he displays his infernal wisdom in various devices to entrap souls to their ruin. He watches every step that is taken, and makes many suggestions, and often these suggestions are followed rather than [57] the counsel of God's word. This finely woven, dangerous net is skillfully prepared to entangle the young and unwary. It may often be disguised under a covering of light; but those who become its victims pierce themselves through with many sorrows. As the result, we see wrecks of humanity everywhere.[5]

Trifling With Hearts—To trifle with hearts is a crime of no small magnitude in the sight of a holy God. And yet some will show preference for young ladies and call out their affections, and then go their way and forget all about the words they have spoken and their effect. A new face attracts them, and they repeat the same words, devote to another the same attentions.

This disposition will reveal itself in the married life. The marriage relation does not always make the fickle mind firm, the wavering steadfast and true to principle. They tire of constancy, and unholy thoughts will manifest themselves in unholy actions. How essential it is, then, that the youth so gird up the loins of their mind and guard their conduct that Satan cannot beguile them from the path of uprightness.[6]

Deceptive Practices in Courtship—A young man who enjoys the society and wins the friendship of a young lady unbeknown to her parents does not act a noble Christian part toward her or toward her parents. Through secret communications and meetings he may gain an influence over her mind, but in so doing he fails to manifest that nobility and integrity of soul which every child of God will possess. In order to accomplish their ends, they act a part that is not frank and open and according to the Bible standard, and prove themselves untrue to those who love them and try to be faithful [58] guardians over them. Marriages contracted under such influences are not according to the word of God. He who would lead a daughter away from duty, who would confuse her ideas of God's plain and positive commands to obey and honor her parents, is not one who would be true to the marriage obligations....

"Thou shalt not steal" was written by the finger of God upon the tables of stone, yet how much underhand stealing of affections is practiced and excused! A deceptive courtship is maintained, private communications are kept up, until the affections of one who is inexperienced, and knows not whereunto these things may grow, are in a measure withdrawn from her parents and placed upon him who shows by the very course he pursues that he is unworthy of her love. The Bible condemns every species of dishonesty....

This underhand way in which courtships and marriages are carried on is the cause of a great amount of misery, the full extent of which is known only to God. On this rock thousands have made shipwreck of their souls. Professed Christians, whose lives are marked with integrity, and who seem sensible upon every other subject, make fearful mistakes here. They manifest a set, determined will that reason cannot change. They become so fascinated with human feelings and impulses that they have no desire to search the Bible and come into close relationship with God.[7]

Avoid the First Downward Step—When one commandment of the Decalogue is broken, the downward steps are almost certain. When once the barriers of female modesty are removed, the basest licentiousness does not appear exceeding sinful. Alas, what terrible results of woman's influence for evil may be witnessed in the world [59] today! Through the allurements of "strange women," thousands are incarcerated in prison cells, many take their own lives, and many cut short the lives of others. How true the words of Inspiration, "Her feet go down to death; her steps take hold on hell."

Beacons of warning are placed on every side in the pathway of life to prevent men from approaching the dangerous, forbidden ground; but, notwithstanding this, multitudes choose the fatal path, contrary to the dictates of reason, regardless of God's law, and in defiance of His vengeance.

Those who would preserve physical health, a vigorous intellect, and sound morals must "flee ... youthful lusts." Those who will put forth zealous and decided efforts to check the wickedness that lifts its bold, presumptuous head in our midst are hated and maligned by all wrongdoers, but they will be honored and recompensed of God.[8]

Sow Wild Oats—Reap a Bitter Crop—You must not imperil your souls by sowing wild oats. You cannot afford to be careless in regard to the companions you choose.[9]

A little time spent in sowing your wild oats, dear young friends, will produce a crop that will embitter your whole life; an hour of thoughtlessness, once yielding to temptation, may turn the whole current of your life in the wrong direction. You can have but one youth; make that useful. When once you have passed over the ground, you can never return to rectify your mistakes. He who refuses to connect with God, and puts himself in the way of temptation will surely fall. God is testing every youth. Many have excused their carelessness and irreverence because of the wrong example given [60] them by more experienced professors. But this should not deter any from right doing. In the day of final accounts you will plead no such [61] excuses as you plead now.[10]

---

[1] Manuscript 4a, 1885.

[2] Fundamentals of Christian Education, 105.

[3] Testimonies For The Church 3, 44, 45.

[4] The Review and Herald, September 25, 1888.

[5] Fundamentals of Christian Education, 103, 104.

[6] The Review and Herald, November 4, 1884.

[7] Fundamentals of Christian Education, 101-103.

[8] The Signs of the Times, July 1, 1903.

[9] Messages to Young People, 164.

[10]Testimonies For The Church 4, 622, 623.

Chapter 9—Forbidden Marriages

Marriage of Christians With Unbelievers—There is in the Christian world an astonishing, alarming indifference to the teaching of God's word in regard to the marriage of Christians with unbelievers. Many who profess to love and fear God choose to follow the bent of their own minds rather than take counsel of Infinite Wisdom. In a matter which vitally concerns the happiness and well-being of both parties for this world and the next, reason, judgment, and the fear of God are set aside; and blind impulse, stubborn determination are allowed to control.

Men and women who are otherwise sensible and conscientious close their ears to counsel; they are deaf to the appeals and entreaties of friends and kindred and of the servants of God. The expression of a caution or warning is regarded as impertinent meddling, and the friend who is faithful enough to utter a remonstrance is treated as an enemy. All this is as Satan would have it. He weaves his spell about the soul, and it becomes bewitched, infatuated. Reason lets fall the reins of self-control upon the neck of lust; unsanctified passion bears sway, until, too late, the victim awakens to a life of misery and bondage. This is not a picture drawn by the imagination, but a recital of facts. God's sanction is not given to unions which He has expressly forbidden.[1]

God's Commands Are Plain—The Lord commanded ancient Israel not to intermarry with the idolatrous nations around them: "Neither shalt thou make marriages with them; thy daughter thou shalt not give unto his son, nor his daughter shalt thou take unto thy son." The reason is given. Infinite Wisdom, foreseeing the result of such unions, declares: "For they will turn away thy son from following Me, that they may serve other gods: so will the anger of the Lord be kindled against you, and destroy thee suddenly." "For thou art an holy people unto the Lord thy God: the Lord thy God hath chosen thee to be a special people unto Himself, above all people that are upon the face of the earth." ...

42

In the New Testament are similar prohibitions concerning the marriage of Christians with the ungodly. The Apostle Paul, in his first letter to the Corinthians, declares: "The wife is bound by the law as long as her husband liveth; but if her husband be dead, she is at liberty to be married to whom she will; *only in the Lord.*" Again, in his second epistle, he writes: "Be ye not unequally yoked together with unbelievers: for what fellowship hath righteousness with unrighteousness? And what communion hath light with darkness? And what concord hath Christ with Belial? Or what part hath he that believeth with an infidel? And what agreement hath the temple of God with idols? For ye are the temple of the living God; as God hath said, I will dwell in them, and walk in them; and I will be their God, and they shall be My people. Wherefore come out from among them, and be ye separate, saith the Lord, and touch not the unclean thing; and I will receive you, and will be a Father unto you, and ye shall be My sons and daughters, saith the Lord Almighty."[2]

The curse of God rests upon many of the ill-timed, inappropriate connections that are formed in this age of the world. If the Bible left these questions in a vague, uncertain light, then the course that many youth of today are pursuing in their attachments for one another would be more excusable. But the requirements of the Bible are not halfway injunctions; they demand perfect purity of thought, of word, and of deed. We are grateful to God that His word is a light to the feet, and that none need mistake the path of duty. The young should make it a business to consult its pages and heed its counsels, for sad mistakes are always made in departing from its precepts.[3]

[63]

God Forbids Believers Marrying Unbelievers—Never should God's people venture upon forbidden ground. Marriage between believers and unbelievers is forbidden by God. But too often the unconverted heart follows its own desires, and marriages unsanctioned by God are formed. Because of this many men and women are without hope and without God in the world. Their noble aspirations are dead; by a chain of circumstances they are held in Satan's net. Those who are ruled by passion and impulse will have a bitter harvest to reap in this life, and their course may result in the loss of their souls.[4]

Those who profess the truth trample on the will of God in marrying unbelievers; they lose His favor and make bitter work for repentance. The unbelieving may possess an excellent moral character, but the fact that he or she has not answered to the claims of God and has neglected so great salvation is sufficient reason why such a union should not be consummated. The character of the unbelieving may be similar to that of the young man to whom Jesus addressed the words, "One thing thou lackest"; that was the one thing needful.[5]

Solomon's Example—There are men of poverty and obscurity whose lives God would accept and make full of usefulness on earth and of glory in heaven, but Satan is working persistently to defeat His purposes and drag them down to perdition by marriage with those whose character is such that they throw themselves directly across the road to life. Very few come out from this entanglement triumphant.[6]

Satan well knew the results that would attend obedience; and during the earlier years of Solomon's reign—years glorious because of the wisdom, the beneficence and the uprightness of the king—he sought to bring in influences that would insidiously undermine Solomon's loyalty to principle and cause him to separate from God. And that the enemy was successful in this effort, we know from the record: "Solomon made affinity with Pharaoh king of Egypt, and took Pharaoh's daughter, and brought her into the city of David."

In forming an alliance with a heathen nation, and sealing the compact by marriage with an idolatrous princess, Solomon rashly disregarded the wise provisions that God had made for maintaining the purity of His people. The hope that this Egyptian wife might be converted was but a feeble excuse for the sin. In violation of a direct command to remain separate from other nations, the king united his strength with the arm of flesh.

For a time God in His compassionate mercy overruled this terrible mistake. Solomon's wife was converted; and the king, by a wise course, might have done much to check the evil forces that his imprudence had set in operation. But Solomon began to lose sight of the Source of his power and glory. Inclination gained the ascendancy over reason. As his self-confidence increased, he sought to carry out the Lord's purpose in his own way....

Many professed Christians think, like Solomon, that they may unite with the ungodly because their influence over those who are in the wrong will be beneficial; but too often they themselves, entrapped and overcome, yield their sacred faith, sacrifice principle, and separate themselves from God. One false step leads to another, till at last they place themselves where they cannot hope to break the chains that bind them.[7]

The Plea—"He Is Favorable to Religion."—The plea is sometimes made that the unbeliever is favorable to religion and is all that could be desired in a companion except in one thing—he is not a Christian. Although the better judgment of the believer may suggest the impropriety of a union for life with an unbeliever, yet, in nine cases out of ten, inclination triumphs. Spiritual declension commences the moment the vow is made at the altar; religious fervor is dampened, and one stronghold after another is broken down, until both stand side by side under the black banner of Satan. Even in the festivities of the wedding the spirit of the world triumphs against conscience, faith, and truth. In the new home the hour of prayer is not respected. The bride and bridegroom have chosen each other and dismissed Jesus.[8]

The Change Is Wrought in the Believing One—At first the unbelieving one may make no show of opposition in the new relation; but when the subject of Bible truth is presented for attention and consideration, the feeling at once arises: "You married me, knowing that I was what I am; I do not wish to be disturbed. From henceforth let it be understood that conversation upon your peculiar views is to be interdicted." If the believer should manifest any special earnestness in regard to his faith, it might seem like unkindness toward the one who has no interest in the Christian experience.

[66]

The believing one reasons that in his new relation he must concede somewhat to the companion of his choice. Social, worldly amusements are patronized. At first there is great reluctance of feeling in doing this, but the interest in the truth becomes less and less, and faith is exchanged for doubt and unbelief. No one would have suspected that the once firm, conscientious believer and devoted follower of Christ could ever become the doubting, vacillating person that he now is. Oh, the change wrought by that unwise marriage![9]

It is a dangerous thing to form a worldly alliance. Satan well knows that the hour that witnesses the marriage of many young men and women closes the history of their religious experience and usefulness. They are lost to Christ. They may for a time make an effort to live a Christian life, but all their strivings are made against a steady influence in the opposite direction. Once it was a privilege and joy to them to speak of their faith and hope; but they become unwilling to mention the subject, knowing that the one with whom they have linked their destiny takes no interest in it. As the result, faith in the precious truth dies out of the heart, and Satan insidiously weaves about them a web of skepticism.[10]

Risking the Enjoyments of Heaven—"Can two walk together, except they be agreed?" "If two of you shall agree on earth as touching any thing that they shall ask, it shall be done for them of My Father which is in heaven." But how strange the sight! While one of those so closely united is engaged in devotion, the other is indifferent and careless; while one is seeking the way to everlasting life, the other is in the broad road to death.

[67] Hundreds have sacrificed Christ and heaven in consequence of marrying unconverted persons. Can it be that the love and fellowship of Christ are of so little value to them that they prefer the companionship of poor mortals? Is heaven so little esteemed that they are willing to risk its enjoyments for one who has no love for the precious Saviour?[11]

To connect with an unbeliever is to place yourself on Satan's ground. You grieve the Spirit of God and forfeit His protection. Can you afford to have such terrible odds against you in fighting the battle for everlasting life?[12]

Ask yourself: "Will not an unbelieving husband lead my thoughts away from Jesus? He is a lover of pleasure more than a lover of God; will he not lead me to enjoy the things that he enjoys?" The path to eternal life is steep and rugged. Take no additional weights to retard your progress.[13]

A Home Where Shadows Are Never Lifted—The heart yearns for human love, but this love is not strong enough, or pure enough, or precious enough to supply the place of the love of Jesus. Only in her Saviour can the wife find wisdom, strength, and grace to meet the cares, responsibilities, and sorrows of life. She should make Him her strength and her guide. Let woman give herself to Christ before giving herself to any earthly friend, and enter into no relation which shall conflict with this. Those who would find true happiness must have the blessing of Heaven upon all that they possess and all that they do. It is disobedience to God that fills so many hearts and homes with misery. My sister, unless you would have a home where the shadows are never lifted, do not unite yourself with one who is an enemy of God.[14]

The Christian's Reasoning—What ought every Christian to do when brought into the trying position which tests the soundness of religious principle? With a firmness worthy of imitation he should say frankly: "I am a conscientious Christian. I believe the seventh day of the week to be the Sabbath of the Bible. Our faith and principles are such that they lead in opposite directions. We cannot be happy together, for if I follow on to gain a more perfect knowledge of the will of God, I shall become more and more unlike the world and assimilated to the likeness of Christ. If you continue to see no loveliness in Christ, no attractions in the truth, you will love the world, which I cannot love, while I shall love the things of God, which you cannot love. Spiritual things are spiritually discerned. Without spiritual discernment you will be unable to see the claims of God upon me, or to realize my obligations to the Master whom I serve; therefore you will feel that I neglect you for religious duties. You will not be happy; you will be jealous on account of the affections which I give to God, and I shall be alone in my religious belief. When your views shall change, when your heart shall respond to the claims of God, and you shall learn to love my Saviour, then our relationship may be renewed." [68]

The believer thus makes a sacrifice for Christ which his conscience approves, and which shows that he values eternal life too highly to run the risk of losing it. He feels that it would be better to remain unmarried than to link his interest for life with one who chooses the world rather than Jesus, and who would lead away from the cross of Christ.[15]

A Safe Marriage Alliance—It is only in Christ that a marriage alliance can be safely formed. Human love should draw its closest bonds from divine love. Only where Christ reigns can there be deep, true, unselfish affection.[16] [69]

When One Partner Is Converted After Marriage—He who has entered the marriage relation while unconverted is by his conversion placed under stronger obligation to be faithful to his companion, however widely they may differ in regard to religious faith; yet the claims of God should be placed above every earthly relationship, even though trials and persecution may be the result. With the spirit of love and meekness, this fidelity may have an influence to win the

[70]   unbelieving one.[17]

---

[1] Testimonies For The Church 5, 365, 366.

[2] Ibid., 5:363, 364.

[3] Fundamentals of Christian Education, 102, 103.

[4] Ibid., 500, 501.

[5] Testimonies For The Church 4, 505.

[6] Testimonies For The Church 5, 124.

[7] Fundamentals of Christian Education, 498-500.

[8] Testimonies For The Church 4, 505.

[9] Ibid., 4:505, 506.

[10] Ibid., 4:504, 505.

[11] Ibid., 4:507.

[12] Ibid., 5:364.

[13] Ibid., 5:363.

[14] Ibid., 5:362, 363.

[15] Ibid., 4:506, 507.

[16] The Ministry of Healing, 358.

[17] Patriarchs and Prophets, 175.

Chapter 10—When Counsel is Needed

Get Counsel From the Bible—Instituted by God, marriage is a sacred ordinance and should never be entered upon in a spirit of selfishness. Those who contemplate this step should solemnly and prayerfully consider its importance and seek divine counsel that they may know whether they are pursuing a course in harmony with the will of God. The instruction given in God's word on this point should be carefully considered. Heaven looks with pleasure upon a marriage formed with an earnest desire to conform to the directions given in the Scripture.[1]

If there is any subject that should be considered with calm reason and unimpassioned judgment, it is the subject of marriage. If ever the Bible is needed as a counselor, it is before taking a step that binds persons together for life. But the prevailing sentiment is that in this matter the feelings are to be the guide, and in too many cases lovesick sentimentalism takes the helm and guides to certain ruin. It is here that the youth show less intelligence than on any other subject; it is here that they refuse to be reasoned with. The question of marriage seems to have a bewitching power over them. They do not submit themselves to God. Their senses are enchained, and they move forward in secretiveness, as if fearful that their plans would be interfered with by someone.[2]

Many are sailing in a dangerous harbor. They need a pilot; but they scorn to accept the much-needed help, feeling that they are competent to guide their own bark, and not realizing that it is about to strike a hidden rock that may cause them to make shipwreck of [71] faith and happiness.... Unless they are diligent students of that word [the Bible], they will make grave mistakes which will mar their happiness and that of others, both for the present and the future life.[3]

Prayer Necessary to Right Decision—If men and women are in the habit of praying twice a day before they contemplate marriage, they should pray four times a day when such a step is anticipated.

Marriage is something that will influence and affect your life, both in this world and in the world to come....

The majority of the marriages of our time and the way in which they are conducted make them one of the signs of the last days. Men and women are so persistent, so headstrong, that God is left out of the question. Religion is laid aside, as if it had no part to act in this solemn and important matter.[4]

When Infatuation Is Deaf to Counsel—Two persons become acquainted; they are infatuated with each other, and their whole attention is absorbed. Reason is blinded, and judgment is overthrown. They will not submit to any advice or control, but insist on having their own way, regardless of consequences. Like some epidemic, or contagion, that must run its course is the infatuation that possesses them; and there seems to be no such thing as putting a stop to it.

Perhaps there are those around them who realize that, should the parties interested be united in marriage, it could only result in lifelong unhappiness. But entreaties and exhortations are given in vain. Perhaps, by such a union, the usefulness of one whom God would bless in His service will be crippled and destroyed; but reasoning and persuasion are alike unheeded. All that can be said by men and women of experience proves ineffectual; it is powerless to change the decision to which their desires have led them. They lose interest in the prayer meeting and in everything that pertains to religion. They are wholly infatuated with each other, and the duties of life are neglected, as if they were matters of little concern.[5]

[72]

Youth Need the Wisdom of Age and Experience—When so much misery results from marriage, why will not the youth be wise? Why will they continue to feel that they do not need the counsel of older and more experienced persons? In business, men and women manifest great caution. Before engaging in any important enterprise, they prepare themselves for their work. Time, money, and much careful study are devoted to the subject, lest they shall make a failure in their undertaking.

How much greater caution should be exercised in entering the marriage relation—a relation which affects future generations and the future life? Instead of this, it is often entered upon with jest and levity, impulse and passion, blindness and lack of calm consideration. The only explanation of this is that Satan loves to see misery and ruin in the world, and he weaves this net to entangle souls. He rejoices to have these inconsiderate persons lose their enjoyment of this world and their home in the world to come.[6]

Matured Judgment of Parents Should Be Valued—Shall children consult only their own desires and inclinations irrespective of the advice and judgment of their parents? Some seem never to bestow a thought upon their parents' wishes or preferences, nor to regard their matured judgment. Selfishness has closed the door of their hearts to filial affection. The minds of the young need to be aroused in regard to this matter. The fifth commandment is the only commandment to which is annexed a promise, but it is held lightly and is even positively ignored by the lover's claim. Slighting a mother's love, dishonoring a father's care are sins that stand registered against many youth. [73]

One of the greatest errors connected with this subject is that the young and inexperienced must not have their affections disturbed, that there must be no interference in their love experience. If there ever was a subject that needed to be viewed from every standpoint, it is this. The aid of the experience of others and a calm, careful weighing of the matter on both sides are positively essential. It is a subject that is treated altogether too lightly by the great majority of people. Take God and your God-fearing parents into your counsel, young friends. Pray over the matter.[7]

Confide in Godly Parents—If you are blessed with God-fearing parents, seek counsel of them. Open to them your hopes and plans; learn the lessons which their life experiences have taught.[8]

If children would be more familiar with their parents, if they would confide in them and unburden to them their joys and sorrows, they would save themselves many a future heartache. When perplexed to know what course is right, let them lay the matter just as they view it before their parents, and ask advice of them. Who are so well calculated to point out their dangers as godly parents? Who can understand their peculiar temperaments so well as they? Children who are Christians will esteem above every earthly blessing the love and approbation of their God-fearing parents. The parents can [74] sympathize with the children and pray for and with them that God will shield and guide them. Above everything else they will point them to their never-failing Friend and Counselor.[9]

Parents to Guide the Affections of Youth—Fathers and mothers should feel that a duty devolves upon them to guide the affections of the youth, that they may be placed upon those who will be suitable companions. They should feel it a duty, by their own teaching and example, with the assisting grace of God, to so mold the character of the children from their earliest years that they will be pure and noble and will be attracted to the good and true. Like attracts like; like appreciates like. Let the love for truth and purity and goodness be early implanted in the soul, and the youth will seek the society of those who possess these characteristics.[10]

The Example Set by Isaac—Parents should never lose sight of their own responsibility for the future happiness of their children. Isaac's deference to his father's judgment was the result of the training that had taught him to love a life of obedience.[11]

Isaac was highly honored by God in being made inheritor of the promises through which the world was to be blessed; yet when he was forty years of age, he submitted to his father's judgment in appointing his experienced, God-fearing servant to choose a wife for him. And the result of that marriage, as presented in the Scriptures, is a tender and beautiful picture of domestic happiness: "Isaac brought her into his mother Sarah's tent, and took Rebekah, and she became his wife; and he loved her: and Isaac was comforted after

[75] his mother's death."[12]

Wise Parents Will Be Considerate—"Should parents," you ask, "select a companion without regard to the mind or feelings of son or daughter?" I put the question to you as it should be: Should a son or daughter select a companion without first consulting the parents, when such a step must materially affect the happiness of parents if they have any affection for their children? And should that child, notwithstanding the counsel and entreaties of his parents, persist in following his own course? I answer decidedly: No; not if he never marries. The fifth commandment forbids such a course. "Honor thy father and thy mother: that thy days may be long upon the land which the Lord thy God giveth thee." Here is a commandment with a promise which the Lord will surely fulfill to those who obey. Wise parents will never select companions for their children without

[76] respect to their wishes.[13]

[77]

[78]

[1]Letter 17, 1896.

[2]Fundamentals of Christian Education. 103.

[3]Ibid., 100.

[4]Messages to Young People, 460.

[5]The Review and Herald, September 25, 1888.

[6]The Review and Herald, February 2, 1886.

[7]Fundamentals of Christian Education, 104.

[8]The Ministry of Healing, 359.

[9]Fundamentals of Christian Education, 105, 106.

[10]Patriarchs and Prophets, 176.

[11]Ibid., 175, 176.

[12]Ibid., 175.

[13]Testimonies For The Church 5. 108.

Section 4—Factors that Make for Success or Failure

Chapter 11—Hasty, Immature Marriages

Dangers of Childhood Attachments—Early marriages are not to be encouraged. A relation so important as marriage and so far-reaching in its results should not be entered upon hastily, without sufficient preparation, and before the mental and physical powers are well developed.[1]

Boys and girls enter upon the marriage relation with unripe love, immature judgment, without noble, elevated feelings, and take upon themselves the marriage vows, wholly led by their boyish, girlish passions....

Attachments formed in childhood have often resulted in very wretched unions or in disgraceful separations. Early connections, if formed without the consent of parents, have seldom proved happy. The young affections should be restrained until the period arrives when sufficient age and experience will make it honorable and safe to unfetter them. Those who will not be restrained will be in danger of dragging out an unhappy existence.

A youth not out of his teens is a poor judge of the fitness of a person as young as himself to be his companion for life. After their judgment has become more matured, they view themselves bound for life to each other and perhaps not at all calculated to make each other happy. Then, instead of making the best of their lot, recriminations take place, the breach widens, until there is settled indifference and neglect of each other. To them there is nothing sacred in the word "home." The very atmosphere is poisoned by unloving words and bitter reproaches.[2]

Immature marriages are productive of a vast amount of the evils that exist today. Neither physical health nor mental vigor is promoted by a marriage that is entered on too early in life. Upon this subject altogether too little reason is exercised. Many youth act from impulse. This step, which affects them seriously for good or ill, to be a lifelong blessing or curse, is too often taken hastily, under the impulse of sentiment. Many will not listen to reason or instruction from a Christian point of view.[3]

Satan is constantly busy to hurry inexperienced youth into a marriage alliance. But the less we glory in the marriages which are now taking place, the better.[4]

In consequence of hasty marriages, even among the professed people of God, there are separations, divorces, and great confusion in the church.[5]

What a contrast between the course of Isaac and that pursued by the youth of our time, even among professed Christians! Young people too often feel that the bestowal of their affections is a matter in which self alone should be consulted—a matter that neither God nor their parents should in any wise control. Long before they have reached manhood or womanhood, they think themselves competent to make their own choice, without the aid of their parents. A few years of married life are usually sufficient to show them their error, but often too late to prevent its baleful results. For the same lack of wisdom and self-control that dictated the hasty choice is permitted to aggravate the evil, until the marriage relation becomes a galling yoke. Many have thus wrecked their happiness in this life and their hope of the life to come.[6]

Potential Workers for God Entangled—Young men have received the truth and run well for a season, but Satan has woven his [81] meshes about them in unwise attachments and poor marriages. This he saw would be the most successful way he could allure them from the path of holiness.[7]

I have been shown that the youth of today have no true sense of their great danger. There are many of the young whom God would accept as laborers in the various branches of His work, but Satan steps in and so entangles them in his web that they become estranged from God and powerless in His work. Satan is a sharp and persevering workman. He knows just how to entrap the unwary, and it is an alarming fact that but few succeed in escaping from his wiles. They see no danger and do not guard against his devices. He prompts them to fasten their affections upon one another without seeking wisdom of God or of those whom He has sent to warn, reprove, and counsel. They feel self-sufficient and will not bear restraint.[8]

Counsel to a Teen-age Youth—Your boyish ideas of love for young girls does not give anyone a high opinion of you. By letting your mind run in this channel, you spoil your thoughts for study. You will be led to form impure associations; your ways and the ways of others will be corrupted. This is just as your case is presented to me, and as long as you persist in following your own way, whoever will seek to guide, influence, or restrain you will meet with the most determined resistance because your heart is not in harmony with truth and righteousness.[9]

[82] **Disparity in Age**—The parties may not have worldly wealth, but they should have the far greater blessing of health. And in most cases there should not be a great disparity in age. A neglect of this rule may result in seriously impairing the health of the younger. And often the children are robbed of physical and mental strength. They cannot receive from an aged parent the care and companionship which their young lives demand, and they may be deprived by death of the father or the mother at the very time when love and guidance

[83] are most needed.[10]

---

[1] The Ministry of Healing, 358.

[2] Messages to Young People, 452.

[3] Ibid., 453.

[4] Testimonies For The Church 2, 252.

[5] The Review and Herald, September 25, 1888.

[6] Patriarchs and Prophets, 175.

[7] Testimonies For The Church 5, 114, 115.

[8] Ibid., 105, 106.

[9] Manuscript 15a, 1896.

[10] The Ministry of Healing, 358.

Chapter 12—Compatibility

Adapted to Each Other—In many families there is not that Christian politeness, that true courtesy, deference, and respect for one another that would prepare its members to marry and make happy families of their own. In the place of patience, kindness, tender courtesy, and Christian sympathy and love, there are sharp words, clashing ideas, and a criticizing, dictatorial spirit.[1]

It is often the case that persons before marriage have little opportunity to become acquainted with each other's habits and disposition; and, so far as everyday life is concerned, they are virtually strangers when they unite their interests at the altar. Many find, too late, that they are not adapted to each other, and lifelong wretchedness is the result of their union. Often the wife and children suffer from the indolence and inefficiency or the vicious habits of the husband and father.[2]

The world is full of misery and sin today in consequence of ill-assorted marriages. In many cases it takes only a few months for husband and wife to realize that their dispositions can never blend; and the result is that discord prevails in the home, where only the love and harmony of heaven should exist.

By contention over trivial matters a bitter spirit is cultivated. Open disagreements and bickering bring inexpressible misery into the home and drive asunder those who should be united in the bonds of love. Thus thousands have sacrificed themselves, soul and body, by unwise marriages and have gone down in the path of perdition.[3]   [84]

Perpetual Differences in a Divided Home—The happiness and prosperity of the married life depend upon the unity of the parties. How can the carnal mind harmonize with the mind that is assimilated to the mind of Christ? One is sowing to the flesh, thinking and acting in accordance with the promptings of his own heart; the other is sowing to the Spirit, seeking to repress selfishness, to overcome inclination, and to live in obedience to the Master, whose servant he professes to be. Thus there is a perpetual difference of taste, of inclination, and of purpose. Unless the believer shall, through his steadfast adherence to principle, win the impenitent, he will, as is much more common, become discouraged and sell his religious principles for the poor companionship of one who has no connection with Heaven.[4]

Marriages Wrecked by Incompatibility—Many marriages can only be productive of misery; and yet the minds of the youth run in this channel because Satan leads them there, making them believe that they must be married in order to be happy, when they have not the ability to control themselves or support a family. Those who are not willing to adapt themselves to each other's disposition, so as to avoid unpleasant differences and contentions, should not take the step. But this is one of the alluring snares of the last days, in which thousands are ruined for this life and the next.[5]

The Aftermath of Blind Love—Every faculty of those who become affected by this contagious disease—blind love—is brought in subjection to it. They seem to be devoid of good sense, and their course of action is disgusting to all who behold it.... With many [85] the crisis of the disease is reached in an immature marriage, and when the novelty is past and the bewitching power of love-making is over, one or both parties awake to their true situation. They then find themselves ill-mated, but united for life. Bound to each other by the most solemn vows, they look with sinking hearts upon the miserable life they must lead. They ought then to make the best of their situation, but many will not do this. They will either prove false to their marriage vows or make the yoke which they persisted in placing upon their own necks so very galling that not a few cowardly put an end to their existence.[6]

It should henceforth be the life study of both husband and wife how to avoid everything that creates contention and to keep unbroken the marriage vows.[7]

Experience of Others a Warning—Mr. A has a nature that Satan plays upon with wonderful success. This case is one that should teach the young a lesson in regard to marriage. His wife followed feeling and impulse, not reason and judgment, in selecting a companion. Was their marriage the result of true love? No, no; it was the result of impulse—blind, unsanctified passion. Neither was at all fitted for the responsibilities of married life. When the novelty of the new order of things wore away, and each became acquainted with the other, did their love become stronger, their affection deeper, and their lives blend together in beautiful harmony? It was entirely the opposite. The worst traits of their characters began to deepen by exercise; and, instead of their married life being one of happiness, it has been one of increasing trouble.[8]

For years I have been receiving letters from different persons who have formed unhappy marriages, and the revolting histories opened before me are enough to make the heart ache. It is no easy [86] thing to decide what advice can be given to these unfortunate ones, or how their hard lot can be lightened; but their sad experience should be a warning to others.[9] [87]

---

[1]The Review and Herald, February 2, 1886.

[2]Patriarchs and Prophets, 189.

[3]Messages to Young People, 453.

[4]Testimonies For The Church 4, 507, 508.

[5]Testimonies For The Church 5, 122, 123.

[6] Testimonies For The Church 5, 110, 111.

[7] Testimonies For The Church 5, 122.

[8] Testimonies For The Church 5, 121, 122.

[9] Testimonies For The Church 5, 366.

Chapter 13—Domestic Training

Preparation for Marriage Is an Essential Part of Education—Upon no account should the marriage relation be entered upon until the parties have a knowledge of the duties of a practical domestic life. The wife should have culture of mind and manners that she may be qualified to rightly train the children that may be given her.[1]

Many ladies, accounted well-educated, having graduated with honors at some institution of learning, are shamefully ignorant of the practical duties of life. They are destitute of the qualifications necessary for the proper regulation of family, and hence essential to its happiness. They may talk of woman's elevated sphere and of her rights, yet they themselves fall far below the true sphere of woman.

It is the right of every daughter of Eve to have a thorough knowledge of household duties, to receive training in every department of domestic labor. Every young lady should be so educated that if called to fill the position of wife and mother, she may preside as a queen in her own domain. She should be fully competent to guide and instruct her children and to direct her servants, or, if need be, to minister with her own hands to the wants of her household. It is her right to understand the mechanism of the human body and the principles of hygiene, the matters of diet and dress, labor and recreation, and countless others that intimately concern the well-being [88] of her household. It is her right to obtain such a knowledge of the best methods of treating disease that she can care for her children in sickness, instead of leaving her precious treasures in the hands of stranger nurses and physicians.

The idea that ignorance of useful employment is an essential characteristic of the true gentleman or lady is contrary to the design of God in the creation of man. Idleness is a sin, and ignorance of common duties is the result of folly, which afterlife will give ample occasion to bitterly regret.[2]

Young women think that it is menial to cook and do other kinds of housework; and, for this reason, many girls who marry and have the care of families have little idea of the duties devolving upon a wife and mother.[3]

It should be a law that young people should not get married unless they know how to care for the children that are brought into their family. They must know how to take care of this house that God has given them. Unless they understand in regard to the laws which God has established in their system, they cannot understand their duty to their God or themselves.[4]

Domestic Training Should Be in the College Curriculum— The education which the young men and women who attend our colleges should receive in the home life is deserving of special attention. It is of great importance in the work of character building that students who attend our colleges be taught to take up the work that is appointed them, throwing off all inclination to sloth. They need to become familiar with the duties of daily life. They should be taught to do their domestic duties thoroughly and well, with as little noise and confusion as possible. Everything should be done decently and in order. The kitchen and all other parts of the building should be kept sweet and clean. Books should be laid aside till their proper season, and no more study should be taken than can be attended to without neglecting the household duties. The study of books is not to engross the mind to the neglect of home duties upon which the comfort of the family depends.

[89]

In the performance of these duties careless, neglectful, disorderly habits should be overcome; for unless corrected, these habits will be carried into every phase of life, and the life will be spoiled for usefulness.[5]

A Knowledge of Homemaking Is Indispensable—Many of the branches of study that consume the student's time are not essential to usefulness or happiness, but it is essential for every youth to have a thorough acquaintance with everyday duties. If need be, a young woman can dispense with a knowledge of French and algebra, or even of the piano; but it is indispensable that she learn to make good bread, to fashion neatly fitting garments, and to perform efficiently the many duties that pertain to homemaking.

To the health and happiness of the whole family nothing is more vital than skill and intelligence on the part of the cook. By ill-prepared, unwholesome food she may hinder and even ruin both the adult's usefulness and the child's development. Or by providing food adapted to the needs of the body, and at the same time inviting and palatable, she can accomplish as much in the right as otherwise she accomplishes in the wrong direction. So, in many ways, life's happiness is bound up with faithfulness in common duties.[6]

[90] **Give Attention to the Principles of Hygiene**—The principles of hygiene as applied to diet, exercise, the care of children, the treatment of the sick, and many like matters should be given much more attention than they ordinarily receive.[7]

In the study of hygiene the earnest teacher will improve every opportunity to show the necessity of perfect cleanliness both in personal habits and in all one's surroundings.... Teach the pupils that a healthful sleeping room, a thoroughly clean kitchen, and a tastefully arranged, wholesomely supplied table will go farther toward securing the happiness of the family and the regard of every sensible visitor than any amount of expensive furnishing in the drawing room. That "the life is more than meat, and the body is more than raiment" [Luke 12:23] is a lesson no less needed now than when given by the divine Teacher eighteen hundred years ago.[8]

A Young Lady Counseled to Acquire Habits of Industry—You have peculiarities of character which need to be sternly disciplined and resolutely controlled before you can with any safety enter the marriage relation. Therefore marriage should be put from your mind until you overcome the defects in your character, for you would not make a happy wife. You have neglected to educate yourself for systematic household labor. You have not seen the necessity of acquiring habits of industry. The habit of enjoying useful labor, once formed, will never be lost. You are then prepared to be placed in any circumstances in life, and you will be fitted for the position. You will learn to love activity. If you enjoy useful labor, your mind will be occupied with your employment, and you will not find time [91] to indulge in dreamy fancies.

Knowledge of useful labor will impart to your restless and dissatisfied mind energy, efficiency, and a becoming, modest dignity, which will command respect.[9]

Value of Practical Education for Girls—Many who consider it necessary for a son to be trained with reference to his own future maintenance seem to consider it entirely optional with herself whether or not their daughter is educated to be independent and self-supporting. She usually learns little at school which can be put to practical use in earning her daily bread; and receiving no instruction at home in the mysteries of the kitchen and domestic life, she grows up utterly useless, a burden upon her parents....

A woman who has been taught to take care of herself is also fitted to take care of others. She will never be a drug in the family or in society. When fortune frowns, there will be a place for her somewhere, a place where she can earn an honest living and assist those who are dependent upon her. Woman should be trained to some business whereby she can gain a livelihood if necessary. Passing over other honorable employments, every girl should learn to take charge of the domestic affairs of home, should be a cook, a housekeeper, a seamstress. She should understand all those things which it is necessary that the mistress of a house should know, whether her family are rich or poor. Then, if reverses come, she is prepared for any emergency; she is, in a manner, independent of circumstances.[10]

A knowledge of domestic duties is beyond price to every woman. There are families without number whose happiness is wrecked by the inefficiency of the wife and mother. It is not so important that our daughters learn painting, fancywork, music, or even "cube root", or the figures of rhetoric, as that they learn how to cut, make, and mend their own clothing, or to prepare food in a wholesome and palatable manner. When a little girl is nine or ten years old, she should be required to take her regular share in household duties, as she is able, and should be held responsible for the manner in which she does her work. That was a wise father who, when asked what he intended to do with his daughters, replied, "I intend to apprentice them to their excellent mother, that they may learn the art of improving time, and be fitted to become wives and mothers, heads of families, and useful members of society."[11]

[92]

The Prospective Husband Should Be Thrifty and Industrious—In early times custom required the bridegroom, before the ratification of a marriage engagement, to pay a sum of money or its equivalent in other property, according to his circumstances, to the father of his wife. This was regarded as a safeguard to the marriage relation. Fathers did not think it safe to trust the happiness of their daughters to men who had not made provision for the support of a family. If they had not sufficient thrift and energy to manage business and acquire cattle or lands, it was feared that their life would prove worthless. But provision was made to test those who had nothing to pay for a wife. They were permitted to labor for the father whose daughter they loved, the length of time being regulated by the value of the dowry required. When the suitor was faithful in his services, and proved in other respects worthy, he obtained the daughter as his wife; and generally the dowry which the father had received was given her at her marriage....

[93] The ancient custom, though sometimes abused, as by Laban, was productive of good results. When the suitor was required to render service to secure his bride, a hasty marriage was prevented, and there was opportunity to test the depth of his affections, as well as his ability to provide for a family. In our time many evils result from pursuing an opposite course.[12]

No man is excusable for being without financial ability. Of many a man it may be said, He is kind, amiable, generous, a good man, a Christian; but he is not qualified to manage his own business. As far as the outlay of means is concerned, he is a mere child. He has not been brought up by his parents to understand and to practice the [94] principles of self-support.[13]

[1] Pacific Health Journal, May, 1890.

[2] Fundamentals of Christian Education, 75.

[3] The Ministry of Healing, 302.

[4] Manuscript 19, 1887.

[5] Testimonies For The Church 6, 169, 170.

[6] Education, 216.

[7] Education, 197.

[8] Education, 200.

[9] Testimonies For The Church 3, 336.

[10] The Health Reformer, December, 1877.

[11] Fundamentals of Christian Education, 74.

[12] Patriarchs and Prophets, 188, 189.

[13] Letter 123, 1900.

Chapter 14—True Conversion a Requisite

Religion Ensures Family Happiness—Family religion is a wonderful power. The conduct of the husband toward the wife and of the wife toward the husband may be such that it will make the home life a preparation for entrance to the family above.[1]

Hearts that are filled with the love of Christ can never get very far apart. Religion is love, and a Christian home is one where love reigns and finds expression in words and acts of thoughtful kindness and gentle courtesy.[2]

Religion is needed in the home. Only this can prevent the grievous wrongs which so often embitter married life. Only where Christ reigns can there be deep, true, unselfish love. Then soul will be knit with soul, and the two lives will blend in harmony. Angels of God will be guests in the home, and their holy vigils will hallow the marriage chamber. Debasing sensuality will be banished. Upward to God will the thoughts be directed; to Him will the heart's devotion ascend.[3]

In every family where Christ abides, a tender interest and love will be manifested for one another; not a spasmodic love expressed only in fond caresses, but a love that is deep and abiding.[4]

Christianity to Be a Controlling Influence—Christianity ought to have a controlling influence upon the marriage relation, but it is too often the case that the motives which lead to this union are not in keeping with Christian principles. Satan is constantly seeking to strengthen his power over the people of God by inducing them to enter into alliance with his subjects, and in order to accomplish [95] this he endeavors to arouse unsanctified passions in the heart. But the Lord has in His word plainly instructed His people not to unite themselves with those who have not His love abiding in them.[5]

Counsel to a Newly Married Couple—Marriage, a union for life, is a symbol of the union between Christ and His church. The spirit that Christ manifests toward His church is the spirit that the husband and wife are to manifest toward each other. If they love God supremely, they will love each other in the Lord, ever treating each other courteously, drawing in even cords. In their mutual self-denial and self-sacrifice they will be a blessing to each other....

Both of you need to be converted. Neither of you have a proper idea of the meaning of obedience to God. Study the words, "He that is not with Me is against Me; and he that gathereth not with Me scattereth abroad." I sincerely hope that you will both become true children of God, servants to whom He can entrust responsibilities. Then peace and confidence and faith will come to you. Yes, you may both be happy, consistent Christians. Cultivate keenness of perception, that you may know how to choose the good and refuse the evil. Make the word of God your study. The Lord Jesus wants you to be saved. He has wonderfully preserved you, my brother, that your life may be one of usefulness. Bring all the good works possible into it.

Unless you have an earnest desire to become children of God, you will not understand clearly how to help each other. To each other ever be tender and thoughtful, giving up your own wishes and purposes to make each other happy. Day by day you may make advancement in self-knowledge. Day by day you may learn better

[96]   how to strengthen your weak points of character. The Lord Jesus will be your light, your strength, your crown of rejoicing, because you yield the will to His will....

You need the subduing grace of God in your heart. Do not desire a life of ease and inactivity. All who are connected with the Lord's work must be constantly on guard against selfishness. Keep your lamp trimmed and burning. Then you will not be reckless of your words and actions. You will both be happy if you try to please each other. Keep the windows of the soul closed earthward and opened heavenward.

Men and women may reach a high standard, if they will but acknowledge Christ as their personal Saviour. Watch and pray, making a surrender of all to God. The knowledge that you are striving for eternal life will strengthen and comfort you both. In thought, in word, in action, you are to be lights in the world. Discipline yourselves in the Lord; for He has committed to you sacred trusts, which you cannot properly fulfill without this discipline. By believing in Jesus, you are not only to save your own souls, but by precept and example you are to seek to save other souls. Take Christ as your pattern. Hold Him up as the One who can give you power to overcome. Utterly destroy the root of selfishness. Magnify God, for you are His children. Glorify your Redeemer, and He will give you a place in His kingdom.[6]

[97]

[98]

[1]Letter 57, 1902.

[2]Testimonies For The Church 5, 355.

[3]Testimonies For The Church 5: 362.

[4]The Review and Herald, February 2, 1886.

[5]Patriarchs and Prophets, 563.

[6]Letter 57, 1902.

Section 5—From the Marriage Altar

Chapter 15—Solemn Promises

God's Purpose for the Husband and Wife—God made from the man a woman, to be a companion and helpmeet for him, to be one with him, to cheer, encourage, and bless him, he in his turn to be her strong helper. All who enter into matrimonial relations with a holy purpose—the husband to obtain the pure affections of a woman's heart, the wife to soften and improve her husband's character and give it completeness—fulfill God's purpose for them.

Christ came not to destroy this institution, but to restore it to its original sanctity and elevation. He came to restore the moral image of God in man, and He began His work by sanctioning the marriage relation.[1]

He who gave Eve to Adam as a helpmeet performed His first miracle at a marriage festival. In the festal hall where friends and kindred rejoiced together, Christ began His public ministry. Thus He sanctioned marriage, recognizing it as an institution that He Himself had established. He ordained that men and women should be united in holy wedlock, to rear families whose members, crowned with honor, should be recognized as members of the family above.[2]

Jesus Wants Happy Marriages—The divine love emanating from Christ never destroys human love, but includes it. By it human love is refined and purified, elevated and ennobled. Human love can never bear its precious fruit until it is united with the divine nature and trained to grow heavenward. Jesus wants to see happy

marriages, happy firesides.[3]

Like every other one of God's good gifts entrusted to the keeping of humanity, marriage has been perverted by sin; but it is the purpose of the gospel to restore its purity and beauty....

The grace of Christ, and this alone, can make this institution what God designed it should be—an agent for the blessing and uplifting of humanity. And thus the families of earth, in their unity and peace and love, may represent the family of heaven.

The condition of society presents a sad comment upon Heaven's ideal of this sacred relation. Yet even for those who have found bitterness and disappointment where they had hoped for companionship and joy, the gospel of Christ offers a solace.[4]

A Joyous Occasion—The Scriptures state that both Jesus and His disciples were called to this marriage feast [at Cana]. Christ has given Christians no sanction to say when invited to a marriage, We ought not to be present on so joyous an occasion. By attending this feast Christ taught that He would have us rejoice with those who do rejoice in the observance of His statutes. He never discouraged the innocent festivities of mankind when carried on in accordance with the laws of Heaven. A gathering that Christ honored by His presence, it is right that His followers should attend. After attending this feast, Christ attended many others, sanctifying them by His presence and instruction.[5]

Display, Extravagance, and Hilarity Are Inappropriate At Weddings—Marriage ceremonies are made matters of display, extravagance, and self-indulgence. But if the contracting parties are agreed in religious belief and practice, and everything is consistent, and the ceremony be conducted without display and extravagance, marriage at this time need not be displeasing to God.[6]

[101]

There is no reason why we should make great parade or display, even if the parties were perfectly suited to each other.[7]

It has always seemed so very inappropriate to me to see the marriage ordinance associated with hilarity and glee and a pretense of something. No. It is an ordinance ordained of God, to be looked upon with the greatest solemnity. As the family relation is formed here below, it is to give a demonstration of what they shall be, the family in heaven above. The glory of God is ever to be made first.[8]

A Wedding in Mrs. White's Home—About 11 a.m. Tuesday our large dining room was prepared for the wedding ceremony. Brother B officiated in the service, and it passed off nicely. The request was made ... that Sister White should offer prayer after the marriage ceremony. The Lord gave me special freedom. My heart was softened and subdued by the Spirit of God. On this occasion there were no light jests or foolish sayings: everything was solemn and sacred in connection with this marriage. Everything was of an elevating character and deeply impressive. The Lord sanctified this marriage, and these two now unite their interests to work in the mission field, to seek and to save them that are lost. God will bless them in their work if they walk humbly with Him, leaning wholly upon His promises.[9]

The Blending of Two Lives [Note: remarks by Mrs. E. G. White on the occasion of a wedding ceremony at Sanitarium California, in 1905.]—This is an important period in the history of the ones who have stood before you to unite their interests, their sympathies, their love, their labor, with each other in the ministry of the saving of souls. In the marriage relation there is a very important step taken—the blending of two lives into one.... It is in accord with the will of God that man and wife should be linked together in His work, to carry it forward in a wholeness and a holiness. They can do this.

The blessing of God in the home where this union shall exist is as the sunshine of heaven, because it is the Lord's ordained will that man and wife should be linked together in holy bonds of union, under Jesus Christ, with Him to control, and His spirit to guide....

God wants the home to be the happiest place on earth, the very symbol of the home in heaven. Bearing the marriage responsibilities in the home, linking their interests with Jesus Christ, leaning upon His arm and His assurance, husband and wife may share a happiness in this union that angels of God commend.

Marriage does not lessen their usefulness, but strengthens it. They may make that married life a ministry to win souls to Christ; and I know whereof I speak, because for thirty-six years my husband and I were united, and we went everywhere that the Lord said Go. In this matter we know that we have the commendation of God in the marriage relation. Therefore it is a solemn ordinance....

And now I can at this time take by the hand this our brother; ... and we take by the hand you, his wife, and urge you to carry on the work of God unitedly. I would say, Make God your counselor. Blend, blend together.[10]

Counsel to a Newly Wedded Pair—My Dear Brother and Sister: You have united in a lifelong covenant. Your education in married life has begun. The first year of married life is a year of experience, a year in which husband and wife learn each other's different traits of character, as a child learns lessons in school. In

[102]

[103]

this, the first year of your married life, let there be no chapters that will mar your future happiness....

My brother, your wife's time and strength and happiness are now bound up with yours. Your influence over her may be a savor of life unto life or of death unto death. Be very careful not to spoil her life.

My sister, you are now to learn your first practical lessons in regard to the responsibilities of married life. Be sure to learn these lessons faithfully day by day.... Guard constantly against giving way to selfishness.

In your life union your affections are to be tributary to each other's happiness. Each is to minister to the happiness of the other. This is the will of God concerning you. But while you are to blend as one, neither of you is to lose his or her individuality in the other. God is the owner of your individuality. Of Him you are to ask: What is right? What is wrong? How may I best fulfill the purpose of my creation?[11]

A Pledge Before Heavenly Witnesses—God has ordained that there should be perfect love and harmony between those who enter into the marriage relation. Let bride and bridegroom, in the presence of the heavenly universe, pledge themselves to love each other as God has ordained they should.... The wife is to respect and reverence her husband, and the husband is to love and cherish his wife.[12]

Men and women, at the beginning of married life, should reconsecrate themselves to God.[13]

[104]

Be as true as steel to your marriage vows, refusing, in thought, word, or deed, to spoil your record as a man who fears God and obeys His commandments.[14]

[105]

[1]Manuscript 16, 1899.

[2]The Ministry of Healing, 356.

[3]The Bible Echo, September 4, 1899.

[4]The Review and Herald, December 10, 1908.

[5]Manuscript 16, 1899.

[6]The Review and Herald, September 25, 1888.

[7]Testimonies For The Church 4, 515.

[8]Manuscript 170, 1905.

[9]Manuscript 23, 1894.

[10]Manuscript 170, 1905.

[11]Testimonies For The Church 7, 45.

[12]The Bible Echo, September 4, 1899.

[13]Manuscript 70, 1903.
[14]Letter 231, 1903.

Chapter 16—A Happy, Successful Partnership

The Real Union Is a Lifelong Experience—To gain a proper understanding of the marriage relation is the work of a lifetime. Those who marry enter a school from which they are never in this life to be graduated.[1]

However carefully and wisely marriage may have been entered into, few couples are completely united when the marriage ceremony is performed. The real union of the two in wedlock is the work of the afteryears.[2]

As life with its burden of perplexity and care meets the newly wedded pair, the romance with which imagination so often invests marriage disappears. Husband and wife learn each other's character as it was impossible to learn it in their previous association. This is a most critical period in their experience. The happiness and usefulness of their whole future life depend upon their taking a right course now. Often they discern in each other unsuspected weaknesses and defects; but the hearts that love has united will discern excellencies also heretofore unknown. Let all seek to discover the excellencies rather than the defects. Often it is our own attitude, the atmosphere that surrounds ourselves, which determines what will be revealed to us in another.[3]

Love Must Be Tested and Tried—Affection may be as clear as crystal and beauteous in its purity, yet it may be shallow because it has not been tested and tried. Make Christ first and last and best in everything. Constantly behold Him, and your love for Him will daily become deeper and stronger as it is submitted to the test of [106] trial. And as your love for Him increases, your love for each other will grow deeper and stronger.[4]

Though difficulties, perplexities, and discouragements may arise, let neither husband nor wife harbor the thought that their union is a mistake or a disappointment. Determine to be all that it is possible to be to each other. Continue the early attentions. In every way encourage each other in fighting the battles of life. Study to advance the happiness of each other. Let there be mutual love, mutual forbearance. Then marriage, instead of being the end of love, will be as it were the very beginning of love. The warmth of true friendship, the love that binds heart to heart, is a foretaste of the joys of heaven.[5]

All should cultivate patience by practicing patience. By being kind and forbearing, true love may be kept warm in the heart, and qualities will be developed that Heaven will approve.[6]

The Enemy Will Seek to Alienate—Satan is ever ready to take advantage when any matter of variance arises, and by moving upon the objectionable, hereditary traits of character in husband or wife, he will try to cause the alienation of those who have united their interests in a solemn covenant before God. In the marriage vows they have promised to be as one, the wife covenanting to love and obey her husband, the husband promising to love and cherish his wife. If the law of God is obeyed, the demon of strife will be kept out of the family, and no separation of interests will take place, no alienation of affection will be permitted.[7]

Counsel to a Strong-willed Couple—Neither husband nor wife is to make a plea for rulership. The Lord has laid down the principle that is to guide in this matter. The husband is to cherish his wife as Christ cherishes the church. And the wife is to respect and love her husband. Both are to cultivate the spirit of kindness, being determined never to grieve or injure the other....

[107]

Do not try to compel each other to do as you wish. You cannot do this and retain each other's love. Manifestations of self-will destroy the peace and happiness of the home. Let not your married life be one of contention. If you do, you will both be unhappy. Be kind in speech and gentle in action, giving up your own wishes. Watch well your words, for they have a powerful influence for good or for ill. Allow no sharpness to come into your voices. Bring into your united life the fragrance of Christlikeness.[8]

Express Love in Words and Deeds—There are many who regard the expression of love as a weakness, and they maintain a reserve that repels others. This spirit checks the current of sympathy. As the social and generous impulses are repressed, they wither, and the heart becomes desolate and cold. We should beware of this error.

Love cannot long exist without expression. Let not the heart of one connected with you starve for the want of kindness and sympathy....

Let each give love rather than exact it. Cultivate that which is noblest in yourselves, and be quick to recognize the good qualities in each other. The consciousness of being appreciated is a wonderful stimulus and satisfaction. Sympathy and respect encourage the striving after excellence, and love itself increases as it stimulates to nobler aims.[9]

The reason there are so many hardhearted men and women in our world is that true affection has been regarded as weakness and has been discouraged and repressed. The better part of the nature of persons of this class was perverted and dwarfed in childhood; and unless rays of divine light can melt away their coldness and hardhearted selfishness, the happiness of such is buried forever. If we would have tender hearts, such as Jesus had when He was upon the earth, and sanctified sympathy, such as the angels have for sinful mortals, we must cultivate the sympathies of childhood, which are simplicity itself. Then we shall be refined, elevated, and directed by heavenly principles.[10]

[108]

Too many cares and burdens are brought into our families, and too little of natural simplicity and peace and happiness is cherished. There should be less care for what the outside world will say and more thoughtful attention to the members of the family circle. There should be less display and affectation of worldly politeness, and much more tenderness and love, cheerfulness and Christian courtesy, among the members of the household. Many need to learn how to make home attractive, a place of enjoyment. Thankful hearts and kind looks are more valuable than wealth and luxury, and contentment with simple things will make home happy if love be there.[11]

The Little Attentions Count—God tests and proves us by the common occurrences of life. It is the little things which reveal the chapters of the heart. It is the little attentions, the numerous small incidents and simple courtesies of life, that make up the sum of life's happiness; and it is the neglect of kindly, encouraging, affectionate words, and the little courtesies of life, which helps compose the sum of life's wretchedness. It will be found at last that the denial of self for the good and happiness of those around us constitutes a large share of the life record in heaven. And the fact will also be revealed

[109]

that the care of self, irrespective of the good and happiness of others, is not beneath the notice of our heavenly Father.[12]

A Husband Who Failed to Express Affection—A house with love in it, where love is expressed in words and looks and deeds, is a place where angels love to manifest their presence and hallow the scene by rays of light from glory. There the humble household duties have a charm in them. None of life's duties will be unpleasant to your wife under such circumstances. She will perform them with cheerfulness of spirit and will be like a sunbeam to all around her, and she will be making melody in her heart to the Lord. At present she feels that she has not your heart's affections. You have given her occasion to feel thus. You perform the necessary duties devolving upon you as head of the family, but there is a lack. There is a serious lack of love's precious influence which leads to kindly attentions. Love should be seen in the looks and manners and heard in the tones of the voice.[13]

A Disappointing, Self-centered Wife—The moral character of those united in marriage is either elevated or degraded by their association; and the work of deterioration accomplished by a low, deceptive, selfish, uncontrollable nature is begun soon after the marriage ceremony. If the young man makes a wise choice, he may have one to stand by his side who will bear to the utmost of her ability her share of the burdens of life, who will ennoble and refine him, and make him happy in her love. But if the wife is fitful in character, self-admiring, exacting, accusing, charging her husband [110] with motives and feelings that originate only in her own perverted temperament; if she has not discernment and nice discrimination to recognize his love and appreciate it, but talks of neglect and lack of love because he does not gratify every whim, she will almost inevitably bring about the very state of things she seems to deplore; she will make all these accusations realities.[14]

Characteristics of a Companionable Wife and Mother—Instead of sinking into a mere household drudge, let the wife and mother take time to read, to keep herself well informed, to be a companion to her husband, and to keep in touch with the developing minds of her children. Let her use wisely the opportunities now hers to influence her dear ones for the higher life. Let her take time to make the dear Saviour a daily Companion and familiar Friend. Let her take time for the study of His word, take time to go with the children into the fields and learn of God through the beauty of His works.

Let her keep cheerful and buoyant. Instead of spending every moment in endless sewing, make the evening a pleasant social season, a family reunion after the day's duties. Many a man would thus be led to choose the society of his home before that of the clubhouse or the saloon. Many a boy would be kept from the street or the corner grocery. Many a girl would be saved from frivolous, misleading associations. The influence of the home would be to parents and children what God designed it should be, a lifelong blessing.[15]

Married life is not all romance; it has its real difficulties and its homely details. The wife must not consider herself a doll, to be tended, but a woman; one to put her shoulder under real, not imaginary, burdens, and live an understanding, thoughtful life, considering that there are other things to be thought of than herself.... Real life has its shadows and its sorrows. To every soul troubles must come. Satan is constantly working to unsettle the faith and destroy the courage and hope of every one.[16]

[111]

Counsel to an Unhappy Couple—Your married life has been very much like a desert—but very few green spots to look back upon with grateful remembrance. It need not have been thus.

Love can no more exist without revealing itself in outward acts than fire can be kept alive without fuel. You, Brother C, have felt that it was beneath your dignity to manifest tenderness by kindly acts and to watch for an opportunity to evince affection for your wife by words of tenderness and kind regard. You are changeable in your feelings and are very much affected by surrounding circumstances.... Leave your business cares and perplexities and annoyances when you leave your business. Come to your family with a cheerful countenance, with sympathy, tenderness, and love. This will be better than expending money for medicines or physicians for your wife. It will be health to the body and strength to the soul. Your lives have been very wretched. You have both acted a part in making them so. God is not pleased with your misery; you have brought it upon yourselves by want of self-control.

You let feelings bear sway. You think it beneath your dignity, Brother C, to manifest love, to speak kindly and affectionately. All these tender words, you think, savor of softness and weakness, and are unnecessary. But in their place come fretful words, words of discord, strife, and censure....

[112]

You have not the elements of a contented spirit. You dwell upon your troubles; imaginary want and poverty far ahead stare you in the face; you feel afflicted, distressed, agonized; your brain seems on fire, your spirits depressed. You do not cherish love to God and gratitude of heart for all the blessings which your kind heavenly Father has bestowed upon you. You see only the discomforts of life. A worldly insanity shuts you in like heavy clouds of thick darkness. Satan exults over you because you will have misery when peace and happiness are at your command.[17]

Mutual Love and Forbearance Rewarded—Without mutual forbearance and love no earthly power can hold you and your husband in the bonds of Christian unity. Your companionship in the marriage relation should be close and tender, holy and elevated, breathing a spiritual power into your lives, that you may be everything to each other that God's word requires. When you reach the condition that the Lord desires you to reach, you will find heaven below and God in your life.[18]

Remember, my dear brother and sister, that God is love and that by His grace you can succeed in making each other happy, as in your marriage pledge you promised to do.[19]

Men and women can reach God's ideal for them if they will take Christ as their helper. What human wisdom cannot do, His grace will accomplish for those who give themselves to Him in loving trust. His providence can unite hearts in bonds that are of heavenly origin. Love will not be a mere exchange of soft and flattering words. The loom of heaven weaves with warp and woof finer, yet more firm, than can be woven by the looms of earth. The result is not a tissue

[113]

fabric, but a texture that will bear wear and test and trial. Heart will

[114]

be bound to heart in the golden bonds of a love that is enduring.[20]

---

[1]Testimonies For The Church 7, 45.

[2]The Ministry of Healing, 359, 360.

[3]Ibid., 360.

[4]Testimonies For The Church 7, 46.

[5]The Ministry of Healing, 360.

[6]The Review and Herald, February 2, 1886.

[7]Letter 18a, 1891.

[8]Testimonies For The Church 7, 47.

[9]The Ministry of Healing, 360, 361.

[10]Testimonies For The Church 3, 539.

[11]Ibid., 4:621, 622.

[12]Ibid., 2:133, 134.

[13]Ibid., 2:417, 418.

[14]Letter 10, 1889.

[15]The Ministry of Healing, 294.

[16]Letter 34, 1890.

[17]Testimonies For The Church 1, 695-697.

[18]Letter 18a, 1891.

[19]Testimonies For The Church 7, 49.

[20]The Ministry of Healing, 362.

Chapter 17—Mutual Obligations

Each Has Individual Responsibilities—The two who unite their interest in life will have distinct characteristics and individual responsibilities. Each one will have his or her work, but women are not to be valued by the amount of work they can do as are beasts of burden. The wife is to grace the family circle as a wife and companion to a wise husband. At every step she should inquire, "Is this the standard of true womanhood?" and, "How shall I make may influence Christlike in my home?" The husband should let his wife know that he appreciates her work.[1]

The wife is to respect her husband. The husband is to love and cherish his wife; and as their marriage vow unites them as one, so their belief in Christ should make them one in Him. What can be more pleasing to God than to see those who enter into the marriage relation seek together to learn of Jesus and to become more and more imbued with His Spirit?[2]

You now have duties to perform that before your marriage you did not have. "Put on therefore, ... kindness, humbleness of mind, meekness, longsuffering." "Walk in love, as Christ also hath loved us." Give careful study to the following instruction: "Wives, submit yourselves unto your own husbands, as unto the Lord. For the husband is the head of the wife, even as Christ is the head of the church.... Therefore as the church is subject unto Christ, so let the wives be to their own husbands in every thing. Husbands, love your wives, even as Christ also loved the church, and gave Himself for it."[3]

[115]

God's Instruction to Eve—Eve was told of the sorrow and pain that must henceforth be her portion. And the Lord said, "Thy desire shall be to thy husband, and he shall rule over thee." In the creation, God had made her the equal of Adam. Had they remained obedient to God—in harmony with His great law of love—they would ever have been in harmony with each other; but sin had brought discord, and now their union could be maintained and harmony preserved

84

only by submission on the part of the one or the other. Eve had been the first in transgression; and she had fallen into temptation by separating from her companion, contrary to the divine direction. It was by her solicitation that Adam sinned, and she was now placed in subjection to her husband. Had the principles enjoined in the law of God been cherished by the fallen race, this sentence, though growing out of the results of sin, would have proved a blessing to them; but man's abuse of the supremacy thus given him has too often rendered the lot of woman very bitter, and made her life a burden.

Eve had been perfectly happy by her husband's side in her Eden home; but, like restless modern Eves, she was flattered with the hope of entering a higher sphere than that which God had assigned her. In attempting to rise above her original position, she fell far below it. A similar result will be reached by all who are unwilling to take up cheerfully their life duties in accordance with God's plan.[4]

Wives Submit; Husbands Love—The question is often asked, "Shall a wife have no will of her own?" The Bible plainly states that the husband is the head of the family. "Wives, submit yourselves unto your own husbands." If this injunction ended here, we might say [116] that the position of the wife is not an enviable one; it is a very hard and trying position in very many cases, and it would be better were there fewer marriages. Many husbands stop at the words, "Wives, submit yourselves," but we will read the conclusion of the same injunction, which is. "As it is fit in the Lord."

God requires that the wife shall keep the fear and glory of God ever before her. Entire submission is to be made only to the Lord Jesus Christ, who has purchased her as His own child by the infinite price of His life. God has given her a conscience, which she cannot violate with impunity. Her individuality cannot be merged into that of her husband, for she is the purchase of Christ. It is a mistake to imagine that with blind devotion she is to do exactly as her husband says in all things, when she knows that in so doing, injury would be worked for her body and her spirit, which have been ransomed from the slavery of Satan. There is One who stands higher than the husband to the wife; it is her Redeemer, and her submission to her husband is to be rendered as God has directed—"as it is fit in the Lord."

When husbands require the complete subjection of their wives, declaring that women have no voice or will in the family, but must render entire submission, they place their wives in a position contrary to the Scripture. In interpreting the Scripture in this way, they do violence to the design of the marriage institution. This interpretation is made simply that they may exercise arbitrary rule, which is not their prerogative. But we read on, "Husbands, love your wives, and be not bitter against them." Why should the husband be bitter against his wife? If the husband has found her erring and full of faults, [117] bitterness of spirit will not remedy the evil.[5]

Wives Subject Only As Husbands Are Subject to Christ— The Lord Jesus has not been correctly represented in His relation to the church by many husbands in their relation to their wives, for they do not keep the way of the Lord. They declare that their wives must be subject to them in everything. But it was not the design of God that the husband should have control, as head of the house, when he himself does not submit to Christ. He must be under the rule of Christ that he may represent the relation of Christ to the church. If he is a coarse, rough, boisterous, egotistical, harsh, and overbearing man, let him never utter the word that the husband is the head of the wife, and that she must submit to him in everything; for he is not the Lord, he is not the husband in the true significance of the term....

Husbands should study the pattern and seek to know what is meant by the symbol presented in Ephesians, the relation Christ sustains to the church. The husband is to be as a Saviour in his family. Will he stand in his noble, God-given manhood, ever seeking to uplift his wife and children? Will he breathe about him a pure, sweet atmosphere? Will he not as assiduously cultivate the love of Jesus, making it an abiding principle in his home, as he will assert his claims to authority?

Let every husband and father study to understand the words of Christ, not in a one-sided manner, merely dwelling upon the subjection of the wife to her husband, but in the light of the cross of Calvary, study as to his own position in the family circle. "Husbands, love your wives, even as Christ also loved the church, and gave Himself for it; that He might sanctify and cleanse it with the washing of water by the word." Jesus gave Himself up to die upon the cross [118] in order that He might cleanse and keep us from all sin and pollution by the influence of the Holy Spirit.[6]

Mutual Forbearance Is Needed—We must have the Spirit of God, or we can never have harmony in the home. The wife, if she has the spirit of Christ, will be careful of her words; she will control her spirit, she will be submissive, and yet will not feel that she is a bondslave, but a companion to her husband. If the husband is a servant of God, he will not lord it over his wife; he will not be arbitrary and exacting. We cannot cherish home affection with too much care; for the home, if the Spirit of the Lord dwells there, is a type of heaven.... If one errs, the other will exercise Christlike forbearance and not draw coldly away.[7]

Neither the husband nor the wife should attempt to exercise over the other an arbitrary control. Do not try to compel each other to yield to your wishes. You cannot do this and retain each other's love. Be kind, patient, and forbearing, considerate, and courteous. By the grace of God you can succeed in making each other happy, as in your marriage vow you promised to do.[8]

Let Each Graciously Yield—In the married life men and women sometimes act like undisciplined, perverse children. The husband wants his way, and the wife wants her way, and neither is willing to yield. Such a condition of things can bring only the greatest unhappiness. Both husband and wife should be willing to yield his or her way or opinion. There is no possibility of happiness while they both persists in doing as they please.[9]

Unless men and women have learned of Christ, His meekness and lowliness, they will reveal the impulsive, unreasonable spirit so often revealed by children. The strong, undisciplined will will seek to rule. Such ones need to study the words of Paul: "When I was a child, I spake as a child, I understood as a child, I thought as a child: but when I became a man, I put away childish things."[10] [119]

Adjusting Family Difficulties—It is a hard matter to adjust family difficulties, even when husband and wife seek to make a fair and just settlement in regard to their several duties, if they have failed to submit the heart to God. How can husband and wife divide the interests of their home life and still keep a loving, firm hold upon each other? They should have a united interest in all that concerns their homemaking, and the wife, if a Christian, will have her interest with her husband as his companion; for the husband is to stand as the head of the household.[11]

Counsel to Discordant Families—Your spirit is wrong. When you take a position, you do not weigh the matter well and consider what must be the effect of your maintaining your views and in an independent manner weaving them into your prayers and conversation, when you know that your wife does not hold the same views that you do. Instead of respecting the feelings of your wife and kindly avoiding, as a gentleman would, those subjects upon which you know you differ, you have been forward to dwell upon objectionable points, and have manifested a persistency in expressing your views regardless of any around you. You have felt that others had no right to see matters differently from yourself. These fruits do not grow upon the Christian tree.[12]

My brother, my sister, open the door of the heart to receive Jesus. Invite him into the soul-temple. Help each other to overcome the obstacles which enter the married life of all. You will have a fierce [120] conflict to overcome your adversary the devil, and if you expect God to help you in this battle, you must both unite in deciding to overcome, to seal your lips against speaking any words of wrong, even if you have to fall upon your knees and cry aloud, "Lord, rebuke the adversary of my soul."[13]

Christ in Each Heart Will Bring Unity—If the will of God is fulfilled, the husband and wife will respect each other and cultivate love and confidence. Anything that would mar the peace and unity of the family should be firmly repressed, and kindness and love should be cherished. He who manifests the spirit of tenderness, forbearance, and love will find that the same spirit will be reflected upon him. Where the Spirit of God reigns, there will be no talk of unsuitability in the marriage relation. If Christ indeed is formed within, the hope of glory, there will be union and love in the home. Christ abiding in the heart of the wife will be at agreement with Christ abiding in the heart of the husband. They will be striving together for the mansions [121] Christ has gone to prepare for those who love Him.[14]

[1] Manuscript 17, 1891.

[2] Manuscript 36, 1899.

[3] Testimonies For The Church 7, 46.

[4] Patriarchs and Prophets, 58, 59.

[5] Letter 18, 1891

[6] Manuscript 17, 1891.

[7] Letter 18, 1891.

[8] The Ministry of Healing, 361.

[9] Manuscript 31, 1911.

[10] Letter 55, 1902.

[11] Manuscript 31, 1911.

[12] Testimonies For The Church 2, 418.

[13] Letter 105, 1893.

[14] The Signs of the Times, November 14, 1892.

Chapter 18—Marital Duties and Privileges

Jesus Did Not Enforce Celibacy—Those who regard the marriage relation as one of God's sacred ordinances, guarded by His holy precept, will be controlled by the dictates of reason.[1]

Jesus did not enforce celibacy upon any class of men. He came not to destroy the sacred relationship of marriage, but to exalt it and restore it to its original sanctity. He looks with pleasure upon the family relationship where sacred and unselfish love bears sway.[2]

Marriage Is Lawful and Holy—There is in itself no sin in eating and drinking, or in marrying and giving in marriage. It was lawful to marry in the time of Noah, and it is lawful to marry now, if that which is lawful is properly treated and not carried to sinful excess. But in the days of Noah men married without consulting God or seeking His guidance and counsel....

The fact that all the relations of life are of a transitory nature should have a modifying influence on all we do and say. In Noah's day it was the inordinate, excessive love of that which in itself was lawful, when properly used, that made marriage sinful before God. There are many who are losing their souls in this age of the world by becoming absorbed in the thoughts of marriage and in the marriage relation itself.[3]

The marriage relation is holy, but in this degenerate age it covers vileness of every description. It is abused and has become a crime [122] which now constitutes one of the signs of the last days, even as marriages, managed as they were previous to the Flood, were then a crime.... When the sacred nature and the claims of marriage are understood, it will even now be approved of Heaven; and the result will be happiness to both parties, and God will be glorified.[4]

The Privileges of the Marriage Relation—Those professing to be Christians ... should duly consider the result of every privilege [Note: On another occasion Mrs. White speaks of the "Privacy And Privileges Of The Family Relation." See Testimonies for the Church

90

2:90.—*Compilers.*] of the marriage relation, and sanctified principle should be the basis of every action.[5]

In very many cases the parents ... have abused their marriage privileges, and by indulgence have strengthened their animal passions.[6]

Duty to Avoid Excesses—It is carrying that which is lawful to excess that makes it a grievous sin.[7]

Many parents do not obtain the knowledge that they should in the married life. They are not guarded lest Satan take advantage of them and control their minds and their lives. They do not see that God requires them to control their married lives from any excesses. But very few feel it to be a religious duty to govern their passions. They have united themselves in marriage to the object of their choice and, therefore, reason that marriage sanctifies the indulgence of the baser passions. Even men and women professing godliness give loose rein to their lustful passions and have no thought that God holds them accountable for the expenditure of vital energy, which weakens their hold on life and enervates the entire system.[8]

[123]

Let Self-denial and Temperance Be the Watchword—Oh, that I could make all understand their obligation to God to preserve the mental and physical organism in the best condition to render perfect service to their Maker! Let the Christian wife refrain, both in word and act, from exciting the animal passions of her husband. Many have no strength at all to waste in this direction. From their youth up they have weakened the brain and sapped the constitution by the gratification of animal passions. Self-denial and temperance should be the watchword in their married life.[9]

We are under solemn obligations to God to keep the spirit pure and the body healthy, that we may be a benefit to humanity and render to God perfect service. The apostle utters these words of warning: "Let not sin therefore reign in your mortal body, that ye should obey it in the lusts thereof." He urges us onward by telling us that "every man that striveth for the mastery is temperate in all things." He exhorts all who call themselves Christians to present their bodies "a living sacrifice, holy, acceptable unto God." He says: "I keep under my body, and bring it into subjection: lest that by any means, when I have preached to others, I myself should be a castaway."[10]

It is not pure love which actuates a man to make his wife an instrument to minister to his lust. It is the animal passions which clamor for indulgence. How few men show their love in the manner specified by the apostle: "Even as Christ also loved the church, and gave Himself for it; that He might [not pollute it, but] sanctify and cleanse it; ... that it should be holy and without blemish." This is the quality of love in the marriage relation which God recognizes as holy. Love is a pure and holy principle, but lustful passion will not

[124]   admit of restraint and will not be dictated to or controlled by reason. It is blind to consequences; it will not reason from cause to effect.[11]

Why Satan Seeks to Weaken Self-control—Satan seeks to lower the standard of purity and to weaken the self-control of those who enter the marriage relation, because he knows that while the baser passions are in the ascendancy, the moral powers grow steadily weaker, and he need have no concern as to their spiritual growth. He knows, too, that in no way can he better stamp his own hateful image upon their offspring, and that he can thus mold their character even more readily than he can the character of the parents.[12]

Results of Excesses—Men and women, you will one day learn what is lust and the result of its gratification. Passion of just as base a quality may be found in the marriage relation as outside of it.[13]

What is the result of giving loose rein to the lower passions? ... The bedchamber, where angels of God should preside, is made unholy by unholy practices. And because shameful animalism rules, bodies are corrupted; loathsome practices lead to loathsome diseases. That which God has given as a blessing is made a curse.[14]

Sexual excess will effectually destroy a love for devotional exercises, will take from the brain the substance needed to nourish the system, and will most effectively exhaust the vitality. No woman should aid her husband in this work of self-destruction. She will not do it if she is enlightened and has true love for him.

The more the animal passions are indulged, the stronger do they

[125]   become, and the more violent will be their clamors for indulgence. Let God-fearing men and women awake to their duty. Many professed Christians are suffering with paralysis of nerve and brain because of their intemperance in this direction.[15]

Husbands to Be Considerate—Husbands should be careful, attentive, constant, faithful, and compassionate. They should manifest love and sympathy. If they fulfill the words of Christ, their love will not be of a base, earthly, sensual character that will lead to the destruction of their own bodies and bring upon their wives debility and disease. They will not indulge in the gratification of base passions, while ringing in the ears of their wives that they must be subject to the husband in everything. When the husband has the nobility of character, purity of heart, elevation of mind that every true Christian must possess, it will be made manifest in the marriage relation. If he has the mind of Christ, he will not be a destroyer of the body, but will be full of tender love, seeking to reach the highest standard in Christ.[16]

When Doubts Creep In—No man can truly love his wife when she will patiently submit to become his slave and minister to his depraved passions. In her passive submission she loses the value she once possessed in his eyes. He sees her dragged down from everything elevating to a low level, and soon he suspects that she will as tamely submit to be degraded by another as by himself. He doubts her constancy and purity, tires of her, and seeks new objects to arouse and intensify his hellish passions. The law of God is not regarded. These men are worse than brutes; they are demons in human form. They are unacquainted with the elevating, ennobling principles of true, sanctified love.

[126]

The wife also becomes jealous of the husband and suspects that if opportunity should offer, he would just as readily pay his addresses to another as to her. She sees that he is not controlled by conscience or the fear of God; all these sanctified barriers are broken down by lustful passions; all that is Godlike in the husband is made the servant of low, brutish lust.[17]

The Problem of Unreasonable Demands—The matter now to be settled is: Shall the wife feel bound to yield implicitly to the demands of her husband when she sees that nothing but base passions control him, and when her reason and judgment are convinced that she does it to the injury of her body, which God has enjoined upon her to possess in sanctification and honor, to preserve as a living sacrifice to God?

It is not pure, holy love which leads the wife to gratify the animal propensities of her husband at the expense of health and life. If she possesses true love and wisdom, she will seek to divert his mind from the gratification of lustful passions to high and spiritual themes by dwelling upon interesting spiritual subjects. It may be necessary to humbly and affectionately urge, even at the risk of his displeasure, that she cannot debase her body by yielding to sexual excess. She should, in a tender, kind manner, remind him that God has the first and highest claim upon her entire being, and that she cannot disregard this claim, for she will be held accountable in the great day of God....

If she will elevate her affections, and in sanctification and honor preserve her refined, womanly dignity, woman can do much by her judicious influence to sanctify her husband, and thus fulfill her high mission. In so doing she can save both her husband and herself, thus [127] performing a double work. In this matter, so delicate and so difficult to manage, much wisdom and patience are necessary, as well as moral courage and fortitude. Strength and grace can be found in prayer. Sincere love is to be the ruling principle of the heart. Love to God and love to the husband can alone be the right ground of action....

When the wife yields her body and mind to the control of her husband, being passive to his will in all things, sacrificing her conscience, her dignity, and even her identity, she loses the opportunity of exerting that mighty influence for good which she should possess to elevate her husband. She could soften his stern nature, and her sanctifying influence could be exerted in a manner to refine and purify, leading him to strive earnestly to govern his passions and be more spiritually minded, that they might be partakers together of the divine nature, having escaped the corruption that is in the world through lust. The power of influence can be great to lead the mind to high and noble themes, above the low, sensual indulgences for which the heart unrenewed by grace naturally seeks. If the wife feels that in order to please her husband she must come down to his standard, when animal passion is the principal basis of his love and controls his actions, she displeases God; for she fails to exert a sanctifying influence upon her husband. If she feels that she must submit to his animal passions without a word of remonstrance, she does not understand her duty to him nor to her God.[18]

Our Bodies a Purchased Possession—The lower passions have their seat in the body and work through it. The words "flesh" or "fleshly" or "carnal lusts" embrace the lower, corrupt nature; the flesh of itself cannot act contrary to the will of God. We are commanded to crucify the flesh, with the affections and lusts. How shall we do it? Shall we inflict pain on the body? No; but put to death the temptation to sin. The corrupt thought is to be expelled. Every thought is to be brought into captivity to Jesus Christ. All animal propensities are to be subjected to the higher powers of the soul. The love of God must reign supreme; Christ must occupy an undivided throne. Our bodies are to be regarded as His purchased possession. The members of the body are to become the instruments of righteousness.[19]

[128]

[129]

[130]

[1] A Solemn Appeal, 139.

[2] Manuscript 126, 1903.

[3] The Review and Herald, September 25, 1888.

[4] Testimonies For The Church 2, 252.

[5] Ibid., 2:380.

[6] Ibid., 2:391.

[7] Testimonies For The Church 4, 505.

[8] Testimonies For The Church 2, 472.

[9] Testimonies For The Church 2, 477, 478.

[10] Testimonies For The Church 2, 381.

[11] Testimonies For The Church 2, 473.

[12] Christian Temperance and Bible Hygiene, 130.

[13] Testimonies For The Church 2, 473.

[14] Manuscript 1, 1888.

[15] Testimonies For The Church 2, 477.

[16] Manuscript 17, 1891.

[17] Testimonies For The Church 2, 474, 475.

[18] Ibid., 2:475-477.

[19] Manuscript 1, 1888.

Section 6—The New Home

Chapter 19—Where Shall the Home Be?

Guiding Principles in Choosing the Location—In choosing a home, God would have us consider, first of all, the moral and religious influences that will surround us and our families.[1]

We should choose the society most favorable to our spiritual advancement, and avail ourselves of every help within our reach; for Satan will oppose many hindrances to make our progress toward heaven as difficult as possible. We may be placed in trying positions, for many cannot have their surroundings what they would; but we should not voluntarily expose ourselves to influences that are unfavorable to the formation of Christian character. When duty calls us to do this, we should be doubly watchful and prayerful, that, through the grace of Christ, we may stand uncorrupted.[2]

The gospel ... teaches us to estimate things at their true value, and to give the most effort to the things of greatest worth—the things that will endure. This lesson is needed by those upon whom rests the responsibility of selecting a home. They should not allow themselves to be diverted from the highest aim....

As the location for a home is sought, let this purpose direct the choice. Be not controlled by the desire for wealth, the dictates of fashion, or the customs of society. Consider what will tend most to simplicity, purity, health, and real worth....

Instead of dwelling where only the works of men can be seen, where the sights and sounds frequently suggest thoughts of evil, where turmoil and confusion bring weariness and disquietude, go where you can look upon the works of God. Find rest of spirit in the beauty and quietude and peace of nature. Let the eye rest on the green fields, the groves, and the hills. Look up to the blue sky, unobscured by the city's dust and smoke, and breathe the invigorating air of heaven.[3]

The First Home a Model—The home of our first parents was to be a pattern for other homes as their children should go forth to occupy the earth. That home, beautified by the hand of God

Himself, was not a gorgeous palace. Men, in their pride, delight in magnificent and costly edifices, and glory in the works of their own hands: but God placed Adam in a garden. This was his dwelling. The blue heavens were its dome; the earth, with its delicate flowers and carpet of living green, was its floor; and the leafy branches of the goodly trees were its canopy. Its walls were hung with the most magnificent adornings—the handiwork of the great Master Artist. In the surroundings of the holy pair was a lesson for all time—that true happiness is found, not in the indulgence of pride and luxury, but in communion with God through His created works. If men would give less attention to the artificial and would cultivate greater simplicity, they would come far nearer to answering the purpose of God in their creation. Pride and ambition are never satisfied, but those who are truly wise will find substantial and elevating pleasure in the sources of enjoyment that God has placed within the reach of all.[4]

God's Choice of an Earthly Home for His Son—Jesus came to this earth to accomplish the greatest work ever accomplished among men. He came as God's ambassador, to show us how to live so as to secure life's best results. What were the conditions chosen by the Infinite Father for His Son? A secluded home in the Galilean hills; a household sustained by honest, self-respecting labor; a life of simplicity; daily conflict with difficulty and hardship; self-sacrifice, economy, and patient, gladsome service; the hour of study at His mother's side, with the open scroll of Scripture; the quiet of dawn or twilight in the green valley; the holy ministries of nature; the study of creation and providence; and the soul's communion with God—these were the conditions and opportunities of the early life of Jesus.[5]

[133]

Rural Homes in the Promised Land—In the Promised Land the discipline begun in the wilderness was continued under circumstances favorable to the formation of right habits. The people were not crowded together in cities, but each family had its own landed possession, ensuring to all the health-giving blessings of a natural, unperverted life.[6]

Effect of Environment on the Character of John—John the Baptist, the forerunner of Christ, received his early training from his parents. The greater portion of his life was spent in the wilderness.... It was John's choice to forego the enjoyments and luxuries of city life for the stern discipline of the wilderness. Here his surroundings were favorable to habits of simplicity and self-denial. Uninterrupted by the clamor of the world, he could here study the lessons of nature, of revelation, and of providence.... From his childhood his mission had been kept before him, and he accepted the holy trust. To him the solitude of the desert was a welcome escape from the society in which suspicion, unbelief, and impurity had become well-nigh all-pervading. He distrusted his own power to withstand temptation and shrank from constant contact with sin lest he should lose the sense of its exceeding sinfulness.[7]

Other Worthies Reared in Country Homes—So with the great majority of the best and noblest men of all ages. Read the history of Abraham, Jacob, and Joseph; of Moses, David, and Elisha. Study the lives of men of later times who have most worthily filled positions of trust and responsibility.

How many of these were reared in country homes. They knew little of luxury. They did not spend their youth in amusement. Many were forced to struggle with poverty and hardship. They early learned to work, and their active life in the open air gave vigor and elasticity to all their faculties. Forced to depend upon their own resources, they learned to combat difficulties and to surmount obstacles, and they gained courage and perseverance. They learned the lessons of self-reliance and self-control. Sheltered in a great degree from evil associations, they were satisfied with natural pleasures and wholesome companionships. They were simple in their tastes and temperate in their habits. They were governed by principle, and they grew up pure and strong and true. When called to their lifework, they brought to it physical and mental power, buoyancy of spirit, ability to plan and execute, and steadfastness in resisting evil that made them a positive power for good in the world.[8]

[134]

[135]

[1]Patriarchs and Prophets, 169.

[2]Messages to Young People, 419.

[3]The Ministry of Healing, 363, 366, 367.

[4]Patriarchs and Prophets, 49, 50.

[5]The Ministry of Healing, 365, 366.

[6]Ibid., 280.

[7]Testimonies For The Church 8, 221.

[8]The Ministry of Healing, 366.

Chapter 20—The Family and the City

Hazards of City Life—Life in the cities is false and artificial. The intense passion for money getting, the whirl of excitement and pleasure seeking, the thirst for display, the luxury and extravagance—all are forces that, with the great masses of mankind, are turning the mind from life's true purpose. They are opening the door to a thousand evils. Upon the youth they have almost irresistible power. One of the most subtle and dangerous temptations that assails the children and youth in the cities is the love of pleasure. Holidays are numerous; games and horse racing draw thousands, and the whirl of excitement and pleasure attracts them away from the sober duties of life. Money that should have been saved for better uses is frittered away for amusements.[1]

Consider the Health Standpoint—The physical surroundings in the cities are often a peril to health. The constant liability to contact with disease, the prevalence of foul air, impure water, impure food, the crowded, dark, unhealthful dwellings, are some of the many evils to be met.

It was not God's purpose that people should be crowded into cities, huddled together in terraces and tenements. In the beginning He placed our first parents amidst the beautiful sights and sounds He desires us to rejoice in today. The more nearly we come into harmony with God's original plan, the more favorable will be our position to secure health of body and mind and soul.[2]

[136]

Hotbeds of Iniquity—The cities are filled with temptation. We should plan our work in such a way as to keep our young people as far as possible from this contamination.[3]

The children and youth should be carefully guarded. They should be kept away from the hotbeds of iniquity that are to be found in our cities.[4]

Turmoil and Confusion—It is not God's will that His people shall settle in the cities, where there is constant turmoil and confusion. Their children should be spared this, for the whole system is demoralized by the hurry and rush and noise.[5]

Labor Troubles—Through the working of trusts and the results of labor unions and strikes, the conditions of life in the city are constantly becoming more and more difficult. Serious troubles are before us, and for many families removal from the cities will become a necessity.[6]

Impending Destruction—The time is near when large cities will be swept away, and all should be warned of these coming judgments.[7]

Oh, that God's people had a sense of the impending destruction of thousands of cities now almost given to idolatry![8]

For Worldly Interests and Love of Gain—It is often the case that parents are not careful to surround their children with right influences. In choosing a home, they think more of their worldly interests than of the moral and social atmosphere, and the children form associations that are unfavorable to the development of piety and the formation of right characters....

[137]

Parents who denounce the Canaanites for offering their children to Moloch, what are you doing? You are making a most costly offering to your mammon god, and then, when your children grow up unloved and unlovely in character, when they show decided impiety and a tendency to infidelity, you blame the faith you profess because it was unable to save them. You are reaping that which you have sown—the result of your selfish love of the world and neglect of the means of grace. You moved your families into places of temptation; and the ark of God, your glory and defense, you did not consider essential; and the Lord has not worked a miracle to deliver your children from temptation.[9]

Cities Offer No Real Benefit—There is not one family in a hundred who will be improved physically, mentally, or spiritually by residing in the city. Faith, hope, love, happiness, can far better be gained in retired places, where there are fields and hills and trees. Take your children away from the sights and sounds of the city, away from the rattle and din of streetcars and teams, and their minds will become more healthy. It will be found easier to bring home to their hearts the truth of the word of God.[10]

Counsel on Moving From Rural to City Areas—Many parents remove from their country homes to the city, regarding it as a more desirable or profitable location. But by making this change, they expose their children to many and great temptations. The boys have no employment, and they obtain a street education and go on from one step in depravity to another, until they lose all interest in anything that is good and pure and holy. How much better had the parents remained with their families in the country, where the influences are most favorable for physical and mental strength. Let the youth be taught to labor in tilling the soil, and let them sleep the sweet sleep of weariness and innocence.

[138]

Through the neglect of parents, the youth in our cities are corrupting their ways and polluting their souls before God. This will ever be the fruit of idleness. The almshouses, the prisons, and the gallows publish the sorrowful tale of the neglected duties of parents.[11]

Better sacrifice any and every worldly consideration than to imperil the precious souls committed to your care. They will be assailed by temptations and should be taught to meet them; but it is your duty to cut off every influence, to break up every habit, to sunder every tie, that keeps you from the most free, open, and hearty committal of yourselves and your family to God.

Instead of the crowded city seek some retired situation where your children will be, so far as possible, shielded from temptation, and there train and educate them for usefulness. The prophet Ezekiel thus enumerates the causes that led to Sodom's sin and destruction: "Pride, fulness of bread, and abundance of idleness was in her and in her daughters, neither did she strengthen the hand of the poor and needy." All who would escape the doom of Sodom must shun the course that brought God's judgments upon that wicked city.[12]

When Lot entered Sodom, he fully intended to keep himself free from iniquity and to command his household after him. But he signally failed. The corrupting influences about him had an effect upon his own faith, and his children's connection with the inhabitants of Sodom bound up his interest in a measure with theirs. The result is before us. Many are still making a similar mistake.[13]

[139]

Let it be your study to select and make your homes as far from Sodom and Gomorrah as you can. Keep out of the large cities. If possible make your homes in the quiet retirement of the country, even if you can never become wealthy by so doing. Locate where there is the best influence.[14]

I am instructed by the Lord to warn our people not to flock to the cities to find homes for their families. To fathers and to mothers I am instructed to say, Fail not to keep your children within your own premises.[15]

Time Now to Move From the Cities—Take your families away from the cities is my message.[16]

The time has come when, as God opens the way, families should move out of the cities. The children should be taken into the country. The parents should get as suitable a place as their means will allow. Though the dwelling may be small, yet there should be land in connection with it that may be cultivated.[17]

Before the overflowing scourge shall come upon the dwellers of the earth, the Lord calls upon all who are Israelites indeed to prepare for that event. To parents He sends the warning cry: Gather your children into your own houses; gather them away from those who are disregarding the commandments of God, who are teaching and practicing evil. Get out of the large cities as fast as possible.[18]

God Will Help His People—Parents can secure small homes in the country, with land for cultivation, where they can have orchards and where they can raise vegetables and small fruits to take the place of flesh meat, which is so corrupting to the lifeblood coursing [140] through the veins. On such places the children will not be surrounded with the corrupting influences of city life. God will help His people [141] to find such homes outside of the cities.[19]

[1] The Ministry of Healing, 364.

[2] Ibid., 365.

[3] Country Living, 30.

[4] Ibid., 12.

[5] Ibid., 29.

[6] The Ministry of Healing, 364.

[7] Evangelism, 29.

[8] The Review and Herald, September 10, 1903.

[9] Testimonies For The Church 5, 320.

[10] Country Living, 13.

[11] The Review and Herald, September 13, 1881

[12] Testimonies For The Church 5, 232, 233.

[13] Patriarchs and Prophets, 168.

[14]Manuscript 57, 1897.

[15]Country Living, 12, 13.

[16]Ibid., 29.

[17]Ibid., 24.

[18]Testimonies For The Church 6, 195.

[19]Medical Ministry, 310.

Chapter 21—Advantages of the Country

With a Piece of Land and a Comfortable Home—Whenever possible, it is the duty of parents to make homes in the country for their children.[1]

Fathers and mothers who possess a piece of land and a comfortable home are kings and queens.[2]

Do not consider it a privation when you are called to leave the cities and move out into the country places. Here there await rich blessings for those who will grasp them.[3]

Contributes to Economic Security—Again and again the Lord has instructed that our people are to take their families away from the cities, into the country, where they can raise their own provisions; for in the future the problem of buying and selling will be a very serious one. We should now begin to heed the instruction given us over and over again: Get out of the cities into rural districts, where the houses are not crowded closely together, and where you will be free from the interference of enemies.[4] (For further detailed counsel on this topic see *Country Living*.)

Advice to a City Dweller—It would be well for you to lay by your perplexing cares and find a retreat in the country, where there is not so strong an influence to corrupt the morals of the young. True, you would not be entirely free from annoyances and perplexing cares in the country; but you would there avoid many evils and close the door against a flood of temptations which threaten to overpower the [142] minds of your children. They need employment and variety. The sameness of their home makes them uneasy and restless, and they have fallen into the habit of mingling with the vicious lads of the town, thus obtaining a street education....

To live in the country would be very beneficial to them; an active, out-of-door life would develop health of both mind and body. They should have a garden to cultivate, where they might find both amusement and useful employment. The training of plants and flowers tends to the improvement of taste and judgment, while an acquaintance with God's useful and beautiful creations has a refining and ennobling influence upon the mind, referring it to the Maker and Master of all.[5]

Rich Blessings Assured Country Dwellers—The earth has blessings hidden in her depths for those who have courage and will and perseverance to gather her treasures.... Many farmers have failed to secure adequate returns from their land because they have undertaken the work as though it was a degrading employment; they do not see that there is a blessing in it for themselves and their families.[6]

Labor That Will Quicken the Mind, Refine the Character— In the cultivation of the soil the thoughtful worker will find that treasures little dreamed of are opening up before him. No one can succeed in agriculture or gardening without attention to the laws involved. The special needs of every variety of plant must be studied. Different varieties require different soil and cultivation, and compliance with the laws governing each is the condition of success. The attention required in transplanting, that not even a root fiber shall be crowded or misplaced, the care of the young plants, the pruning and watering, the shielding from frost at night and sun by day, keeping out weeds, disease, and insect pests, the training and arranging, not only teach important lessons concerning the development of character, but the work itself is a means of development. In cultivating carefulness, patience, attention to detail, obedience to law, it imparts a most essential training. The constant contact with the mystery of life and the loveliness of nature, as well as the tenderness called forth in ministering to these beautiful objects of God's creation, tends to quicken the mind and refine and elevate the character.[7]

[143]

God Will Instruct and Teach—He who taught Adam and Eve in Eden how to tend the garden would instruct men today. There is wisdom for him who holds the plow and plants and sows the seed. The earth has its concealed treasures, and the Lord would have thousands and tens of thousands working upon the soil who are crowded into the cities to watch for a chance to earn a trifle.... Those who will take their families into the country place them where they have fewer temptations. The children who are with parents that love and fear God are in every way much better situated to learn of the

Great Teacher, who is the source and fountain of wisdom. They have a much more favorable opportunity to gain a fitness for the kingdom of heaven.[8]

God's Plan for Israel's Land—Through disobedience to God Adam and Eve had lost Eden, and because of sin the whole earth was cursed. But if God's people followed His instruction, their land would be restored to fertility and beauty. God Himself gave them directions in regard to the culture of the soil, and they were to co-operate with Him in its restoration. Thus the whole land, under God's control, would become an object lesson of spiritual truth. As in obedience to His natural laws the earth should produce its treasures, so in obedience to His moral law the hearts of the people were to reflect the attributes of His character.[9]

Find Spiritual Lessons in Daily Living—God has surrounded us with nature's beautiful scenery to attract and interest the mind. It is His design that we should associate the glories of nature with His character. If we faithfully study the book of nature, we shall find it a fruitful source for contemplating the infinite love and power of God.[10]

Christ has linked His teaching, not only with the day of rest, but with the week of toil.... In the plowing and sowing, the tilling and reaping, He teaches us to see an illustration of His work of grace in the heart. So in every line of useful labor and every association of life, He desires us to find a lesson of divine truth. Then our daily toil will no longer absorb our attention and lead us to forget God; it will continually remind us of our Creator and Redeemer. The thought of God will run like a thread of gold through all our homely cares and occupations. For us the glory of His face will again rest upon the face of nature. We shall ever be learning new lessons of heavenly truth and growing into the image of His purity.[11]

Identical Laws Govern Nature and Mankind—The Great Teacher brought His hearers in contact with nature, that they might listen to the voice which speaks in all created things; and as their hearts became tender and their minds receptive, He helped them to interpret the spiritual teaching of the scenes upon which their eyes rested.... In His lessons there was something to interest every mind, to appeal to every heart. Thus the daily task, instead of being a mere

[144]

[145]

round of toil, bereft of higher thoughts, was brightened and uplifted by constant reminders of the spiritual and the unseen.

So we should teach. Let the children learn to see in nature an expression of the love and the wisdom of God; let the thought of Him be linked with bird and flower and tree; let all things seen become to them the interpreters of the unseen, and all the events of life be a means of divine teaching.

As they learn thus to study the lessons in all created things and in all life's experiences, show that the same laws which govern the things of nature and the events of life are to control us, that they are given for our good, and that only in obedience to them can we find true happiness and success.[12]

Give Practical Lessons in Agriculture—Of the almost innumerable lessons taught in the varied processes of growth, some of the most precious are conveyed in the Saviour's parable of the growing seed. It has lessons for old and young....

The germination of the seed represents the beginning of spiritual life, and the development of the plant is a figure of the development of character.... As parents and teachers try to teach these lessons, the work should be made practical. Let the children themselves prepare the soil and sow the seed. As they work, the parent or teacher can explain the garden of the heart, with the good or bad seed sown there, and that as the garden must be prepared for the natural seed, so the heart must be prepared for the seed of truth.... No one settles upon a raw piece of land with the expectation that it will at once yield a harvest. Diligent, persevering labor must be put forth in the preparation of the soil, the sowing of the seed, and the culture of the crop. So it must be in the spiritual sowing.[13]

[146]

Wrong Habits Seen as Weeds—If possible, the home should be out of the city, where the children can have ground to cultivate. Let them each have a piece of ground of their own; and as you teach them how to make a garden, how to prepare the soil for seed, and the importance of keeping all the weeds pulled out, teach them also how important it is to keep unsightly, injurious practices out of the life. Teach them to keep down wrong habits as they keep down the weeds in their gardens. It will take time to teach these lessons, but it will pay, greatly pay.[14]

Home Surroundings to Exemplify Our Beliefs—Parents are under obligation to God to make their surroundings such as will correspond to the truth they profess. They can then give correct lessons to their children, and the children will learn to associate the home below with the home above. The family here must, as far as possible, be a model of the one in heaven. Then temptations to indulge in what is low and groveling will lose much of their force. Children should be taught that they are only probationers here, and educated to become inhabitants of the mansions which Christ is preparing for those who love Him and keep His commandments. This is the highest duty which parents have to perform.[15]

Parents: Get Homes in the Country—So long as God gives me power to speak to our people, I shall continue to call upon parents to leave the cities and get homes in the country, where they can cultivate the soil and learn from the book of nature the lessons of

[147] purity and simplicity. The things of nature are the Lord's silent ministers, given to us to teach us spiritual truths. They speak to us of the love of God and declare the wisdom of the great Master Artist.

I love the beautiful flowers. They are memories of Eden, pointing to the blessed country into which, if faithful, we shall soon enter. The Lord is leading my mind to the health-giving properties of the

[148] flowers and trees.[16]

---

[1]Country Living, 12.

[2]Fundamentals of Christian Education, 327.

[3]Country Living, 14.

[4]Ibid., 9, 10.

[5]Testimonies For The Church 4, 136.

[6]Fundamentals of Christian Education, 326, 327.

[7]Education, 111, 112.

[8]Fundamentals of Christian Education, 326.

[9]Christ's Object Lessons, 289.

[10]Messages to Young People, 365, 366.

[11]Christ's Object Lessons, 26, 27.

[12]Education, 102, 103.

[13]Ibid., 104, 105, 111.

[14]Counsels to Teachers, Parents, and Students, 124.

[15]Christian Temperance and Bible Hygiene, 144.

[16]Letter 47, 1903.

Chapter 22—Building and Furnishing the Home

Provide Ventilation, Sunlight, and Drainage—In the construction of buildings, whether for public purposes or as dwellings, care should be taken to provide for good ventilation and plenty of sunlight. Churches and schoolrooms are often faulty in this respect. Neglect of proper ventilation is responsible for much of the drowsiness and dullness that destroy the effect of many a sermon and make the teacher's work toilsome and ineffective.

So far as possible, all buildings intended for human habitation should be placed on high, well-drained ground. This will ensure a dry site.... This matter is often too lightly regarded. Continuous ill health, serious diseases, and many deaths result from the dampness and malaria of low-lying, ill-drained situations.

In the building of houses it is especially important to secure thorough ventilation and plenty of sunlight. Let there be a current of air and an abundance of light in every room in the house. Sleeping rooms should be so arranged as to have a free circulation of air day and night. No room is fit to be occupied as a sleeping room unless it can be thrown open daily to the air and sunshine. In most countries bedrooms need to be supplied with conveniences for heating, that they may be thoroughly warmed and dried in cold or wet weather.

The guestchamber should have equal care with the rooms intended for constant use. Like the other bedrooms, it should have air and sunshine and should be provided with some means of heating to dry out the dampness that always accumulates in a room not in [149] constant use. Whoever sleeps in a sunless room or occupies a bed that has not been thoroughly dried and aired does so at the risk of health, and often of life....

Those who have the aged to provide for should remember that these especially need warm, comfortable rooms. Vigor declines as years advance, leaving less vitality with which to resist unhealthful influences; hence the greater necessity for the aged to have plenty of sunlight and fresh, pure air.[1]

Avoid Lowlands—If we would have our homes the abiding place of health and happiness, we must place them above the miasma and fog of the lowlands and give free entrance to heaven's life-giving agencies. Dispense with heavy curtains, open the windows and the blinds, allow no vines, however beautiful, to shade the windows, and permit no trees to stand so near the house as to shut out the sunshine. The sunlight may fade the drapery and the carpets and tarnish the picture frames, but it will bring a healthy glow to the cheeks of the children.[2]

The Yard Surrounding the House—A yard beautified with scattering trees and some shrubbery, at a proper distance from the house, has a happy influence upon the family, and, if well taken care of, will prove no injury to the health. But shade trees and shrubbery close and dense around a house make it unhealthful, for they prevent the free circulation of air and shut out the rays of the sun. In consequence, a dampness gathers in the house, especially in wet seasons.[3]

[150] **The Effect of Natural Beauty on the Household**—God loves the beautiful. He has clothed the earth and the heavens with beauty, and with a Father's joy He watches the delight of His children in the things that He has made. He desires us to surround our homes with the beauty of natural things.

Nearly all dwellers in the country, however poor, could have about their homes a bit of grassy lawn, a few shade trees, flowering shrubbery, or fragrant blossoms. And far more than any artificial adorning will they minister to the happiness of the household. They will bring into the home life a softening, refining influence, strengthening the love of nature and drawing the members of the household nearer to one another and nearer to God.[4]

Let the Home Furnishings Be Simple—Our artificial habits deprive us of many blessings and much enjoyment, and unfit us for living the most useful lives. Elaborate and expensive furnishings are a waste not only of money but of that which is a thousandfold more precious. They bring into the home a heavy burden of care and labor and perplexity....

Furnish your home with things plain and simple, things that will bear handling, that can be easily kept clean, and that can be replaced without great expense. By exercising taste, you can make a very simple home attractive and inviting, if love and contentment are there.[5]

Happiness is not found in empty show. The more simple the order of a well-regulated household, the happier will that home be.[6]

Avoid the Spirit of Rivalry—Life is a disappointment and a weariness to many persons because of the unnecessary labor with which they burden themselves in meeting the claims of custom. Their minds are continually harassed with anxiety as to supplying wants which are the offspring of pride and fashion.... [151]

The expense, the care, and labor lavished on that which, if not positively injurious, is unnecessary would go far toward advancing the cause of God if applied to a worthier object. People crave what are called the luxuries of life, and sacrifice health, strength, and means to obtain them. A lamentable spirit of rivalry is manifested among persons of the same class as to who shall make the greatest display in matters of dress and of household expenditure. The sweet word "Home" is perverted to mean "something with four walls, filled with elegant furniture and adornments," while its inmates are on a continual strain to meet the requirements of custom in the different departments of life.[7]

Many are unhappy in their home life because they are trying so hard to keep up appearances. They expend large sums of money and labor unremittingly that they may make a display and gain the praise of their associates—those who really care nothing for them or their prosperity. One article after another is considered indispensable to the household appointments, until many expensive additions are made that, while they please the eye and gratify pride and ambition, do not in the least increase the comfort of the family. And yet these things have taxed the strength and patience, and consumed valuable time which should have been given to the service of the Lord.

The precious grace of God is made secondary to matters of no real importance; and many, while collecting material for enjoyment, lose the capacity for happiness. They find that their possessions fail to give the satisfaction they had hoped to derive from them. This endless round of labor, this unceasing anxiety to embellish the home [152] for visitors and strangers to admire, never pays for the time and means thus expended. It is placing upon the neck a yoke of bondage grievous to be borne.[8]

Two Visits are Contrasted—In some families there is too much done. Neatness and order are essential to comfort, but these virtues should not be carried to such an extreme as to make life a period of unceasing drudgery and to render the inmates of the home miserable. In the houses of some whom we highly esteem, there is a stiff precision about the arrangement of the furniture and belongings that is quite as disagreeable as a lack of order would be. The painful propriety which invests the whole house makes it impossible to find there that rest which one expects in the true home.

It is not pleasant, when making a brief visit to dear friends, to see the broom and the duster in constant requisition, and the time which you had anticipated enjoying with your friends in social converse spent by them in a general tidying up and peering into corners in search of a concealed speck of dust or a cobweb. Although this may be done out of respect to your presence in the house, yet you feel a painful conviction that your company is of less consequence to your friends than their ideas of excessive neatness.

In direct contrast to such homes was one that we visited during the last summer [1876]. Here the few hours of our stay were not spent in useless labor or in doing that which could be done as well at some other time, but were occupied in a pleasant and profitable manner, restful alike to mind and body. The house was a model of comfort, although not extravagantly furnished. The rooms were all well lighted and ventilated, ... which is of more real value than the most costly adornments. The parlors were not furnished with that precision which is so tiresome to the eye, but there was a pleasing variety in the articles of furniture.

[153]

The chairs were mostly rockers or easy chairs, not all of the same fashion, but adapted to the comfort of the different members of the family. There were low, cushioned rocking chairs and high, straight-backed ones; wide, capacious lounging chairs and snug, little ones; there were also comfortable sofas; and all seemed to say, Try me, rest in me. There were tables strewn with books and papers. All was neat and attractive, but without that precise arrangement that seems to warn all beholders not to touch anything for fear of getting it out of place.

The proprietors of this pleasant home were in such circumstances that they might have furnished and embellished their residence expensively, but they had wisely chosen comfort rather than display. There was nothing in the house considered too good for general use, and the curtains and blinds were not kept closed to keep the carpets from fading and the furniture from tarnishing. The God-given sunlight and air had free ingress, with the fragrance of the flowers in the garden. The family were, of course, in keeping with the home; they were cheerful and entertaining, doing everything needful for our comfort, without oppressing us with so much attention as to make us fear that we were causing extra trouble. We felt that here was a place of rest. This was a home in the fullest sense of the word.[9]

A Principle Used in Decorating—The rigid precision which we have mentioned as being a disagreeable feature of so many homes is not in accordance with the great plan of nature. God has not caused the flowers of the fields to grow in regular beds, with set borders, but He has scattered them like gems over the greensward, and they beautify the earth with their variety of form and color. The trees of the forest are not in regular order. It is restful to eye and mind to range over the scenes of nature, over forest, hill, and valley, plain and river, enjoying the endless diversity of form and color, and the beauty with which trees, shrubs, and flowers are grouped in nature's garden, making it a picture of loveliness. Childhood, youth, and age can alike find rest and gratification there.

[154]

This law of variety can be in a measure carried out in the home. There should be a proper harmony of colors and a general fitness of things in the furnishings of a house; but it is not necessary to good taste that every article of furniture in a room should be of the same pattern in design, material, or upholstery; but, on the contrary, it is more pleasing to the eye that there should be a harmonious variety.

But whether the home be humble or elegant, its appointments costly or the reverse, there will be no happiness within its walls unless the spirit of its inmates is in harmony with the divine will. Contentment should reign within the household.[10]

The very best part of the house, the sunniest and most inviting rooms, and the most comfortable furniture should be in a daily use by those who really live in the house. This will make home attractive to the inmates and also to that class of friends who really care for us, whom we could benefit, and by whom we could be benefited.[11]

Consider the Children's Comfort and Welfare—It does not require costly surroundings and expensive furniture to make children contented and happy in their homes, but it is necessary that the parents give them tender love and careful attention.[12]

Four walls and costly furniture, velvet carpets, elegant mirrors, and fine pictures do not make a "home" if sympathy and love are wanting. That sacred word does not belong to the glittering mansion where the joys of domestic life are unknown....

In fact the comfort and welfare of the children are the last things thought of in such a home. They are neglected by the mother, whose whole time is devoted to keeping up appearances and meeting the claims of fashionable society. Their minds are untrained; they acquire bad habits and become restless and dissatisfied. Finding no pleasure in their own homes, but only uncomfortable restrictions, they break away from the family circle as soon as possible. They launch out into the great world with little reluctance, unrestrained by home influence and the tender counsel of the hearthstone.[13]

Don't say to them as I have heard many mothers say, "There is no room for you here in the parlor. Don't sit on that sofa that is covered with satin damask. We don't want you to sit down on that sofa." And when they go into another room, "We don't want your noise here." And they go into the kitchen, and the cook says, "I cannot be bothered with you here. Go out from here with your noise; you pester me so, and bother me." Where do they go to receive their education? Into the street.[14]

Kindness and Love More Precious Than Luxury—Too many cares and burdens are brought into our families, and too little of natural simplicity and peace and happiness is cherished. There should be less care for what the outside world will say, and more thoughtful attention to the members of the family circle. There should be less display and affectation of worldly politeness, and much more tenderness and love, cheerfulness and Christian courtesy among the members of the household. Many need to learn how to make home attractive, a place of enjoyment. Thankful hearts and kind looks are more valuable than wealth and luxury, and contentment with simple things will make home happy if love be there.

Jesus, our Redeemer, walked the earth with the dignity of a king; yet He was meek and lowly of heart. He was a light and blessing in every home because He carried cheerfulness, hope, and courage with Him. Oh, that we could be satisfied with less heart longings, less striving for things difficult to obtain wherewith to beautify our homes, while that which God values above jewels, the meek and quiet spirit, is not cherished. The grace of simplicity, meekness, and true affection would make a paradise of the humblest home. It is better to endure cheerfully every inconvenience than to part with peace and contentment.[15]

[157]

[158]

[1] The Ministry of Healing, 274, 275.

[2] Ibid., 275.

[3] Christian Temperance and Bible Hygiene, 107.

[4] The Ministry of Healing, 370.

[5] Ibid., 367, 370.

[6] The Signs of the Times, August 23, 1877.

[7] The Signs of the Times, August 23, 1877.

[8] The Signs of the Times, October 2, 1884.

[9] The Signs of the Times, August 23, 1877.

[10] The Signs of the Times, August 23, 1877.

[11] The Signs of the Times, October 2, 1884.

[12] The Signs of the Times, October 2, 1884.

[13] The Signs of the Times, October 2, 1884.

[14] Manuscript 43a, 1894.

[15] Testimonies For The Church 4, 621, 622.

Section 7—Heritage of the Lord

Chapter 23—Children a Blessing

God Planned for Families—He who gave Eve to Adam as a helpmeet ... ordained that men and women should be united in holy wedlock, to rear families whose members, crowned with honor, should be recognized as members of the family above.[1]

Children are the heritage of the Lord, and we are answerable to Him for our management of His property.... In love, faith, and prayer let parents work for their households, until with joy they can come to God saying, "Behold, I and the children whom the Lord hath given me."[2]

A childless house is a desolate place. The hearts of the inmates are in danger of becoming selfish, of cherishing a love for their own ease, and consulting their own desires and conveniences. They gather sympathy to themselves, but have little to bestow upon others.[3]

Counsel to a Childless Couple—Selfishness, which manifests itself in a variety of ways according to circumstances and the peculiar organization of individuals, must die. If you had children, and your mind were compelled to be called away from yourself to care for them, to instruct them, and be an example to them, it would be an advantage to you.... When two compose a family, as in your case, and there are no children to call into exercise patience, forbearance, and true love, there is need of constant watchfulness lest selfishness obtain the supremacy, lest you yourselves become the center, and you require attention, care, and interest, which you feel under no

obligation to bestow upon others.[4]

Many are diseased physically, mentally, and morally because their attention is turned almost exclusively to themselves. They might be saved from stagnation by the healthy vitality of younger and varying minds and the restless energy of children.[5]

Noble Traits Are Developed in Caring for Children—I have a very tender interest in all children, for I became a sufferer at a very early age. I have taken many children to care for, and I have always felt that association with the simplicity of childhood was a great blessing to me....

The sympathy, forbearance, and love required in dealing with children would be a blessing in any household. They would soften and subdue set traits of character in those who need to be more cheerful and restful. The presence of a child in a home sweetens and refines. A child brought up in the fear of the Lord is a blessing.[6]

Care and affection for dependent children removes the roughness from our natures, makes us tender and sympathetic, and has an influence to develop the nobler elements of our character.[7]

A Child's Influence on Enoch—After the birth of his first son, Enoch reached a higher experience; he was drawn into a closer relationship with God. He realized more fully his own obligations and responsibility as a son of God. And as he saw the child's love for its father, its simple trust in his protection; as he felt the deep, yearning tenderness of his own heart for that first-born son, he learned a precious lesson of the wonderful love of God to men in the gift of His Son, and the confidence which the children of God may repose in their heavenly Father.[8]

[161]

A Precious Trust—Children are committed to their parents as a precious trust, which God will one day require at their hands. We should give to their training more time, more care, and more prayer. They need more of the right kind of instruction....

Remember that your sons and daughters are younger members of God's family. He has committed them to your care, to train and educate for heaven. You must render an account to Him for the manner in which you discharge your sacred trust.[9]

[162]

---

[1]The Ministry of Healing, 356.

[2]Christ's Object Lessons, 195, 196.

[3]Testimonies For The Church 2:647.

[4]Ibid., 2:230, 231.

[5]Ibid., 2:647.

[6]Letter 329, 1904.

[7]Testimonies For The Church 2:647.

[8]Patriarchs and Prophets, 84.

[9]The Review and Herald, June 13, 1882.

Chapter 24—Size of the Family

A Grievous Wrong to Mothers, Children, and Society— There are parents who, without consideration as to whether or not they can do justice to a large family, fill their houses with these helpless little beings, who are wholly dependent upon their parents for care and instruction.... This is a grievous wrong, not only to the mother, but to her children and to society....

Parents should always bear in mind the future good of their children. They should not be compelled to devote every hour to taxing labor in order to provide the necessaries of life.[1]

Before increasing their family, they should take into consideration whether God would be glorified or dishonored by their bringing children into the world. They should seek to glorify God by their union from the first, and during every year of their married life.[2]

The Mother's Health Is Important— In view of the responsibility that devolves upon parents, it should be carefully considered whether it is best to bring children into the family. Has the mother sufficient strength to care for her children? And can the father give such advantages as will rightly mold and educate the child? How little is the destiny of the child considered! The gratification of passion is the only thought, and burdens are brought upon the wife and mother which undermine her vitality and paralyze her spiritual power. In broken health and with discouraged spirits she finds herself surrounded by a little flock whom she cannot care for as she should. Lacking the instruction they should have, they grow up to dishonor God and to communicate to others the evil of their own natures, and thus an army is raised up whom Satan manages as he pleases.[3]

Other Factors to Be Considered— God would have parents act as rational beings and live in such a manner that each child may be properly educated, that the mother may have strength and time to employ her mental powers in disciplining her little ones for the society of the angels. She should have courage to act nobly her part

[163]

122

and to do her work in the fear and love of God, that her children may prove a blessing to the family and to society.

The husband and father should consider all these things lest the wife and mother of his children be overtaxed and thus overwhelmed with despondency. He should see to it that the mother of his children is not placed in a position where she cannot possibly do justice to her numerous little ones, so that they have to come up without proper training.[4]

Parents should not increase their families any faster than they know that their children can be well cared for and educated. A child in the mother's arms from year to year is great injustice to her. It lessens, and often destroys, social enjoyment and increases domestic wretchedness. It robs their children of that care, education, and happiness which parents should feel it their duty to bestow upon them.[5]

Counsel to Parents of a Large Family—The question to be settled by you is, "Am I raising a family of children to strengthen the influence and swell the ranks of the powers of darkness, or am I bringing up children for Christ?"

[164]

If you do not govern your children and mold their characters to meet the requirements of God, then the fewer children there are to suffer from your defective training the better it will be for you, their parents, and the better it will be for society. Unless children can be trained and disciplined from their babyhood by a wise and judicious mother who is conscientious and intelligent, and who rules her household in the fear of the Lord, molding and shaping their characters to meet the standard of righteousness, it is a sin to increase your family. God has given you reason, and He requires you to use it.[6]

Fathers and mothers, when you know that you are deficient in a knowledge of how to train your children for the Master, why do you not learn your lessons? Why do you continue to bring children into the world to swell the numbers in Satan's ranks? Is God pleased with this showing? When you see that a large family will severely tax your resources, when you see that it is giving the mother her hands full of children, and that she has not time intervening between their births to do the work every mother needs to do, why do you not consider the sure result? Every child draws upon the vitality of the mother, and when fathers and mothers do not use their reason in this matter, what chance is given to parents or children to be properly disciplined? The Lord calls upon parents to consider this matter in the light of future eternal realities.[7]

Economic Considerations—[Parents] should calmly consider what provision can be made for their children. They have no right to bring children into the world to be a burden to others. Have they a business that they can rely upon to sustain a family so that they need not become a burden to others? If they have not, they commit a crime in bringing children into the world to suffer for want of proper care, food, and clothing.[8]

[165]

Those who are seriously deficient in business tact, and who are the least qualified to get along in the world, generally fill their houses with children; while men who have ability to acquire property generally have no more children than they can well provide for. Those who are not qualified to take care of themselves should not have children.[9]

How Perplexity Is Sometimes Brought to the Church—Many who can but barely live when they are single choose to marry and raise a family when they know they have nothing with which to support them. And worse than this, they have no family government. Their whole course in their family is marked with their loose, slack habits. They have but little control over themselves and are passionate, impatient, and fretful. When such embrace the message, they feel that they are entitled to assistance from their more wealthy brethren; and if their expectations are not met, they complain of the church and accuse them of not living out their faith. Who must be the sufferers in this case? Must the cause of God be sapped, and the treasury in different places exhausted, to take care of these large families of poor? No. The parents must be the sufferers. They will not, as a general thing, suffer any greater lack after they embrace the Sabbath than they did before.[10]

How Missionary Service May Be Restricted—In sending missionaries to distant countries, those men should be selected who know how to economize, who have not large families, and who, realizing the shortness of time and the great work to be accomplished, will not fill their hands and houses with children, but will keep themselves as free as possible from everything that will divert their minds

[166]

from their one great work. The wife, if devoted and left free to do so, can, by standing by the side of her husband, accomplish as much as he. God has blessed woman with talents to be used to His glory in bringing many sons and daughters to God; but many who might be efficient laborers are kept at home to care for their little ones.

We want missionaries who are missionaries in the fullest sense of the word; who will put aside selfish considerations and let the cause of God come first; and who, working with an eye single to His glory, will keep themselves as minute men to go where He shall bid and to work in any capacity to spread the knowledge of the truth. Men who have wives that love and fear God and that can help them in the work are needed in the missionary field. Many who have families go out to labor, but they do not give themselves entirely to the work. Their minds are divided. Wife and children draw them from their labor and often keep them out of fields that they might enter were it not that they think they must be near their home.[11]

[167]

---

[1] The Review and Herald, June 24, 1890.

[2] Testimonies For The Church 2:380.

[3] The Review and Herald, October 25, 1892.

[4] The Review and Herald, June 24, 1890.

[5] A Solemn Appeal, 110, 111

[6] Testimonies For The Church 5, 323, 324.

[7] Letter 107, 1898.

[8] Testimonies For The Church 2, 380.

[9] A Solemn Appeal, 103.

[10] Testimonies For The Church 1, 273.

[11] The Review and Herald, December 8, 1885.

Chapter 25—Caring for Needy Children

Orphaned Children—Many a father who has died in the faith, resting upon the eternal promise of God, has left his loved ones in full trust that the Lord would care for them. And how does the Lord provide for these bereaved ones? He does not work a miracle in sending manna from heaven; He does not send ravens to bring them food; but He works a miracle upon human hearts, expelling selfishness from the soul and unsealing the fountains of benevolence. He tests the love of His professed followers by committing to their tender mercies the afflicted and bereaved ones.

Let those who have the love of God open their hearts and homes to take in these children....

There is a wide field of usefulness before all who will work for the Master in caring for these children and youth who have been deprived of the watchful guidance of parents and the subduing influence of a Christian home. Many of them have inherited evil traits of character; and if left to grow up in ignorance, they will drift into associations that lead to vice and crime. These unpromising children need to be placed in a position favorable for the formation of a right character, that they may become children of God.[1]

Responsibility of the Church—Fatherless and motherless children are thrown into the arms of the church, and Christ says to His followers: Take these destitute children, bring them up for Me, and ye shall receive your wages. I have seen much selfishness exhibited

[168] in these things. Unless there is some special evidence that they *themselves* are to be benefited by adopting into their family those who need homes, some turn away and answer: No. They do not seem to know or care whether such are saved or lost. That, they think, is not their business. With Cain they say: "Am I my brother's keeper?" They are not willing to be put to inconvenience or to make any sacrifice for the orphans, and they indifferently thrust such ones into the arms of the world, who are sometimes more willing to receive them than are these professed Christians. In the day of God inquiry

126

will be made for those whom Heaven gave them the opportunity of saving. But they wished to be excused, and would not engage in the good work unless they could make it a matter of profit to them. I have been shown that those who refuse these opportunities for doing good will hear from Jesus: "As ye did it not to one of the least of these, ye did it not to Me." Please read Isaiah 58: [verses 5-11].[2]

An Appeal to Childless Couples—Some who have not children of their own should educate themselves to love and care for the children of others. They may not be called to go to a foreign field of labor, but they may be called to work in the very locality in which they live. In place of giving so much attention to pets, lavishing affection upon dumb animals, let them exercise their talent upon human beings who have a heaven to win and a hell to shun. Let them give their attention to little children whose characters they may mold and fashion after the divine similitude. Place your love upon the homeless little ones that are around you. Instead of closing your heart to the members of the human family, see how many of these little homeless ones you can bring up in the nurture and admonition of the Lord. There is an abundance of work for everyone who wants work to do. By engaging in this line of Christian endeavor, the church may be increased in members and enriched in spirit. The work of saving the homeless and the fatherless is everyone's business.[3]

[169]

If those who have no children and whom God has made stewards of means would expand their hearts to care for children who need love, care, and affection, and assistance with this world's goods, they would be far happier than they are today. So long as youth who have not a father's pitying care nor a mother's tender love are exposed to the corrupting influences of these last days, it is somebody's duty to supply the place of father and mother to some of them. Learn to give them love, affection, and sympathy. All who profess to have a Father in heaven, who they hope will care for them and finally take them to the home He has prepared for them, ought to feel a solemn obligation resting upon them to be friends to the friendless and fathers to the orphans, to aid the widows, and be of some practical use in this world by benefiting humanity.[4]

Should Ministers' Wives Adopt Children?—The question has been asked whether a minister's wife should adopt infant children. I answer: if she has no inclination or fitness to engage in missionary work outside her home, and feels it her duty to take orphan children and care for them, she may do a good work. But let the choice of children be first made from among those who have been left orphans by Sabbathkeeping parents. God will bless men and women as they with willing hearts share their homes with these homeless ones. But if the minister's wife can herself act a part in the work of educating [170] others, she should consecrate her powers to God as a Christian worker. She should be a true helper to her husband, assisting him in his work, improving her intellect, and helping to give the message. The way is open for humble, consecrated women, dignified by the grace of Christ, to visit those in need of help and shed light into discouraged souls. They can lift up the bowed down by praying with them and pointing them to Christ. Such should not devote their time and strength to one helpless little mortal that requires constant care and attention. They should not thus voluntarily tie their hands.[5]

Open Homes to Orphans and Friendless—As far as lies in your power, make a home for the homeless. Let everyone stand ready to act a part in helping forward this work. The Lord said to Peter: "Feed My lambs." This command is to us, and by opening our homes for the orphans we aid in its fulfillment. Let not Jesus be disappointed in you.

Take these children and present them to God as a fragrant offering. Ask His blessing upon them and then mold and fashion them according to Christ's order. Will our people accept this holy trust.?[6] [Note: for further detailed counsel on this topic see *Welfare Ministry*.]

A Test for God's People—Years ago I was shown that God's people would be tested upon this point of making homes for the homeless; that there would be many without homes in consequence of their believing the truth. Opposition and persecution would deprive believers of their homes, and it was the duty of those who had homes to open a wide door to those who had not. I have been shown more recently that God would specially test His professed people in [171] reference to this matter. Christ for our sakes became poor that we through His poverty might be made rich. He made a sacrifice that He might provide a home for pilgrims and strangers in the world [172] seeking for a better country, even an heavenly.[7]

[1] Testimonies For The Church 6, 281, 282.

[2] Ibid., 2:33.

[3] Manuscript 38, 1895.

[4] Testimonies For The Church 2, 329.

[5] Ibid., 6:285.

[6] Ibid., 6:284.

[7] Ibid., 2:27, 28.

Chapter 26—Parents' Legacy to Children

The Law of Heredity—The physical and mental condition of the parents is perpetuated in their offspring. This is a matter that is not duly considered. Wherever the habits of the parents are contrary to physical law, the injury done to themselves will be repeated in the future generations....

By physical, mental, and moral culture all may become co-workers with Christ. Very much depends upon the parents. It lies with them whether they shall bring into the world children who will prove a blessing or a curse.[1]

The nobler the aims, the higher the mental and spiritual endowments, and the better developed the physical powers of the parents, the better will be the life equipment they give their children. In cultivating that which is best in themselves, parents are exerting an influence to mold society and to uplift future generations.[2]

Many Parents Are Lamentably Ignorant—Those who have charge of God's property in the souls and bodies of the children formed in His image should erect barriers against the sensual indulgence of this age which is ruining the physical and moral health of thousands. If the many crimes of this time were traced to their true cause, it would be seen that they are chargeable to the ignorance of fathers and mothers who are indifferent on this subject. Health and life itself is being sacrificed to this lamentable ignorance. Parents, if you fail to give your children the education that God makes it your duty to give them, both by precept and example, you must answer to [173] your God for the results. These results will not be confined merely to your children. They will reach through generations. Just as the one thistle permitted to grow in the field produces a harvest of its kind, the sins resulting from your neglect will work to ruin all who come within the sphere of their influence.[3]

Evils of Intemperance Are Perpetuated—Luxurious living and the use of wine corrupt the blood, inflame the passions, and produce diseases of every kind. But the evil does not end here. Parents leave maladies as a legacy to their children. As a rule, every intemperate man who rears children transmits his inclinations and evil tendencies to his offspring; he gives them disease from his own inflamed and corrupted blood. Licentiousness, disease, and imbecility are transmitted as an inheritance of woe from father to son and from generation to generation, and this brings anguish and suffering into the world and is no less than a repetition of the fall of man....

And yet with scarcely a thought or care, men and women of the present generation indulge intemperance by surfeiting and drunkenness and thereby leave, as a legacy for the next generation, disease, enfeebled intellects, and polluted morals.[4]

There Is Reason for Double Understanding and Patience— Fathers and mothers may study their own character in their children. They may often read humiliating lessons as they see their own imperfections reproduced in their sons and daughters. While seeking to repress and correct in their children hereditary tendencies to evil, parents should call to their aid double patience, perseverance, and love.[5]

When a child reveals the wrong traits which it has inherited from its parents, shall they storm over this reproduction of their own defects? No, no! Let parents keep a careful watch over themselves, guarding against all coarseness and roughness, lest these defects be seen once more in their children.[6]

Manifest the meekness and gentleness of Christ in dealing with the wayward little ones. Always bear in mind that they have received their perversity as an inheritance from the father or mother. Then bear with the children who have inherited your own trait of character.[7]

Parents must trust implicitly in the power of Christ to transform the tendencies to wrong which have been transmitted to their children.[8]

Have patience, fathers and mothers. Often your past neglect will make your work hard. But God will give you strength if you will trust in Him. Deal wisely and tenderly with your children.[9]

[174]

[175]

[176]

[1]Manuscript 3, 1897.

[2]The Ministry of Healing, 371.

[3]Manuscript 58, 1899.

[4]Testimonies For The Church 4, 30, 31.

[5]The Review and Herald, August 30, 1881.

[6]The Signs of the Times, September 25, 1901.

[7]Manuscript 142, 1898.

[8]Manuscript 79, 1901.

[9]Manuscript 80, 1901.

Section 8—The Successful Family

Chapter 27—A Sacred Circle

Sanctity of the Family Circle—There is a sacred circle around every family which should be preserved. No other one has any right in that sacred circle. The husband and wife should be all to each other. The wife should have no secrets to keep from her husband and let others know, and the husband should have no secrets to keep from his wife to relate to others. The heart of his wife should be the grave for the faults of the husband, and the heart of the husband the grave for his wife's faults. Never should either party indulge in a joke at the expense of the other's feelings. Never should either the husband or wife in sport or in any other manner complain of each other to others, for frequently indulging in this foolish and what may seem perfectly harmless joking will end in trial with each other and perhaps estrangement. I have been shown that there should be a sacred shield around every family.[1]

The home circle should be regarded as a sacred place, a symbol of heaven, a mirror in which to reflect ourselves. Friends and acquaintances we may have, but in the home life they are not to meddle. A strong sense of proprietorship should be felt, giving a sense of ease, restfulness, trust.[2]

Tongues, Ears, and Eyes to Be Sanctified—Let those composing the family circle pray that God will sanctify their tongues, their ears, their eyes, and every member of their body. When brought into
contact with evil, it is not necessary to be overcome of evil. Christ has made it possible for the character to be fragrant with good....

How many dishonor Christ and misrepresent His character in the home circle! How many do not manifest patience, forbearance, forgiveness, and true love! Many have their likes and dislikes and feel at liberty to manifest their own perverse disposition rather than to reveal the will, the works, the character of Christ. The life of Jesus is full of kindness and love. Are we growing into His divine nature?[3]

Unity, Love, and Peace—Let fathers and mothers make a solemn promise to God, whom they profess to love and obey, that by His grace they will not disagree between themselves, but will in their own life and temper manifest the spirit that they wish their children to cherish.[4]

Parents should be careful not to allow the spirit of dissension to creep into the home; for this is one of Satan's agents to make his impression on the character. If parents will strive for unity in the home by inculcating the principles that governed the life of Christ, dissension will be driven out, and unity and love will abide there. Parents and children will partake of the gift of the Holy Spirit.[5]

Let the husband and wife remember that they have burdens enough to carry without making their lives wretched by allowing differences to come in. Those who give place to little differences invite Satan into their home. The children catch the spirit of contention over mere trifles. Evil agencies do their part to make parents and children disloyal to God.[6]

Although trials may arise in the married life, the husband and the wife are to keep their souls in the love of God. The father should look upon the mother of his children as one deserving of all kindness, tenderness, and sympathy.[7]

[179]

The Secret of Family Unity—The cause of division and discord in families and in the church is separation from Christ. To come near to Christ is to come near to one another. The secret of true unity in the church and in the family is not diplomacy, not management, not a superhuman effort to overcome difficulties—though there will be much of this to do—but union with Christ.

Picture a large circle, from the edge of which are many lines all running to the center. The nearer these lines approach the center, the nearer they are to one another.

Thus it is in the Christian life. The closer we come to Christ, the nearer we shall be to one another. God is glorified as His people unite in harmonious action.[8]

Let Each Help the Other—The family firm is a sacred, social society, in which each member is to act a part, each helping the other. The work of the household is to move smoothly, like the different parts of well-regulated machinery.[9]

Every member of the family should realize that a responsibility rests upon him individually to do his part in adding to the comfort, order, and regularity of the family. One should not work against another. All should unitedly engage in the good work of encouraging one another; they should exercise gentleness, forbearance, and patience; speak in low, calm tones, shunning confusion; and each

[180] doing his utmost to lighten the burdens of the mother....

Each member of the family should understand just the part he is expected to act in union with the others. All, from the child six years old and upward, should understand that it is required of them to bear their share of life's burdens.[10]

A Fitting Resolve—I must grow in grace at home and wherever I may be, in order to give moral power to all my actions. At home I must guard my spirit, my actions, my words. I must give time to personal culture, to training and educating myself in right principles. I must be an example to others. I must meditate upon the word of God night and day and bring it into my practical life. The sword of the Spirit, which is the word of God, is the only sword which I can

[181] safely use.[11]

---

[1]Manuscript 1, 1855.
[2]Letter 17, 1895.
[3]Manuscript 18, 1891.
[4]Manuscript 38, 1895.
[5]Manuscript 53, 1912.
[6]Letter 133, 1904.
[7]Letter 198, 1901.
[8]Letter 49, 1904.
[9]Manuscript 129, 1903.
[10]Testimonies For The Church 2, 699, 700.
[11]Manuscript 13, 1891.

Chapter 28—The Child's First School

God's Original Plan for Education—The system of education established in Eden centered in the family. Adam was "the son of God" (Luke 3:38), and it was from their Father that the children of the Highest received instruction. Theirs, in the truest sense, was a family school.

In the divine plan of education as adapted to man's condition after the fall, Christ stands as the representative of the Father, the connecting link between God and man; He is the great teacher of mankind. And He ordained that men and women should be His representatives. The family was the school, and the parents were the teachers.

The education centering in the family was that which prevailed in the days of the patriarchs. For the schools thus established, God provided the conditions most favorable for the development of character. The people who were under His direction still pursued the plan of life that He had appointed in the beginning. Those who departed from God built for themselves cities, and, congregating in them, gloried in the splendor, the luxury, and the vice that make the cities of today the world's pride and its curse. But the men who held fast God's principles of life dwelt among the fields and hills. They were tillers of the soil and keepers of flocks and herds; and in this free, independent life, with its opportunities for labor and study and meditation, they learned of God and taught their children of His works and ways. This was the method of education that God desired to establish in Israel.[1]

In ordinary life the family was both a school and a church, the parents being the instructors in secular and in religious lines.[2]

The Family Circle a School—In His wisdom the Lord has decreed that the family shall be the greatest of all educational agencies. It is in the home that the education of the child is to begin. Here is his first school. Here, with his parents as instructors, he is to learn the lessons that are to guide him throughout life—lessons of respect,

[182]

137

obedience, reverence, self-control. The educational influences of the home are a decided power for good or for evil. They are in many respects silent and gradual, but if exerted on the right side, they become a far-reaching power for truth and righteousness. If the child is not instructed aright here, Satan will educate him through agencies of his choosing. How important, then, is the school in the home![3]

Look upon the family circle as a training school, where you are preparing your children for the performance of their duties at home, in society, and in the church.[4]

Home Education First in Importance—It is a sad fact, almost universally admitted and deplored, that the home education and training of the youth of today have been neglected.[5]

There is no more important field of effort than that committed to the founders and guardians of the home. No work entrusted to human beings involves greater or more far-reaching results than does the work of fathers and mothers.

It is by the youth and children of today that the future of society is to be determined, and what these youth and children shall be depends upon the home. To the lack of right home training may be traced the larger share of the disease and misery and crime that curse humanity. If the home life were pure and true, if the children who went forth from its care were prepared to meet life's responsibilities and dangers, what a change would be seen in the world![6]

[183]

All Else to Be Secondary—Every child brought into the world is the property of Jesus Christ, and should be educated by precept and example to love and obey God; but by far the largest number of parents have neglected their God-given work, by failing to educate and train their children, from the first dawning of reason, to know and love Christ. By painstaking effort parents are to watch the opening, receptive mind and make everything in the home life secondary to the positive duty enjoined upon them by God—to train their children in the nurture and admonition of the Lord.[7]

Parents should not permit business cares, worldly customs and maxims, and fashion to have a controlling power over them, so that they neglect their children in babyhood and fail to give their children proper instruction as they increase in years.[8]

One great reason why there is so much evil in the world today is that parents occupy their minds with other things than that which is all-important—how to adapt themselves to the work of patiently and kindly teaching their children the way of the Lord. If the curtain could be drawn aside, we should see that many, many children who have gone astray have been lost to good influences through this neglect. Parents, can you afford to have it so in your experience? You should have no work so important that it will prevent you from giving to your children all the time that is necessary to make them understand what it means to obey and trust the Lord fully.... [184]

And what will you reap as a reward of your effort? You will find your children right by your side, willing to take hold and co-operate with you in the lines th___ ___ou suggest. You will find your work made easy.[9]

God's Te__ ___ in the Home School—Parents should in a speci__ ___hemselves as agents of God to instruct their chi__ ___ham, to keep the way of the Lord. They need to ___es diligently, to know what is the way of the I__ ___ach it to their household. Micah says, "Wha___ ___of thee, but to do justly, and to love mer___ ___ith thy God?" [Micah 6:8.] In order ___learners, gathering light constantly ___precept and example bringing this ___of their children.[10]

___iven me, I know that the husband a___ ___ minister, physician, nurse, and te___ ___iemselves and to God, training th___ ___any way militate against God's w___ ___ to care for every part of the li___

___ninent in this work of train-in___ ___ortant duties rest upon the fat___ ___ociation with her children, esp___ ___, must always be their special ins___ ___. She should take great care to cultivate nea___ ___er in her children, to direct them in forming correct habi__ and tastes; she should train them to be industrious, self-reliant, [185] and helpful to others; to live and act and labor as though always in the sight of God.[12]

The elder sisters can exert a strong influence upon the younger members of the family. The younger, witnessing the example of the older, will be led more by the principle of imitation than by oft-repeated precepts. The eldest daughter should ever feel it a Christian duty devolving upon her to aid the mother in bearing her many toilsome burdens.[13]

Parents should be much at home. By precept and example they should teach their children the love and the fear of God; teach them to be intelligent, social, affectionate; to cultivate habits of industry, economy, and self-denial. By giving their children love, sympathy, and encouragement at home, parents may provide for them a safe and welcome retreat from many of the world's temptations.[14]

Preparation for the Church School—It is in the home school that our boys and girls are to be prepared to attend the church school. Parents should constantly keep this in mind and, as teachers in the home, should consecrate every power of the being to God, that they may fulfill their high and holy mission. Diligent, faithful instruction in the home is the best preparation that children can receive for school life.[15]

God's Injunctions to Be Paramount—We have Bible rules for the guidance of all, both parents and children, a high and holy standard from which there can be no swerving. God's injunctions must be paramount. Let the father and mother of the family spread out God's word before Him, the searcher of hearts, and ask in sincerity, [186] "What hath God said?"[16]

Teach your children to love truth because it is truth, and because they are to be sanctified through the truth and fitted to stand in the grand review that shall erelong determine whether they are qualified to enter into higher work and become members of the royal family, children of the heavenly King.[17]

Prepare for the Coming Conflict—Satan is marshaling his hosts; and are we individually prepared for the fearful conflict that is just before us? Are we preparing our children for the great crisis? Are we preparing ourselves and our households to understand the position of our adversaries and their modes of warfare? Are our children forming habits of decision, that they may be firm and unyielding in every matter of principle and duty? I pray that we all may understand the signs of the times, and that we may so prepare ourselves and our children that in the time of conflict God may be our refuge and defense.[18]

[187]

[1]Education, 33, 34.

[2]Ibid., 41.

[3]Counsels to Teachers, Parents, and Students, 107.

[4]The Signs of the Times, September 10, 1894.

[5]The Review and Herald, August 30, 1881.

[6]The Ministry of Healing, 351.

[7]Manuscript 126, 1896.

[8]The Signs of the Times, September 17, 1894.

[9]Manuscript 53, 1912.

[10]Christian Temperance and Bible Hygiene, 145.

[11]Manuscript 100, 1902.

[12]Pacific Health Journal, January, 1890.

[13]Testimonies For The Church 3, 337.

[14]Fundamentals of Christian Education, 65.

[15]Counsels to Teachers, Parents, and Students, 150.

[16]The Review and Herald, September 15, 1891.

[17]The Signs of the Times, September 10, 1894.

[18]The Review and Herald, April 23, 1889.

Chapter 29—A Work That Cannot Be Transferred

Parental Responsibilities Which No One Else Can Bear— Parents, you carry responsibilities that no one can bear for you. As long as you live, you are accountable to God to keep His way.... Parents who make the word of God their guide, and who realize how much their children depend upon them for the characters they form, will set an example that it will be safe for their children to follow.[1]

Fathers and mothers are responsible for the health, the constitution, the development of the character of their children. No one else should be left to see to this work. In becoming the parents of children, it devolves upon you to co-operate with the Lord in educating them in sound principles.[2]

How sad it is that many parents have cast off their God-given responsibility to their children, and are willing that strangers should bear it for them! They are willing that others should labor for their children and relieve them of all burden in the matter.[3]

Many who are now bemoaning the waywardness of their children have only themselves to blame. Let these look to their Bibles and see what God enjoins upon them as parents and guardians. Let them take up their long-neglected duties. They need to humble themselves and to repent before God for their neglect to follow His directions in the training of their children. They need to change their own course of action and to follow the Bible strictly and carefully as their guide [188] and counselor.[4]

The Church Alone Cannot Assume These Responsibilities— Oh, that the youth and children would give their hearts to Christ! What an army might then be raised up to win others to righteousness! But parents should not leave this work for the church to do alone.[5]

Nor Can the Minister— You roll vast responsibilities upon the preacher and hold him accountable for the souls of your children; but you do not sense your own responsibility as parents and as instructors.... Your sons and daughters are corrupted by your own example and lax precepts; and, notwithstanding this lack of domestic

142

training, you expect the minister to counteract your daily work and accomplish the wonderful achievement of training their hearts and lives to virtue and piety. After the minister has done all he can do for the church by faithful, affectionate admonition, patient discipline, and fervent prayer to reclaim and save the soul, yet is not successful, the fathers and mothers often blame him because their children are not converted, when it may be because of their own neglect. The burden rests with the parents; and will they take up the work that God has entrusted to them and with fidelity perform it? Will they move onward and upward, working in a humble, patient, persevering way to reach the exalted standard themselves and to bring their children up with them?[6]

Are not many fathers and mothers placing their responsibilities into others' hands? Do not many of them think that the minister should take the burden and see to it that their children are converted and that the seal of God is placed upon them?"[7]

Nor Can the Sabbath School—It is their [the parents'] privilege to help their children obtain that knowledge which they may [189] carry with them into the future life. But for some reason many parents dislike to give their children religious instruction. They leave them to pick up in Sabbath school the knowledge they should impart concerning their responsibility to God. Such parents need to understand that God desires them to educate, discipline, and train their children, ever keeping before them the fact that they are forming characters for the present and the future life.[8]

Do not depend upon the teachers of the Sabbath school to do your work of training your children in the way they should go. The Sabbath school is a great blessing; it may help you in your work, but it can never take your place. God has given to all fathers and mothers the responsibility of bringing their children to Jesus, teaching them how to pray and believe in the word of God.

In the education of your children lay not the grand truths of the Bible to one side, supposing that the Sabbath school and the minister will do your neglected work. The Bible is not too sacred and sublime to be opened daily and studied diligently. The truths of the word of God are to be brought into contact with the supposed little things of life. If rightly regarded they will brighten the common life, supplying motives for obedience and principles for the formation of a right character.[9]

[1]Letter 356, 1907.

[2]Manuscript 126, 1897.

[3]The Review and Herald, October 25, 1892.

[4]Manuscript 57, 1897.

[5]The Signs of the Times, August 13, 1896.

[6]Testimonies For The Church 5, 494, 495.

[7]The Review and Herald, May 21, 1895.

[8]The Review and Herald, June 6, 1899.

[9]Manuscript 5, 1896.

[190]

Chapter 30—Family Companionship

Parents to Become Acquainted With Children—Some parents do not understand their children and are not really acquainted with them. There is often a great distance between parents and children. If the parents would enter more fully into the feelings of their children and draw out what is in their hearts, it would have a beneficial influence upon them.[1]

The father and the mother should work together in full sympathy with each other. They should make themselves companions to their children.[2]

Parents should study the best and most successful manner of winning the love and confidence of their children, that they may lead them in the right path. They should reflect the sunshine of love upon the household.[3]

Encouragement and Commendation—Young children love companionship and can seldom enjoy themselves alone. They yearn for sympathy and tenderness. That which they enjoy they think will please mother also, and it is natural for them to go to her with their little joys and sorrows. The mother should not wound their sensitive hearts by treating with indifference matters that, though trifling to her, are of great importance to them. Her sympathy and approval are precious. An approving glance, a word of encouragement or commendation, will be like sunshine in their hearts, often making the whole day happy.[4]

Parents to Be Child's Confidants—Parents should encourage their children to confide in *them* and unburden to them their heart griefs, their little daily annoyances and trials.[5] [191]

Kindly instruct them and bind them to your hearts. It is a critical time for children. Influences will be thrown around them to wean them from you which you must counteract. Teach them to make you their confidant. Let them whisper in your ear their trials and joys.[6]

Children would be saved from many evils if they would be more familiar with their parents. Parents should encourage in their children

145

a disposition to be open and frank with them, to come to them with their difficulties and, when they are perplexed as to what course is right, to lay the matter just as they view it before the parents and ask their advice. Who are so well calculated to see and point out their dangers as godly parents? Who can understand the peculiar temperaments of their own children as well as they? The mother who has watched every turn of the mind from infancy, and is thus acquainted with the natural disposition, is best prepared to counsel her children. Who can tell as well what traits of character to check and restrain as the mother, aided by the father?[7]

"No Time"—"No time," says the father; "I have no time to give to the training of my children, no time for social and domestic enjoyments." Then you should not have taken upon yourself the responsibility of a family. By withholding from them the time which is justly theirs, you rob them of the education which they should have at your hands. If you have children, you have a work to do, in union with the mother, in the formation of their characters.[8]

[192]

It is the cry of many mothers: "I have no time to be with my children." Then for Christ's sake spend less time on your dress. Neglect if you will to adorn your apparel. Neglect to receive and make calls. Neglect to cook an endless variety of dishes. But never, never neglect your children. What is the chaff to the wheat? Let nothing interpose between you and the best interests of your children.[9]

Burdened with many cares, mothers sometimes feel that they cannot take time patiently to instruct their little ones and give them love and sympathy. But they should remember that if the children do not find in their parents and in their home that which will satisfy their desire for sympathy and companionship, they will look to other sources, where both mind and character may be endangered.[10]

With Your Children in Work and Play—Give some of your leisure hours to your children; associate with them in their work and in their sports, and win their confidence. Cultivate their friendship.[11]

Let parents devote the evenings to their families. Lay off care and perplexity with the labors of the day.[12]

Counsel to Reserved, Dictatorial Parents—There is danger of both parents and teachers commanding and dictating too much, while they fail to come sufficiently into social relation with their children or scholars. They often hold themselves too much reserved and exercise their authority in a cold, unsympathizing manner which cannot win the hearts of their children and pupils. If they would gather the children close to them and show that they love them, and would manifest an interest in all their efforts and even in their sports, sometimes even being a child among children, they would make the children very happy and would gain their love and win their confidence. And the children would sooner respect and love the authority of their parents and teachers.[13] [193]

Evil Associates as Competitors of the Home—Satan and his host are making most powerful efforts to sway the minds of the children, and they must be treated with candor, Christian tenderness, and love. This will give you a strong influence over them, and they will feel that they can repose unlimited confidence in you. Throw around your children the charms of home and of your society. If you do this, they will not have so much desire for the society of young associates.... Because of the evils now in the world, and the restriction necessary to be placed upon the children, parents should have double care to bind them to their hearts and let them see that they wish to make them happy.[14]

Parents to Be Acquainted With Their Children—No barrier of coldness and reserve should be allowed to arise between parents and children. Let parents become acquainted with their children, seeking to understand their tastes and dispositions, entering into their feelings, and drawing out what is in their hearts.

Parents, let your children see that you love them and will do all in your power to make them happy. If you do so, your necessary restrictions will have far greater weight in their young minds. Rule your children with tenderness and compassion, remembering that "their angels do always behold the face of My Father which is in heaven." If you desire the angels to do for your children the work given them of God, co-operate with them by doing your part.

Brought up under the wise and loving guidance of a true home, children will have no desire to wander away in search of pleasure and companionship. Evil will not attract them. The spirit that prevails in the home will mold their characters; they will form habits and principles that will be a strong defense against temptation when they shall leave the home shelter and take their place in the world.[15] [195]

[194]

[1]Testimonies For The Church 1: 395.

[2]Manuscript 45, 1912.

[3]The Review and Herald, August 30, 1881.

[4]The Ministry of Healing, 388.

[5]Testimonies For The Church 1, 391.

[6]Testimonies For The Church 1, 387.

[7]Testimonies For The Church 1, 392.

[8]Fundamentals of Christian Education, 65, 66.

[9]The Signs of the Times, April 3, 1901.

[10]The Ministry of Healing, 389.

[11]Counsels to Teachers, Parents, and Students, 124.

[12]Christian Temperance and Bible Hygiene, 65.

[13]Testimonies For The Church 3, 134, 135.

[14]Ibid., 1:387, 388.

[15]The Ministry of Healing, 394.

Chapter 31—Security Through Love

The Power of Love's Ministry—Love's agencies have wonderful power, for they are divine. The soft answer that "turneth away wrath," the love that "suffereth long, and is kind," the charity that "covereth a multitude of sins"—would we learn the lesson, with what power for healing would our lives be gifted! How life would be transformed and the earth become a very likeness and foretaste of heaven!

These precious lessons may be so simply taught as to be understood even by little children. The heart of the child is tender and easily impressed; and when we who are older become "as little children," when we learn the simplicity and gentleness and tender love of the Saviour, we shall not find it difficult to touch the hearts of the little ones and teach them love's ministry of healing.[1]

From a worldly point of view, money is power; but from the Christian standpoint, love is power. Intellectual and spiritual strength are involved in this principle. Pure love has special efficacy to do good, and can do nothing but good. It prevents discord and misery and brings the truest happiness. Wealth is often an influence to corrupt and destroy; force is strong to do hurt; but truth and goodness are the properties of pure love.[2]

Love Is a Plant to Be Nourished—Home is to be the center of the purest and most elevated affection. Peace, harmony, affection, and happiness should be perseveringly cherished every day, until these precious things abide in the hearts of those who compose the family. The plant of love must be carefully nourished, else it will die. [196] Every good principle must be cherished if we would have it thrive in the soul. That which Satan plants in the heart—envy, jealousy, evil surmising, evil speaking, impatience, prejudice, selfishness, covetousness, and vanity—must be uprooted. If these evil things are allowed to remain in the soul, they will bear fruit by which many shall be defiled. Oh, how many cultivate the poisonous plants that kill out the precious fruits of love and defile the soul![3]

149

Remember Your Own Childhood—Do not treat your children only with sternness, forgetting your own childhood and forgetting that they are but children. Do not expect them to be perfect or try to make them men and women in their acts at once. By so doing, you will close the door of access which you might otherwise have to them and will drive them to open a door for injurious influences, for others to poison their young minds before you awake to their danger....

Parents should not forget their childhood years, how much they yearned for sympathy and love, and how unhappy they felt when censured and fretfully chided. They should be young again in their feelings, and bring their minds down to understand the wants of their children.[4]

They need gentle, encouraging words. How easy it is for mothers to speak words of kindness and affection which will send a sunbeam to the hearts of the little ones, causing them to forget their troubles![5]

Parents, give your children love: love in babyhood, love in childhood, love in youth. Do not give them frowns, but ever keep a sunshiny countenance.[6]

[197]

Keep Children in a Sunny Atmosphere—The little ones must be carefully soothed when in trouble. Children between babyhood and manhood and womanhood do not generally receive the attention that they should have. Mothers are needed who will so guide their children that they will regard themselves as a part of the family. Let the mother talk with her children regarding their hopes and their perplexities. Let parents remember that their children are to be cared for in preference to strangers. They are to be kept in a sunny atmosphere, under the mother's guidance.[7]

Help your children to gain victories.... Surround them with an atmosphere of love. Thus you can subdue their stubborn dispositions.[8]

When Children Need Love Rather Than Food—Many mothers shamefully neglect their children that they may gain time to embroider the clothing or to put needless trimming upon the little garments of their children. When the children are tired and really need their care, they are neglected or given something to eat. They not only did not need the food but it was a positive injury to them. What they did need was the mother's soothing embrace. Every mother should have time to give her children these little endearments which are so essential during infancy and childhood. In this way the mother would bind up the children's hearts and happiness with her own. She is to them what God is to us.[9]

Reasonable Desires to Be Gratified—You should ever impress upon your children the fact that you love them; that you are laboring for their interest; that their happiness is dear to you; and that you design to do only that which is for their good. You should gratify their little wants whenever you can reasonably do so.[10]

[198]

Never act from impulse in governing children. Let authority and affection be blended. Cherish and cultivate all that is good and lovely, and lead them to desire the higher good by revealing Christ to them. While you deny them those things that would be an injury to them, let them see that you love them and want to make them happy. The more unlovely they are, the greater pains you should take to reveal your love for them. When the child has confidence that you want to make him happy, love will break every barrier down. This is the principle of the Saviour's dealing with man; it is the principle that must be brought into the church.[11]

Love Should Be Expressed—In many families there is a great lack in expressing affection one for another. While there is no need of sentimentalism, there is need of expressing love and tenderness in a chaste, pure, dignified way. Many absolutely cultivate hardness of heart and in word and action reveal the satanic side of the character. Tender affection should ever be cherished between husband and wife, parents and children, brothers and sisters. Every hasty word should be checked, and there should not be even the appearance of the lack of love one for another. It is the duty of everyone in the family to be pleasant, to speak kindly.[12]

Cultivate tenderness, affection, and love that have expression in little courtesies, in speech, in thoughtful attentions.[13]

The best way to educate children to respect their father and mother is to give them the opportunity of seeing the father offering kindly attentions to the mother and the mother rendering respect and reverence to the father. It is by beholding love in their parents that children are led to obey the fifth commandment and to heed the injunction, "Children, obey your parents in the Lord: for this is right."[14]

[199]

The Love of Jesus to Be Mirrored in the Parents—When the mother has gained the confidence of her children and taught them to love and obey her, she has given them the first lesson in the Christian life. They must love and trust and obey their Saviour as they love and trust and obey their parents. The love which in faithful care and right training the parent manifests for the child faintly mirrors the love of Jesus for His faithful people.[15]

[200]

[1] Education, 114.

[2] Testimonies For The Church 4, 138.

[3] The Signs of the Times, June 20, 1911.

[4] Testimonies For The Church 1, 387, 388.

[5] The Review and Herald, July 9, 1901.

[6] Manuscript 129, 1898.

[7] Manuscript 127, 1998.

[8] Manuscript 114, 1903.

[9] Manuscript 43, 1900.

[10] Testimonies For The Church 4, 140.

[11] Manuscript 4, 1993.

[12] The Signs of the Times, November 14, 1892.

[13] The Youth's Instructor, April 21, 1886.

[14] The Review and Herald, November 15, 1892.

[15] The Signs of the Times, April 4, 1911.

Chapter 32—Preoccupy the Garden of the Heart

Parents as Gardeners—The Lord has entrusted to parents a solemn, sacred work. They are to cultivate carefully the soil of the heart. Thus they may be laborers together with God. He expects them to guard and tend carefully the garden of their children's hearts. They are to sow the good seed, weeding out every unsightly weed. Every defect in character, every fault in disposition, needs to be cut away; for if allowed to remain, these will mar the beauty of the character.[1]

Parents, your own home is the first field in which you are called to labor. The precious plants in the home garden demand your first care. To you it is appointed to watch for souls as they that must give account. Carefully consider your work, its nature, its bearing, and its results.[2]

You have before your own door a little plot of ground to care for, and God will hold you responsible for this work which He has left in your hands.[3]

Tending the Garden—The prevailing influence in the world is to suffer the youth to follow the natural turn of their own minds. And if very wild in youth, parents say they will come right after a while and, when sixteen or eighteen years of age, will reason for themselves and leave off their wrong habits and become at last useful men and women. What a mistake! For years they permit an enemy to sow the garden of the heart; they suffer wrong principles to grow, [201] and in many cases all the labor afterward bestowed on that soil will avail nothing....

Some parents have suffered their children to form wrong habits, the marks of which may be seen all through life. Upon the parents lies this sin. These children may profess to be Christians; yet without a special work of grace upon the heart and a thorough reform in life, their past habits will be seen in all their experience, and they will exhibit just the character which their parents allowed them to form.[4]

153

The young should not be suffered to learn good and evil indiscriminately, with the idea that at some future time the good will predominate and the evil lose its influence. The evil will increase faster than the good. It is possible that after many years the evil they have learned may be eradicated; but who will venture this? Time is short. It is easier and much safer to sow clean, good seed in the hearts of your children than to pluck up the weeds afterward. Impressions made upon the minds of the young are hard to efface. How important, then, that these impressions be of the right sort, that the elastic faculties of youth be bent in the right direction.[5]

Seed Sowing, Weeding—In the earliest years of the child's life the soil of the heart should be carefully prepared for the showers of God's grace. Then the seeds of truth are to be carefully sown and diligently tended. And God, who rewards every effort made in His name, will put life into the seed sown; and there will appear first the blade, then the ear, then the full corn in the ear.

Too often, because of the wicked neglect of parents, Satan sows his seeds in the hearts of children, and a harvest of shame and sorrow is borne. The world today is destitute of true goodness because parents have failed to gather their children to themselves in the home. They have not kept them from association with the careless and reckless. Therefore the children have gone forth into the world to sow the seeds of death.[6]

[202]

The great work of instruction, of weeding out worthless and poisonous weeds, is a most important one. For if left to themselves, these weeds will grow until they choke out the precious plants of moral principle and truth.[7]

If a field is left uncultivated, a crop of noxious weeds is sure to appear which will be very difficult to exterminate. Then the soil must be worked and the weeds subdued before the precious plants can grow. Before these valuable plants can grow, the seed must first be carefully sown. If mothers neglect the sowing of the precious seed and then expect a harvest of precious grain, they will be disappointed; for they will reap briars and thorns. Satan is ever watching, prepared to sow seeds which will spring up and bear a plentiful harvest after his own satanic character.[8]

Eternal vigilance must be manifested with regard to our children. With his manifold devices Satan begins to work with their tempers and their wills as soon as they are born. Their safety depends upon the wisdom and the vigilant care of the parents. They must strive in the love and fear of God to preoccupy the garden of the heart, sowing the good seeds of a right spirit, correct habits, and the love and fear of God.[9]

Unfolding Natural Beauty—Parents and teachers should seek most earnestly for that wisdom which Jesus is ever ready to give; for they are dealing with human minds at the most interesting and impressible period of their development. They should aim so to cultivate the tendencies of the youth that at each stage of their life [203] they may represent the natural beauty appropriate to that period, unfolding gradually, as do the plants and flowers in the garden.[10] [204]

[1]Manuscript 138, 1898.

[2]The Signs of the Times, July 1, 1886.

[3]The Review and Herald, September 15, 1891.

[4]Testimonies For The Church 1, 403.

[5]Christian Temperance and Bible Hygiene, 138, 139.

[6]Manuscript 49, 1901.

[7]The Review and Herald, April 14, 1885.

[8]Manuscript 43, 1900.

[9]Manuscript 7, 1899.

[10]Testimonies For The Church 6, 204, 205.

Chapter 33—Promises of Divine Guidance

How Sweet the Consciousness of a Divine Friend—Your compassionate Redeemer is watching you with love and sympathy, ready to hear your prayers and to render you the assistance which you need. He knows the burdens of every mother's heart and is her best friend in every emergency. His everlasting arms support the God-fearing, faithful mother. When upon earth, He had a mother that struggled with poverty, having many anxious cares and perplexities, and He sympathizes with every Christian mother in her cares and anxieties. That Saviour who took a long journey for the purpose of relieving the anxious heart of a woman whose daughter was possessed by an evil spirit will hear the mother's prayers and will bless her children.

He who gave back to the widow her only son as he was carried to the burial is touched today by the woe of the bereaved mother. He who wept tears of sympathy at the grave of Lazarus and gave back to Martha and Mary their buried brother; who pardoned Mary Magdalene; who remembered His mother when He was hanging in agony upon the cross; who appeared to the weeping women and made them His messengers to spread the first glad tidings of a risen Saviour—He is woman's best friend today and is ready to aid her in all the relations of life.[1]

No work can equal that of the Christian mother. She takes up her work with a sense of what it is to bring up her children in the nurture and admonition of the Lord. How often will she feel her burden's weight heavier than she can bear; and then how precious the privilege of taking it all to her sympathizing Saviour in prayer! She may lay her burden at His feet and find in His presence a strength that will sustain her and give her cheerfulness, hope, courage, and wisdom in the most trying hours. How sweet to the careworn mother is the consciousness of such a friend in all her difficulties! If mothers would go to Christ more frequently and trust Him more fully, their burdens would be easier, and they would find rest to their souls.[2]

[205]

156

The God of Heaven Hears Your Prayers—You cannot bring up your children as you should without divine help; for the fallen nature of Adam always strives for the mastery. The heart must be prepared for the principles of truth, that they may root in the soul and find nourishment in the life.[3]

Parents may understand that as they follow God's directions in the training of their children, they will receive help from on high. They receive much benefit; for as they teach, they learn. Their children will achieve victories through the knowledge that they have acquired in keeping the way of the Lord. They are enabled to overcome natural and hereditary tendencies to evil.[4]

Parents, are you working with unflagging energy in behalf of your children? The God of heaven marks your solicitude, your earnest work, your constant watchfulness. He hears your prayers. With patience and tenderness train your children for the Lord. All heaven is interested in your work.... God will unite with you, crowning your efforts with success.[5]

As you try to make plain the truths of salvation, and point the children to Christ as a personal Saviour, angels will be by your side. The Lord will give to fathers and mothers grace to interest their little ones in the precious story of the Babe of Bethlehem, who is indeed the hope of the world.[6]

[206]

Ask and Receive—In their important work parents must ask and receive divine aid. Even if the character, habits, and practices of parents have been cast in an inferior mold, if the lessons given them in childhood and youth have led to an unhappy development of character, they need not despair. The converting power of God can transform inherited and cultivated tendencies; for the religion of Jesus is uplifting. "Born again" means a transformation, a new birth in Christ Jesus.[7]

Let us instruct our children in the teachings of the word. If you will call, the Lord will answer you. He will say, Here I am; what would you have Me do for you? Heaven is linked with earth that every soul may be enabled to fulfill his mission. The Lord loves these children. He wants them brought up with an understanding of their high calling.[8]

The Holy Spirit Will Guide—The mother should feel her need of the Holy Spirit's guidance, that she herself may have a genuine experience in submission to the way and will of God. Then, through the grace of Christ, she can be a wise, gentle, loving teacher.[9]

Christ has made every provision that every parent who will be controlled by the Holy Spirit will be given strength and grace to be a teacher in the home. This education and discipline in the home will have a molding and fashioning influence.[10]

Divine Power Will Unite With Human Effort—Without human effort divine effort is in vain. God will work with power when in trustful dependence upon Him parents will awake to the sacred responsibility resting upon them and seek to train their children aright. He will co-operate with those parents who carefully and prayerfully educate their children, working out their own and their children's salvation. He will work in them to will and to do of His own good pleasure.[11]

[207]

Human effort alone will not result in helping your children to perfect a character for heaven; but with divine help a grand and holy work may be accomplished.[12]

When you take up your duties as a parent in the strength of God, with a firm determination never to relax your efforts nor to leave your post of duty in striving to make your children what God would have them, then God looks down upon you with approbation. He knows that you are doing the best you can, and He will increase your power. He will Himself do the part of the work that the mother or father cannot do; He will work with the wise, patient, well-directed efforts of the God-fearing mother. Parents, God does not propose to do the work that He has left for you to do in your home. You must not give up to indolence and be slothful servants, if you would have your children saved from the perils that surround them in the world.[13]

Cling to Jesus When Trials Come—Parents, gather the rays of divine light which are shining upon your pathway. Walk in the light as Christ is in the light. As you take up the work of saving your children and maintaining your position on the highway of holiness, the most provoking trials will come. But do not lose your hold. Cling to Jesus. He says, "Let him take hold of My strength, that he may make peace with Me; and he shall make peace with Me." Difficulties will arise. You will meet with obstacles. Look constantly to Jesus. When an emergency arises, ask, Lord, what shall I do now?[14]

[208]

The harder the battle, the greater their [parents] need of help from their heavenly Father, and the more marked will be the victory gained.[15]

Then Work in Faith.—Patiently, lovingly, as faithful stewards of the manifold grace of Christ, parents are to do their appointed work. It is expected of them that they will be found faithful. Everything is to be done in faith. Constantly they must pray that God will impart His grace to their children. Never must they become weary, impatient, or fretful in their work. They must cling closely to their children and to God. If parents work in patience and love, earnestly endeavoring to help their children to reach the highest standard of purity and modesty, they will succeed.[16]

[209]

[210]

---

[1]The Signs of the Times, September 9, 1886.

[2]The Signs of the Times, September 13, 1877.

[3]The Review and Herald, October 25, 1892.

[4]The Review and Herald, June 6, 1899.

[5]The Review and Herald, January 29, 1901.

[6]The Desire of Ages, 517.

[7]The Review and Herald, April 13, 1897.

[8]Manuscript 31, 1909.

[9]Counsels to Teachers, Parents, and Students, 128.

[10]Manuscript 36, 1899.

[11]The Signs of the Times, September 25, 1901.

[12]The Review and Herald, October 25, 1892.

[13]The Review and Herald, July 10, 1888.

[14]Manuscript 67, 1901.

[15]The Review and Herald, August 30, 1881.

[16]Manuscript 138, 1898.

Section 9—Father—The House-Band

Chapter 34—Father's Position and Responsibilities

True Definition of Husband—The home is an institution of God. God designed that the family circle, father, mother, and children, should exist in this world as a firm.[1]

The work of making home happy does not rest upon the mother alone. Fathers have an important part to act. The husband is the house-band of the home treasures, binding by his strong, earnest, devoted affection the members of the household, mother and children, together in the strongest bonds of union.[2]

His name, "house-band," is the true definition of husband.... I saw that but few fathers realize their responsibility.[3]

The Head of the Family Firm—The husband and father is the head of the household. The wife looks to him for love and sympathy and for aid in the training of the children; and this is right. The children are his as well as hers, and he is equally interested in their welfare. The children look to the father for support and guidance; he needs to have a right conception of life and of the influences and associations that should surround his family; above all, he should be controlled by the love and fear of God and by the teaching of His word, that he may guide the feet of his children in the right way....

The father should do his part toward making home happy. What-ever his cares and business perplexities, they should not be permitted to overshadow his family; he should enter his home with smiles and pleasant words.[4]

The Lawmaker and Priest—All members of the family center in the father. He is the lawmaker, illustrating in his own manly bearing the sterner virtues: energy, integrity, honesty, patience, courage, diligence, and practical usefulness. The father is in one sense the priest of the household, laying upon the altar of God the morning and evening sacrifice. The wife and children should be encouraged to unite in this offering and also to engage in the song of praise. Morning and evening the father, as priest of the household, should confess to God the sins committed by himself and his children through the day. Those sins which have come to his knowledge and also those which are secret, of which God's eye alone has taken cognizance, should be confessed. This rule of action, zealously carried out by the father when he is present or by the mother when he is absent, will result in blessings to the family.[5]

The father represents the divine Lawgiver in his family. He is a laborer together with God, carrying out the gracious designs of God and establishing in his children upright principles, enabling them to form pure and virtuous characters, because he has preoccupied the soul with that which will enable his children to render obedience not only to their earthly parent but also to their heavenly Father.[6]

The father must not betray his sacred trust. He must not, on any point, yield up his parental authority.[7]

To Walk With God—The father ... will bind his children to the throne of God by living faith. Distrusting his own strength, he hangs his helpless soul on Jesus and takes hold of the strength of the Most High. Brethren, pray at home, in your family, night and morning; pray earnestly in your closet; and while engaged in your daily labor, lift up the soul to God in prayer. It was thus that Enoch walked with God. The silent, fervent prayer of the soul will rise like holy incense to the throne of grace and will be as acceptable to God as if offered in the sanctuary. To all who thus seek Him, Christ becomes a present help in time of need. They will be strong in the day of trial.[8]

[213]

Maturity of Experience Called For—A father must not be as a child, moved merely by impulse. He is bound to his family by sacred, holy ties.[9]

What his influence will be in the home will be determined by his knowledge of the only true God and Jesus Christ whom He has sent. "When I was a child," Paul says, "I spake as a child, I understood as a child, I thought as a child: but when I became a man, I put away childish things." The father is to stand at the head of his family, not as an overgrown, undisciplined boy, but as a man with manly character and with his passions controlled. He is to obtain an education in correct morals. His conduct in his home life is to be directed and restrained by the pure principles of the word of God. Then he will grow up to the full stature of a man in Christ Jesus.[10]

Submit the Will to God—To the man who is a husband and a father, I would say, Be sure that a pure, holy atmosphere surrounds your soul.... You are to learn daily of Christ. Never, never are you to show a tyrannical spirit in the home. The man who does this is working in partnership with satanic agencies. Bring your will into [214] submission to the will of God. Do all in your power to make the life of your wife pleasant and happy. Take the word of God as the man of your counsel. In the home live out the teachings of the word. Then you will live them out in the church and will take them with you to your place of business. The principles of heaven will ennoble all your transactions. Angels of God will cooperate with you, helping you to reveal Christ to the world.[11]

A Fitting Prayer for a Quick-tempered Husband—Do not allow the vexations of your business to bring darkness into your home life. If, when little things occur that are not exactly as you think they should be, you fail to reveal patience, long forbearance, kindness, and love, you show that you have not chosen as a companion Him who so loved you that He gave His life for you, that you might be one with Him.

In the daily life you will meet with sudden surprises, disappointments, and temptations. What saith the word? "Resist the devil," by firm reliance upon God, "and he will flee from you. Draw nigh to God, and He will draw nigh to you." "Let him take hold of My strength, that he may make peace with Me; and he shall make peace with Me." Look unto Jesus at all times and in all places, offering a silent prayer from a sincere heart that you may know how to do His will. Then when the enemy comes in like a flood, the Spirit of the Lord will lift up a standard for you against the enemy. When you are almost ready to yield, to lose patience and self-control, to be hard and denunciatory, to find fault and accuse—this is the time for you to send to heaven the prayer, "Help me, O God, to resist temptation, to put all bitterness and wrath and evilspeaking out of my heart. Give me Thy meekness, Thy lowliness, Thy long-suf- [215] fering, and Thy love. Leave me not to dishonor my Redeemer, to misinterpret the words and motives of my wife, my children, and my brethren and sisters in the faith. Help me that I may be kind, pitiful, tenderhearted, forgiving. Help me to be a real house-band in my home and to represent the character of Christ to others."[12]

Exercise Authority With Humility—It is no evidence of manliness in the husband for him to dwell constantly upon his position as head of the family. It does not increase respect for him to hear him quoting Scripture to sustain his claims to authority. It will not make him more manly to require his wife, the mother of his children, to act upon his plans as if they were infallible. The Lord has constituted the husband the head of the wife to be her protector; he is the house-band of the family, binding the members together, even as Christ is the head of the church and the Saviour of the mystical body. Let every husband who claims to love God carefully study the requirements of God in his position. Christ's authority is exercised in wisdom, in all kindness and gentleness; so let the husband exercise his power and imitate the great Head of the church.[13]

[216]

[1]Manuscript 36, 1899.

[2]The Signs of the Times, September 13, 1877.

[3]Testimonies For The Church 1, 547.

[4]The Ministry of Healing, 390, 392.

[5]Testimonies For The Church 2, 701.

[6]The Signs of the Times, September 10, 1894.

[7]Letter 9, 1904.

[8]Testimonies for the Church 4:616.

[9]Testimonies For The Church 1, 547.

[10]Manuscript 36, 1899.

[11]Letter 272, 1903.

[12]Letter 105, 1893.

[13]Letter 18b, 1891.

Chapter 35—Sharing the Burdens

Father's Duty Cannot Be Transferred—The father's duty to his children cannot be transferred to the mother. If she performs her own duty, she has burden enough to bear. Only by working in unison can the father and mother accomplish the work which God has committed to their hands.[1]

The father should not excuse himself from his part in the work of educating his children for life and immortality. He must share in the responsibility. There is obligation for both father and mother. There must be love and respect manifested by the parents for one another, if they would see these qualities developed in their children.[2]

The father should encourage and sustain the mother in her work of care by his cheerful looks and kind words.[3]

Try to help your wife in the conflict before her. Be careful of your words, cultivate refinement of manners, courtesy, gentleness, and you will be rewarded for so doing.[4]

Tender Ministration Will Lighten the Mother's Load—Whatever may be his calling and its perplexities, let the father take into his home the same smiling countenance and pleasant tones with which he has all day greeted visitors and strangers. Let the wife feel that she can lean upon the large affections of her husband—that his arms will strengthen and uphold her through all her toils and cares, that his influence will sustain hers—and her burden will lose half its weight. Are the children not his as well as hers?[5]

[217]

The wife may gather to herself burdens which she may suppose to be of greater importance than to help her husband in bearing his portion of responsibility; and the same is true of the husband. Tender ministrations are of value. There is a tendency for the husband to feel free to go out and come into his home more as a boarder than a husband of the family circle.[6]

Domestic duties are sacred and important; yet they are often attended by a weary monotony. The countless cares and perplexities become irritating without the variety of change and cheerful relaxation which the husband and father frequently has ... in his power to grant her if he chose—or rather if he thought it necessary or desirable to do so. The life of a mother in the humbler walks of life is one of unceasing self-sacrifice, made harder if the husband fails to appreciate the difficulties of her position and to give her his support.[7]

Show Consideration for a Feeble Wife—The husband should manifest great interest in his family. Especially should he be very tender of the feelings of a feeble wife. He can shut the door against much disease. Kind, cheerful, and encouraging words will prove more effective than the most healing medicines. These will bring courage to the heart of the desponding and discouraged, and the happiness and sunshine brought into the family by kind acts and encouraging words will repay the effort tenfold. The husband should remember that much of the burden of training his children rests upon the mother, that she has much to do with molding their minds. This should call into exercise his tenderest feelings, and with care should he lighten her burdens. He should encourage her to lean upon his large affections and direct her mind to heaven, where there is strength and peace and a final rest for the weary. He should not come to his home with a clouded brow, but should with his presence bring sunlight into the family and should encourage his wife to look up and believe in God. Unitedly they can claim the promises of God and bring His rich blessing into the family.[8]

[218]

"Lead on Softly"—Many a husband and father might learn a helpful lesson from the carefulness of the faithful shepherd. Jacob, when urged to undertake a rapid and difficult journey, made answer:

"The children are tender, and the flocks and herds with young are with me: and if men should overdrive them one day, all the flock will die." "I will lead on softly, according as the cattle that goeth before me and the children be able to endure."

In life's toilsome way let the husband and father "lead on softly," as the companion of his journey is able to endure. Amidst the world's eager rush for wealth and power, let him learn to stay his steps, to comfort and support the one who is called to walk by his side....

Let the husband aid his wife by his sympathy and unfailing affection. If he wishes to keep her fresh and gladsome, so that she will be as sunshine in the home, let him help her bear her burdens. His kindness and loving courtesy will be to her a precious encouragement, and the happiness he imparts will bring joy and peace to his own heart....

If the mother is deprived of the care and comforts she should have, if she is allowed to exhaust her strength through overwork or through anxiety and gloom, her children will be robbed of the vital-force and of the mental elasticity and cheerful buoyancy they should inherit. Far better will it be to make the mother's life bright [219] and cheerful, to shield her from want, wearing labor, and depressing care, and let the children inherit good constitutions, so that they may [220] battle their way through life with their own energetic strength.[9]

---

[1] Fundamentals of Christian Education, 69.

[2] The Signs of the Times, July 22, 1889.

[3] The Signs of the Times, September 13, 1877.

[4] Testimonies For The Church 2, 84.

[5] Christian Temperance and Bible Hygiene, 70.

[6] Manuscript 80, 1898.

[7] The Signs of the Times, December 6, 1877.

[8] Testimonies For The Church 1, 306, 307.

[9] The Ministry of Healing, 374.

Chapter 36—A Companion With His Children

Spend Time With Children—The average father wastes many golden opportunities to attract and bind his children to him. Upon returning home from his business, he should find it a pleasant change to spend some time with his children.[1]

Fathers should unbend from their false dignity, deny themselves some slight self-gratification in time and leisure, in order to mingle with the children, sympathizing with them in their little troubles, binding them to their hearts by the strong bonds of love, and establishing such an influence over their expanding minds that their counsel will be regarded as sacred.[2]

Take Special Interest in the Boys—The father of boys should come into close contact with his sons, giving them the benefit of his larger experience and talking with them in such simplicity and tenderness that he binds them to his heart. He should let them see that he has their best interest, their happiness, in view all the time.[3]

He who has a family of boys must understand that, whatever his calling, he is never to neglect the souls placed in his care. He has brought these children into the world and has made himself responsible to God to do everything in his power to keep them from unsanctified associations, from evil companionship. He should not leave his restless boys wholly to the care of the mother. This is too heavy a burden for her. He must arrange matters for the best interests of the mother and the children. It may be very hard for the mother to exercise self-control and to manage wisely in the training of her [221] children. If this is the case, the father should take more of the burden upon his soul. He should be determined to make the most decided efforts to save his children.[4]

Train Children for Usefulness—The father, as the head of his own household, should understand how to train his children for usefulness and duty. This is his special work, above every other. During the first few years of a child's life the molding of the disposition is committed principally to the mother; but she should ever feel that

169

in her work she has the co-operation of the father. If he is engaged in business which almost wholly closes the door of usefulness to his family, he should seek other employment which will not prevent him from devoting some time to his children. If he neglects them, he is unfaithful to the trust committed to him of God.

The father may exert an influence over his children which shall be stronger than the allurements of the world. He should study the disposition and character of the members of his little circle, that he may understand their needs and their dangers and thus be prepared to repress the wrong and encourage the right.[5]

Whatever may be the character of his business, it is not of so great importance that he be excused in neglecting the work of educating and training his children to keep the way of the Lord.[6]

Become Acquainted With Varied Dispositions—The father should not become so absorbed in business life or in the study of books that he cannot take time to study the natures and necessities of his children. He should help in devising ways by which they may be kept busy in useful labor agreeable to their varying dispositions.[7]

[222]

Fathers, spend as much time as possible with your children. Seek to become acquainted with their various dispositions, that you may know how to train them in harmony with the word of God. Never should a word of discouragement pass your lips. Do not bring darkness into the home. Be pleasant, kind, and affectionate toward your children, but not foolishly indulgent. Let them bear their little disappointments, as every one must. Do not encourage them to come to you with their petty complaints of one another. Teach them to bear with one another and to seek to maintain each other's confidence and respect.[8]

Associate With Them in Work and Sports—Fathers, ... combine affection with authority, kindness and sympathy with firm restraint. Give some of your leisure hours to your children; become acquainted with them; associate with them in their work and in their sports, and win their confidence. Cultivate friendship with them, especially with your sons. In this way you will be a strong influence for good.[9]

Teach Them Lessons From Nature—Let the father seek to lighten the mother's task.... Let him point them to the beautiful flowers, the lofty trees, in whose very leaves they can trace the work and love of God. He should teach them that the God who made all these things loves the beautiful and the good. Christ pointed His disciples to the lilies of the field and the birds of the air, showing how God cares for them and presenting this as evidence that He will care for man, who is of higher consequence than birds or flowers. Tell the children that however much time may be wasted in attempts at display, our appearance can never compare, for grace and beauty, [223] with that of the simplest flowers of the field. Thus their minds may be drawn from the artificial to the natural. They may learn that God has given them all these beautiful things to enjoy, and that He wants them to give Him the heart's best and holiest affections.[10]

He may take them into the garden and show them the opening buds and the varied tints of the blooming flowers. Through such mediums he may give them the most important lessons concerning the Creator, by opening before them the great book of nature, where the love of God is expressed in every tree and flower and blade of grass. He may impress upon their minds the fact that if God cares so much for the trees and flowers, He will care much more for the creatures formed in His image. He may lead them early to understand that God wants children to be lovely, not with artificial adornment, but with beauty of character, the charms of kindness and affection, which will make their hearts bound with joy and happiness.[11] [224]

[1]The Signs of the Times, December 6, 1877.

[2]Ibid..

[3]Counsels to Teachers, Parents, and Students, 128.

[4]Manuscript 79, 1901.

[5]The Review and Herald, August 30, 1881.

[6]The Signs of the Times, September 10, 1894.

[7]Counsels to Teachers, Parents, and Students, 127, 128.

[8]Manuscript 60, 1903.

[9]The Ministry of Healing, 391, 392.

[10]Christian Temperance and Bible Hygiene, 70.

[11]The Signs of the Times, December 6, 1877.

Chapter 37—The Kind of Husband Not To Be

The Husband Who Expects Wife to Carry Double Burdens—In most families there are children of various ages, some of whom need not only the attention and wise discipline of the mother but also the sterner, yet affectionate, influence of the father. Few fathers consider this matter in its due importance. They fall into neglect of their own duty and thus heap grievous burdens upon the mother, at the same time feeling at liberty to criticize and condemn her actions according to their judgment. Under this heavy sense of responsibility and censure, the poor wife and mother often feels guilty and remorseful for that which she has done innocently or ignorantly, and frequently when she has done the very best thing possible under the circumstances. Yet when her wearisome efforts should be appreciated and approved and her heart made glad, she is obliged to walk under a cloud of sorrow and condemnation because her husband, while ignoring his own duty, expects her to fulfill both her own and his to his satisfaction, regardless of preventing circumstances.[1]

[225] Many husbands do not sufficiently understand and appreciate the cares and perplexities which their wives endure, generally confined all day to an unceasing round of household duties. They frequently come to their homes with clouded brows, bringing no sunshine to the family circle. If the meals are not on time, the tired wife, who is frequently housekeeper, nurse, cook, and housemaid, all in one, is greeted with faultfinding. The exacting husband may condescend to take the worrying child from the weary arms of its mother that her arrangements for the family meal may be hastened; but if the child is restless and frets in the arms of its father, he will seldom feel it his duty to act the nurse and seek to quiet and soothe it. He does not pause to consider how many hours the mother has endured the little one's fretfulness, but calls out impatiently, "Here, Mother, take *your* child." Is it not *his* child as well as hers? Is he not under a

172

natural obligation to patiently bear his part of the burden of rearing his children?[2]

A Dictatorial and Dominating Husband; Words of Counsel—Your life would be much happier if you did not feel that absolute authority is vested in you because you are a husband and father. Your practice shows that you misinterpret your position—houseband. You are nervous and dictatorial and often manifest great lack of judgment, so that however you may regard your course at such times, it cannot be made to appear consistent to your wife and children. When once you have taken a position, you are seldom willing to withdraw from it. You are determined to carry out your plans, when many times you are not pursuing the right course and should see it. What you need is more, far more, of love, of forbearance, and less of a determination to have your way both in word and in deed. In the course you are now pursuing, instead of being a house-band, you will be as a vise to compress and distress others....

In trying to force others to carry out your ideas in every particular, you often do greater harm than if you were to yield these points. This is true even when your ideas are right in themselves, but in many things they are not correct; they are overstrained as the result of the peculiarities of your organization; therefore you drive the wrong thing in a strong, unreasonable manner.[3]

[226]

You have peculiar views in regard to managing your family. You exercise an independent, arbitrary power which permits no liberty of will around you. You think yourself sufficient to be head in your family and feel that your head is sufficient to move every member, as a machine is moved in the hands of the workmen. You dictate and assume authority. This displeases Heaven and grieves the pitying angels. You have conducted yourself in your family as though you alone were capable of self-government. It has offended you that your wife should venture to oppose your opinion or question your decisions.[4]

Fretful and Querulous Husbands—Husbands, give your wives a chance for their spiritual life.... By many the disposition to fret is encouraged until they become like grown-up children. They do not leave this portion of their child life behind them. They cherish these feelings until they cramp and dwarf the whole life by their querulous complaints. And not only their own lives but the lives of others also. They carry with them the spirit of Ishmael, whose hand was against everybody, and everybody's hand against him.[5]

The Selfish and Morose Husband—Brother B is not of a temperament to bring sunshine into his family. Here is a good place for him to begin to work. He is more like a cloud than a beam of light. He is too selfish to speak words of approval to the members of his family, especially to the one of all others who should have his love and tender respect. He is morose, overbearing, dictatorial; his words are frequently cutting, and leave a wound that he does not try to heal by softening spirit, acknowledging his faults, and confessing his wrongdoings....

[227]

Brother B should soften; he should cultivate refinement and courtesy. He should be very tender and gentle toward his wife, who is his equal in every respect; he should not utter a word that would cast a shadow upon her heart. He should begin the work of reformation at home; he should cultivate affection and overcome the coarse, harsh, unfeeling, and ungenerous traits of his disposition.[6]

The husband and father who is morose, selfish, and overbearing is not only unhappy himself, but he casts gloom upon all the inmates of his home. He will reap the result in seeing his wife dispirited and sickly and his children marred with his own unlovely temper.[7]

An Egotistical and Intolerant Husband—You expect too much of your wife and children. You censure too much. If you would encourage a cheerful, happy temper yourself and speak kindly and tenderly to them, you would bring sunlight into your dwelling instead of clouds, sorrow, and unhappiness. You think too much of your opinion; you have taken extreme positions, and have not been willing that your wife's judgment should have the weight it should in your family. You have not encouraged respect for your wife yourself nor educated your children to respect her judgment. You have not made her your equal, but have rather taken the reins of government and control into your own hands and held them with a firm grasp. You have not an affectionate, sympathetic disposition. These traits of character you need to cultivate if you want to be an overcomer and if you want the blessing of God in your family.[8]

[228]

To One Who Disregards Christian Courtesy—You have looked upon it as a weakness to be kind, tender, and sympathetic and have thought it beneath your dignity to speak tenderly, gently, and lovingly to your wife. Here you mistake in what true manliness and dignity consist. The disposition to leave deeds of kindness undone is a manifest weakness and defect in your character. That which you would look upon as weakness God regards as true Christian courtesy that should be exercised by every Christian; for this was the spirit which Christ manifested.[9]

Husbands Should Merit Love and Affection—If the husband is tyrannical, exacting, critical of the actions of his wife, he cannot hold her respect and affection, and the marriage relation will become odious to her. She will not love her husband, because he does not try to make himself lovable. Husbands should be careful, attentive, constant, faithful, and compassionate. They should manifest love and sympathy.... When the husband has the nobility of character, purity of heart, elevation of mind, that every true Christian must possess, it will be made manifest in the marriage relation.... He will seek to keep his wife in health and courage. He will strive to speak words of comfort, to create an atmosphere of peace in the home circle.[10]

[229]

[230]

[1]The Signs of the Times, December 6, 1877.
[2]Ibid..
[3]Letter 19a, 1891.
[4]Testimonies For The Church 2, 253.
[5]Letter 107, 1898.
[6]Testimonies For The Church 4, 36, 37.
[7]The Ministry of Healing, 374, 375.
[8]Testimonies For The Church 4, 255.
[9]Testimonies For The Church 4, 256.
[10]Manuscript 17, 1891.

Section 10—Mother—Queen of the Household

Chapter 38—Mother's Position and Responsibilities

The Husband's Equal—Woman should fill the position which God originally designed for her, as her husband's equal. The world needs mothers who are mothers not merely in name but in every sense of the word. We may safely say that the distinctive duties of woman are more sacred, more holy, than those of man. Let woman realize the sacredness of her work and in the strength and fear of God take up her life mission. Let her educate her children for usefulness in this world and for a home in the better world.[1]

The wife and mother should not sacrifice her strength and allow her powers to lie dormant, leaning wholly upon her husband. Her individuality cannot be merged in his. She should feel that she is her husband's equal—to stand by his side, she faithful at her post of duty and he at his. Her work in the education of her children is in every respect as elevating and ennobling as any post of duty he may be called to fill, even if it is to be the chief magistrate of the nation.[2]

The Queen of the Home—The king upon his throne has no higher work than has the mother. The mother is queen of her household. She has in her power the molding of her children's characters, that they may be fitted for the higher, immortal life. An angel could not ask for a higher mission; for in doing this work she is doing service for God. Let her only realize the high character of her task, and it will inspire her with courage. Let her realize the worth of her work and put on the whole armor of God, that she may resist the temptation to conform to the world's standard. Her work is for time and for eternity.[3]

The mother is the queen of the home, and the children are her subjects. She is to rule her household wisely, in the dignity of her motherhood. Her influence in the home is to be paramount; her word, law. If she is a Christian, under God's control, she will command the respect of her children.[4]

The children are to be taught to regard their mother, not as a slave whose work it is to wait on them, but as a queen who is to guide and direct them, teaching them line upon line, precept upon precept.[5]

A Graphic Comparison of Values—The mother seldom appreciates her own work and frequently sets so low an estimate upon her labor that she regards it as domestic drudgery. She goes through the same round day after day, week after week, with no special marked results. She cannot tell at the close of the day the many little things she has accomplished. Placed beside her husband's achievement, she feels that she has done nothing worth mentioning.

The father frequently comes in with a self-satisfied air and proudly recounts what he has accomplished through the day. His remarks show that now he must be waited upon by the mother, for she has not done much except take care of the children, cook the meals, and keep the house in order. She has not acted the merchant, bought nor sold; she has not acted the farmer, in tilling the soil; she has not acted the mechanic—therefore she has done nothing to make her weary. He criticizes and censures and dictates as though he was the lord of creation. And this is all the more trying to the wife and mother, because she has become very weary at her post of duty during the day, and yet she cannot see what she has done and is really disheartened.

[233]

Could the veil be withdrawn and father and mother see as God sees the work of the day, and see how His infinite eye compares the work of the one with that of the other, they would be astonished at the heavenly revelation. The father would view his labors in a more modest light, while the mother would have new courage and energy to pursue her labor with wisdom, perseverance, and patience. Now she knows its value. While the father has been dealing with the things which must perish and pass away, the mother has been dealing with developing minds and character, working not only for time but for eternity.[6]

God Has Appointed Her Work—Would that every mother could realize how great are her duties and her responsibilities and how great will be the reward of faithfulness.[7]

The mother who cheerfully takes up the duties lying directly in her path will feel that life is to her precious, because God has given her a work to perform. In this work she need not necessarily dwarf her mind nor allow her intellect to become enfeebled.[8]

The mother's work is given her of God, to bring up her children in the nurture and admonition of the Lord. The love and fear of God should ever be kept before their tender minds. When corrected, they should be taught to feel that they are admonished of God, that He is displeased with deception, untruthfulness, and wrongdoing. Thus the minds of little ones may be so connected with God that all they [234] do and say will be in reference to His glory; and in after years they will not be like the reed in the wind, continually wavering between inclination and duty.[9]

To lead them to Jesus is not all that is required.... These children are to be educated and trained to become disciples of Christ, "that our sons may be as plants grown up in their youth; that our daughters may be as corner stones, polished after the similitude of a palace." This work of molding, refining, and polishing is the mother's. The character of the child is to be developed. The mother must engrave upon the tablet of the heart lessons as enduring as eternity; and she will surely meet the displeasure of the Lord if she neglects this sacred work or allows anything to interfere with it.... The Christian mother has her God-appointed work, which she will not neglect if she is closely connected with God and imbued with His Spirit.[10]

Her Grand and Noble Commission—There are opportunities of inestimable worth, interests infinitely precious, committed to every mother. The humble round of duties which women have come to regard as a wearisome task should be looked upon as a grand and noble work. It is the mother's privilege to bless the world by her influence, and in doing this she will bring joy to her own heart. She may make straight paths for the feet of her children through sunshine and shadow to the glorious heights above. But it is only when she seeks, in her own life, to follow the teachings of Christ that the mother can hope to form the character of her children after the divine pattern.[11]

Amid all the activities of life the mother's most sacred duty is to her children. But how often is this duty put aside that some selfish [235] gratification may be followed! Parents are entrusted with the present and eternal interests of their children. They are to hold the reins of government and guide their households to the honor of God. God's law should be their standard, and love should rule in all things.[12]

No Work Is Greater or Holier—If married men go into the work, leaving their wives to care for the children at home, the wife and mother is doing fully as great and important a work as the husband and father. Although one is in the missionary field, the other is a home missionary, whose cares and anxieties and burdens frequently far exceed those of the husband and father. Her work is a solemn and important one.... The husband in the open missionary field may receive the honors of men, while the home toiler may receive no earthly credit for her labor. But if she works for the best interest of her family, seeking to fashion their characters after the divine Model, the recording angel writes her name as one of the greatest missionaries in the world. God does not see things as man's finite vision views them.[13]

The mother is God's agent to Christianize her family. She is to exemplify Biblical religion, showing how its influence is to control us in its everyday duties and pleasures, teaching her children that by grace alone can they be saved, through faith, which is the gift of God. This constant teaching as to what Christ is to us and to them, His love, His goodness, His mercy, revealed in the great plan of redemption, will make a hallowed, sacred impress on the heart.[14]

The training of children constitutes an important part of God's plan for demonstrating the power of Christianity. A solemn responsibility rests upon parents to so train their children that when they go forth into the world, they will do good and not evil to those with whom they associate.[15]

[236]

A Co-worker With the Minister—The minister has his line of work, and the mother has hers. She is to bring her children to Jesus for His blessing. She is to cherish the words of Christ and teach them to her children. From their babyhood she is to discipline them to self-restraint and self-denial, to habits of neatness and order. The mother can bring up her children so that they will come with open, tender hearts to hear the words of God's servants. The Lord has need of mothers who in every line of the home life will improve their God-given talents and fit their children for the family of heaven.

The Lord is served as much, yea, more, by faithful home work than by the one who teaches the word. As verily as do the teachers in the school, fathers and mothers are to feel that they are the educators of their children.[16]

The Christian mother's sphere of usefulness should not be narrowed by her domestic life. The salutary influence which she exerts in the home circle she may and will make felt in more widespread usefulness in her neighborhood and in the church of God. Home is not a prison to the devoted wife and mother.[17]

She Has a Life Mission—Let woman realize the sacredness of her work and, in the strength and fear of God, take up her life mission. Let her educate her children for usefulness in this world and for a fitness for the better world. We address Christian mothers. We entreat that you feel your responsibility as mothers and that you live not to please yourselves, but to glorify God. Christ pleased not Himself, but took upon Him the form of a servant.[18]

[237]

The world teems with corrupting influences. Fashion and custom exert a strong power over the young. If the mother fails in her duty to instruct, guide, and restrain, her children will naturally accept the evil and turn from the good. Let every mother go often to her Saviour with the prayer, "Teach us, how shall we order the child, and what shall we do unto him?" Let her heed the instruction which God has given in His word, and wisdom will be given her as she shall have need.[19]

Sculpturing a Likeness of the Divine—There is a God above, and the light and glory from His throne rests upon the faithful mother as she tries to educate her children to resist the influence of evil. No other work can equal hers in importance. She has not, like the artist, to paint a form of beauty upon canvas; nor, like the sculptor, to chisel it from marble. She has not, like the author, to embody a noble thought in words of power; nor, like the musician, to express a beautiful sentiment in melody. It is hers, with the help of God, to develop in a human soul the likeness of the divine.

The mother who appreciates this will regard her opportunities as priceless. Earnestly will she seek, in her own character and by her methods of training, to present before her children the highest ideal. Earnestly, patiently, courageously, she will endeavor to improve her own abilities, that she may use aright the highest powers of the mind in the training of her children. Earnestly will she inquire at every step, "What hath God spoken?" Diligently she will study His word. She will keep her eyes fixed upon Christ, that her own daily experience, in the lowly round of care and duty, may be a true reflection of the one true Life.[20] [238]

The Faithful Mother Enrolled in Book of Immortal Fame— Self-denial and the cross are our portion. Will we accept it? None of us need expect that when the last great trials come upon us, a self-sacrificing, patriotic spirit will be developed in a moment because needed. No, indeed, this spirit must be blended with our daily experience and infused into the minds and hearts of our children, both by precept and example. Mothers in Israel may not be warriors themselves, but they may raise up warriors who shall gird on the whole armor and fight manfully the battles of the Lord.[21]

Mothers, to a great degree the destiny of your children rests in your hands. If you fail in duty, you may place them in the ranks of the enemy and make them his agents to ruin souls; but by a godly example and faithful discipline you may lead them to Christ and make them the instruments in His hands of saving many souls.[22]

Her work [the Christian mother's], if done faithfully in God, will be immortalized. The votaries of fashion will never see or understand the immortal beauty of that Christian mother's work, and will sneer at her old-fashioned notions and her plain, unadorned dress; while the Majesty of heaven will write the name of that faithful mother in the book of immortal fame.[23]

The Moments Are Priceless—The whole future life of Moses, the great mission which he fulfilled as the leader of Israel, testifies to the importance of the work of the Christian mother. There is no other work that can equal this... Parents should direct the instruction and training of their children while very young, to the end that they may be Christians. They are placed in our care to be trained, not as heirs to the throne of an earthly empire, but as kings unto God, to reign through unending ages. [239]

Let every mother feel that her moments are priceless; her work will be tested in the solemn day of accounts. Then it will be found that many of the failures and crimes of men and women have resulted from the ignorance and neglect of those whose duty it was to guide their childish feet in the right way. Then it will be found that many who have blessed the world with the light of genius and truth and holiness owe the principles that were the mainspring of their influence and success to a praying, Christian mother.[24] [240]

[1] Christian Temperance and Bible Hygiene, 77.

[2] Pacific Health Journal, June, 1890.

[3] The Signs of the Times, March 16, 1891.

[4] Counsels to Teachers, Parents, and Students, 111.

[5] Letter 272, 1903.

[6] The Signs of the Times, September 13, 1877.

[7] The Signs of the Times, October 11, 1910.

[8] Pacific Health Journal, June, 1890.

[9] Good Health, January, 1880.

[10] Ibid.

[11] Patriarchs and Prophets, 572.

[12] The Signs of the Times, March 16, 1891.

[13] Testimonies For The Church 5, 594.

[14] The Review and Herald, September 15, 1891.

[15] Manuscript 49, 1901.

[16] Manuscript 32, 1899.

[17] Pacific Health Journal, June, 1890.

[18] Testimonies For The Church 3, 565.

[19] Patriarchs and Prophets, 572, 573.

[20] The Ministry of Healing, 377, 378.

[21] Testimonies For The Church 5, 135.

[22] The Signs of the Times, March 11, 1886.

[23] The Signs of the Times, September 13, 1877.

[24] Patriarchs and Prophets, 244.

Chapter 39—Influence of the Mother

Mother's Influence Reaches Into Eternity—The sphere of the mother may be humble; but her influence, united with the father's, is as abiding as eternity. Next to God, the mother's power for good is the strongest known on earth.[1]

The mother's influence is an unceasing influence; and if it is always on the side of right, her children's characters will testify to her moral earnestness and worth. Her smile, her encouragement, may be an inspiring force. She may bring sunshine to the heart of her child by a word of love, a smile of approval....

When her influence is for truth, for virtue, when she is guided by divine wisdom, what a power for Christ will be her life! Her influence will reach on through time into eternity. What a thought is this—that the mother's looks and words and actions bear fruit in eternity, and the salvation or ruin of many will be the result of her influence![2]

Little does the mother realize that her influence in the judicious training of her children reaches with such power through the vicissitudes of this life, stretching forward into the future, immortal life. To fashion a character after the heavenly Model requires much faithful, earnest, persevering labor; but it will pay, for God is a rewarder of all well-directed labor in securing the salvation of souls.[3]

Like Mother—Like Children—The tenderest earthly tie is that between the mother and her child. The child is more readily impressed by the life and example of the mother than by that of the father, for a stronger and more tender bond of union unites them.[4] [241]

The thoughts and feelings of the mother will have a powerful influence upon the legacy she gives her child. If she allows her mind to dwell upon her own feelings, if she indulges in selfishness, if she is peevish and exacting, the disposition of her child will testify to the fact. Thus many have received as a birthright almost unconquerable tendencies to evil. The enemy of souls understands this matter much better than do many parents. He will bring his temptations to bear

185

upon the mother, knowing that if she does not resist him, he can through her affect her child. The mother's only hope is in God. She may flee to Him for strength and grace; and she will not seek in vain.[5]

A Christian mother will ever be wide awake to discern the dangers that surround her children. She will keep her own soul in a pure, holy atmosphere; she will regulate her temper and principles by the word of God and will faithfully do her duty, living above the petty temptations which will always assail her.[6]

The Wholesome Influence of a Patient Mother—Many times in the day is the cry of, Mother, mother, heard, first from one little troubled voice and then another. In answer to the cry, mother must turn here and there to attend to their demands. One is in trouble and needs the wise head of the mother to free him from his perplexity. Another is so pleased with some of his devices he must have his mother see them, thinking she will be as pleased as he is. A word of approval will bring sunshine to the heart for hours. Many precious beams of light and gladness can the mother shed here and there among her precious little ones. How closely can she bind these dear ones to her heart, that her presence will be to them the sunniest place in the world.

[242]

But frequently the patience of the mother is taxed with these numerous little trials that seem scarcely worth attention. Mischievous hands and restless feet create a great amount of labor and perplexity for the mother. She has to hold fast the reins of self-control, or impatient words will slip from her tongue. She almost forgets herself time and again, but a silent prayer to her pitying Redeemer calms her nerves, and she is enabled to hold the reins of self-control with quiet dignity. She speaks with calm voice, but it has cost her an effort to restrain harsh words and subdue angry feelings which, if expressed, would have destroyed her influence, which it would have taken time to regain.

The perception of children is quick, and they discern patient, loving tones from the impatient, passionate command, which dries up the moisture of love and affection in the hearts of children. The true Christian mother will not drive her children from her presence by her fretfulness and lack of sympathizing love.[7]

To Shape Minds and Mold Characters—Especially does responsibility rest upon the mother. She, by whose lifeblood the child is nourished and its physical frame built up, imparts to it also mental and spiritual influences that tend to the shaping of mind and character. It was Jochebed, the Hebrew mother, who, strong in faith, was "not afraid of the king's commandment," of whom was born Moses, the deliverer of Israel. It was Hannah, the woman of prayer and self-sacrifice and heavenly inspiration, who gave birth to Samuel, the heaven-instructed child, the incorruptible judge, the founder of Israel's sacred schools. It was Elizabeth, the kinswoman and kindred spirit of Mary of Nazareth, who was the mother of the Saviour's herald.[8] [243]

The World's Debt to Mothers—The day of God will reveal how much the world owes to godly mothers for men who have been unflinching advocates of truth and reform—men who have been bold to do and dare, who have stood unshaken amid trials and temptations; men who chose the high and holy interests of truth and the glory of God before worldly honor or life itself.[9]

Mothers, awake to the fact that your influence and example are affecting the character and destiny of your children; and in view of your responsibility, develop a well-balanced mind and a pure character, reflecting only the true, the good, and the beautiful.[10] [244]

---

[1] Good Health, March 1, 1880, par. 12.

[2] The Signs of the Times, March 16, 1891.

[3] Good Health, July, 1880.

[4] Testimonies For The Church 2, 536.

[5] The Signs of the Times, September 13, 1910.

[6] Letter 69, 1896.

[7] The Signs of the Times, September 13, 1877.

[8] The Ministry of Healing, 372.

[9] The Signs of the Times, October 11, 1910.

[10] The Signs of the Times, September 9, 1886.

Chapter 40—Misconception of the Mother's Work

Mother Tempted to Feel That Her Work Is Unimportant—The mother's work often seems to her an unimportant service. It is a work that is rarely appreciated. Others know little of her many cares and burdens. Her days are occupied with a round of little duties, all calling for patient effort, for self-control, for tact, wisdom, and self-sacrificing love; yet she cannot boast of what she has done as any great achievement. She has only kept things in the home running smoothly. Often weary and perplexed, she has tried to speak kindly to the children, to keep them busy and happy, and to guide their little feet in the right path. She feels that she has accomplished nothing. But it is not so. Heavenly angels watch the careworn mother, noting the burdens she carries day by day. Her name may not have been heard in the world, but it is written in the Lamb's book of life.[1]

The true wife and mother ... will perform her duties with dignity and cheerfulness, not considering it degrading to do with her own hands whatever it is necessary to do in a well-ordered household.[2]

Regarded as Inferior to Mission Service—What an important work! And yet we hear mothers sighing for missionary work! If they could only go to some foreign country, they would feel that they were doing something worth while. But to take up the daily duties of the home life and carry them forward seems to them like [245] an exhausting and thankless task.[3]

Mothers who sigh for a missionary field have one at hand in their own home circle.... Are not the souls of her own children of as much value as the souls of the heathen? With what care and tenderness should she watch their growing minds and connect God with all their thoughts! Who can do this as well as a loving, God-fearing mother?[4]

There are some who think that unless they are directly connected with active religious work, they are not doing the will of God; but this is a mistake. Everyone has a work to do for the Master; it is a wonderful work to make home pleasant and all that it ought to be. The humblest talents, if the heart of the recipient is given to God,

188

will make the home life all that God would have it. A bright light will shine forth as the result of wholehearted service to God. Men and women can just as surely serve God by giving earnest heed to the things which they have heard, by educating their children to live and fear to offend God, as can the minister in the pulpit.[5]

These women who are doing with ready willingness what their hands find to do, with cheerfulness of spirit aiding their husbands to bear their burdens and training their children for God, are missionaries in the highest sense.[6]

Religious Activities Should Not Supersede Care of Family— If you ignore your duty as a wife and mother and hold out your hands for the Lord to put another class of work in them, be sure that He will not contradict Himself; He points you to the duty you have to do at home. If you have the idea that some work greater and holier than this has been entrusted to you, you are under a deception. By faithfulness in your own home, working for the souls of those who are nearest to you, you may be gaining a fitness to work for Christ in a wider field. But be sure that those who are neglectful of their duty in the home circle are not prepared to work for other souls.[7]

[246]

The Lord has not called you to neglect your home and your husband and children. He never works in this way; and He never will.... Never for a moment suppose that God has given you a work that will necessitate a separation from your precious little flock. Do not leave them to become demoralized by improper associations and to harden their hearts against their mother. This is letting your light shine in a wrong way, altogether; you are making it more difficult for your children to become what God would have them and win heaven at last. God cares for them, and so must you if you claim to be His child.[8]

During the first years of their lives is the time in which to work and watch and pray and encourage every good inclination. This work must go on without interruption. You may be urged to attend mothers' meetings and sewing circles, that you may do missionary work; but unless there is a faithful, understanding instructor to be left with your children, it is your duty to answer that the Lord has committed to you another work which you can in no wise neglect. You cannot overwork in any line without becoming disqualified for the work of training your little ones and making them what God would have them be. As Christ's co-worker you must bring them to Him disciplined and trained.[9]

Much of the malformation of an ill-trained child's character lies at the mother's door. The mother should not accept burdens in the church work which compel her to neglect her children. The best work in which a mother can engage is to see that no stitches are dropped in the training of her children....

[247]

In no other way can a mother help the church more than by devoting her time to those who are dependent upon her for instruction and training.[10]

Aspirations for a Broader Mission Field Are Vain—Some mothers long to engage in missionary labor, while they neglect the simplest duties lying directly in their path. The children are neglected, the home is not made cheerful and happy for the family, scolding and complaining are of frequent occurrence, and the young people grow up feeling that home is the most uninviting of all places. As a consequence, they impatiently look forward to the time when they shall leave it, and it is with little reluctance that they launch out into the great world, unrestrained by home influence and the tender counsel of the hearthstone.

The parents, whose aim should have been to bind these young hearts to themselves and guide them aright, squander their God-given opportunities, are blind to the most important duties of their lives, and vainly aspire to work in the broad missionary field.[11]

[248]

---

[1] Counsels to Teachers, Parents, and Students, 144.

[2] The Signs of the Times, September 9, 1886.

[3] The Review and Herald, July 9, 1901.

[4] Manuscript 43, 1900.

[5] Manuscript 32, 1899.

[6] Testimonies For The Church 2, 466.

[7] The Review and Herald, September 15, 1891, **par. 2.**

[8] Letter 28, 1890.

[9] Manuscript 32, 1899.

[10] Manuscript 75, 1901.

[11] The Health Reformer, October, 1876.

Chapter 41—Imperfect Patterns of Motherhood

A Fancied Martyr—Many a home is made very unhappy by the useless repining of its mistress, who turns with distaste from the simple, homely tasks of her unpretending domestic life. She looks upon the cares and duties of her lot as hardships; and that which, through cheerfulness, might be made not only pleasant and interesting, but profitable, becomes the merest drudgery. She looks upon the slavery of her life with repugnance and imagines herself a martyr.

It is true that the wheels of domestic machinery will not always run smoothly; there is much to try the patience and tax the strength. But while mothers are not responsible for circumstances over which they have no control, it is useless to deny that circumstances make a great difference with mothers in their lifework. But their condemnation is when circumstances are allowed to rule and to subvert their principle, when they grow tired and unfaithful to their high trust and neglect their known duty.

The wife and mother who nobly overcomes difficulties under which others sink for want of patience and fortitude to persevere not only becomes strong herself in doing her duty, but her experience in overcoming temptations and obstacles qualifies her to be an efficient help to others, both by words and example. Many who do well under favorable circumstances seem to undergo a transformation of character under adversity and trial; they deteriorate in proportion to their troubles. God never designed that we should be the sport of circumstances.[1]

[249]

Nourishing a Sinful Discontent—Very many husbands and children who find nothing attractive at home, who are continually greeted by scolding and murmuring, seek comfort and amusement away from home, in the dramshop or in other forbidden scenes of pleasure. The wife and mother, occupied with her household cares, frequently becomes thoughtless of the little courtesies that make home pleasant to the husband and children, even if she avoids

191

dwelling upon her peculiar vexations and difficulties in their presence. While she is absorbed in preparing something to eat or to wear, the husband and sons go in and come out as strangers.

While the mistress of the household may perform her outward duties with exactitude, she may be continually crying out against the slavery to which she is doomed, and exaggerate her responsibilities and restrictions by comparing her lot with what she styles the higher life of woman.... While she is fruitlessly yearning for a different life, she is nourishing a sinful discontent and making her home very unpleasant for her husband and children.[2]

Occupied With the World's Follies—Satan has prepared pleasing attractions for parents as well as for children. He knows that if he can exert his deceptive power upon mothers, he has gained much. The ways of the world are full of deceitfulness and fraud and misery, but they are made to appear inviting; and if the children and youth are not carefully trained and disciplined, they will surely go astray. Having no fixed principles, it will be hard for them to resist temptation.[3]

[250]

Assuming Unnecessary Burdens—Many mothers spend their time in doing needless nothings. They give their whole attention to the things of time and sense' and do not pause to think of the things of eternal interest. How many neglect their children, and the little ones grow up coarse, rough, and uncultivated![4]

When parents, especially mothers, have a true sense of the important, responsible work which God has left for them to do, they will not be so much engaged in the business which concerns their neighbors, with which they have nothing to do. They will not go from house to house to engage in fashionable gossip, dwelling upon the faults, wrongs, and inconsistencies of their neighbors. They will feel so great a burden of care for their own children that they can find no time to take up a reproach against their neighbor.[5]

If woman looks to God for strength and comfort and in His fear seeks to perform her daily duties, she will win the respect and confidence of her husband and see her children coming to maturity honorable men and women, having moral stamina to do right. But mothers who neglect present opportunities, and let their duties and burdens fall upon others, will find that their responsibility remains the same, and they will reap in bitterness what they have sown in carelessness and neglect. There is no chance work in this life; the harvest will be determined by the character of the seed sown.[6] [251]

---

[1]The Signs of the Times, November 29, 1877.
[2]Ibid.
[3]The Review and Herald, June 27, 1899.
[4]The Signs of the Times, July 22, 1889.
[5]Testimonies For The Church 2, 466.
[6]The Signs of the Times, April 4, 1911.

Chapter 42—Mother's Health and Personal Appearance

Mother's Health to Be Cherished—The strength of the mother should be tenderly cherished. Instead of spending her precious strength in exhausting labor, her care and burdens should be lessened. Often the husband and father is unacquainted with the physical laws which the well-being of his family requires him to understand. Absorbed in the struggle for a livelihood, or bent on acquiring wealth, and pressed with cares and perplexities, he allows to rest upon the wife and mother burdens that overtax her strength at the most critical period and cause feebleness and disease.[1]

It is for her own interest, and that of her family, to save herself all unnecessary taxation and to use every means at her command to preserve life, health, and the energies which God has given her; for she will need the vigor of all her faculties for her great work. A portion of her time should be spent out-of-doors, in physical exercise, that she may be invigorated to do her work indoors with cheerfulness and thoroughness, being the light and blessing of the home.[2]

Mothers to Be Advocates of Health Reform—The will of God has been plainly expressed to all mothers; He would have them, by precept and example, advocates of health reform. They should plant their feet firmly upon principle, in no case to violate the physical laws which God has implanted in their beings. "Standing by a purpose true," with firm integrity, mothers will have moral power and grace from Heaven to let their light shine forth to the world, both in their own upright course and in the noble character of their children.[3]

[252]

To Exercise Self-control in Diet—The mother needs the most perfect self-control; and in order to secure this, she should take all precautions against any physical or mental disorder. Her life should be ordered according to the laws of God and of health. As the diet materially affects the mind and disposition, she should be very careful in that particular, eating that which is nourishing but not stimulating, that her nerves may be calm and her temper equable. She will then find it easier to exercise patience in dealing with the varying tendencies of her children and to hold the reins of government firmly yet affectionately.[4]

To Radiate Sunshine Under All Circumstances—The mother can and should do much toward controlling her nerves and mind when depressed; even when she is sick, she can, if she only schools herself, be pleasant and cheerful and can bear more noise than she would once have thought possible. She should not make the children feel her infirmities and cloud their young, sensitive minds by her depression of spirits, causing them to feel that the house is a tomb and the mother's room the most dismal place in the world. The mind and nerves gain tone and strength by the exercise of the will. The power of the will in many cases will prove a potent soother of the nerves. Do not let your children see you with a clouded brow.[5]

To Regard the Esteem of Husband and Children—Sisters, when about their work, should not put on clothing which would make them look like images to frighten the crows from the corn. It is more gratifying to their husbands and children to see them in a becoming, well-fitting attire than it can be to mere visitors or strangers. Some wives and mothers seem to think it is no matter how they look when about their work and when they are seen only by their husbands and children, but they are very particular to dress in taste for the eyes of those who have no special claims upon them. Is not the esteem and love of husband and children more to be prized than that of strangers or common friends? The happiness of husband and children should be more sacred to every wife and mother than that of all others.[6]

[253]

Wear clothing that is becoming to you. This will increase the respect of your children for you. See to it that they, too, are dressed in a becoming manner. Do not allow them to fall into habits of untidiness.[7]

Not to Be in Bondage to Public Opinion—Too often mothers show a morbid sensitiveness as to what others may think of their habits, dress, and opinions; and, to a great extent, they are slaves to the thought of how others may regard them. Is it not a sad thing that judgment-bound creatures should be controlled more by the thought of what their neighbors will think of them than by the thought of their obligation to God? We too often sacrifice the truth in order to be in harmony with custom, that we may avoid ridicule....

A mother cannot afford to be in bondage to opinion; for she is to train her children for this life and for the life to come. In dress, mothers should not seek to make a display by needless ornamentation.[8]

To Give Lessons in Neatness and Purity—If mothers allow

[254]   themselves to wear untidy garments at home, they are teaching their children to follow in the same slovenly way. Many mothers think that anything is good enough for home wear, be it ever so soiled and shabby. But they soon lose their influence in the family. The children draw comparisons between their mother's dress and that of others who dress neatly, and their respect for her is weakened.

Mothers, make yourselves as attractive as possible; not by elaborate trimming, but by wearing clean, well-fitting garments. Thus you will give to your children constant lessons in neatness and purity. The love and respect of her children should be of the highest value to every mother. Everything upon her person should teach cleanliness and order and should be associated in their minds with purity. There is a sense of fitness, an idea of the appropriateness of things, in the minds of even very young children; and how can they be impressed with the desirability of purity and holiness when their eyes daily rest on untidy dresses and disorderly rooms? How can the heavenly guests, whose home is where all is pure and holy, be invited into such a dwelling?[9]

Order and cleanliness is the law of heaven; and in order to come into harmony with the divine arrangement, it is our duty to be neat

[255]   and tasty.[10]

---

[1] The Ministry of Healing, 373.

[2] Pacific Health Journal, June, 1890.

[3] Good Health, February, 1880.

[4] Pacific Health Journal, May, 1890.

[5] Testimonies For The Church 1. 387.

[6] Ibid., 1:464, 465.

[7] Letter 47a. 1902.

[8] The Review and Herald, March 31, 1891.

[9] Christian Temperance and Bible Hygiene, 143, 144.

[10] Testimonies For The Church 4, 142, 143.

Chapter 43—Prenatal Influences

Women Should Be Qualified to Become Mothers—Women have need of great patience before they are qualified to become mothers. God has ordained that they shall be fitted for this work. The work of the mother becomes infinite through her connection with Christ. It is beyond understanding. Woman's office is sacred. The presence of Jesus is needed in the home; for the mother's ministries of love may shape the home into a Bethel. The husband and the wife are to co-operate. What a world we would have if all mothers would consecrate themselves on the altar of God, and would consecrate their offspring to God, both before and after its birth![1]

Importance of Prenatal Influences—The effect of prenatal influences is by many parents looked upon as a matter of little moment; but heaven does not so regard it. The message sent by an angel of God, and twice given in the most solemn manner, shows it to be deserving of our most careful thought.

In the words spoken to the Hebrew mother [the wife of Manoah], God speaks to all mothers in every age. "Let her beware," the angel said; "all that I commanded her let her observe." The well-being of the child will be affected by the habits of the mother. Her appetites and passions are to be controlled by principle. There is something for her to shun, something for her to work against, if she fulfills God's purpose for her in giving her a child.[2]

The world is full of snares for the feet of the young. Multitudes are attracted by a life of selfish and sensual pleasure. They cannot discern the hidden dangers or the fearful ending of the path that seems to them the way of happiness. Through the indulgence of appetite and passion, their energies are wasted, and millions are ruined for this world and for the world to come. Parents should remember that their children must encounter these temptations. Even before the birth of the child, the preparation should begin that will enable it to fight successfully the battle against evil.[3]

[256]

197

If before the birth of her child she is self-indulgent, if she is selfish, impatient, and exacting, these traits will be reflected in the disposition of the child. Thus many children have received as a birthright almost unconquerable tendencies to evil.

But if the mother unswervingly adheres to right principles, if she is temperate and self-denying, if she is kind, gentle, and unselfish, she may give her child these same precious traits of character.[4]

Essentials of Prenatal Care—It is an error generally committed to make no difference in the life of a woman previous to the birth of her children. At this important period the labor of the mother should be lightened. Great changes are going on in her system. It requires a greater amount of blood, and therefore an increase of food of the most nourishing quality to convert into blood. Unless she has an abundant supply of nutritious food, she cannot retain her physical strength, and her offspring is robbed of vitality. [Note: see *Counsels On Diet And Foods,* section, "Diet During Pregnancy," for further instruction on this point.] Her clothing also demands attention. Care should be taken to protect the body from a sense of chilliness. She should not call vitality unnecessarily to the surface to supply the want of sufficient clothing. If the mother is deprived of an abundance of wholesome, nutritious food, she will lack in the quantity and quality of blood. Her circulation will be poor, and her child will lack in the very same things. There will be an inability in the offspring to appropriate food which it can convert into good blood to nourish the system. The prosperity of mother and child depends much upon good, warm clothing and a supply of nourishing food.[5]

[257]

Great care should be exercised to have the surroundings of the mother pleasant and happy. The husband and father is under special responsibility to do all in his power to lighten the burden of the wife and mother. He should bear, as much as possible, the burden of her condition. He should be affable, courteous, kind, and tender, and specially attentive to all her wants. Not half the care is taken of some women while they are bearing children that is taken of animals in the stable.[6]

Appetite Alone Not a Safe Guide—The idea that women, because of their special condition, may let the appetite run riot is a mistake based on custom, but not on sound sense. The appetite of women in this condition may be variable, fitful, and difficult to gratify; and custom allows her to have anything she may fancy, without consulting reason as to whether such food can supply nutrition for her body and for the growth of her child. The food should be nutritious, but should not be of an exciting quality.... If ever there is need of simplicity of diet and special care as to the quality of food eaten, it is in this important period.

Women who possess principle, and who are well instructed, will not depart from simplicity of diet at this time of all others. They will consider that another life is dependent upon them and will be careful in all their habits and especially in diet. They should not eat [258] that which is innutritious and exciting, simply because it tastes good. There are too many counselors ready to persuade them to do things which reason would tell them they ought not to do. Diseased children are born because of the gratification of appetite by the parents....

If so much food is taken into the stomach that the digestive organs are compelled to overwork in order to dispose of it and to free the system from irritating substances, the mother does injustice to herself and lays the foundation of disease in her offspring. If she chooses to eat as she pleases and what she may fancy, irrespective of consequences, she will bear the penalty, but not alone. Her innocent child must suffer because of her indiscretion.[7]

Self-control and Temperance Are Necessary—The mother's physical needs should in no case be neglected. Two lives are depending upon her, and her wishes should be tenderly regarded, her needs generously supplied. But at this time above all others she should avoid, in diet and in every other line, whatever would lessen physical or mental strength. By the command of God Himself she is placed under the most solemn obligation to exercise self-control.[8]

The basis of a right character in the future man is made firm by habits of strict temperance in the mother prior to the birth of her child.... This lesson should not be regarded with indifference.[9]

Encourage Cheerful, Contented Disposition—Every woman about to become a mother, whatever may be her surroundings, should encourage constantly a happy, cheerful, contented disposition, knowing that for all her efforts in this direction she will be repaid tenfold in the physical, as well as the moral, character of her offspring. Nor [259] is this all. She can, by habit, accustom herself to cheerful thinking, and thus encourage a happy state of mind and cast a cheerful reflection of her own happiness of spirit upon her family and those with whom she associates. And in a very great degree will her physical health be improved. A force will be imparted to the lifesprings, the blood will not move sluggishly, as would be the case if she were to yield to despondency and gloom. Her mental and moral health are invigorated by the buoyancy of her spirits. The power of the will can resist impressions of the mind and will prove a grand soother of the nerves. Children who are robbed of that vitality which they should have inherited of their parents should have the utmost care. By close attention to the laws of their being a much better condition of things can be established.[10]

Maintain a Peaceful, Trustful Attitude—She who expects to become a mother should keep her soul in the love of God. Her mind should be at peace; she should rest in the love of Jesus, practicing the words of Christ. She should remember that the mother is a laborer together with God.[11]

[260]

---

[1] Manuscript 43, 1900.

[2] The Ministry of Healing, 372.

[3] Ibid., 371.

[4] Ibid., 372, 373.

[5] Testimonies For The Church 2, 381, 382.

[6] Ibid., 2:383.

[7] Ibid., 382, 383.

[8] The Ministry of Healing, 373.

[9] Good Health, February, 1880.

[10] A Solemn Appeal, 123, 124.

[11] The Signs of the Times, April 9, 1896.

Chapter 44—Care Of Little Children

Correct Attitudes for the Nursing Mother—The best food for the infant is the food that nature provides. Of this it should not be needlessly deprived. It is a heartless thing for a mother, for the sake of convenience or social enjoyment, to seek to free herself from the tender office of nursing her little one.[1]

The period in which the infant receives its nourishment from the mother is critical. Many mothers, while nursing their infants, have been permitted to overlabor and to heat their blood in cooking; and the nursling has been seriously affected, not only with fevered nourishment from the mother's breast, but its blood has been poisoned by the unhealthy diet of the mother, which has fevered her whole system, thereby affecting the food of the infant. The infant will also be affected by the condition of the mother's mind. If she is unhappy, easily agitated, irritable, giving vent to outbursts of passion, the nourishment the infant receives from its mother will be inflamed, often producing colic, spasms, and in some instances causing convulsions and fits.

The character also of the child is more or less affected by the nature of the nourishment received from the mother. How important then that the mother, while nursing her infant, should preserve a happy state of mind, having the perfect control of her own spirit. By thus doing, the food of the child is not injured, and the calm, self-possessed course the mother pursues in the treatment of her child has very much to do in molding the mind of the infant. If it is nervous and easily agitated, the mother's careful, unhurried manner will have a soothing and correcting influence, and the health of the infant can be very much improved.[2]

[261]

The more quiet and simple the life of the child, the more favorable it will be to both physical and mental development. At all times the mother should endeavor to be quiet, calm, and self-possessed.[3]

Food Is Not a Substitute for Attention—Infants have been greatly abused by improper treatment. If fretful, they have generally

201

been fed to keep them quiet, when, in most cases, the very reason of their fretfulness was because of their having received too much food, made injurious by the wrong habits of the mother. More food only made the matter worse, for their stomachs were already overloaded.

Children are generally brought up from the cradle to indulge the appetite and are taught that they live to eat. The mother does much toward the formation of the character of her children in their childhood. She can teach them to control the appetite, or she can teach them to indulge the appetite and become gluttons. The mother often arranges her plans to accomplish a certain amount through the day; and when the children trouble her, instead of taking time to soothe their little sorrows and divert them, something is given them to eat to keep them still, which answers the purpose for a short time but eventually makes things worse. The children's stomachs have been pressed with food, when they had not the least want of it. All that was required was a little of the mother's time and attention. But she regarded her time as altogether too precious to devote to the amusement of her children. Perhaps the arrangement of her house in a tasteful manner for visitors to praise, and to have her food cooked [262] in a fashionable style, are with her higher considerations than the happiness and health of her children.[4]

Food to Be Wholesome and Inviting, but Simple—Food should be so simple that its preparation will not absorb all the time of the mother. It is true, care should be taken to furnish the table with healthful food prepared in a wholesome and inviting manner. Do not think that anything you can carelessly throw together to serve as food is good enough for the children. But less time should be devoted to the preparation of unhealthful dishes for the table, to please a perverted taste, and more time to the education and training of the children.[5]

Preparing the Baby's Layette—In the preparation of the baby's wardrobe, convenience, comfort, and health should be sought before fashion or a desire to excite admiration. The mother should not spend time in embroidery and fancywork to make the little garments beautiful, thus taxing herself with unnecessary labor at the expense of her own health and the health of her child. She should not bend over sewing that severely taxes eyes and nerves, at a time when she needs much rest and pleasant exercise. She should realize her obligation to cherish her strength, that she may be able to meet the demands that will be made upon her.[6]

Insure Cleanliness, Warmth, Fresh Air—Babies require warmth, but a serious error is often committed in keeping them in overheated rooms, deprived to a great degree of fresh air....

The baby should be kept free from every influence that would tend to weaken or to poison the system. The most scrupulous care should be taken to have everything about it sweet and clean. While it may be necessary to protect the little ones from sudden or too great changes of temperature, care should be taken that, sleeping or waking, day or night, they breathe a pure, invigorating atmosphere.[7]

[263]

The Care of Children in Sickness—In many cases the sickness of children can be traced to errors in management. Irregularities in eating, insufficient clothing in the chilly evening, lack of vigorous exercise to keep the blood in healthy circulation, or lack of abundance of air for its purification, may be the cause of the trouble. Let the parents study to find the causes of the sickness and then remedy the wrong conditions as soon as possible.

All parents have it in their power to learn much concerning the care and prevention, and even the treatment, of disease. Especially ought the mother to know what to do in common cases of illness in her family. She should know how to minister to her sick child. Her love and insight should fit her to perform services for it which could not so well be trusted to a stranger's hand.[8]

[264]

---

[1] The Ministry of Healing, 383.

[2] Counsels on Diet and Foods, 228.

[3] The Ministry of Healing, 381.

[4] A Solemn Appeal, 125, 126.

[5] Christian Temperance and Bible Hygiene, 141.

[6] The Ministry of Healing, 381, 382.

[7] Ibid., 381.

[8] Ibid., 385.

Chapter 45—Mother's First Duty Is To Train Children

The Possibilities in a Properly Trained Child—God sees all the possibilities in that mite of humanity. He sees that with proper training the child will become a power for good in the world. He watches with anxious interest to see whether the parents will carry out His plan or whether by mistaken kindness they will destroy His purpose, indulging the child to its present and eternal ruin. To transform this helpless and apparently insignificant being into a blessing to the world and an honor to God is a great and grand work. Parents should allow nothing to come between them and the obligation they owe to their children.[1]

A Work for God and Country—Those who keep the law of God look upon their children with indefinable feelings of hope and fear, wondering what part they will act in the great conflict that is just before them. The anxious mother questions, "What stand will they take? What can I do to prepare them to act well their part, so that they will be the recipients of eternal glory?" Great responsibilities rest upon you, mothers. Although you may not stand in national councils, ... you may do a great work for God and your country. You may educate your children. You may aid them to develop characters that will not be swayed or influenced to do evil, but will sway and influence others to do right. By your fervent prayers of faith you can [265] move the arm that moves the world.[2]

It is in childhood and youth that instruction should be given. The children should be educated for usefulness. They should be taught to do those things that are needful in the home life; and the parents should make these duties as pleasant as possible with kindly words of instruction and approval.[3]

Home Training Is Neglected by Many—Notwithstanding boasted advancement that has been made in educational methods, the training of children at the present day is sadly defective. It is the home training that is neglected. Parents, and especially mothers,

204

do not realize their responsibility. They have neither the patience to instruct nor the wisdom to control the little ones entrusted to their keeping.[4]

It is too true that mothers are not standing at their post of duty, faithful to their motherhood. God requires of us nothing that we cannot in His strength perform, nothing that is not for our own good and the good of our children.[5]

Mothers to Seek Divine Aid—Did mothers but realize the importance of their mission, they would be much in secret prayer, presenting their children to Jesus, imploring His blessing upon them, and pleading for wisdom to discharge aright their sacred duties. Let the mother improve every opportunity to mold and fashion the disposition and habits of her children. Let her watch carefully the development of character, repressing traits that are too prominent, encouraging those that are deficient. Let her make her own life a pure and noble example to her precious charge.

The mother should enter upon her work with courage and energy, relying constantly upon divine aid in all her efforts. She should never rest satisfied until she sees in her children a gradual elevation of character, until they have a higher object in life than merely to seek their own pleasure.[6]

[266]

It is impossible to estimate the power of a praying mother's influence. She acknowledges God in all her ways. She takes her children before the throne of grace and presents them to Jesus, pleading for His blessing upon them. The influence of those prayers is to those children as "a wellspring of life." These prayers, offered in faith, are the support and strength of the Christian mother. To neglect the duty of praying with our children is to lose one of the greatest blessings within our reach, one of the greatest helps amid the perplexities, cares, and burdens of our lifework.[7]

The power of a mother's prayers cannot be too highly estimated. She who kneels beside her son and daughter through the vicissitudes of childhood, through the perils of youth, will never know till the judgment the influence of her prayers upon the life of her children. If she is connected by faith with the Son of God, the mother's tender hand may hold back her son from the power of temptation, may restrain her daughter from indulging in sin. When passion is warring for the mastery, the power of love, the restraining, earnest, determined influence of the mother, may balance the soul on the side of right.[8]

When Visitors Interrupt—You should take time to talk and pray with your little ones, and you should allow nothing to interrupt that season of communion with God and with your children. You can say to your visitors, "God has given me a work to do, and I have no time for gossiping." You should feel that you have a work to do for time and for eternity. You owe your first duty to your children.[9]

[267]

Before visitors, before every other consideration, your children should come first.... The labor due your child during its early years will admit of no neglect. There is no time in its life when the rule should be forgotten.[10]

Do not send them out-of-doors that you may entertain your visitors, but teach them to be quiet and respectful in the presence of visitors.[11]

Mothers to Be Models of Goodness and Nobility—Mothers, be careful of your precious moments. Remember that your children are passing forward where they may be beyond your educating and training. You may be to them the very model of all that is good and pure and noble. Identify your interest with theirs.[12]

If you fail in everything else, be thorough, be efficient, here. If your children come forth from the home training pure and virtuous, if they fill the least and lowest place in God's great plan of good for the world, your life can never be called a failure and can never be reviewed with remorse.[13]

Infant children are a mirror for the mother in which she may see reflected her own habits and deportment. How careful, then, should be her language and behavior in the presence of these little learners! Whatever traits of character she wishes to see developed in them she must cultivate in herself.[14]

Aim Higher Than the World's Standard—The mother should not be governed by the world's opinion, nor labor to reach its standard. She should decide for herself what is the great end and aim of life and then bend all her efforts to attain that end. She may, for want of time, neglect many things about her house, with no serious evil results; but she cannot with impunity neglect the proper discipline of her children. Their defective characters will publish her unfaithfulness. The evils which she permits to pass uncorrected, the

[268]

coarse, rough manners, the disrespect and disobedience, the habits of idleness and inattention, will reflect dishonor upon her and embitter her life. Mothers, the destiny of your children rests to a great extent in your hands. If you fail in duty, you may place them in Satan's ranks, and make them his agents to ruin other souls. Or your faithful discipline and godly example may lead them to Christ, and they in turn will influence others, and thus many souls may be saved through your instrumentality.[15]

Cultivate the Good; Repress the Evil—Parents are to co-operate with God by bringing their children up in His love and fear. They cannot displease Him more than by neglecting to train their children aright.... They are to carefully guard the words and actions of their little ones, lest the enemy shall gain an influence over them. This he is intensely desirous of doing, that he may counterwork the purpose of God. Kindly, interestedly, tenderly, parents are to work for their children, cultivating every good thing and repressing every evil thing which develops in the characters of their little ones.[16]

The Joy of Work Satisfactorily Done—Children are the heritage of the Lord, and we are answerable to Him for our management of His property. The education and training of their children to be Christians is the highest service that parents can render to God. It is a work that demands patient labor—a lifelong, diligent, and persevering effort. By a neglect of this trust we prove ourselves unfaithful stewards.... [269]

In love, faith, and prayer let parents work for their households, until with joy they can come to God saying, "Behold, I and the children whom the Lord hath given me."[17] [270]

---

[1] The Signs of the Times, September 25, 1901.

[2] The Review and Herald, April 23, 1889.

[3] Manuscript 12, 1898.

[4] The Signs of the Times, March 11, 1886.

[5] The Signs of the Times, February 9, 1882.

[6] The Signs of the Times, May 25, 1882.

[7] Good Health, July, 1880.

[8] The Signs of the Times, March 16, 1891.

[9] The Signs of the Times, July 22, 1889.

[10] Counsels to Teachers, Parents, and Students, 129.

[11] The Signs of the Times, August 23, 1899.

[12] The Review and Herald, September 15, 1891.

[13]Testimonies For The Church 5, 44.

[14]The Signs of the Times, September 9, 1886.

[15]The Signs of the Times, February 9, 1882.

[16]Manuscript 49, 1901.

[17]Christ's Object Lessons, 195, 196.

Chapter 46—The Stepmother

Counsel to a Stepmother—Your marriage to one who is a father of children will prove to be a blessing to you.... You were in danger of becoming self-centered. You had precious traits of character that needed to be awakened and exercised.... Through your new relations you will gain an experience that will teach you how to deal with minds. By the care of children affection, love, and tenderness are developed. The responsibilities resting upon you in your family may be a means of great blessing to you. These children will be to you a precious lesson book. They will bring you many blessings if you read them aright. The train of thought awakened by their care will call into exercise tenderness, love, and sympathy. Although these children are not a part of your flesh and blood, yet through your marriage to their father, they have become yours, to be loved, cherished, instructed, and ministered to by you. Your connection with them will call into exercise thoughts and plans that will be of genuine benefit to you.... By the experience that you will gain in your home, you will lose the self-centered ideas that threatened to mar your work and will change the set plans that have needed softening and subduing....

You have needed to develop greater tenderness and larger sympathy, that you might come close to those in need of gentle, sympathetic, loving words. Your children will call out these traits of character and will help you to develop breadth of mind and judgment. Through loving association with them, you will learn to be more tender and sympathetic in your ministry for suffering humanity.[1]   [271]

Reproof to a Stepmother Who Lacked Love—You loved your husband and married him. You knew that when you married him you covenanted to become a mother to his children. But I saw a lack in you in this matter. You are sadly deficient. You do not love the children of your husband, and unless there is an entire change, a thorough reformation in you and in your manner of government, these precious jewels are ruined. Love, manifestation of affection, is not a part of your discipline....

You are making the lives of those dear children very bitter, especially the daughter's. Where is the affection, the loving caress, the patient forbearance? Hatred lives in your unsanctified heart more than love. Censure leaps from your lips more than praise and encouragement. Your manners, your harsh ways, your unsympathizing nature, are to that sensitive daughter like desolating hail upon a tender plant; it bends to every blast until its life is crushed out, and it lies bruised and broken.

Your administration is drying up the channel of love, hopefulness, and joy in your children. A settled sadness is expressed in the countenance of the girl, but, instead of awakening sympathy and tenderness in you, this arouses impatience and positive dislike. You can change this expression to animation and cheerfulness if you choose....

Children read the countenance of the mother; they understand whether love or dislike is there expressed. You know not the work you are doing. Does not the little sad face, the heaving sigh welling up from a pressed heart in its yearning call for love, awaken pity?[2]

Results of Undue Severity—Some time ago I was shown the [272] case of J. Her errors and wrongs were faithfully portrayed before her; but in the last view given me I saw that the wrongs still existed, that she was cold and unsympathizing with her husband's children. Correction and reproof are not given by her for grave offenses merely, but for trivial matters that should be passed by unnoticed. Constant faultfinding is wrong, and the Spirit of Christ cannot abide in the heart where it exists. She is disposed to pass over the good in her children without a word of approval, but is ever ready to bear down with censure if any wrong is seen. This ever discourages children and leads to habits of heedlessness. It stirs up the evil in the heart and causes it to cast up mire and dirt. In children who are habitually censured there will be a spirit of "I don't care," and evil passions will frequently be manifested, regardless of consequences....

Sister J should cultivate love and sympathy. She should manifest tender affection for the motherless children under her care. This would be a blessing to these children of God's love and would be reflected back upon her in affection and love.[3]

When Double Care is Needed—Children who have lost the one in whose breasts maternal love has flowed have met with a loss that can never be supplied. But when one ventures to stand in the place of mother to the little stricken flock, a double care and burden rests upon her to be even more loving if possible, more forbearing of censure and threatening than their own mother could have been, and in this way supply the loss which the little flock have sustained.[4]   [273]

---

[1]Letter 329, 1904.

[2]Testimonies For The Church 2, 56-58.

[3]Ibid., 3:531, 532.

[4]Ibid., 2:58.

Chapter 47—Christ's Encouragement to Mothers

Jesus Blessed the Children—In the days of Christ mothers brought their children to Him, that He might lay His hands upon them in blessing. By this act they showed their faith in Jesus and the intense anxiety of their hearts for the present and future welfare of the little ones committed to their care. But the disciples could not see the need of interrupting the Master just for the sake of noticing the children, and as they were sending these mothers away, Jesus rebuked the disciples and commanded the crowd to make way for these faithful mothers with their little children. Said He, "Suffer little children, and forbid them not, to come unto Me: for of such is the kingdom of heaven."

As the mothers passed along the dusty road and drew near the Saviour, He saw the unbidden tear and the quivering lip, as they offered a silent prayer in behalf of the children. He heard the words of rebuke from the disciples and promptly countermanded the order. His great heart of love was open to receive the children. One after another, He took them in His arms and blessed them, while one little child lay fast asleep, reclining against His bosom. Jesus spoke words of encouragement to the mothers in reference to their work, and, oh, what a relief was thus brought to their minds! With what joy they dwelt upon the goodness and mercy of Jesus, as they looked back to that memorable occasion! His gracious words had removed [274] the burden from their hearts and inspired them with fresh hope and courage. All sense of weariness was gone.

This is an encouraging lesson to mothers for all time. After they have done the best they can do for the good of their children, they may bring them to Jesus. Even the babes in the mother's arms are precious in His sight. And as the mother's heart yearns for the help she knows she cannot give, the grace she cannot bestow, and she casts herself and children into the merciful arms of Christ, He will receive and bless them; He will give peace, hope, and happiness to mother and children. This is a precious privilege which Jesus has granted to all mothers.[1]

Jesus Still Invites the Mothers—Christ, the Majesty of heaven, said, "Suffer the little children to come unto Me, and forbid them not: for of such is the kingdom of God." Jesus does not send the children to the rabbis; He does not send them to the Pharisees; for He knows that these men would teach them to reject their best Friend. The mothers that brought their children to Jesus did well.... Let mothers now lead their children to Christ. Let ministers of the gospel take the little children in their arms and bless them in the name of Jesus. Let words of tenderest love be spoken to the little ones; for Jesus took the lambs of the flock in His arms and blessed them.[2]

Let mothers come to Jesus with their perplexities. They will find grace sufficient to aid them in the management of their children. The gates are open for every mother who would lay her burdens at the Saviour's feet.... He ... still invites the mothers to lead up their little ones to be blessed by Him. Even the babe in its mother's arms may dwell under the shadow of the Almighty through the faith of the praying mother. John the Baptist was filled with the Holy Spirit from his birth. If we live in communion with God, we too may expect the divine Spirit to mould our little ones, even from their earliest moments.[3]

[275]

Hearts of Young Are Susceptible—He [Christ] identified Himself with the lowly, the needy, and the afflicted. He took little children in His arms and descended to the level of the young. His large heart of love could comprehend their trials and necessities, and He enjoyed their happiness. His spirit, wearied with the bustle and confusion of the crowded city, tired of association with crafty and hypocritical men, found rest and peace in the society of innocent children. His presence never repulsed them. The Majesty of heaven condescended to answer their questions and simplified His important lessons to meet their childish understanding. He planted in their young, expanding minds the seeds of truth that would spring up and produce a plentiful harvest in their riper years.[4]

He knew that these children would listen to His counsel and accept Him as their Redeemer, while those who were worldly-wise and hardhearted would be less likely to follow Him and find a place in the kingdom of God. These little ones, by coming to Christ and receiving His advice and benediction, had His image and His gracious words stamped upon their plastic minds, never to be effaced. We should learn a lesson from this act of Christ, that the hearts of the young are most susceptible to the teachings of Christianity, easy to influence toward piety and virtue, and strong to retain the impressions received.[5]

"Suffer the little children to come unto Me, and forbid them not: for of such is the kingdom of heaven." These precious words are to be cherished, not only by every mother, but by every father as well.

[276]   These words are an encouragement to parents to press their children into His notice, to ask in the name of Christ that the Father may let His blessing rest upon their entire family. Not only are the best beloved to receive particular attention, but also the restless, wayward

[277]   children, who need careful training and tender guidance.[6]

[278]

---

[1] Good Health. January, 1880.

[2] The Review and Herald, March 24, 1896.

[3] The Desire of Ages, 512.

[4] Testimonies For The Church 4, 141.

[5] Ibid., 4:142.

[6] The Signs of the Times, August 13, 1896.

Section 11—Children—The Junior Partners

Chapter 48—Heaven's Estimate of Children

Children Are the Purchase of Christ's Blood—Christ placed such a high estimate upon your children that He gave His life for them. Treat them as the purchase of His blood. Patiently and firmly train them for Him. Discipline with love and forbearance. As you do this, they will become a crown of rejoicing to you and will shine as lights in the world.[1]

The youngest child that loves and fears God is greater in His sight than the most talented and learned man who neglects the great salvation. The youth who consecrate their hearts and lives to God have, in so doing, placed themselves in connection with the Fountain of all wisdom and excellence.[2]

"Of Such Is the Kingdom of Heaven."—The soul of the little child that believes in Christ is as precious in His sight as are the angels about His throne. They are to be brought to Christ and trained for Christ. They are to be guided in the path of obedience, not indulged in appetite or vanity.[3]

If we would but learn the wonderful lessons which Jesus sought to teach His disciples from a little child, how many things that now seem insurmountable difficulties would wholly disappear! When the disciples came to Jesus, saying, "Who is the greatest in the kingdom of heaven? ... Jesus called a little child unto Him, and set him in the midst of them, and said, Verily I say unto you, Except ye be converted, and become as little children, ye shall not enter into the kingdom of heaven.[4] Whosoever therefore shall humble himself as this little child, the same is greatest in the kingdom of heaven."

God's Property Entrusted to Parents—Children derive life and being from their parents, and yet it is through the creative power of God that your children have life, for God is the Life-giver. Let it be remembered that children are not to be treated as though they were our own personal property. Children are the heritage of the Lord, and the plan of redemption includes their salvation as well as ours. They have been entrusted to parents in order that they might be brought up in the nurture and admonition of the Lord, that they might be qualified to do their work in time and eternity.[5]

Mothers, deal gently with your little ones. Christ was once a little child. For His sake honor the children. Look upon them as a sacred charge, not to be indulged, petted, and idolized, but to be taught to live pure, noble lives. They are God's property; He loves them, and calls upon you to co-operate with Him in helping them to form perfect characters.[6]

If you would meet God in peace, feed His flock now with spiritual food; for every child has the possibility of attaining unto eternal life. Children and youth are God's peculiar treasure.[7]

The youth need to be impressed with the truth that their endowments are not their own. Strength, time, intellect, are but lent treasures. They belong to God, and it should be the resolve of every youth to put them to the highest use. He is a branch, from which God expects fruit; a steward, whose capital must yield increase; a light, to illuminate the world's darkness. Every youth, every child, has a work to do for the honor of God and the uplifting of humanity.[8]   [281]

The Path to Heaven Is Suited to Children's Capacity—I saw that Jesus knows our infirmities and has Himself shared our experience in all things but in sin; therefore He has prepared for us a path suited to our strength and capacity and, like Jacob, has marched softly and in evenness with the children as they were able to endure, that He might entertain us by the comfort of His company and be to us a perpetual guide. He does not despise, neglect, or leave behind the children of the flock. He has not bidden us move forward and leave them. He has not traveled so hastily as to leave us with our children behind. Oh, no; but He has evened the path to life, even for children. And parents are required in His name to lead them along the narrow way. God has appointed us a path suited to the strength and capacity of children.[9]   [282]

---

[1]The Signs of the Times, April 3, 1901.

[2]Messages to Young People, 329.

[3]The Review and Herald, March 30, 1897.

[4]Manuscript 13, 1891.

[5]The Signs of the Times, September 10, 1894.

[6]The Signs of the Times, August 23, 1899.

[7]Letter 105, 1893.

[8]Education, 57, 58.
[9]Testimonies For The Church 1, 388, 389.

Chapter 49—Mother's Helpers

Children to Be Partners in the Home Firm—Children as well as parents have important duties in the home. They should be taught that they are a part of the home firm. They are fed and clothed and loved and cared for; and they should respond to these many mercies by bearing their share of the home burdens and bringing all the happiness possible into the family of which they are members.[1]

Let every mother teach her children that they are members of the family firm and must bear their share of the responsibilities of this firm. Every member of the family should bear these responsibilities as faithfully as church members bear the responsibilities of church relationships.

Let the children know that they are helping father and mother by doing little errands. Give them some work to do for you, and tell them that afterward they can have a time to play.[2]

Children have active minds, and they need to be employed in lifting the burdens of practical life.... They should never be left to pick up their own employment. Parents should control this matter themselves.[3]

Parents and Children Have Obligations—Parents are under obligation to feed and clothe and educate their children, and children are under obligation to serve their parents with cheerful, earnest fidelity. When children cease to feel their obligation to share the toil and burden with their parents, then how would it suit them to have their parents cease to feel their obligation to provide for them? In ceasing to do the duties that devolve upon them to be useful to their parents, to lighten their burdens by doing that which may be disagreeable and full of toil, children miss their opportunity of obtaining a most valuable education that will fit them for future usefulness.[4]

God wants the children of all believers to be trained from their earliest years to share the burdens that their parents must bear in caring for them. To them is given a portion of the home for their

[283]

219

rooms and the right and privilege of having a place at the family board. God requires parents to feed and clothe their children. But the obligations of parents and children are mutual. On their part children are required to respect and honor their parents.[5]

Parents are not to be slaves to their children, doing all the sacrificing, while the children are permitted to grow up careless and unconcerned, letting all the burdens rest upon their parents.[6]

Indolence Taught Through Mistaken Kindness—Children should be taught very young to be useful, to help themselves, and to help others. Many daughters of this age can, without remorse of conscience, see their mothers toiling, cooking, washing, or ironing, while they sit in the parlor and read stories, knit edging, crochet, or embroider. Their hearts are as unfeeling as a stone.

But where does this wrong originate? Who are the ones usually most to blame in this matter? The poor, deceived parents. They overlook the future good of their children and, in their mistaken fondness, let them sit in idleness or do that which is of but little account, which requires no exercise of the mind or muscles, and then excuse their indolent daughters because they are weakly. What has made them weakly? In many cases it has been the wrong course of the parents. A proper amount of exercise about the house would improve both mind and body. But children are deprived of this through false ideas, until they are averse to work.[7]

[284]

If your children have been unaccustomed to labor, they will soon become weary. They will complain of side ache, pain in the shoulders, and tired limbs; and you will be in danger, through sympathy, of doing the work yourselves rather than have them suffer a little. Let the burden upon the children be very light at first, and then increase it a little every day, until they can do a proper amount of labor without becoming so weary.[8]

Perils of Idleness—I have been shown that much sin has resulted from idleness. Active hands and minds do not find time to heed every temptation which the enemy suggests, but idle hands and brains are all ready for Satan to control. The mind, when not properly occupied, dwells upon improper things. Parents should teach their children that idleness is sin.[9]

There is nothing which more surely leads to evil than to lift all burdens from children, leaving them to an idle, aimless life, to do nothing, or to occupy themselves as they please. The minds of children are active, and if not occupied with that which is good and useful, they will inevitably turn to what is bad. While it is right and necessary for them to have recreation, they should be taught to work, to have regular hours for physical labor and also for reading and study. See that they have employment suited to their years and are supplied with useful and interesting books.[10]

The Surest Safeguard Is Useful Occupation—One of the surest safeguards for the young is useful occupation. Had they been trained to industrious habits, so that all their hours were usefully employed, they would have no time for repining at their lot or for idle daydreaming. They would be in little danger of forming vicious habits or associations.[11]

[285]

If parents are so occupied with other things that they cannot keep their children usefully employed, Satan will keep them busy.[12]

Children Should Learn to Bear Burdens—Parents should awaken to the fact that the most important lesson for their children to learn is that they must act their part in bearing the burdens of the home.... Parents should teach their children to take a common-sense view of life, to realize that they are to be useful in the world. In the home, under the supervision of a wise mother, boys and girls should receive their first instruction in bearing the burdens of life.[13]

The education of the child for good or for evil begins in its earliest years.... As the older children grow up, they should help to care for the younger members of the family. The mother should not wear herself out by doing work that her children might do and should do.[14]

Sharing Burdens Gives Satisfaction—Help your children, parents, to do the will of God by being faithful in the performance of the duties which really belong to them as members of the family. This will give them a most valuable experience. It will teach them that they are not to center their thoughts upon themselves, to do their own pleasure, or to amuse themselves. Patiently educate them to act their part in the family circle, to make a success of their efforts to share the burdens of father and mother and brothers and sisters. Thus they will have the satisfaction of knowing that they are really useful.[15]

[286]

Children can be educated to be helpful. They are naturally active and inclined to be busy; and this activity is susceptible of being trained and directed in the right channel. Children may be taught, when young, to lift daily their light burdens, each child having some particular task for the accomplishment of which he is responsible to his parents or guardian. They will thus learn to bear the yoke of duty while young; and the performance of their little tasks will become a pleasure, bringing them a happiness that is only gained by well-doing. They will become accustomed to work and responsibility and will relish employment, perceiving that life holds for them more important business than that of amusing themselves....

Work is good for children; they are happier to be usefully employed a large share of the time; their innocent amusements are enjoyed with a keener zest after the successful completion of their tasks. Labor strengthens both the muscles and the mind. Mothers may make precious little helpers of their children; and, while teaching them to be useful, they may themselves gain knowledge of human nature and how to deal with these fresh, young beings and keep their hearts warm and youthful by contact with the little ones. And as their children look to them in confidence and love, so may they look to the dear Saviour for help and guidance. Children that are properly trained, as they advance in years, learn to love that labor which makes the burdens of their friends lighter.[16]

Assures Mental Balance—In the fulfillment of their apportioned tasks strength of memory and a right balance of mind may be

[287] gained, as well as stability of character and dispatch. The day, with its round of little duties, calls for thought, calculation, and a plan of action. As the children become older, still more can be required of them. It should not be exhaustive labor, nor should their work be so protracted as to fatigue and discourage them; but it should be judiciously selected with reference to the physical development most desirable and the proper cultivation of the mind and character.[17]

Links With Workers in Heaven—If children were taught to regard the humble round of everyday duties as the course marked out for them by the Lord, as a school in which they were to be trained to render faithful and efficient service, how much more pleasant and honorable would their work appear! To perform every duty as unto the Lord throws a charm around the humblest employment and links the workers on earth with the holy beings who do God's will in heaven.[18]

Work is constantly being done in heaven. There are no idlers there. "My Father worketh hitherto," said Christ, "and I work." We cannot suppose that when the final triumph shall come, and we have the mansions prepared for us, that idleness will be our portion, that we shall rest in a blissful, do-nothing state.[19]

Strengthens Home Ties—In the home training of the youth the principle of co-operation is invaluable.... The older ones should be their parents' assistants, entering into their plans and sharing their responsibilities and burdens. Let fathers and mothers take time to teach their children; let them show that they value their help, desire their confidence, and enjoy their companionship; and the children will not be slow to respond. Not only will the parents' burden be lightened, and the children receive a practical training of inestimable [288] worth, but there will be a strengthening of the home ties and a deepening of the very foundations of character.[20]

Makes for Growth in Mental, Moral, Spiritual Excellence—Children and youth should take pleasure in making lighter the cares of father and mother, showing an unselfish interest in the home. As they cheerfully lift the burdens that fall to their share, they are receiving a training which will fit them for positions of trust and usefulness. Each year they are to make steady advancement, gradually but surely laying aside the inexperience of boyhood and girlhood for the experience of manhood and womanhood. In the faithful performance of the simple duties of the home boys and girls lay the foundation for mental, moral, and spiritual excellence.[21]

Gives Health of Body, Peace of Mind—The approval of God rests with loving assurance upon the children who cheerfully take their part in the duties of domestic life, sharing the burdens of father and mother. They will be rewarded with health of body and peace of mind; and they will enjoy the pleasure of seeing their parents take their share of social enjoyment and healthful recreation, thus prolonging their lives. Children trained to the practical duties of life will go out from the home to be useful members of society, with an education far superior to that gained by close confinement in the schoolroom at an early age, when neither the mind nor the body is strong enough to endure the strain.[22]

In some cases it would be better if children had less work in the school and more training in the performance of home duties. Above all else they should be taught to be thoughtful and helpful. Many [289] things to be learned from books are far less essential than the lessons of practical industry and discipline.[23]

Insures Restful Sleep—Mothers should take their daughters with them into the kitchen and patiently educate them. Their constitution will be better for such labor, their muscles will gain tone and strength, and their meditations will be more healthy and elevated at the close of the day. They may be weary, but how sweet is rest after a proper amount of labor! Sleep, nature's sweet restorer, invigorates the weary body and prepares it for the next day's duties. Do not intimate to your children that it is no matter whether they labor or not. Teach them that their help is needed, that their time is of value, and that you depend on their labor.[24]

It is a sin to let children grow up in idleness. Let them exercise their limbs and muscles, even if it wearies them. If they are not overworked, how can weariness harm them more than it harms you? There is quite a difference between weariness and exhaustion. Children need more frequent change of employment and intervals of rest than grown persons do; but even when quite young, they may begin learning to work, and they will be happy in the thought that they are making themselves useful. Their sleep will be sweet after healthful labor, and they will be refreshed for the next day's work.[25]

Do Not Say, "My Children Bother Me."—"Oh," say some mothers, "my children bother me when they try to help me." So did mine, but do you think I let them know it? Praise your children. Teach them, line upon line, precept upon precept. This is better than reading novels, better than making calls, better than following the [290] fashions of the world.[26]

A View of the Pattern—For a period of time the Majesty of heaven, the King of glory, was only a Babe in Bethlehem and could only represent the babe in its mother's arms. In childhood He could only do the work of an obedient child, fulfilling the wishes of His parents, in doing such duties as would correspond to His ability as a child. This is all that children can do, and they should be so educated and instructed that they may follow Christ's example. Christ acted in a manner that blessed the household in which He was found, for

He was subject to His parents and thus did missionary work in His home life. It is written, "And the child grew, and waxed strong in spirit, filled with wisdom: and the grace of God was upon Him." "And Jesus increased in wisdom and stature, and in favor with God and man."[27]

It is the precious privilege of teachers and parents to co-operate in teaching the children how to drink in the gladness of Christ's life by learning to follow His example. The Saviour's early years were useful years. He was His mother's helper in the home; and He was just as verily fulfilling His commission when performing the duties of the home and working at the carpenter's bench as when He engaged in His public work of ministry.[28]

In His earth life Christ was an example to all the human family, and He was obedient and helpful in the home. He learned the carpenter's trade and worked with His own hands in the little shop at Nazareth.... As He worked in childhood and youth, mind and body were developed. He did not use His physical powers recklessly, but in such a way as to keep them in health, that He might do the best work in every line.[29]

[291]

[292]

---

[1]The Ministry of Healing, 394.

[2]The Review and Herald, June 23, 1903.

[3]Manuscript 57, 1897.

[4]The Youth's Instructor, July 20, 1893.

[5]Manuscript 128, 1901.

[6]Manuscript 126, 1897.

[7]Testimonies For The Church 1:686.

[8]Ibid., 1:686.

[9]Ibid., 1:395.

[10]Christian Temperance and Bible Hygiene, 134, 135.

[11]The Review and Herald, September 13, 1881.

[12]The Signs of the Times, April 3, 1901.

[13]Letter 106, 1901.

[14]Manuscript 126, 1903.

[15]Manuscript 27, 1896.

[16]The Health Reformer, December, 1877.

[17]Ibid.

[18]Patriarchs and Prophets, 574.

[19]Manuscript 126, 1897.

[20]Education, 285.

[21]Messages to Young People, 211, 212.

[22] Counsels to Teachers, Parents, and Students, 148.

[23] Manuscript 126, 1903.

[24] Testimonies For The Church 1, 395.

[25] Christian Temperance and Bible Hygiene, 135.

[26] Manuscript 31, 1901.

[27] The Signs of the Times, September 17, 1894.

[28] The Review and Herald, May 6, 1909.

[29] Counsels to Teachers, Parents, and Students, 147.

Chapter 50—The Honor Due Parents

The Child's Indebtedness to Parents—Children should feel that they are indebted to their parents, who have watched over them in infancy and nursed them in sickness. They should realize that their parents have suffered much anxiety on their account. Especially have conscientious, godly parents felt the deepest interest that their children should take a right course. As they have seen faults in their children, how heavy have been their hearts! If the children who caused those hearts to ache could see the effect of their course, they would certainly relent. If they could see their mother's tears and hear her prayers to God in their behalf, if they could listen to her suppressed and broken sighs, their hearts would feel and they would speedily confess their wrongs and ask to be forgiven.[1]

Children, when they become of age, will prize the parent who labored faithfully, and would not permit them to cherish wrong feelings or indulge in evil habits.[2]

A Command Binding on All—"Honor thy father and thy mother: that thy days may be long upon the land which the Lord thy God giveth thee." This is the first commandment with promise. It is binding upon childhood and youth, upon the middle-aged and the aged. There is no period in life when children are excused from honoring their parents. This solemn obligation is binding upon every son and daughter and is one of the conditions to their prolonging their lives upon the land which the Lord will give the faithful. This is not a subject unworthy of notice, but a matter of vital importance. The promise is upon condition of obedience. If you obey, you shall live long in the land which the Lord your God gives you. If you disobey, you shall not prolong your life in that land.[3] [293]

Parents are entitled to a degree of love and respect which is due to no other person. God Himself, who has placed upon them a responsibility for the souls committed to their charge, has ordained that during the earlier years of life parents shall stand in the place of God to their children. And he who rejects the rightful authority

227

of his parents is rejecting the authority of God. The fifth commandment requires children not only to yield respect, submission, and obedience to their parents, but also to give them love and tenderness, to lighten their cares, to guard their reputation, and to succor and comfort them in old age.[4]

God cannot prosper those who go directly contrary to the plainest duty specified in His word, the duty of children to their parents.... If they disrespect and dishonor their earthly parents, they will not respect and love their Creator.[5]

When children have unbelieving parents, and their commands contradict the requirements of Christ, then, painful though it may be, they must obey God and trust the consequences with Him.[6]

Many Are Breaking the Fifth Commandment—In these last days children are so noted for their disobedience and disrespect that God has especially noticed it, and it constitutes a sign that the end is near. It shows that Satan has almost complete control of the minds of the young. By many, age is no more respected.[7]

[294] There are many children who profess to know the truth who do not render to their parents the honor and affection that are due to them, who manifest but little love to father and mother, and fail to honor them in deferring to their wishes or in seeking to relieve them of anxiety. Many who profess to be Christians do not know what it means to "honor thy father and thy mother" and consequently will know just as little what it means, "that thy days may be long upon the land which the Lord thy God giveth thee."[8]

In this rebellious age children who have not received right instruction and discipline have but little sense of their obligations to their parents. It is often the case that the more their parents do for them, the more ungrateful they are and the less they respect them. Children who have been petted and waited upon always expect it; and if their expectations are not met, they are disappointed and discouraged. This same disposition will be seen through their whole lives; they will be helpless, leaning upon others for aid, expecting others to favor them and yield to them. And if they are opposed, even after they have grown to manhood and womanhood, they think themselves abused; and thus they worry their way through the world, hardly able to bear their own weight, often murmuring and fretting because everything does not suit them.[9]

No Place in Heaven for Ungrateful Children—I saw that Satan had blinded the minds of the youth that they could not comprehend the truths of God's word. Their sensibilities are so blunted that they regard not the injunctions of the holy apostle:

"Children, obey your parents in the Lord: for this is right. Honour thy father and mother; which is the first commandment with promise; that it may be well with thee, and thou mayest live long on the [new] earth." "Children, obey your parents in all things: for this is well pleasing unto the Lord." Children who dishonor and disobey their parents, and disregard their advice and instructions, can have no part in the earth made new. The purified new earth will be no place for the rebellious, the disobedient, the ungrateful son or daughter. Unless such learn obedience and submission here, they will never learn it; the peace of the ransomed will not be marred by disobedient, unruly, unsubmissive children. No commandment breaker can inherit the kingdom of heaven.[10] [295]

Love to Be Manifested—I have seen children who seemed to have no affection to give to their parents, no expressions of love and endearment, which are due them and which they would appreciate; but they lavish an abundance of affection and caresses to select ones for whom they show preference. Is this as God would have it? No, no. Bring all the rays of sunshine, of love, and of affection into the home circle. Your father and mother will appreciate these little attentions you can give. Your efforts to lighten the burdens, and to repress every word of fretfulness and ingratitude, show that you are not a thoughtless child, and that you do appreciate the care and love that has been bestowed upon you in the years of your helpless infancy and childhood.[11]

Children, it is necessary that your mothers love you, or else you would be very unhappy. And is it not also right that children love their parents, and show this love by pleasant looks, pleasant words, and cheerful, hearty cooperation, helping the father out-of-doors and the mother indoors?[12]

Deeds Considered As Though Done to Jesus—If you are truly converted, if you are children of Jesus, you will honor your parents; [296] you will not only do what they tell you but will watch for opportunities to help them. In doing this you are working for Jesus. He considers all these care-taking, thoughtful deeds as done to Himself.

This is the most important kind of missionary work; and those who are faithful in these little everyday duties are gaining a valuable

experience.[13]

[1]Testimonies For The Church 1, 395, 396.

[2]The Signs of the Times, July 13, 1888.

[3]Testimonies For The Church 2, 80, 81.

[4]Patriarchs and Prophets, 308.

[5]Testimonies For The Church 3, 232.

[6]The Review and Herald, November 15, 1892.

[7]Testimonies for the Church 1:217, 218.

[8]Messages to Young People, 331.

[9]Testimonies For The Church 1, 392, 393.

[10]Ibid., 1:497, 498.

[11]The Youth's Instructor, April 21, 1886.

[12]Manuscript 129, 1898.

[13]The Youth's Instructor, January 30, 1884.

Chapter 51—Counsel to Children

Seek God Early—Children and youth should begin early to seek God; for early habits and impressions will frequently exert a powerful influence upon the life and character. Therefore the youth who would be like Samuel, John, and especially like Christ, must be faithful in the things which are least, turning away from the companions who plan evil and who think that their life in the world is to be one of pleasure and selfish indulgence. Many of the little home duties are overlooked as of no consequence; but if the small things are neglected, the larger duties will be also. You want to be whole men and women, with pure, sound, noble characters. Begin the work at home; take up the little duties and do them with thoroughness and exactness. When the Lord sees you are faithful in that which is least, He will entrust you with larger responsibilities. Be careful how you build, and what kind of material you put into the building. The characters you are now forming will be lasting as eternity.

Let Jesus take possession of your mind, your heart, and your affections; and work as Christ worked, doing conscientiously the home duties, little acts of self-denial and deeds of kindness, employing the moments diligently, keeping a careful watch against little sins and a grateful heart for little blessings, and you will have at last such a testimony for yourself as was given of John and Samuel, and especially of Christ: "And Jesus increased in wisdom and stature, and in favor with God and man."[1]

"Give Me Thine Heart."—The Lord says to the young, "My son, give Me thine heart." The Saviour of the world loves to have children and youth give their hearts to Him. There may be a large army of children who shall be found faithful to God, because they walk in the light as Christ is in the light. They will love the Lord Jesus, and it will be their delight to please Him. They will not be impatient if reproved, but will make glad the heart of father and mother by their kindness, their patience, their willingness to do

[298]

231

all they can in helping to bear the burdens of daily life. Through childhood and youth they will be found faithful disciples of our Lord.[2]

An Individual Choice to Be Made—Watch and pray, and obtain a personal experience in the things of God. Your parents may teach you, they may try to guide your feet into safe paths; but it is impossible for them to change your heart. You must give your heart to Jesus and walk in the precious light of truth that He has given you. Faithfully take up your duties in the home life, and, through the grace of God, you may grow up unto the full stature of what Christ would have a child grow to be in Him. The fact that your parents keep the Sabbath, and obey the truth, will not insure your salvation. For though Noah and Job and Daniel were in the land, "As I live, saith the Lord God, they shall deliver neither son nor daughter; they shall but deliver their own souls by their righteousness."

In childhood and youth you may have an experience in the service of God. Do the things that you know to be right. Be obedient to your parents. Listen to their counsels; for if they love and fear God, upon them will be laid the responsibility of educating, disciplining, and training your soul for the immortal life. Thankfully receive the help they want to give you, and make their hearts glad by cheerfully submitting yourselves to the dictates of their wiser judgments. In this way you will honor your parents, glorify God, and become a blessing to those with whom you associate.[3]

[299]

Fight the battle, children; remember every victory places you above the enemy.[4]

Children to Pray for Help—Children should pray for grace to resist the temptations which will come to them—temptations to have their own way and to do their own selfish pleasure. As they ask Christ to help them in their life service to be truthful, kind, obedient, and to bear their responsibilities in the family circle, He will hear their simple prayer.[5]

Jesus would have the children and the youth come to Him with the same confidence with which they go to their parents. As a child asks his mother or father for bread when he is hungry, so the Lord would have you ask Him for the things which you need....

Jesus knows the needs of children, and He loves to listen to their prayers. Let the children shut out the world and everything that would attract the thoughts from God; and let them feel that they are alone with God, that His eye looks into the inmost heart and reads the desire of the soul, and that they may talk with God....

Then, children, ask God to do for you those things that you cannot do for yourselves. Tell Jesus everything. Lay open before Him the secrets of your heart; for His eye searches the inmost recesses of the soul, and He reads your thoughts as an open book. When you have asked for the things that are necessary for your soul's good, believe that you receive them, and you shall have them.[6]

Perform the Home Duties Cheerfully—Children and youth should be missionaries at home by doing those things that need to be done and that someone must do.... You can prove by faithful performance of the little things that seem to you unimportant that you have a true missionary spirit. It is the willingness to do the duties that lie in your path, to relieve your overburdened mother, that will prove you worthy of being entrusted with larger responsibilities. You do not think that washing dishes is pleasant work, yet you would not like to be denied the privilege of eating food that has been placed on those dishes. Do you think that it is more pleasant work for your mother to do those things than it is for you? Are you willing to leave what you consider a disagreeable task for your careworn mother to do, while you play the lady? There is sweeping to be done, there are rugs to take up and shake, and the rooms are to be put in order; and while you are neglecting to do these things, is it consistent for you to desire larger responsibilities? Have you considered how many times mother has to attend to all these household duties while you are excused to attend school or amuse yourself?[7]

Many children go about their home duties as though they were disagreeable tasks, and their faces plainly show the disagreeable. They find fault and murmur, and nothing is done willingly. This is not Christlike; it is the spirit of Satan, and if you cherish it, you will be like him. You will be miserable yourselves and will make all about you miserable. Do not complain of how much you have to do and how little time you have for amusement, but be thoughtful and care-taking. By employing your time in some useful work, you will be closing a door against Satan's temptations. Remember that Jesus lived not to please Himself, and you must be like Him. Make this matter one of religious principle, and ask Jesus to help you.

[300]

[301]

By exercising your mind in this direction, you will be preparing to become burden bearers in the cause of God as you have been caretakers in the home circle. You will have a good influence upon others and may win them to the service of Christ.[8]

Give Mothers Change and Rest—It is difficult for a loving mother to urge her children to help her when she sees they have no heart in the work and will frame any and every excuse to get rid of doing a disagreeable task Children and youth, Christ is looking upon you, and shall He see you neglecting the trust He has put into your hands? If you want to be useful, the opportunity is yours. Your first duty is to help your mother who has done so much for you. Lift her burdens, give her pleasant days of rest; for she has had few holidays and very little variety in her life. You have claimed all the pleasure and amusement as your right, but the time has come for you to shed sunshine in the home. Take up your duty; go right to work. Through your self-denying devotion give her rest and pleasure.[9]

God's Reward for the Daniels of Today—There is now need of men who, like Daniel, will do and dare. A pure heart and a strong, fearless hand are wanted in the world today. God designed that man should be constantly improving, daily reaching a higher point in the scale of excellence. He will help us if we seek to help ourselves. Our hope of happiness in two worlds depends upon our improvement in one....

Dear youth, God calls upon you to do a work which through His grace you can do. "Present your bodies a living sacrifice, holy, acceptable unto God, which is your reasonable service." Stand forth in your God-given manhood and womanhood. Show a purity of tastes, appetite, and habits that bears comparison with Daniel's. God will reward you with calm nerves, a clear brain, an unimpaired judgment, keen perceptions. The youth of today whose principles are firm and unwavering will be blessed with health of body, mind, and soul.[10]

Begin Now to Redeem the Past—The youth are now deciding their own eternal destiny, and I would appeal to you to consider the commandment to which God has annexed such a promise, "That thy days may be long upon the land which the Lord thy God giveth thee." Children, do you desire eternal life? Then respect and honor your parents. Do not wound and grieve their hearts and cause them

[302]

to spend sleepless nights in anxiety and distress over your case. If you have sinned in not rendering love and obedience to them, begin now to redeem the past. You cannot afford to take any other course; for it means to you the loss of eternal life.[11]

[1]The Youth's Instructor, November 3, 1886.

[2]Messages to Young People, 333.

[3]The Youth's Instructor, August 17, 1893.

[4]Manuscript 19, 1887.

[5]The Review and Herald, November 17, 1896.

[6]The Youth's Instructor, July 7, 1892.

[7]The Youth's Instructor, March 2, 1893.

[8]The Youth's Instructor, January 30, 1884.

[9]The Youth's Instructor, March 2, 1893.

[10]The Youth's Instructor, July 9, 1903.

[11]The Youth's Instructor, June 22, 1893.

Section 12—Standards of Family Living

Chapter 52—Home Government

The Guiding Principle for Parents—Many in the world have their affections on things that may be good in themselves, but their minds are satisfied with these things and do not seek the greater and higher good that Christ desires to give them. Now we must not rudely seek to deprive them of what they hold dear. Reveal to them the beauty and preciousness of truth. Lead them to behold Christ and His loveliness; then they will turn aside from everything that will draw their affections away from Him. This is the principle upon which parents should work in the training of their children. By your manner of dealing with the little ones you can by the grace of Christ mold their characters for everlasting life.[1]

Fathers and mothers should make it their life study that their children may become as nearly perfect in character as human effort, combined with divine aid, can make them. This work, with all its importance and responsibility, they have accepted, in that they have brought children into the world.[2]

Rules Necessary for Government in the Home—Every Christian home should have rules; and parents should, in their words and in their deportment toward each other, give to the children a precious living example of what they desire them to be.... Teach the children and youth to respect themselves, to be true to God, true to principle; teach them to respect and obey the law of God. Then these principles will control their lives and will be carried out in their association

with others.[3]

Bible Principles to Be Followed—There is need for constant watching that the principles which lie at the foundation of family government are not disregarded. The Lord designs that the families on earth shall be symbols of the family in heaven. And when earthly families are conducted in right lines, the same sanctification of the Spirit will be brought into the church.[4]

Parents should themselves be converted and know what it is to be in submission to God's will, as little children, bringing into captivity their thoughts to the will of Jesus Christ, before they can rightly represent the government that God designed should exist in the family.[5]

God Himself established the family relations. His word is the only safe guide in the management of children. Human philosophy has not discovered more than God knows or devised a wiser plan of dealing with children than that given by our Lord. Who can better understand all the needs of children than their Creator? Who can feel a deeper interest in their welfare than He who bought them with His own blood? If the word of God were carefully studied and faithfully obeyed, there would be less soul anguish over the perverse conduct of wicked children.[6]

Respect the Children's Rights—Remember that children have rights which must be respected.[7]

Children have claims which their parents should acknowledge and respect. They have a right to such an education and training as will make them useful, respected, and beloved members of society here, and give them a moral fitness for the society of the pure and holy hereafter. The young should be taught that both their present and their future well-being depend to a great degree on the habits they form in childhood and youth. They should be early accustomed to submission, self-denial, and a regard for others' happiness. They should be taught to subdue the hasty temper, to withhold the passionate word, to manifest unvarying kindness, courtesy, and self-control.[8]

[307]

To a Parent Deluded by Blind Affection—Blind affection, a cheap manifestation of love, goes a long ways with you. To encircle the arms about the neck is easy; but manifestations should not be encouraged by you unless they are proved to be of real value by perfect obedience. Your indulgence, your disregard of God's requirements is the veriest cruelty. You encourage and excuse disobedience by saying, "My boy loves me." Such love is cheap and deceptive. It is no love at all. The love, the genuine love, to be cultivated in the family is of value because it is verified by obedience....

If you love the souls of your children, bring them into order. But abundant kisses and tokens of love blind your eyes, and your children know it. Make less of these outward demonstrations of embracing and kissing and go down to the bottom of things and show what constitutes filial love. Refuse these manifestations as a fraud, a deception, unless backed up by obedience and respect for your commands.[9]

Manifest Neither Blind Affection nor Undue Severity— While we are not to indulge blind affection, neither are we to manifest undue severity. Children cannot be brought to the Lord by force. They can be led, but not driven. "My sheep hear My voice, and I know them, and they follow Me," Christ declares. He did not say, My sheep hear My voice and are forced into the path of obedience. In the government of children love must be shown. Never should parents cause their children pain by harshness or unreasonable exactions. Harshness drives souls into Satan's net.[10]

[308]

The combined influence of authority and love will make it possible to hold firmly and kindly the reins of family government. An eye single to the glory of God and to what our children owe Him will keep us from looseness and from sanctioning evil.[11]

Harshness Not Requisite to Obedience— Let none imagine ... that harshness and severity are necessary to secure obedience. I have seen the most efficient family government maintained without a harsh word or look. I have been in other families where commands were constantly given in an authoritative tone, and harsh rebukes and severe punishments were often administered. In the first case the children followed the course pursued by the parents and seldom spoke to one another in harsh tones. In the second also the parental example was imitated by the children; and cross words, faultfindings, and disputes were heard from morning till night.[12]

Words that intimidate, creating fear and expelling love from the soul, are to be restrained. A wise, tender, God-fearing father will bring, not a slavish fear, but an element of love into the home. If we drink of the water of life, the fountain will send forth sweet water, not bitter.[13]

Harsh words sour the temper and wound the hearts of children, and in some cases these wounds are difficult to heal. Children are sensitive to the least injustice, and some become discouraged under it and will neither heed the loud, angry voice of command nor care for threatenings of punishment.[14]

There is danger of too severely criticizing small things. Criticism that is too severe, rules that are too rigid, lead to the disregard of

[309]

all regulations; and by and by children thus educated will show the same disrespect for the laws of Christ.[15]

Uniform Firmness, Unimpassioned Control Necessary—Children have sensitive, loving natures. They are easily pleased and easily made unhappy. By gentle discipline in loving words and acts mothers may bind their children to their hearts. To manifest severity and to be exacting with children are great mistakes. Uniform firmness and unimpassioned control are necessary to the discipline of every family. Say what you mean calmly, move with consideration, and carry out what you say without deviation.

It will pay to manifest affection in your association with your children. Do not repel them by lack of sympathy in their childish sports, joys, and griefs. Never let a frown gather upon your brow or a harsh word escape your lips. God writes all these words in His book of records.[16]

Restraint and Caution Not Enough—Dear brethren, as a church you have sadly neglected your duty toward the children and youth. While rules and restrictions are laid upon them, great care should be taken to show them the Christlike side of your character and not the satanic side. Children need constant watchcare and tender love. Bind them to your hearts, and keep the love as well as the fear of God before them. Fathers and mothers do not control their own spirit and therefore are not fit to govern others. To restrain and caution your children is not all that is required. You have yet to learn to do justly and love mercy, as well as to walk humbly with God.[17]

Counsel to the Mother of a Strong-willed Child—Your child is not your own; you cannot do with her as you like, for she is the property of the Lord. Exercise a steady persevering control over her; teach her that she belongs to God. With such a training she will grow up to be a blessing to those around her. But clear, sharp discernment will be necessary in order that you may repress her inclination to rule you both, to have her own will and way, and to do as she pleases.[18]

[310]

Even, Steady Management—I have seen many families shipwrecked through overmanagement on the part of their head, whereas through consultation and agreement all might have moved off harmoniously and well.[19]

Unsteadiness in family government is productive of great harm, in fact is nearly as bad as no government at all. The question is often asked, Why are the children of religious parents so often headstrong, defiant, and rebellious? The reason is to be found in the home training. Too often the parents are not united in their family government.[20]

A fitful government—at one time holding the lines firmly, and at another allowing that which has been condemned—is ruination to a child.[21]

Mutual Law for Parents and Children—God is our Lawgiver and King, and parents are to place themselves under His rule. This rule forbids all oppression from parents and all disobedience from children. The Lord is full of lovingkindness, mercy, and truth. His law is holy, just, and good, and must be obeyed by parents and children. The rules which should regulate the lives of parents and children flow from a heart of infinite love, and God's rich blessing will rest upon those parents who administer His law in their homes,

[311] and upon the children who obey this law. The combined influence of mercy and justice is to be felt. "Mercy and truth are met together; righteousness and peace have kissed each other." Households under this discipline will walk in the way of the Lord, to do justice and

[312] judgment.[22]

---

[1]Manuscript 4, 1893.

[2]Fundamentals of Christian Education, 67.

[3]Letter 74, 1896.

[4]Manuscript 80, 1898.

[5]The Review and Herald, March 13, 1894.

[6]The Signs of the Times, November 24, 1881.

[7]Letter 47a, 1902.

[8]Fundamentals of Christian Education, 67.

[9]Letter 52, 1886.

[10]The Review and Herald, January 29, 1901.

[11]Manuscript 24, 1887.

[12]The Signs of the Times, March 11, 1886.

[13]Letter 8a, 1896.

[14]Testimonies For The Church 3, 532.

[15]Manuscript 7, 1899.

[16]Testimonies for the Church 3:532.

[17]Ibid., 4:621.

[18]Letter 69, 1896.

[19]Testimonies For The Church 4, 127.1.

[20]The Signs of the Times, February 9, 1882.

[21]Letter 69. 1896.

[22]Manuscript 133, 1898.

Chapter 53—A United Front

Responsibilities in Government to Be Shared—Unitedly and prayerfully the father and mother should bear the grave responsibility of guiding their children aright.[1]

Parents are to work together as a unit. There must be no division. But many parents work at cross-purposes, and thus the children are spoiled by mismanagement.... It sometimes happens that, of the mother and father, one is too indulgent and the other too severe. This difference works against good results in the formation of the characters of their children. No harsh force is to be exercised in carrying out reforms, but at the same time no weak indulgence must be shown. The mother is not to seek to blind the eyes of the father to the faults of the children, neither is she to influence them to do those things which the father has forbidden them to do. Not one seed of doubt should the mother plant in her children's minds in regard to the wisdom of the father's management. She should not, by her course of action, counteract the work of the father.[2]

If fathers and mothers are at variance, one working against the other to counteract each other's influence, the family will be in a demoralized condition, and neither the father nor the mother will receive the respect and confidence that are essential to a well-governed family.... Children are quick to discern anything that will cast a reflection upon the rules and regulations of a household, especially those regulations that restrict their actions.[3]

[313]

The father and mother should unite in disciplining their children; each should bear a share of the responsibility, acknowledging themselves under solemn obligations to God to train up their offspring in such a way as to secure to them, as far as possible, good physical health and well-developed characters.[4]

How Lessons in Deception May Be Given—Some fond mothers suffer wrongs in their children which should not be allowed in them for a moment. The wrongs of the children are sometimes concealed from the father. Articles of dress or some other indulgence

244

is granted by the mother with the understanding that the father is to know nothing about it, for he would reprove for these things.

Here a lesson of deception is effectually taught the children. Then if the father discovers these wrongs, excuses are made and but half the truth told. The mother is not openhearted. She does not consider as she should that the father has the same interest in the children as herself, and that he should not be kept ignorant of the wrongs or besetments that ought to be corrected in them while young. Things have been covered. The children know the lack of union in their parents, and it has its effect. The children begin young to deceive, cover up, tell things in a different light from what they are to their mother as well as their father. Exaggeration becomes habit, and blunt falsehoods come to be told with but little conviction or reproof of conscience.

These wrongs commenced by the mother's concealing things from the father, who has an equal interest with her in the character their children are forming. The father should have been consulted freely. All should have been laid open to him. But the opposite course, taken to conceal the wrongs of the children, encourages in them a disposition to deceive, a lack of truthfulness and honesty.[5]

[314]

There should always be a fixed principle with Christian parents to be united in the government of their children. There is a fault in this respect with some parents—a lack of union. The fault is sometimes with the father, but oftener with the mother. The fond mother pets and indulges her children. The father's labor calls him from home often, and from the society of his children. The mother's influence tells. Her example does much toward forming the character of the children.[6]

Children Are Confused by Parents at Variance—The family firm must be well organized. Together the father and mother must consider their responsibilities, and with a clear comprehension undertake their task. There is to be no variance. The father and mother should never in the presence of their children criticize each other's plans and judgment.

If the mother is inexperienced in the knowledge of God, she should reason from cause to effect, finding out whether her discipline is of a nature to increase the difficulties of the father as he labors for the salvation of the children. Am I following the way of the Lord? This should be the all-important question.[7]

If parents do not agree, let them absent themselves from the presence of their children until an understanding can be arrived at.[8]

Too often the parents are not united in their family government. The father, who is with his children but little, and is ignorant of their peculiarities of disposition and temperament, is harsh and severe. He does not control his temper, but corrects in passion. The child [315] knows this, and instead of being subdued, the punishment fills him with anger. The mother allows misdemeanors to pass at one time for which she will severely punish at another. The children never know just what to expect, and are tempted to see how far they can transgress with impunity. Thus are sown seeds of evil that spring up and bear fruit.[9]

If parents are united in this work of discipline, the child will understand what is required of him. But if the father, by word or look, shows that he does not approve of the discipline the mother gives; if he feels that she is too strict and thinks that he must make up for the harshness by petting and indulgence, the child will be ruined. He will soon learn that he can do as he pleases. Parents who commit this sin against their children are accountable for the ruin of their souls.[10]

The angels look with intense interest upon every family, to see how the children are treated by parents, guardians, or friends. What strange mismanagement they witness in a family where father and mother are at variance! The tones of the voice of father and mother, their looks, their words—all make it manifest that they are not united in the management of their children. The father casts reflections upon the mother and leads the children to hold in disrespect the mother's tenderness and affection for the little ones. The mother thinks she is compelled to give large affection to the children, to gratify and indulge them, because she thinks the father is harsh and impatient and she must work to counteract the influence of his severity.[11]

Much Prayer, Sober Reflection Needed—Affection cannot be lasting, even in the home circle, unless there is a conformity of the will and disposition to the will of God. All the faculties and passions [316] are to be brought into harmony with the attributes of Jesus Christ. If the father and mother in the love and fear of God unite their interests to have authority in the home, they will see the necessity of much prayer, much sober reflection. And as they seek God, their eyes will be opened to see heavenly messengers present to protect them in answer to the prayer of faith. They will overcome the weaknesses of their character and go on unto perfection.[12]

Hearts to Be Bound by the Silken Cord of Love .—Father and mother, bind your hearts in closest, happiest union. Do not grow apart, but bind yourselves more closely to each other; then you are prepared to bind your children's hearts to you by the silken cord of love.[13]

Keep sowing the seed for time and eternity. All heaven is watching the efforts of the Christian parent.[14]

[317]

[1] Counsels to Teachers, Parents, and Students, 127.

[2] The Review and Herald, March 30, 1897.

[3] The Review and Herald, March 13, 1894.

[4] Pacific Health Journal, April, 1890.

[5] Testimonies For The Church 1, 156, 157.

[6] Testimonies For The Church 1, 156.

[7] Manuscript 79, 1901.

[8] The Review and Herald, March 30, 1897.

[9] The Signs of the Times, March 11, 1886.

[10] The Review and Herald, June 27, 1899.

[11] The Review and Herald, March 13, 1894.

[12] Manuscript 36, 1899.

[13] The Review and Herald, September 15, 1891.

[14] Ibid.

Chapter 54—Religion in the Family

Family Religion Defined—Family religion consists in bringing up the children in the nurture and admonition of the Lord. Every one in the family is to be nourished by the lessons of Christ, and the interest of each soul is to be strictly guarded, in order that Satan shall not deceive and allure away from Christ. This is the standard every family should aim to reach, and they should determine not to fail or to be discouraged. When parents are diligent and vigilant in their instruction, and train their children with an eye single to the glory of God, they co-operate with God, and God co-operates with them in the saving of the souls of the children for whom Christ has died.[1]

Religious instruction means much more than ordinary instruction. It means that you are to pray with your children, teaching them how to approach Jesus and tell Him all their wants. It means that you are to show in your life that Jesus is everything to you, and that His love makes you patient, kind, forbearing, and yet firm in commanding your children after you, as did Abraham.[2]

Just as you conduct yourself in your home life, you are registered in the books of heaven. He who would become a saint in heaven must first become a saint in his own family. If fathers and mothers are true Christians in the family, they will be useful members of the church and be able to conduct affairs in the church and in society after the same manner in which they conduct their family concerns. Parents, let not your religion be simply a profession, but let it become a reality.[3]

[318]

Religion to Be a Part of Home Education—Home religion is fearfully neglected. Men and women show much interest in foreign missions. They give liberally to them and thus seek to satisfy their conscience, thinking that giving to the cause of God will atone for their neglect to set a right example in the home. But the home is their special field, and no excuse is accepted by God for neglecting this field.[4]

Where religion is a practical thing in the home, great good is accomplished. Religion will lead the parents to do the very work God designed should be done in the home. Children will be brought up in the fear and admonition of the Lord.[5]

The reason why the youth of the present age are not more religiously inclined is that their education is defective. True love is not exercised toward children when they are allowed to indulge passion, or when disobedience of your laws is permitted to go unpunished. As the twig is bent, the tree is inclined.[6]

If religion is to influence society, it must first influence the home circle. If children were trained to love and fear God at home, when they go forth into the world, they would be prepared to train their own families for God, and thus the principles of truth would become implanted in society and would exert a telling influence in the world. Religion should not be divorced from home education.[7]

Home Religion Precedes That in the Church—In the home the foundation is laid for the prosperity of the church. The influences that rule in the home life are carried into the church life; therefore church duties should first begin in the home.[8]

[319]

When we have good home religion, we will have excellent meeting religion. Hold the fort at home. Consecrate your family to God, and then speak and act at home as a Christian. Be kind and forbearing and patient at home, knowing that you are teachers. Every mother is a teacher, and every mother should be a learner in the school of Christ that she may know how to teach, that she may give the right mold, the right form of character to her children.[9]

Where there is a lack of home religion, a profession of faith is valueless.... Many are deceiving themselves by thinking that the character will be transformed at the coming of Christ, but there will be no conversion of heart at His appearing. Our defects of character must here be repented of, and through the grace of Christ we must overcome them while probation shall last. This is the place for fitting up for the family above.[10]

Home religion is greatly needed, and our words in the home should be of a right character, or our testimonies in the church will amount to nothing. Unless you manifest meekness, kindness, and courtesy in your home, your religion will be vain. If there were more genuine home religion, there would be more power in the church.[11]

Terrible Mistake to Delay Religious Instruction—It is a most grievous thing to let children grow up without the knowledge of God.[12]

Parents make a most terrible mistake when they neglect the work of giving their children religious training, thinking that they will come out all right in the future and, as they get older, will of themselves be anxious for a religious experience. Cannot you see, parents, that if you do not plant the precious seeds of truth, of love, of heavenly attributes, in the heart, Satan will sow the field of the

[320]   heart with tares?[13]

Too often children are allowed to grow up without religion because their parents think they are too young to have Christian duties enjoined upon them....

The question of the duty of children in regard to religious matters is to be decided absolutely and without hesitancy while they are members of the family.[14]

Parents stand in the place of God to their children to tell them what they must do and what they must not do with firmness and perfect self-control. Every effort made for them with kindness and self-control will cultivate in their characters the elements of firmness and decision.... Fathers and mothers are in duty bound to settle this question early so that the child will no more think of breaking the Sabbath, neglecting religious worship and family prayer than he would think of stealing. Parents' own hands must build the barrier.[15]

From the earliest age a wise education in Christ's lines is to be begun and carried forward. When the children's hearts are impressible, they are to be taught concerning eternal realities. Parents should remember that they are living, speaking, and acting in the presence of God.[16]

Parents, what course are you pursuing? Are you acting upon the idea that in religious matters your children should be left free of all restraint? Are you leaving them without counsel or admonition through childhood and youth? Are you leaving them to do as they please? If so, you are neglecting your God-given responsibilities.[17]

Adapt Instruction to the Child's Age—As soon as the little ones are intelligent to understand, parents should tell them the story of Jesus that they may drink in the precious truth concerning the Babe of Bethlehem. Impress upon the children's minds sentiments of simple piety that are adapted to their years and ability. Bring your [321] children in prayer to Jesus, for He has made it possible for them to learn religion as they learn to frame the words of the language.[18]

When very young, children are susceptible to divine influences. The Lord takes these children under His special care; and when they are brought up in the nurture and admonition of the Lord, they are a help and not a hindrance to their parents.[19]

Parents Jointly Foster Religion in the Home—The father and the mother are responsible for the maintenance of religion in the home.[20]

Let not the mother gather to herself so many cares that she cannot give time to the spiritual needs of her family. Let parents seek God for guidance in their work. On their knees before Him they will gain a true understanding of their great responsibilities, and there they can commit their children to One who will never err in counsel and instruction....

The father of the family should not leave to the mother all the care of imparting spiritual instruction. A large work is to be done by fathers and mothers, and both should act their individual part in preparing their children for the grand review of the judgment.[21]

Parents, take your children with you into your religious exercises. Throw around them the arms of your faith, and consecrate them to Christ. Do not allow anything to cause you to throw off your responsibility to train them aright; do not let any worldly interest induce you to leave them behind. Never let your Christian life isolate them from you. Bring them with you to the Lord; educate their minds to become familiar with divine truth. Let them associate with those that love God. Bring them to the people of God as children whom [322] you are seeking to help to build characters fit for eternity.[22]

Religion in the home—what will it not accomplish? It will do the very work that God designed should be done in every family. Children will be brought up in the nurture and admonition of the Lord. They will be educated and trained, not to be society devotees, but members of the Lord's family.[23]

Children Look to Parents for Consistent Life—Everything leaves its impress upon the youthful mind. The countenance is studied, the voice has its influence, and the deportment is closely imitated by them. Fretful and peevish fathers and mothers are giving their children lessons which at some period in their lives they would give all the world, were it theirs, could they unlearn. Children must see in the lives of their parents that consistency which is in accordance with their faith. By leading a consistent life and exercising self-control, parents may mold the characters of their children.[24]

God Honors a Well-ordered Family—Fathers and mothers who make God first in their households, who teach their children that the fear of the Lord is the beginning of wisdom, glorify God before angels and before men by presenting to the world a well-ordered, well-disciplined family, a family that love and obey God instead of rebelling against Him. Christ is not a stranger in their homes; His name is a household name, revered and glorified. Angels delight in a home where God reigns supreme, and the children are taught to reverence religion, the Bible, and their Creator. Such families can claim the promise: "Them that honour Me I will honour."[25]

[323]

How Christ Is Brought Into the Home—When Christ is in the heart, He is brought into the family. The father and mother feel the importance of living in obedience to the Holy Spirit so that the heavenly angels, who minister to those who shall be heirs of salvation, will minister to them as teachers in the home, educating and training them for the work of teaching their children. In the home it is possible to have a little church which will honor and glorify the Redeemer.[26]

Make Religion Attractive—Make the Christian life an attractive one. Speak of the country in which the followers of Christ are to make their home. As you do this, God will guide your children into all truth, filling them with a desire to fit themselves for the mansions which Christ has gone to prepare for those that love Him.[27]

Parents are not to compel their children to have a form of religion, but they are to place eternal principles before them in an attractive light.[28]

Parents are to make the religion of Christ attractive by their cheerfulness, their Christian courtesy, and their tender, compassionate sympathy; but they are to be firm in requiring respect and obedience. Right principles must be established in the mind of the child.[29]

We need to present to the youth an inducement for right doing. Silver and gold is not sufficient for this. Let us reveal to them the love and mercy and grace of Christ, the preciousness of His word, and the joys of the overcomer. In efforts of this kind you will do a work that will last throughout eternity.[30]

Why Some Parents Fail—Some parents, although they profess to be religious, do not keep before their children the fact that God is to be served and obeyed, that convenience, pleasure, or inclination should not interfere with His claims upon them. "The fear of the Lord is the beginning of wisdom." This fact should be woven into the very life and character. The right conception of God through the knowledge of Christ, who died that we might be saved, should be impressed upon their minds.[31]

You may think, parents, that you have not time to do all this, but you must take time to do your work in your family, else Satan will supply the deficiency. Cut out everything else from your life that prevents this work from being done, and train your children after His order. Neglect anything of a temporal nature, be satisfied to live economically, bind about your wants, but for Christ's sake do not neglect the religious training of yourselves and your children.[32]

Every Member of the Family to Be Dedicated to God—The directions that Moses gave concerning the Passover feast are full of significance, and have an application to parents and children in this age of the world....

The father was to act as the priest of the household, and if the father was dead, the eldest son living was to perform this solemn act of sprinkling the doorpost with blood. This is a symbol of the work to be done in every family. Parents are to gather their children into the home and to present Christ before them as their Passover. The father is to dedicate every inmate of his home to God and to do a work that is represented by the feast of the Passover. It is perilous to leave this solemn duty in the hands of others.[33]

Let Christian parents resolve that they will be loyal to God, and let them gather their children into their homes with them and strike the doorpost with blood, representing Christ as the only One who can shield and save, that the destroying angel may pass over the cherished circle of the household. Let the world see that a more than human influence is at work in the home. Let parents maintain a vital connection with God, set themselves on Christ's side, and show by His grace what great good may be accomplished through parental agency.[34]

[324]

[325]

[326]

[1] Manuscript 24b, 1894.

[2] Letter 8a, 1896.

[3] Manuscript 53, Undated.

[4] The Signs of the Times, August 23, 1899.

[5] The Review and Herald, March 13, 1894.

[6] Testimonies For The Church 2, 701.

[7] The Signs of the Times, April 8, 1886.

[8] The Signs of the Times, September 1, 1898.

[9] Manuscript 70, Undated.

[10] The Signs of the Times, November 14, 1892.

[11] Messages to Young People, 327.

[12] The Signs of the Times, April 23, 1894.

[13] The Signs of the Times, August 6, 1912.

[14] The Review and Herald, April 13, 1897.

[15] Manuscript 119, 1899.

[16] The Review and Herald, March 13, 1894.

[17] Ibid.

[18] The Signs of the Times, August 27, 1912.

[19] The Signs of the Times, April 23, 1912.

[20] Manuscript 47, 1908.

[21] Letter 90, 1911.

[22] The Signs of the Times, April 23, 1912.

[23] Manuscript 7, 1899.

[24] Testimonies For The Church 4, 621.

[25] Ibid., 5:424.

[26] Manuscript 102, 1901.

[27] The Review and Herald, January 29, 1901.

[28] The Signs of the Times, August 27, 1912.

[29] The Review and Herald, June 27, 1899.

[30] Manuscript 93, 1909.

[31] The Review and Herald, June 24, 1890.

[32] Manuscript 12, 1898.

[33] The Review and Herald, May 21, 1895.

[34] The Review and Herald, February 19, 1895.

Chapter 55—Moral Standards

Satan Seeks to Pervert the Marriage Institution—It was Satan's studied effort [in the antediluvian age] to pervert the marriage institution, to weaken its obligations and lessen its sacredness; for in no surer way could he deface the image of God in man and open the door to misery and vice.[1]

Satan well knows the material with which he has to deal in the human heart. He knows—for he has studied with fiendish intensity for thousands of years—the points most easily assailed in every character; and through successive generations he has wrought to overthrow the strongest men, princes in Israel, by the same temptations that were so successful at Baal-peor. All along through the ages there are strewn wrecks of character that have been stranded upon the rocks of sensual indulgence.[2]

Tragedy in Israel—The crime that brought the judgments of God upon Israel was that of licentiousness. The forwardness of women to entrap souls did not end at Baal-peor. Notwithstanding the punishment that followed the sinners in Israel, the same crime was repeated many times. Satan was most active in seeking to make Israel's overthrow complete.[3]

The licentious practice of the Hebrews accomplished for them that which all the warfare of nations and the enchantments of Balaam could not do. They became separated from their God. Their covering and protection were removed from them. God turned to be their enemy. So many of the princes and people were guilty of licentiousness that it became a national sin, for God was wroth with the whole congregation.[4] [327]

The History to Be Repeated—Near the close of this earth's history Satan will work with all his powers in the same manner and with the same temptations wherewith he tempted ancient Israel just before their entering the Land of Promise. He will lay snares for those who claim to keep the commandments of God, and who are almost on the borders of the heavenly Canaan. He will use his powers

255

to their utmost in order to entrap souls and to take God's professed people upon their weakest points. Those who have not brought the lower passions into subjection to the higher powers of their being, those who have allowed their minds to flow in a channel of carnal indulgence of the baser passions, Satan is determined to destroy with his temptations—to pollute their souls with licentiousness. He is not aiming especially at the lower and less important marks, but he makes use of his snares through those whom he can enlist as his agents to allure or attract men to take liberties which are condemned in the law of God. And men in responsible positions, teaching the claims of God's law, whose mouths are filled with arguments in vindication of His law, against which Satan has made such a raid—over such he sets his hellish powers and his agencies at work and overthrows them upon the weak points in their character, knowing that he who offends on one point is guilty of all, thus obtaining complete mastery over the entire man. Mind, soul, body, and conscience are involved in the ruin. If he be a messenger of righteousness and has had great light, or if the Lord has used him as His special worker in the cause of truth, then how great is the triumph of Satan! How he exults! How God is dishonored![5]

[328]

Prevalence of Immorality Today—A terrible picture of the condition of the world has been presented before me. Immorality abounds everywhere. Licentiousness is the special sin of this age. Never did vice lift its deformed head with such boldness as now. The people seem to be benumbed, and the lovers of virtue and true goodness are nearly discouraged by its boldness, strength, and prevalence. The iniquity which abounds is not merely confined to the unbeliever and the scoffer. Would that this were the case, but it is not. Many men and women who profess the religion of Christ are guilty. Even some who profess to be looking for His appearing are no more prepared for that event than Satan himself. They are not cleansing themselves from all pollution. They have so long served their lust that it is natural for their thoughts to be impure and their imaginations corrupt. It is as impossible to cause their minds to dwell upon pure and holy things as it would be to turn the course of Niagara and send its waters pouring up the falls.... Every Christian will have to learn to restrain his passions and be controlled by principle. Unless he does this, he is unworthy of the Christian name.[6]

Lovesick sentimentalism prevails. Married men receive attention from married or unmarried women; women also appear to be charmed and lose reason and spiritual discernment and good common sense; they do the very things that the word of God condemns, the very things that the testimonies of the Spirit of God condemn. Warnings and reproofs are before them in clear lines, yet they go over the same path that others have traveled before them. It is like an infatuating game at which they are playing. Satan leads them on to ruin themselves, to imperil the cause of God, to crucify the Son of God afresh and put Him to an open shame.[7]

[329]

Ignorance, pleasure loving, and sinful habits, corrupting soul, body, and spirit, make the world full of moral leprosy; a deadly moral malaria is destroying thousands and tens of thousands. What shall be done to save our youth? We can do little, but God lives and reigns, and He can do much.[8]

God's People to Stand in Contrast to the World—The liberties taken in this age of corruption should be no criterion for Christ's followers. These fashionable exhibitions of familiarity should not exist among Christians fitting for immortality. If lasciviousness, pollution, adultery, crime, and murder are the order of the day among those who know not the truth, and who refuse to be controlled by the principles of God's word, how important that the class professing to be followers of Christ, closely allied to God and angels, should show them a better and nobler way! How important that by their chastity and virtue they stand in marked contrast to that class who are controlled by brute passions![9]

Increasing Perils and Dangers—In this degenerate age many will be found who are so blinded to the sinfulness of sin that they choose a licentious life because it suits the natural and perverse inclination of the heart. Instead of facing the mirror of the law of God and bringing their hearts and characters up to God's standard, they allow Satan's agents to erect his standard in their hearts. Corrupt men think it easier to misinterpret the Scriptures to sustain them in their iniquity than to yield up their corruption and sin and be pure in heart and life.

There are more men of this stamp than many have imagined, and they will multiply as we draw near the end of time.[10]

[330]

When Satan's bewitching power controls a person, God is forgotten, and man who is filled with corrupt purposes is extolled. Secret licentiousness is practiced by these deceived souls as a virtue. This is a species of witchcraft.... There is always a bewitching power in heresies and in licentiousness. The mind is so deluded that it cannot reason intelligently, and an illusion is continually leading it from purity. The spiritual eyesight becomes blurred, and persons of hitherto untainted morals become confused under the delusive sophistry of those agents of Satan who profess to be messengers of light. It is this delusion which gives these agents power. Should they come out boldly and make their advances openly, they would be repulsed without a moment's hesitation; but they work first to gain sympathy and secure confidence in themselves as holy, self-sacrificing men of God. As his special messengers they then begin their artful work of drawing away souls from the path of rectitude by attempting to make void the law of God.[11]

Both Men and Women Must Keep Their Place and Live Above Reproach—The mind of a man or woman does not come down in a moment from purity and holiness to depravity, corruption, and crime. It takes time to transform the human to the divine, or to degrade those formed in the image of God to the brutal or the satanic. By beholding we become changed. Though formed in the image of his Maker, man can so educate his mind that sin which he once loathed will become pleasant to him. As he ceases to watch and pray, he ceases to guard the citadel, the heart, and engages in sin and crime. The mind is debased, and it is impossible to elevate it from corruption while it is being educated to enslave the moral and intellectual powers and bring them in subjection to grosser passions. Constant war against the carnal mind must be maintained; and we must be aided by the refining influence of the grace of God, which will attract the mind upward and habituate it to meditate upon pure and holy things.[12]

[331]

There is no safety for any man, young or old, unless he feels the necessity of seeking God for counsel at every step. Those only who maintain close communion with God will learn to place His estimate upon men, to reverence the pure, the good, the humble, and the meek. The heart must be garrisoned as was that of Joseph. Then temptations to depart from integrity will be met with decision: "How then can I do this great wickedness, and sin against God?" The strongest temptation is no excuse for sin. No matter how severe the pressure brought to bear upon you, sin is your own act. The seat of the difficulty is the unrenewed heart.[13]

In view of the dangers of this time, shall not we, as God's commandment-keeping people, put away from among us all sin, all iniquity, all perverseness? Shall not the women professing the truth keep strict guard over themselves, lest the least encouragement be given to unwarrantable familiarity? They may close many a door of temptation if they will observe at all times strict reserve and propriety of deportment.[14]

Women Must Uphold High Standard of Conduct—I write with a distressed heart that the women in this age, both married and unmarried, too frequently do not maintain the reserve that is necessary. They act like coquettes. They encourage the attentions of single and married men, and those who are weak in moral power will be ensnared. These things, if allowed, deaden the moral senses and blind the mind so that crime does not appear sinful. Thoughts are awakened that would not have been if woman had kept her place in all modesty and sobriety. She may have had no unlawful purpose or motive herself, but she has given encouragement to men who are tempted, and who need all the help they can get from those associated with them. By being circumspect, reserved, taking no liberties, receiving no unwarrantable attentions, but preserving a high moral tone and becoming dignity, much evil might be avoided.[15]

[332]

I have long been designing to speak to my sisters and tell them that, from what the Lord has been pleased to show me from time to time, there is a great fault among them. They are not careful to abstain from all appearance of evil. They are not all circumspect in their deportment, as becometh women professing godliness. Their words are not as select and well chosen as those of women who have received the grace of God should be. They are too familiar with their brethren. They linger around them, incline toward them, and seem to choose their society. They are highly gratified with their attention.

From the light which the Lord has given me, our sisters should pursue a very different course. They should be more reserved, manifest less boldness, and encourage in themselves "shamefacedness and sobriety." Both brethren and sisters indulge in too much jovial talk when in each other's society. Women professing godliness indulge in much jesting, joking, and laughing. This is unbecoming and grieves the Spirit of God. These exhibitions reveal a lack of true Christian refinement. They do not strengthen the soul in God, but bring great darkness; they drive away the pure, refined, heavenly angels and bring those who engage in these wrongs down to a low

[333]   level.[16]

Women are too often tempters. On one pretense or another they engage the attention of men, married or unmarried, and lead them on till they transgress the law of God, till their usefulness is ruined, and their souls are in jeopardy.... If women would only elevate their lives and become workers with Christ, there would be less danger through their influence; but with their present feelings of unconcern in regard to home responsibilities and in regard to the claims that God has upon them, their influence is often strong in the wrong direction, their powers are dwarfed, and their work does not bear the divine impress.[17]

There are so many forward misses and bold, forward women who have a faculty of insinuating themselves into notice, putting themselves in the company of young men, courting the attentions, inviting flirtations from married or unmarried men, that unless your face is set Christward, firm as steel, you will be drawn into Satan's net.[18]

As Christ's ambassador, I entreat you who profess present truth to promptly resent any approach to impurity and forsake the society of those who breathe an impure suggestion. Loathe these defiling sins with the most intense hatred. Flee from those who would, even in conversation, let the mind run in such a channel, "for out of the abundance of the heart the mouth speaketh." ...

You should not for one moment give place to an impure, covert suggestion, for even this will stain the soul, as impure water defiles the channel through which it passes.[19]

A woman who will allow an unchaste word or hint to be uttered in her presence is not as God would have her; one that will permit any undue familiarity or impure suggestion does not preserve her

[334]   godlike womanhood.[20]

Protected by a Sacred Circle of Purity—Our sisters should encourage true meekness; they should not be forward, talkative, and bold, but modest and unassuming, slow to speak. They may cherish courteousness. To be kind, tender, pitiful, forgiving, and humble would be becoming and well pleasing to God. If they occupy this position, they will not be burdened with undue attention from gentlemen in the church or out. All will feel that there is a sacred circle of purity around these God-fearing women which shields them from any unwarrantable liberties.

With some women professing godliness, there is a careless, coarse freedom of manner which leads to wrong and evil. But those godly women whose minds and hearts are occupied in meditating upon themes which strengthen purity of life, and which elevate the soul to commune with God, will not be easily led astray from the path of rectitude and virtue. Such will be fortified against the sophistry of Satan; they will be prepared to withstand his seductive arts.[21]

I appeal to you, as followers of Christ making an exalted profession, to cherish the precious, priceless gem of modesty. This will guard virtue.[22]

Control the Thoughts—You should control your thoughts. This will not be an easy task; you cannot accomplish it without close and even severe effort. Yet God requires this of you; it is a duty resting upon every accountable being. You are responsible to God for your thoughts. If you indulge in vain imaginations, permitting your mind to dwell upon impure subjects, you are, in a degree, as guilty before God as if your thoughts were carried into action. All that prevents the action is the lack of opportunity. Day and night dreaming and castle-building are bad and exceedingly dangerous habits. When once established, it is next to impossible to break up such habits and direct the thoughts to pure, holy, elevated themes.[23]

Beware of Flattery—I am pained when I see men praised, flattered, and petted. God has revealed to me the fact that some who receive these attentions are unworthy to take His name upon their lips; yet they are exalted to heaven in the estimation of finite beings, who read only from outward appearance. My sisters, never pet and flatter poor, fallible, erring men, either young or old, married or unmarried. You know not their weaknesses, and you know not but

[335]

that these very attentions and this profuse praise may prove their ruin. I am alarmed at the shortsightedness, the want of wisdom, that many manifest in this respect.

Men who are doing God's work, and who have Christ abiding in their hearts, will not lower the standard of morality, but will ever seek to elevate it. They will not find pleasure in the flattery of women or in being petted by them. Let men, both single and married, say: "Hands off! I will never give the least occasion that my good should be evil spoken of. My good name is capital of far more value to me than gold or silver. Let me preserve it untarnished. If men assail that name, it shall not be because I have given them occasion to do so, but for the same reason that they spoke evil of Christ—because they hated the purity and holiness of His character, for it was a constant rebuke to them."[24]

If the Minister Tempts—The slightest insinuations, from whatever source they may come, inviting you to indulge in sin or to allow the least unwarrantable liberty with your persons should be resented as the worst of insults to your dignified womanhood. The kiss upon your cheek, at an improper time and place, should lead you to repel the emissary of Satan with disgust. If it is from one in high places, who is dealing in sacred things, the sin is of tenfold greater magnitude and should lead a God-fearing woman or youth to recoil with horror, not only from the sin he would have you commit, but from the hypocrisy and villainy of one whom the people respect and honor as God's servant.[25]

[336]

If a minister of the gospel does not control his baser passions, if he fails to follow the example of the apostle and so dishonors his profession and faith as to even name the indulgence of sin, our sisters who profess godliness should not for an instant flatter themselves that sin or crime loses its sinfulness in the least because their minister dares to engage in it. The fact that men who are in responsible places show themselves to be familiar with sin should not lessen the guilt and enormity of the sin in the minds of any. Sin should appear just as sinful, just as abhorrent, as it had been heretofore regarded; and the minds of the pure and elevated should abhor and shun the one who indulges in sin as they would flee from a serpent whose sting was deadly. If the sisters were elevated and possessed purity of heart, any corrupt advances, even from their minister, would be repulsed with such positiveness as would never need a repetition.[26]

Be Faithful to Marriage Vows—How careful should the husband and father be to maintain his loyalty to his marriage vows! How circumspect should be his character, lest he shall encourage thoughts in young girls, or even in married women, that are not in accordance with the high, holy standard—the commandments of God! Those commandments Christ shows to be exceedingly broad, reaching even the thoughts, intents, and purposes of the heart. Here is where many are delinquent. Their heart imaginings are not of the pure, holy character which God requires; and however high their calling, however talented they may be, God will mark iniquity against them and will count them as far more guilty and deserving of His wrath than those who have less talent, less light, less influence.[27]

[337]

To married men I am instructed to say, It is to your wives, the mothers of your children, that your respect and affection are due. Your attentions are to be given to them, and your thoughts are to dwell upon plans for their happiness.[28]

I have been shown families where the husband and father has not preserved that reserve, that dignified, godlike manhood which is befitting a follower of Christ. He has failed to perform the kind, tender, courteous acts due to his wife, whom he has promised before God and angels to love, respect, and honor while they both shall live. The girl employed to do the work has been free and somewhat forward to dress his hair and to be affectionately attentive, and he is pleased, foolishly pleased. In his love and attention to his wife he is not as demonstrative as he once was. Be sure that Satan is at work here. Respect your hired help, treat them kindly, considerately, but go no farther. Let your deportment be such that there will be no advances to familiarity from them.[29]

Maintain Family Privacy—Oh, how many lives are made bitter by the breaking down of the walls which inclose the privacies of every family, and which are calculated to preserve its purity and sanctity! A third person is taken into the confidence of the wife, and her private family matters are laid open before the special friend. This is the device of Satan to estrange the hearts of the husband and wife. Oh, that this would cease! What a world of trouble would be saved! Lock within your own hearts the knowledge of each other's

[338]

faults. Tell your troubles alone to God. He can give you right counsel and sure consolation which will be pure, having no bitterness in it.[30]

When a woman relates her family troubles or complains of her husband to another man, she violates her marriage vows; she dishonors her husband and breaks down the wall erected to preserve the sanctity of the marriage relation; she throws wide open the door and invites Satan to enter with his insidious temptations. This is just as Satan would have it. If a woman comes to a Christian brother with a tale of her woes, her disappointments and trials, he should ever advise her, if she must confide her troubles to someone, to select sisters for her confidants, and then there will be no appearance of evil whereby the cause of God may suffer reproach.[31]

How to Be Kept From Straying—I speak to our people. If you draw close to Jesus and seek to adorn your profession by a well-ordered life and godly conversation, your feet will be kept from straying into forbidden paths. If you will only watch, continually watch unto prayer, if you will do everything as if you were in the immediate presence of God, you will be saved from yielding to temptation and may hope to be kept pure, spotless, and undefiled till the last. If you hold the beginning of your confidence firm unto the end, your ways will be established in God; and what grace has begun, glory will crown in the kingdom of our God. The fruits of

[339] the Spirit are love, joy, peace, long-suffering, gentleness, goodness, faith, meekness, temperance; against such there is no law. If Christ

[340] be within us, we shall crucify the flesh with the affections and lusts.[32]

[1] Patriarchs and Prophets, 338.

[2] Ibid., 457.

[3] The Review and Herald, May 17, 1887.

[4] Ibid.

[5] Ibid.

[6] Testimonies For The Church 2, 346, 347.

[7] Manuscript 19 a, 1890.

[8] Manuscript 8, 1894.

[9] Testimonies For The Church 2, 459.

[10] Testimonies For The Church 5, 141.

[11] Testimonies For The Church 5, 142, 143.

[12] Testimonies For The Church 2, 478, 479.

[13] Manuscript 19a, 1890.

[14] Testimonies For The Church 5, 601, 602.

[15]Manuscript 4a. 1885.

[16]Testimonies For The Church 2, 455.

[17]Testimonies For The Church 5, 596, 597.

[18]Medical Ministry, 145.

[19]Testimonies For The Church 5, 146, 147.

[20]Manuscript 4a, 1885.

[21]Testimonies For The Church 2, 456.

[22]Testimonies For The Church 1. 458.1.

[23]Testimonies For The Church 1. 561.

[24]Testimonies For The Church 5, 595.

[25]Testimonies For The Church 2, 458. 459.

[26]Testimonies For The Church 2, 457.

[27]Testimonies For The Church 5, 594, 595.

[28]Letter 231. 1903.

[29]Testimonies For The Church 2, 461.

[30]Testimonies For The Church 2, 462.

[31]Testimonies For The Church 2. 306.

[32]Testimonies For The Church 5. 148.

Chapter 56—Divorce

Marriage Is a Contract for Life—In the youthful mind marriage is clothed with romance, and it is difficult to divest it of this feature, with which imagination covers it, and to impress the mind with a sense of the weighty responsibilities involved in the marriage vow. This vow links the destinies of the two individuals with bonds which naught but the hand of death should sever.[1]

Every marriage engagement should be carefully considered, for marriage is a step taken for life. Both the man and the woman should carefully consider whether they can cleave to each other through the vicissitudes of life as long as they both shall live.[2]

Jesus Corrected Misconceptions of Marriage—Among the Jews a man was permitted to put away his wife for the most trivial offenses, and the woman was then at liberty to marry again. This practice led to great wretchedness and sin. In the Sermon on the Mount Jesus declared plainly that there could be no dissolution of the marriage tie except for unfaithfulness to the marriage vow. "Every one," He said, "that putteth away his wife, saving for the cause of fornication, maketh her an adulteress: and whosoever shall marry her when she is put away committeth adultery."

When the Pharisees afterward questioned Him concerning the lawfulness of divorce, Jesus pointed His hearers back to the marriage institution as ordained at creation. "Because of the hardness of your hearts," He said, Moses "suffered you to put away your wives: but [341] from the beginning it was not so." He referred them to the blessed days of Eden when God pronounced all things "very good." Then marriage and the Sabbath had their origin, twin institutions for the glory of God in the benefit of humanity. Then, as the Creator joined the hands of the holy pair in wedlock, saying, A man shall "leave his father and his mother, and shall cleave unto his wife: and they shall be one," He enunciated the law of marriage for all the children of Adam to the close of time. That which the eternal Father Himself had

266

pronounced good was the law of highest blessing and development for man.[3]

Jesus came to our world to rectify mistakes and to restore the moral image of God in man. Wrong sentiments in regard to marriage had found a place in the minds of the teachers of Israel. They were making of none effect the sacred institution of marriage. Man was becoming so hardhearted that he would for the most trivial excuse separate from his wife, or, if he chose, he would separate her from the children and send her away. This was considered a great disgrace and was often accompanied by the most acute suffering on the part of the discarded one.

Christ came to correct these evils, and His first miracle was wrought on the occasion of the marriage. Thus He announced to the world that marriage when kept pure and undefiled is a sacred institution.[4]

Counsel to One Contemplating Divorce—Your ideas in regard to the marriage relation have been erroneous. Nothing but the violation of the marriage bed can either break or annul the marriage vow. We are living in perilous times, when there is no assurance in anything save in firm, unwavering faith in Jesus Christ. There is no heart that may not be estranged from God through the devices of Satan, if one does not watch unto prayer.

[342]

Your health would have been in a far better condition had your mind been at peace and rest; but it became confused and unbalanced, and you reasoned incorrectly in regard to the matter of divorce. Your views cannot be sustained on the ground from which you reason. Men are not at liberty to make a standard of law for themselves, to avoid God's law and please their own inclination. They must come to God's great moral standard of righteousness....

God gave only one cause why a wife should leave her husband, or the husband leave his wife, which was adultery. Let this ground be prayerfully considered.[5]

Advice to a Separated Couple—My brother, my sister, for some time you have not been living together. You should not have pursued this course and would not have done so if both of you had been cultivating the patience, kindness, and forbearance that should ever exist between husband and wife. Neither of you should set up your own will and try to carry out your individual ideas and plans whatever the consequences may be. Neither of you should be determined to do as you please. Let the softening, subduing influence of the Spirit of God work upon your hearts and fit you for the work of training your children.... Appeal to your heavenly Father to keep you from yielding to the temptation to speak in an impatient, harsh, willful manner to each other, the husband to the wife, and the wife to the husband. Both of you have imperfect characters. Because you have not been under God's control, your conduct toward each other has been unwise.

[343] I beseech you to bring yourselves under God's control. When tempted to speak provokingly, refrain from saying anything. You will be tempted on this point because you have never overcome this objectionable trait of character. But every wrong habit must be overcome. Make a complete surrender to God. Fall on the Rock, Christ Jesus, and be broken. As husband and wife, discipline yourselves. Go to Christ for help. He will willingly supply you with His divine sympathy, His free grace....

Repent before God for your past course. Come to an understanding, and reunite as husband and wife. Put away the disagreeable, unhappy experience of your past life. Take courage in the Lord. Close the windows of the soul earthward, and open them heavenward. If your voices are uplifted in prayer to heaven for light, the Lord Jesus, who is light and life, peace and joy, will hear your cry. He, the Sun of Righteousness, will shine into the chambers of your mind, lighting up the soul temple. If you welcome the sunshine of His presence into your home, you will not utter words of a nature to cause feelings of unhappiness.[6]

To a Hopelessly Mistreated Wife—I have received your letter, and in reply to it I would say, I cannot advise you to return to D unless you see decided changes in him. The Lord is not pleased with the ideas he has had in the past of what is due to a wife.... If [he] holds to his former views, the future would be not better for you than the past has been. He does not know how to treat a wife.

I feel very sad about this matter. I feel indeed sorry for D, but I cannot advise you to go to him against your judgment. I speak to you as candidly as I spoke to him; it would be perilous for you to again place yourself under his dictation. I had hoped that he would change....

The Lord understands all about your experiences.... Be of good courage in the Lord; He will not leave you nor forsake you. My heart goes out in tenderest sympathy for you.[7] [344]

To a Deserted Husband—"Shoulder Your Cross."—I cannot see what more can be done in this case, and I think that the only thing that you can do is to give up your wife. If she is thus determined not to live with you, both she and you would be most miserable to attempt it. And as she has fully and determinedly set her stakes, you can only shoulder your cross and show yourself a man.[8]

Still Married in God's Sight, Although Divorced—A woman may be legally divorced from her husband by the laws of the land and yet not divorced in the sight of God and according to the higher law. There is only one sin, which is adultery, which can place the husband or wife in a position where they can be free from the marriage vow in the sight of God. Although the laws of the land may grant a divorce, yet they are husband and wife still in the Bible light, according to the laws of God.

I saw that Sister _____, as yet, has no right to marry another man; but if she, or any other woman, should obtain a divorce legally on the ground that her husband was guilty of adultery, then she is free to be married to whom she chooses.[9]

Separation From an Unbelieving Companion—If the wife is an unbeliever and an opposer, the husband cannot, in view of the law of God, put her away on this ground alone. In order to be in harmony with the law of Jehovah, he must abide with her unless she chooses of herself to depart. He may suffer opposition and be oppressed and annoyed in many ways; he will find his comfort and his strength and support from God, who is able to give grace for every emergency. [345] He should be a man of pure mind, of truly decided, firm principles, and God will give him wisdom in regard to the course which he should pursue. Impulse will not control his reason, but reason will hold the lines of control in her firm hand, that lust shall be held under bit and bridle.[10]

A Wife Urged to Change Disposition, Not the Marriage Status—I have received a letter from your husband. I would say that there is only one thing for which a husband may lawfully separate from his wife or a wife from her husband, and that is adultery.

If your dispositions are not congenial, would it not be for the glory of God for you to change these dispositions?

A husband and wife should cultivate respect and affection for each other. They should guard the spirit, the words, and the actions so that nothing will be said or done to irritate or annoy. Each is to have a care for the other, doing all in their power to strengthen their mutual affection.

I tell you both to seek the Lord. In love and kindness do your duty one to the other. The husband should cultivate industrious habits, doing his best to support his family. This will lead his wife to have respect for him....

My sister, you cannot please God by maintaining your present attitude. Forgive your husband. He is your husband, and you will be blessed in striving to be a dutiful, affectionate wife. Let the law of kindness be on your lips. You can and must change your attitude.[11]

You must both study how you can assimilate, instead of differing, with one another.... The use of mild, gentle methods will make a surprising difference in your lives.[12]

[346]

Adultery, Divorce, and Church Membership—In regard to the case of the injured sister, A.G., we would say in reply to the questions of——that it is a feature in the cases of most who have been overtaken in sin, as her husband has, that they have no real sense of their villainy. Some, however, do and are restored to the church, but not till they have merited the confidence of the people of God by unqualified confessions and a period of sincere repentance. This case presents difficulties not found in some, and we would add only the following:

1. In cases of the violation of the seventh commandment where the guilty party does not manifest true repentance, if the injured party can obtain a divorce without making their own cases and that of their children, if they have them, worse by so doing, they should be free.

2. If they would be liable to place themselves and their children in worse condition by a divorce, we know of no scripture that would make the innocent party guilty by remaining.

3. Time and labor and prayer and patience and faith and a godly life might work a reform. To live with one who has broken the marriage vows and is covered all over with the disgrace and shame

of guilty love, and realizes it not, is an eating canker to the soul; and yet a divorce is a lifelong, heartfelt sore. God pity the innocent party! Marriage should be considered well before contracted.

4. Why! oh, why! will men and women who might be respectable and good and reach heaven at last sell themselves to the devil so cheap, wound their bosom friends, disgrace their families, bring a reproach upon the cause, and go to hell at last? God have mercy! Why will not those who are overtaken in crime manifest repentance proportionate to the enormity of their crime and fly to Christ for mercy and heal, as far as possible, the wounds they have made?[13]

[347]

5. But, if they will not do as they should, and if the innocent have forfeited the legal right to a divorce, by living with the guilty after his guilt is known, we do not see that sin rests upon the innocent in remaining, and her moral right in departing seems questionable, if her health and life be not greatly endangered in so remaining. [Note: this is one of the very few statements to be issued jointly by James and Ellen White. Inasmuch as it was signed by both, it is evident that the views expressed had full sanction of Mrs. White. It should be noted that the restoration of church membership referred to in the introductory paragraph of the section is not against a background of divorce, but of adultery. The paragraph makes no reference whatsoever to divorce. The references to divorce and church membership in the succeeding paragraphs relate, not to the offending husband, but to the offended wife and her church membership should she decide to divorce or should she decide to remain with her husband.—*Compilers.*]

[348]

[1] Testimonies For The Church 4, 507.

[2] Letter 17, 1896.

[3] Thoughts from the Mount of Blessing, 99, 100.

[4] Manuscript 16, 1899.

[5] Letter 8, 1888.

[6] Letter 47, 1902.

[7] Letter 148, 1907.

[8] Letter 40, 1888.

[9] Letter 4a, 1863.

[10] Letter 8, 1888.

[11] Letter 168, 1901.

[12] Letter 157, 1903.

[13]The Review and Herald, March 24, 1868.

Chapter 57—Attitude Toward an Unbelieving Companion

[Note: this chapter is largely communications to distressed believers seeking counsel.—*Compilers*.]

Should a Christian Wife Leave an Unbelieving Husband?—Letters have come to me from mothers, relating their trials at home and asking my counsel. One of these cases will serve to represent many. The husband and father is not a believer, and everything is made hard for the mother in the training of her children. The husband is a profane man, vulgar and abusive in his language to her, and he teaches the children to disregard her authority. When she is trying to pray with them, he will come in and make all the noise he can and break out into cursing God and heaping vile epithets upon the Bible. She is so discouraged that life is a burden to her. What good can she do? What benefit is it to her children for her to remain at home? She has felt an earnest desire to do some work in the Lord's vineyard and has thought that it might be best to leave her family rather than to remain while the husband and father is constantly teaching the children to disrespect and disobey her.

In such cases my advice would be, Mothers, whatever trials you may be called to endure through poverty, through wounds and bruises of the soul, from the harsh, overbearing assumption of the husband and father, do not leave your children; do not give them up to the influence of a godless father. Your work is to counteract the work of the father, who is apparently under the control of Satan.[1]   [349]

Give a Living Example of Self-control—You have trials, I know, but there is such a thing as showing a spirit of driving rather than of drawing. Your husband needs each day to see a living example of patience and self-control. Make every effort to please him, and yet do not yield up one principle of the truth....

Christ requires the whole being in His service—heart, soul, mind, and strength. As you give Him what He asks of you, you will represent Him in character. Let your husband see the Holy Spirit

273

working in you. Be careful and considerate, patient and forbearing. Do not urge the truth upon him. Do your duty as a wife should, and then see if his heart is not touched. Your affections must not be weaned from your husband. Please him in every way possible. Let not your religious faith draw you apart. Conscientiously obey God, and please your husband wherever you can....

Let all see that you love Jesus and trust in Him. Give your husband and your believing and unbelieving friends evidence that you desire them to see the beauty of truth. But do not show that painful, worrying anxiety which often spoils a good work....

Never let a word of reproach or faultfinding fall upon the ears of your husband. You sometimes pass through strait places, but do not talk of these trials. Silence is eloquence. Hasty speech will only increase your unhappiness. Be cheerful and happy. Bring all the sunshine possible into your home, and shut out the shadows. Let the bright beams of the Sun of Righteousness shine into the chambers of your soul temple. Then the fragrance of the Christian life will be brought into your family. There will be no dwelling upon disagreeable things, which many times have no truth in them.[2]

[350]

A Burdened Wife Counseled to Keep Cheerful—You now have a double responsibility because your husband has turned his face away from Jesus....

I know it must be a great grief for you to stand alone, as far as the doing of the word is concerned. But how knowest thou, O wife, but that your consistent life of faith and obedience may win back your husband to the truth? Let the dear children be brought to Jesus. In simple language speak the words of truth to them. Sing to them pleasant, attractive songs which reveal the love of Christ. Bring your children to Jesus, for He loves little children.

Keep cheerful. Do not forget that you have a Comforter, the Holy Spirit, which Christ has appointed. You are never alone. If you will listen to the voice that now speaks to you, if you will respond without delay to the knocking at the door of your heart, "Come in, Lord Jesus, that I may sup with Thee, and Thee with me," the heavenly Guest will enter. When this element, which is all divine, abides with you, there is peace and rest.[3]

Maintain Christian Principles—The household where God is not worshiped is like a ship in the midst of the sea without a pilot or a helm. The tempest beats and breaks upon it, and there is danger that all on board may perish. Regard your life and the lives of your children as precious for Christ's sake, for you must meet them and your husband before the throne of God. Your steadfast Christian principles must not become weak, but stronger and stronger. However much your husband may be annoyed, however strongly he may oppose you, you must show a consistent, faithful, Christian steadfastness. And then whatever he may say, in heart and judgment he can but respect you, if he has a heart of flesh.[4]

[351]

God's Claims to Come First [Note: taken from chapter "Warnings and Reproofs," in which are found testimonies to a number of members in a certain church. This follows a message addressed to a brother T.—*Compilers.*]—I was then shown his daughter-in-law. She is beloved of God, but held in servile bondage, fearing, trembling, desponding, doubting, and very nervous. This sister should not feel that she must yield her will to a godless youth who has less years upon his head than herself. She should remember that her marriage does not destroy her individuality. God has claims upon her higher than any earthly claim. Christ has bought her with His own blood. She is not her own. She fails to put her entire trust in God and submits to yield her convictions, her conscience, to an overbearing, tyrannical man, fired up by Satan whenever his satanic majesty can work effectually through him to intimidate this trembling, shrinking soul. She has so many times been thrown into agitation that her nervous system is shattered, and she is merely a wreck. Is it the will of the Lord that this sister should be in this state and God be robbed of her service? No. Her marriage was a deception of the devil. Yet now she should make the best of it, treat her husband with tenderness, and make him as happy as she can without violating her conscience; for if he remains in his rebellion, this world is all the heaven he will have. But to deprive herself of the privilege of meetings, to gratify an overbearing husband possessing the spirit of the dragon, is not according to God's will.[5]

"And another said, I have married a wife, and therefore I cannot come." The sin of this man was not in marrying, but in marrying one who divorced his mind from the higher and more important interests of life. Never should a man allow wife and home to draw his thoughts away from Christ or to lead him to refuse to accept the

[352]

gracious invitations of the gospel.[6]

Better Save Part Than Lose All—Brother K, you have had many discouragements; but you must be earnest, firm, and decided to do your duty in your family, and take them with you if possible. You should spare no effort to prevail upon them to accompany you on your heavenward journey. But if the mother and the children do not choose to accompany you, but rather seek to draw you away from your duties and religious privileges, you must go forward even if you go alone. You must live in the fear of God. You must improve your opportunities of attending the meetings and gaining all the spiritual strength you can, for you will need it in the days to come. Lot's property was all consumed. If you should meet with loss, you should not be discouraged; and if you can save only a *part* of your [353]   family, it is much better than to lose all.[7]

[1]Letter 28, 1890.

[2]Letter 145, 1900.

[3]Letter 124, 1897.

[4]Letter 76, 1896.

[5]Testimonies For The Church 2, 99, 100.

[6]Manuscript 24, 1891.

[7]Testimonies For The Church 4, 112, 113.

Chapter 58—The Minister's Family

Home Life of Minister to Exemplify Message—God designs that in his home life the teacher of the Bible shall be an exemplification of the truths that he teaches. What a man is has greater influence than what he says. Piety in the daily life will give power to the public testimony. Patience, consistency, and love will make an impression on hearts that sermons fail to reach.[1]

If properly carried on, the training of the children of a minister will illustrate the lessons he gives in the desk. But if, by the wrong education he has given his children, a minister shows his incapacity to govern and control, he needs to learn that God requires him to properly discipline the children given him before he can do his duty as shepherd of the flock of God.[2]

His First Duty Is to His Children—The minister's duties lie around him, nigh and afar off; but his first duty is to his children. He should not become so engrossed with his outside duties as to neglect the instruction which his children need. He may look upon his home duties as of lesser importance, but in reality they lie at the very foundation of the well-being of individuals and of society. To a large degree the happiness of men and women and the success of the church depend upon home influence....

Nothing can excuse the minister for neglecting the inner circle for the larger circle outside. The spiritual welfare of his family comes first. In the day of final reckoning God will inquire what he did to win to Christ those whom he took the responsibility of bringing into the world. Great good done for others cannot cancel the debt that he owes to God to care for his own children.[3]

[354]

The Magnitude of the Minister's Influence—Ministers' children are in some cases the most neglected children in the world, for the reason that the father is with them but little, and they are left to choose their own employment and amusement.[4]

Great as are the evils of parental unfaithfulness under any circumstances, they are tenfold greater when they exist in the families

277

of those appointed as teachers of the people. When these fail to control their own households, they are, by their wrong example, misleading many. Their guilt is as much greater than that of others as their position is more responsible.[5]

Wife and Children Best Judge of His Piety—It is not so much the religion of the pulpit as the religion of the family that reveals our real character. The minister's wife, his children, and those who are employed as helpers in his family are best qualified to judge of his piety. A good man will be a blessing to his household. Wife, children, and helpers will all be the better for his religion.

Brethren, carry Christ into the family, carry Him into the pulpit, carry Him with you wherever you go. Then you need not urge upon others the necessity of appreciating the ministry, for you will bear the heavenly credentials which will prove to all that you are servants of Christ.[6]

The Minister's Wife, a Helper or a Hindrance?—When a man accepts the responsibilities of a minister, he claims to be a mouthpiece for God, to take the words from the mouth of God and give them to the people. How closely, then, he should keep at the side of the Great Shepherd; how humbly he should walk before God, keeping self out of sight and exalting Christ! And how important it is that the character of his wife be after the Bible pattern, and that his children be in subjection with all gravity!

[355]

The wife of a minister of the gospel can be either a most successful helper and a great blessing to her husband or a hindrance to him in his work. It depends very much on the wife whether a minister will rise from day to day in his sphere of usefulness, or whether he will sink to the ordinary level.[7]

I saw that the wives of the ministers should help their husbands in their labors and be exact and careful what influence they exert, for they are watched, and more is expected of them than of others. Their dress should be an example. Their lives and conversation should be an example, savoring of life rather than of death. I saw that they should take a humble, meek, yet exalted stand, not having their conversation upon things that do not tend to direct the mind heavenward. The great inquiry should be: "How can I save my own soul and be the means of saving others?" I saw that no halfhearted work in this matter is accepted of God. He wants the whole heart and interest, or He will have none. Their influence tells, decidedly, unmistakably, in favor of the truth or against it. They gather with Jesus or scatter abroad. An unsanctified wife is the greatest curse that a minister can have.[8]

Satan is ever at work to dishearten and lead astray ministers whom God has chosen to preach the truth. The most effectual way in which he can work is through home influences, through unconsecrated companions. If he can control their minds, he can through them the more readily gain access to the husband, who is laboring in word and doctrine to save souls.... Satan has had much to do with controlling the labors of the ministers through the influence of selfish, ease-loving companions.[9]

Words of Counsel to Ministers Regarding Family Management—You have a duty to do at home which you cannot shun and yet be true to God and to your God-given trust.... The gospel field is the world. You wish to sow the field with gospel truth, waiting for God to water the seed sown that it may bring forth fruit. You have entrusted to you a little plot of ground; but your own dooryard is left to grow up with brambles and thorns, while you are engaged in weeding others' gardens. This is not a small work, but one of great moment. You are preaching the gospel to others; practice it yourself at home.[10]

Until you can be united in the work of properly disciplining your child, let the wife remain with her child away from the scene of her husband's labors; for no example of lax, loose discipline should be given to the church of God.

I have known many ministers who were unwise enough to travel about, taking with them an unruly child. Their labors in the pulpit were counteracted by the unlovely tempers manifested by their children.[11]

Take an Interest in Others' Children—Your interest should not be swallowed up in your own family to the exclusion of others. If you share the hospitalities of your brethren, they may reasonably expect something in return. Identify your interests with those of parents and children, and seek to instruct and bless. Sanctify yourself to the work of God, and be a blessing to those who entertain you, conversing with parents and in no case overlooking the children. Do

[356]

[357]

not feel that your own little one is more precious in the sight of God than other children.[12]

An Appeal to a Minister's Wayward Son—Your father is a minister of the gospel, and Satan works most zealously to lead the children of ministers to dishonor their parents. If possible he will bring them into captivity to his will and imbue them with his evil propensities. Will you allow Satan to work through you to destroy the hope and comfort of your parents? Will they be obliged to look upon you with continual sadness because you give yourself into Satan's control? Will you leave them to the discouragement of thinking that they have brought up children who refuse to be instructed by them, who follow their own inclinations whatever happens? ...

You have good impulses, and you awaken hope and expectation in the minds of your parents; but, so far, you have been powerless to resist temptation, and Satan exults in your readiness to do just as he wills. Often you make statements which inspire your parents with hope, but just as often you fail because you will not resist the enemy. You cannot know how it pains your father and mother when you are found on Satan's side. Many times you say, "I cannot do this," and "I cannot do that," when you know that the things you say you cannot do are right for you to do. You can fight against the enemy, not in your own strength, but in the strength God is ever ready to give you. Trusting in His word, you will never say, "I can't." ...

I appeal to you in the name of the Lord to turn before it is too late. Because you are the son of parents who are co-workers with God, you are supposed to be a well-disposed boy; but often, by your waywardness, you dishonor your father and mother and counteract [358] the work they are seeking to do. Has not your mother sufficient to oppress and crush her spirits without your waywardness? Will you still pursue such a course of action that your father's heart will be weighed down with grief? Is it a pleasure for you to have all heaven looking upon you with displeasure? Is it a satisfaction for you to place yourself in the ranks of the enemy, to be ordered and controlled by him?

Oh, that now, while it is called today, you would turn to the Lord! Your every deed is making you either better or worse. If your actions are on Satan's side, they leave behind them an influence that continues to work its baleful results. Only the pure, the clean, and the holy can enter the city of God, "Today if ye will hear His voice, harden not your hearts," but turn to the Lord, that the path you travel may not leave desolation in its track.[13]

Minister to Treat Children With Kindness and Courtesy—Let the kindness and courtesy of the minister be seen in his treatment of children. He should ever bear in mind that they are miniature men and women, younger members of the Lord's family. These may be very near and dear to the Master and, if properly instructed and disciplined, will do service for Him, even in their youth. Christ is grieved with every harsh, severe, and inconsiderate word spoken to children. Their rights are not always respected, and they are frequently treated as though they had not an individual character which needs to be properly developed that it may not be warped and the purpose of God in their lives prove a failure.[14]

Let the church take a special care of the lambs of the flock, exerting every influence in their power to win the love of the children and to bind them to the truth. Ministers and church members should second the efforts of parents to lead the children into safe paths. The Lord is calling for the youth, for He would make them His helpers to do good service under His banner.[15]

[359]

An Effectual Sermon on Godliness—The minister should instruct the people upon the government of children, and his own children should be examples of proper subjection.[16]

There should exist in the minister's family a unity that will preach an effectual sermon on practical godliness. As the minister and his wife faithfully do their duty in the home, restraining, correcting, advising, counseling, guiding, they are becoming better fitted to labor in the church and are multiplying agencies for the accomplishment of God's work outside the home. The members of the family become members of the family above and are a power for good, exerting a far-reaching influence.[17]

[360]

---

[1] Gospel Workers, 204.
[2] Letter 1, 1877.
[3] Gospel Workers, 204.
[4] Ibid., 206.
[5] Patriarchs and Prophets, 579.
[6] Testimonies For The Church 5, 161.

[7]Letter 1, 1877.

[8]Testimonies For The Church 1, 139.

[9]Testimonies For The Church 1, 449, 451.

[10]Testimonies For The Church 4, 381.

[11]Letter 1, 1877.

[12]Testimonies For The Church 4, 382.

[13]Letter 15a, 1896.

[14]Testimonies For The Church 4, 397, 398.

[15]The Review and Herald, October 25, 1892.

[16]Letter 1, 1877.

[17]Gospel Workers, 204, 205.

Chapter 59—The Aged Parents

"Honor Thy Father and Thy Mother."—The obligation resting upon children to honor their parents is of lifelong duration. If the parents are feeble and old, the affection and attention of the children should be bestowed in proportion to the need of father and mother. Nobly, decidedly, the children should shape their course of action even if it requires self-denial, so that every thought of anxiety and perplexity may be removed from the minds of the parents....

Children should be educated to love and care tenderly for father and mother. Care for them, children, yourselves; for no other hand can do the little acts of kindness with the acceptance that you can do them. Improve your precious opportunity to scatter seeds of kindness.[1]

Our obligation to our parents never ceases. Our love for them, and theirs for us, is not measured by years or distance, and our responsibility can never be set aside.[2]

Let children carefully remember that at the best the aged parents have but little joy and comfort. What can bring greater sorrow to their hearts than manifest neglect on the part of their children? What sin can be worse in children than to bring grief to an aged, helpless father or mother?[3]

Smooth the Pathway—After children grow to years of maturity, some of them think their duty is done in providing an abode for their parents. While giving them food and shelter, they give them no love or sympathy. In their parents' old age, when they long for expression of affection and sympathy, children heartlessly deprive them of their attention. There is no time when children should withhold respect and love from their father and mother. While the parents live, it should be the children's joy to honor and respect them. They should bring all the cheerfulness and sunshine into the life of the aged parents that they possibly can. They should smooth their pathway to the grave. There is no better recommendation in this world than

[361]

283

that a child has honored his parents, no better record in the books of heaven than that he has loved and honored father and mother.[4]

Ingratitude to Parents—Is it possible that children can become so dead to the claims of father and mother that they will not willingly remove all causes of sorrow in their power, watching over them with unwearying care and devotion? Can it be possible that they will not regard it a pleasure to make the last days of their parents their best days? How can a son or daughter be willing to leave father or mother on the hands of strangers for them to care for! Even were the mother an unbeliever and disagreeable, it would not release the child from the obligation that God has placed upon him to care for his parent.[5]

Some Parents Are Responsible for Disrespect—When parents permit a child to show them disrespect in childhood, allowing them to speak pettishly and even harshly, there will be a dreadful harvest to be reaped in after years. When parents fail to require prompt and perfect obedience in their children, they fail to lay the right foundation of character in their little ones. They prepare their children to dishonor them when they are old, and bring sorrow to their hearts when they are nearing the grave, unless the grace of Christ changes [362] the hearts and transforms the characters of their children.[6]

Show No Retaliation Against Unjust Parents—Said one of her mother, "I always hated my mother, and my mother hated me." These words stand registered in the books of heaven to be opened and revealed in the day of judgment when everyone shall be rewarded according to his works.

If children think that they were treated with severity in their childhood, will it help them to grow in grace and in the knowledge of Christ, will it make them reflect His image, to cherish a spirit of retaliation and revenge against their parents, especially when they are old and feeble? Will not the very helplessness of the parents plead for the children's love? Will not the necessities of the aged father and mother call forth the noble feelings of the heart, and through the grace of Christ, shall not the parents be treated with kind attention and respect by their offspring? Oh, let not the heart be made as adamant as steel against father and mother! How can a daughter professing the name of Christ cherish hatred against her mother, especially if that mother is sick and old? Let kindness and love, the sweetest fruits of Christian life, find a place in the heart of children toward their parents.[7]

Be Patient With Infirmities—Especially dreadful is the thought of a child turning in hatred upon a mother who has become old and feeble, upon whom has come those infirmities of disposition attendant upon second childhood. How patiently, how tenderly, should children bear with such a mother! Tender words which will not irritate the spirit should be spoken. A true Christian will never be unkind, never under any circumstances be neglectful of his father or mother, but will heed the command, "Honour thy father and thy mother." God has said, "Thou shalt rise up before the hoary head, and honour the face of the old man." ... [363]

Children, let your parents, infirm and unable to care for themselves, find their last days filled with contentment, peace, and love. For Christ's sake let them go down to the grave receiving from you only words of kindness, love, mercy, and forgiveness. You desire the Lord to love and pity and forgive you, and to make all your bed in your sickness, and will you not treat others as you would wish to be treated yourself?[8]

God's Plan of Caring for the Aged—The matter of caring for our aged brethren and sisters who have no homes is constantly being urged. What can be done for them? The light which the Lord has given me has been repeated: It is not best to establish institutions for the care of the aged, that they may be in a company together. Nor should they be sent away from home to receive care. Let the members of every family minister to their own relatives. When this is not possible, the work belongs to the church, and it should be accepted both as a duty and as a privilege. All who have Christ's spirit will regard the feeble and aged with special respect and tenderness.[9]

A Privilege That Brings Satisfaction and Joy—The thought that children have ministered to the comfort of their parents is a thought of satisfaction all through the life, and will especially bring them joy when they themselves are in need of sympathy and love. Those whose hearts are filled with love will regard the privilege of smoothing the passage to the grave for their parents an inestimable privilege. They will rejoice that they had a part in bringing comfort and peace to the last days of their loved parents. To do otherwise [364] than this, to deny to the helpless aged ones the kindly ministrations of sons and daughters, would fill the soul with remorse, the days with regret, if our hearts were not hardened and cold as a stone.[10]

[365]

[366]

[1]Manuscript 18, 1891.

[2]The Review and Herald, November 15, 1892.

[3]Ibid.

[4]Ibid.

[5]Ibid.

[6]Manuscript 18, 1891.

[7]Ibid.

[8]Ibid.

[9]Testimonies For The Church 6, 272.

[10]The Review and Herald, November 15, 1892.

Section 13—The Use of Money

Chapter 60—Stewards of God

We Are to Recognize God's Ownership—That which lies at the foundation of business integrity and of true success is the recognition of God's ownership. The Creator of all things, He is the original proprietor. We are His stewards. All that we have is a trust from Him, to be used according to His direction.

This is an obligation that rests upon every human being. It has to do with the whole sphere of human activity. Whether we recognize it or not, we are stewards, supplied from God with talents and facilities and placed in the world to do a work appointed by Him.[1]

Money is not ours; houses and grounds, pictures and furniture, garments and luxuries, do not belong to us. We are pilgrims, we are strangers. We have only a grant of those things that are necessary for health and life.... Our temporal blessings are given us in trust, to prove whether we can be entrusted with eternal riches. If we endure the proving of God, then we shall receive that purchased possession which is to be our own—glory, honor, and immortality.[2]

We Must Give an Account—If our own people would only put into the cause of God the money that has been lent them in trust, that portion which they spend in selfish gratification, in idolatry, they would lay up treasure in heaven, and would be doing the very work God requires them to do. But like the rich man in the parable, they live sumptuously. The money God has lent them in trust, to be used to His name's glory, they spend extravagantly. They do not stop to consider their accountability to God. They do not stop to consider that there is to be a reckoning day not far hence, when they must give an account of their stewardship.[3]

We should ever remember that in the judgment we must meet the record of the way we use God's money. Much is spent in self-pleasing, self-gratification, that does us no real good, but positive injury. If we realize that God is the giver of all good things, that the money is His, then we shall exercise wisdom in its expenditure, conforming to His holy will. The world, its customs, its fashions, will not be our standard. We shall not have a desire to conform to its practices; we shall not permit our own inclinations to control us.[4]

In our use of money we can make it an agent of spiritual improvement by regarding it as a sacred trust, not to be employed to administer to pride, vanity, appetite, or passion.[5]

I was shown that the recording angel makes a faithful record of every offering dedicated to God and put into the treasury and also of the final result of the means thus bestowed. The eye of God takes cognizance of every farthing devoted to His cause and of the willingness or reluctance of the giver. The motive in giving is also chronicled.[6]

Systematic Giving for the Family—"Let every one of you lay by him in store, as God hath prospered him." Every member of the family, from the oldest down to the youngest, may take part in this work of benevolence.... The plan of systematic benevolence [Note: reference is here made to plans followed early by the church in laying aside weekly the tithes and offerings.—*Compilers.*] will prove a safeguard to every family against temptations to spend means for needless things, and especially will it prove a blessing to the rich by guarding them from indulging in extravagances.

[369]

Every week the demands of God upon each family are brought to mind by each of its members fully carrying out the plan; and as they have denied themselves some superfluity in order to have means to put into the treasury, lessons of value in self-denial for the glory of God have been impressed upon the heart. Once a week each is brought face to face with the doings of the past week—the income that he might have had if he had been economical, and the means that he does not have because of indulgence. His conscience is reined up, as it were, before God and either commends or accuses him. He learns that if he retains peace of mind and the favor of God, he must eat and drink and dress to His glory.[7]

Make God's Requirements First—God's requirements come first. We are not doing His will if we consecrate to Him what is left of our income after all our imaginary wants have been supplied. Before any part of our earnings is consumed, we should take out and present to Him that portion which He claims. In the old dispensation an offering of gratitude was kept continually burning upon the altar, thus showing man's endless obligation to God. If we have prosperity in our secular business, it is because God blesses us. A part of this income is to be devoted to the poor, and a large portion to be applied to the cause of God. When that which God claims is rendered to Him, the remainder will be sanctified and blessed to our own use. But when a man robs God by withholding that which He requires,

[370] His curse rests upon the whole.[8]

Remember the Needy Poor—If we represent the character of Christ, every particle of selfishness must be expelled from the soul. In carrying forward the work He gave to our hands, it will be necessary for us to give every jot and tittle of our means that we can spare. Poverty and distress in families will come to our knowledge, and afflicted and suffering ones will have to be relieved. We know very little of the human suffering that exists everywhere about us; but as we have opportunity, we should be ready to render immediate assistance to those who are under a severe pressure.[9]

The squandering of money in luxuries deprives the poor of the means necessary to supply them with food and clothing. That which is spent for the gratification of pride in dress, in buildings, in furniture, and in decorations would relieve the distress of many wretched, suffering families. God's stewards are to minister to the needy.[10]

God's Remedy for Selfishness and Covetousness—The giving that is the fruit of self-denial is a wonderful help to the giver. It imparts an education that enables us more fully to comprehend the work of Him who went about doing good, relieving the suffering, and supplying the needs of the destitute.[11]

Constant, self-denying benevolence is God's remedy for the cankering sins of selfishness and covetousness. God has arranged systematic benevolence to sustain His cause and relieve the necessities of the suffering and needy. He has ordained that giving should become a habit, that it may counteract the dangerous and deceitful sin of covetousness. Continual giving starves covetousness to death. Systematic benevolence is designed in the order of God to

[371] tear away treasures from the covetous as fast as they are gained, and to consecrate them to the Lord, to whom they belong....

The constant practice of God's plan of systematic benevolence weakens covetousness and strengthens benevolence. If riches increase, men, even those professing godliness, set their hearts upon them; and the more they have, the less they give to the treasury of the Lord. Thus riches make men selfish, and hoarding feeds covetousness; and these evils strengthen by active exercise. God knows our danger and has hedged us about with means to prevent our own ruin. He requires the constant exercise of benevolence, that the force of habit in good works may break the force of habit in an opposite direction.[12]

[372]

[1] Education, 137.

[2] Letter 8, 1889.

[3] Letter 21. 1898.

[4] Letter 8, 1889.

[5] Ibid.

[6] Testimonies For The Church 2, 518, 519.

[7] Ibid., 3:412.

[8] Ibid., 4:477.

[9] Manuscript 25, 1894.

[10] The Review and Herald. December 8. 1896.

[11] The Youth's Instructor, September 10. 1907.

[12] Testimonies For The Church 3, 548.

Chapter 61—Principles of Family Finance

Money May Be a Blessing or a Curse—Money is not necessarily a curse; it is of high value because if rightly appropriated, it can do good in the salvation of souls, in blessing others who are poorer than ourselves. By an improvident or unwise use, ... money will become a snare to the user. He who employs money to gratify pride and ambition makes it a curse rather than a blessing. Money is a constant test of the affections. Whoever acquires more than sufficient for his real needs should seek wisdom and grace to know his own heart and to keep his heart diligently, lest he have imaginary wants and become an unfaithful steward, using with prodigality his Lord's entrusted capital.

When we love God supremely, temporal things will occupy their right place in our affections. If we humbly and earnestly seek for knowledge and ability in order to make a right use of our Lord's goods, we shall receive wisdom from above. When the heart leans to its own preferences and inclinations, when the thought is cherished that money can confer happiness without the favor of God, then the money becomes a tyrant, ruling the man; it receives his confidence and esteem and is worshiped as a god. Honor, truth, righteousness, and justice are sacrificed upon its altar. The commands of God's word are set aside, and the world's customs and usages, which King Mammon has ordained, become a controlling power.[1]

Seek Security in Home Ownership—If the laws given by God had continued to be carried out, how different would be the present condition of the world, morally, spiritually, and temporally. Selfishness and self-importance would not be manifested as now, but each would cherish a kind regard for the happiness and welfare of others.... Instead of the poorer classes being kept under the iron heel of oppression by the wealthy, instead of having other men's brains to think and plan for them in temporal as well as in spiritual things, they would have some chance for independence of thought and action.

[373]

292

The sense of being owners of their own homes would inspire them with a strong desire for improvement. They would soon acquire skill in planning and devising for themselves; their children would be educated to habits of industry and economy, and the intellect would be greatly strengthened. They would feel that they are men, not slaves, and would be able to regain to a great degree their lost self-respect and moral independence.[2]

Educate our people to get out of the cities into the country, where they can obtain a small piece of land and make a home for themselves and their children.[3]

Caution Regarding Selling Homes—There are poor men and women who are writing to me for advice as to whether they shall sell their homes and give the proceeds to the cause. They say the appeals for means stir their souls, and they want to do something for the Master, who has done everything for them. I would say to such: "It may not be your duty to sell your little homes just now, but go to God for yourselves; the Lord will certainly hear your earnest prayers for wisdom to understand your duty."[4]

God does not now call for the houses His people need to live in; but if those who have an abundance do not hear His voice, cut loose from the world, and sacrifice for God, He will pass them by and will call for those who are willing to do anything for Jesus, even to sell their homes to meet the wants of the cause.[5]

[374]

A Praiseworthy Independence—Independence of one kind is praiseworthy. To desire to bear your own weight and not to eat the bread of dependence is right. It is a noble, generous ambition that dictates the wish to be self-supporting. Industrious habits and frugality are necessary.[6]

Balancing the Budget—Many, very many, have not so educated themselves that they can keep their expenditures within the limit of their income. They do not learn to adapt themselves to circumstances, and they borrow and borrow again and again and become overwhelmed in debt, and consequently they become discouraged and disheartened.[7]

Keep a Record of Expenditures—Habits of self-indulgence or a want of tact and skill on the part of the wife and mother may be a constant drain upon the treasury; and yet that mother may think she is doing her best because she has never been taught to restrict her wants or the wants of her children and has never acquired skill and tact in household matters. Hence one family may require for its support twice the amount that would suffice for another family of the same size.

All should learn how to keep accounts. Some neglect this work as nonessential, but this is wrong. All expenses should be accurately stated.[8]

[375]

The Evils of Spendthrift Habits—The Lord has been pleased to present before me the evils which result from spendthrift habits, that I might admonish parents to teach their children strict economy. Teach them that money spent for that which they do not need is perverted from its proper use.[9]

If you have extravagant habits, cut them away from your life at once. Unless you do this, you will be bankrupt for eternity. Habits of economy, industry, and sobriety are a better portion for your children than a rich dowry.

We are pilgrims and strangers on the earth. Let us not spend our means in gratifying desires that God would have us repress. Let us fitly represent our faith by restricting our wants.[10]

A Parent Reproved for Extravagance—You do not know how to use money economically and do not learn to bring your wants within your income.... You have an eager desire to get money, that you may freely use it as your inclination shall dictate, and your teaching and example have proved a curse to your children. How little they care for principle! They are more and more forgetful of God, less fearful of His displeasure, more impatient of restraint. The more easily money is obtained, the less thankfulness is felt.[11]

To a Family Living Beyond Its Means—You ought to be careful that your expenses do not exceed your income. Bind about your wants.

It is a great pity that your wife is so much like you in this matter of expending means so that she cannot be a help to you in this direction, to watch the little outgoes in order to avoid the larger leaks. Needless expenses are constantly brought about in your family management.

[376]

Your wife loves to see her children dress in a manner beyond their means, and because of this, tastes and habits are cultivated in your children which will make them vain and proud. If you would learn the lesson of economy and see the peril to yourselves and to your children and to the cause of God in this free use of means, you would obtain an experience essential to the perfection of your Christian character. Unless you do obtain such an experience, your children will bear the mold of a defective education as long as they live....

I would not influence you to hoard up means—it would be difficult for you to do this—but I would counsel you both to expend your money carefully and let your daily example teach lessons of frugality, self-denial, and economy to your children. They need to be educated by precept and example.[12]

A Family Called to Self-denial—I was shown that you, my brother and sister, have much to learn. You have not lived within your means. You have not learned to economize. If you earn high wages, you do not know how to make it go as far as possible. You consult taste or appetite instead of prudence. At times you expend money for a quality of food in which your brethren cannot afford to indulge. Dollars slip from your pocket very easily.... Self-denial is a lesson which you both have yet to learn.[13]

Parents should learn to live within their means. They should cultivate self-denial in their children, teaching them by precept and example. They should make their wants few and simple, that there may be time for mental improvement and spiritual culture.[14]

Indulgence Not an Expression of Love—Do not educate your children to think that your love for them must be expressed by indulgence of their pride, extravagance, and love of display. There is no time now to invent ways for using up money. Use your inventive faculties in seeking to economize.[15]

[377]

Economy Consistent With Generosity—The natural turn of youth in this age is to neglect and despise economy and to confound it with stinginess and narrowness. But economy is consistent with the most broad and liberal views and feelings; there can be no true generosity where it is not practiced. No one should think it beneath him to study.[16]

The Other Extreme—Unwise Economy—God is not honored when the body is neglected or abused and is thus unfitted for His service. To care for the body by providing for it food that is relishable and strengthening is one of the first duties of the householder. It is far better to have less expensive clothing and furniture than to stint the supply of food.

Some householders stint the family table in order to provide expensive entertainment for visitors. This is unwise. In the entertainment of guests there should be greater simplicity. Let the needs of the family have first attention.

Unwise economy and artificial customs often prevent the exercise of hospitality where it is needed and would be a blessing. The regular supply of food for our tables should be such that the unexpected guest can be made welcome without burdening the housewife to make extra preparation.[17]

[378]   Our economy must never be of that kind which would lead to providing meager meals. Students should have an abundance of wholesome food. But let those in charge of the cooking gather up the fragments that nothing be lost.[18]

Economy does not mean niggardliness, but a prudent expenditure of means because there is a great work to be done.[19]

Provide Conveniences to Lighten Wife's Labor—Brother E's family live in accordance with the principles of strictest economy.... Brother E had conscientiously decided not to build a convenient woodshed and kitchen for his large family, because he did not feel free to invest means in personal conveniences when the cause of God needed money to carry it forward. I tried to show him that it was necessary for the health as well as the morals of his children that he should make home pleasant and provide conveniences to lighten the labor of his wife.[20]

Wife's Allowance for Personal Use—You must help each other. Do not look upon it as a virtue to hold fast the purse strings, refusing to give your wife money.[21]

You should allow your wife a certain sum weekly and should let her do what she please with this money. You have not given her opportunity to exercise her tact or her taste because you have not a proper realization of the position that a wife should occupy. Your wife has an excellent and a well-balanced mind.[22]

Give your wife a share of the money that you receive. Let her have this as her own, and let her use it as she desires. She should have been allowed to use the means that she earned as she in her judgment deemed best. If she had had a certain sum to use as her own, without being criticized, a great weight would have been lifted [379]   from her mind.[23]

Seek Comfort and Health—Brother P has not made a judicious use of means. Wise judgment has not influenced him as much as have the voices and desires of his children. He does not place the estimate that he should upon the means in his hands, and expend it cautiously for the most needful articles, for the very things he must have for comfort and health. The entire family need to improve in this respect. Many things are needed in the family for convenience and comfort. The lack of appreciating order and system in the arrangement of family matters leads to destructiveness and working to great disadvantage.[24]

We cannot make the heart purer or holier by clothing the body in sackcloth or depriving the home of all that ministers to comfort, taste, or convenience.[25]

God does not require that His people should deprive themselves of that which is really necessary for their health and comfort, but He does not approve of wantonness and extravagance and display.[26]

Learn When to Spare and When to Spend—You should learn to know when to spare and when to spend. We cannot be Christ's followers unless we deny self and lift the cross. We should pay up squarely as we go; gather up the dropped stitches; bind off your raveling edges, and know just what you can call your own. You should reckon up all the littles spent in self-gratification. You should notice what is used simply to gratify taste and in cultivating a perverted, epicurean appetite. The money expended for useless delicacies might be used to add to your substantial home comforts and conveniences. You are not to be penurious; you are to be honest with yourself and your brethren. Penuriousness is an abuse of God's bounties. Lavishness is also an abuse. The little outgoes that you think of as [380] not worth mentioning amount to considerable in the end.[27]

The Surrendered Heart Will Be Guided—It is not necessary to specify here how economy may be practiced in every particular. Those whose hearts are fully surrendered to God, and who take His word as their guide, will know how to conduct themselves in all the duties of life. They will learn of Jesus, who is meek and lowly of heart; and in cultivating the meekness of Christ, they will close the door against innumerable temptations.[28] [381]

[1]Letter 8, 1889.

[2]Historical Sketches of The S.D.A. Foreign Mission, 165, 166.

[3] General Conference Bulletin, Church and Sabbath School, April 6, 1903.

[4]Testimonies For The Church 5, 734.

[5]The Review and Herald, September 16, 1884.

[6]Testimonies For The Church 2, 308.

[7]The Review and Herald, December 19, 1983.

[8]Gospel Workers, 460.

[9]Christian Temperance and Bible Hygiene, 63.

[10]The Review and Herald, December 24, 1903.

[11]Letter 8, 1889.

[12]Letter 23, 1888.

[13]Testimonies For The Church 2, 431, 432.

[14]The Review and Herald, June 24, 1890.

[15]Testimonies For The Church 6: 451.

[16]Ibid., 5:400.

[17]The Ministry of Healing, 322.

[18]Testimonies For The Church 6, 209.

[19]Letter 151, 1899.

[20]Letter 9, 1888.

[21]Letter 65, 1904.

[22]Letter 47, 1904.

[23]Letter 157, 1903.

[24]Testimonies For The Church 2, 699.

[25]The Review and Herald, May 16, 1882.

[26]The Review and Herald, December 19, 1893.

[27]Letter 11, 1888.

[28]Christian Temperance and Bible Hygiene, 63.

Chapter 62—Economy to be Practiced

"Gather Up the Fragments."—Christ once gave His disciples a lesson upon economy which is worthy of careful attention. He wrought a miracle to feed the hungry thousands who had listened to His teachings; yet after all had eaten and were satisfied, He did not permit the fragments to be wasted. He who could, in their necessity, feed the vast multitude by His divine power bade His disciples gather up the fragments, that nothing might be lost. This lesson was given as much for our benefit as for those living in Christ's day. The Son of God has a care for the necessities of temporal life. He did not neglect the broken fragments after the feast, although He could make such a feast whenever He chose.[1]

The lessons of Jesus Christ are to be carried into every phase of practical life. Economy is to be practiced in all things. Gather up the fragments, that nothing be lost. There is a religion that does not touch the heart and therefore becomes a form of words. It is not brought into practical life. Religious duty and the highest human prudence in business lines must be co-mingled.[2]

Follow Christ in Self-denial—In order to become acquainted with the disappointments and trials and griefs that come to human beings, Christ reached to the lowest depths of woe and humiliation. He has traveled the path that He asks His followers to travel. He says to them, "If any man will come after Me, let him deny himself, and take up his cross daily, and follow Me." But professing Christians are not always willing to practice the self-denial that the Saviour calls for. They are not willing to bind about their wishes and desires [382] in order that they may have more to give to the Lord. One says, "My family are expensive in their tastes, and it costs much to keep them." This shows that he and they need to learn the lessons of economy taught by the life of Christ....

To all comes the temptation to gratify selfish, extravagant desires, but let us remember that the Lord of life and glory came to this world to teach humanity the lesson of self-denial.[3]

299

Those who do not live for self will not use up every dollar meeting their supposed wants and supplying their conveniences, but will bear in mind that they are Christ's followers, and that there are others who are in need of food and clothing.[4]

Economize to Help God's Cause—Much might be said to the young people regarding their privilege to help the cause of God by learning lessons of economy and self-denial. Many think that they must indulge in this pleasure and that, and in order to do this, they accustom themselves to live up to the full extent of their income. God wants us to do better in this respect. We sin against ourselves when we are satisfied with enough to eat and drink and wear. God has something higher than this before us. When we are willing to put away our selfish desires and give the powers of heart and mind to the work of the cause of God, heavenly agencies will co-operate with us, making us a blessing to humanity.

Even though he may be poor, the youth who is industrious and economical can save a little for the cause of God.[5]

[383] **When Tempted to Needless Spending**—When you are tempted to spend money for knickknacks, you should remember the self-denial and self-sacrifice that Christ endured to save fallen man. Our children should be taught to exercise self-denial and self-control. The reason so many ministers feel that they have a hard time in financial matters is that they do not bind about their tastes, their appetites and inclinations. The reason so many men become bankrupt and dishonestly appropriate means is because they seek to gratify the extravagant tastes of their wives and children. How careful should fathers and mothers be to teach economy by precept and example to their children![6]

I wish I could impress on every mind the grievous sinfulness of wasting the Lord's money on fancied wants. The expenditure of sums that look small may start a train of circumstances that will reach into eternity. When the judgment shall sit, and the books are opened, the losing side will be presented to your view—the good that you might have done with the accumulated mites and the larger sums that were used for wholly selfish purposes.[7]

Watch the Pennies and Nickels—Waste not your pennies and your shillings in purchasing unnecessary things. You may think these little sums do not amount to much, but these many littles will prove a great whole. If we could, we would plead for the means that is spent in needless things, in dress and selfish indulgence. Poverty in every shape is on every hand. And God has made it our duty to relieve suffering humanity in every way possible.

The Lord would have His people thoughtful and caretaking. He would have them study economy in everything, and waste nothing.[8]   [384]

The amount daily spent in needless things, with the thought, "It is only a nickel," "It is only a dime," seems very little; but multiply these littles by the days of the year, and as the years go by, the array of figures will seem almost incredible.[9]

Do Not Emulate Fashionable Neighbors—It is not best to pretend to be rich, or anything above what we are—humble followers of the meek and lowly Saviour. We are not to feel disturbed if our neighbors build and furnish their houses in a manner that we are not authorized to follow. How must Jesus look upon our selfish provision for the indulgence of appetite, to please our guests, or to gratify our own inclination! It is a snare to us to aim at making a display or to allow our children, under our control, to do so.[10]

Personal Experience in Mrs. White's Girlhood—When I was only twelve years old, I knew what it was to economize. With my sister I learned a trade, and although we would earn only twenty-five cents a day, from this sum we were able to save a little to give to missions. We saved little by little until we had thirty dollars. Then when the message of the Lord's soon coming came to us, with a call for men and means, we felt it a privilege to hand over the thirty dollars to father, asking him to invest it in tracts and pamphlets to send the message to those who were in darkness....

With the money that we had earned at our trade, my sister and I provided ourselves with clothes. We would hand our money to mother, saying, "Buy so that, after we have paid for our clothing, there will be something left to give for missionary work." And she would do this, thus encouraging in us a missionary spirit.[11]   [385]

Practice Economy From Principle—Those whose hands are open to respond to the calls for means to sustain the cause of God and to relieve the suffering and the needy are not the ones who are found loose and lax and dilatory in their business management. They are always careful to keep their outgoes within their income. They are economical from principle; they feel it their duty to save, that [386] they may have something to give.[12]

[1] Testimonies For The Church 4, 572, 573.

[2] Manuscript 31, 1897.

[3] Letter 4a, 1902.

[4] The Review and Herald, August 21, 1894.

[5] The Youth's Instructor, September 10, 1907.

[6] Letter 11, 1888.

[7] The Review and Herald, August 11, 1891.

[8] Letter 21, 1898.

[9] Christian Temperance and Bible Hygiene, 63.

[10] Letter 8, 1889.

[11] The Youth's Instructor, September 10, 1907.

[12] Testimonies For The Church 4, 573.

Chapter 63—Instructing Children How to Earn and Use Money

Teach Simple Habits in Daily Life—Parents are to bring up and educate and train their children in habits of self-control and self-denial. They are ever to keep before them their obligation to obey the word of God and to live for the purpose of serving Jesus. They are to educate their children that there is need of living in accordance with simple habits in their daily life, and to avoid expensive dress, expensive diet, expensive houses, and expensive furniture.[1]

When very young, children should be educated to read, to write, to understand figures, to keep their own accounts. They may go forward, advancing step by step in this knowledge. But before everything else, they should be taught that the fear of the Lord is the beginning of wisdom.[2]

Youth to Be Considerate of Family Finance—Through erroneous ideas regarding the use of money the youth are exposed to many dangers. They are not to be carried along and supplied with money as if there were an inexhaustible supply from which they could draw to gratify every supposed need. Money is to be regarded as a gift entrusted to us of God to do His work, to build up His kingdom, and the youth should learn to restrict their desires.[3]

Do not make your wants many, especially if the income for home expenses is limited. Bring your wants within your parents' means. The Lord will recognize and commend your unselfish efforts.... Be [387] faithful in that which is least. You will then be in no danger of neglecting greater responsibilities. God's word declares, "He that is faithful in that which is least is faithful also in much."[4]

Give Lessons in Money Values—Money which comes to the young with but little effort on their part will not be valued. Some have to obtain money by hard work and privation, but how much safer are those youth who know just where their spending money comes from, who know what their clothing and food costs, and what it takes to purchase a home!

303

There are many ways in which children can earn money themselves and can act their part in bringing thank offerings to Jesus, who gave His own life for them.... They should be taught that the money which they earn is not theirs to spend as their inexperienced minds may choose, but to use judiciously and to give to missionary purposes. They should not be satisfied to take money from their father or mother and put it into the treasury as an offering, when it is not theirs. They should say to themselves, "Shall I give of that which costs me nothing?"[5]

There is such a thing as giving unwise help to our children. Those who work their way through college appreciate their advantages more than those who are provided with them at someone else's expense, for they know their cost. We must not carry our children until they become helpless burdens.[6]

Parents mistake their duty when they freely hand out money to any youth who has physical strength to enter on a course of study to become a minister or a physician before he has had an experience in useful, taxing labor.[7]

[388] **Encourage Children to Earn Their Own Money**—Many a child who lives out of the city can have a little plot of land where he can learn to garden. He can be taught to make this a means of securing money to give to the cause of God. Both boys and girls can engage in this work; and it will, if they are rightly instructed, teach them the value of money and how to economize. It is possible for the children, besides raising money for missionary purposes, to be able to help in buying their own clothes, and they should be encouraged to do this.[8]

Discourage the Reckless Use of Money—Oh, how much money we waste on useless articles in the house, on ruffles and fancy dress, and on candies and other articles we do not need! Parents, teach your children that it is wrong to use God's money in self-gratification.... Encourage them to save their pennies wherever possible, to be used in missionary work. They will gain rich experiences through the practice of self-denial, and such lessons will often keep them from acquiring habits of intemperance.[9]

The children may learn to show their love for Christ by denying themselves needless trifles, for the purchase of which much money slips through their fingers. In every family this work should be done.

It requires tact and method, but it will be the best education the children can receive. And if all the little children would present their offerings to the Lord, their gifts would be as little rivulets which, when united and set flowing, would swell into a river.[10]

Keep a little money box on the mantel or in some safe place where it can be seen, in which the children can place their offerings for the Lord.... Thus they may be trained for God.[11]

[389]

Teach Children to Pay Tithe and Offerings—Not only does the Lord claim the tithe as His own, but He tells us how it should be reserved for Him. He says, "Honour the Lord with thy substance, and with the firstfruits of all thine increase." This does not teach that we are to spend our means on ourselves and bring to the Lord the remnant, even though it should be otherwise an honest tithe. Let God's portion be first set apart. The directions given by the Holy Spirit through the Apostle Paul in regard to gifts present a principle that applies also to tithing. "Upon the first day of the week let every one of you lay by him in store, as God hath prospered him." Parents and children are here included.[12]

A Mistake Sometimes Made by Wealthy Fathers—The circumstances in which a child is placed will often have a more effective influence on him than even the example of parents. There are wealthy men who expect their children to be what they were in their youth, and blame the depravity of the age if they are not. But they have no right to expect this of their children unless they place them in circumstances similar to those in which they themselves have lived. The circumstances of the father's life have made him what he is. In his youth he was pressed with poverty and had to work with diligence and perseverance. His character was molded in the stern school of poverty. He was forced to be modest in his wants, active in his work, simple in his tastes. He had to put his faculties to work in order to obtain food and clothing. He had to practice economy.

Fathers labor to place their children in a position of wealth, rather than where they themselves began. This is a common mistake. Had children today to learn in the same school in which their fathers learned, they would become as useful as they. The fathers have altered the circumstances of their children. Poverty was the father's master; abundance of means surrounds the son. All his wants are supplied. His father's character was molded under the severe dis-

[390]

cipline of frugality; every trifling good was appreciated. His son's habits and character will be formed, not by the circumstances which once existed, but by the present situation—ease and indulgence.... When luxury abounds on every side, how can it be denied him?[13]

Parents' Best Legacy to Children—The very best legacy which parents can leave their children is a knowledge of useful labor and the example of a life characterized by disinterested benevolence. By such a life they show the true value of money, that it is only to be appreciated for the good that it will accomplish in relieving their own wants and the necessities of others, and in advancing [391] the cause of God.[14]

[1] The Review and Herald, November 13, 1894.

[2] Counsels to Teachers, Parents, and Students, 168, 169.

[3] Testimonies For The Church 6, 214, 215.

[4] Manuscript 2, 1903.

[5] Letter 11, 1888.

[6] Letter 50, 1895.

[7] Letter 103, 1900.

[8] Letter 356, 1907.

[9] The Youth's Instructor, November 1, 1904.

[10] The Review and Herald, December 25, 1900.

[11] Manuscript 128, 1901.

[12] The Review and Herald, November 10, 1896.

[13] Manuscript 58, 1899.

[14] Testimonies For The Church 3, 399.

Chapter 64—Business Integrity

The Bible a Source Book of Business Principles—There is no branch of legitimate business for which the Bible does not afford an essential preparation. Its principles of diligence, honesty, thrift, temperance, and purity are the secret of true success. These principles, as set forth in the Book of Proverbs, constitute a treasury of practical wisdom. Where can the merchant, the artisan, the director of men in any department of business, find better maxims for himself or for his employees than are found in these words of the wise man:

"Seest thou a man diligent in his business? He shall stand before kings; he shall not stand before mean men."

"In all labour there is profit: but the talk of the lips tendeth only to penury."

"The soul of the sluggard desireth, and hath nothing."

"The drunkard and the glutton shall come to poverty: and drowsiness shall clothe a man with rags." ...

How many a man might have escaped financial failure and ruin by heeding the warnings so often repeated and emphasized in the Scriptures:

"He that maketh haste to be rich shall not be innocent."

"Wealth gotten in haste shall be diminished; but he that gathereth by labor shall have increase."

"The getting of treasures by a lying tongue is a vanity tossed to and fro of them that seek death."

"The borrower is servant to the lender."

"He that is surety for a stranger shall smart for it: and he that hateth suretiship is sure."[1]

The eighth commandment condemns ... theft and robbery. It demands strict integrity in the minutest details of the affairs of life. It forbids overreaching in trade and requires the payment of just debts or wages."[2]

Mind and Character Degraded by Dishonesty—He [one who utters falsehood or practices deception] loses his own self-respect.

[392]

307

He may not be conscious that God sees him and is acquainted with every business transaction, that holy angels are weighing his motives and listening to his words, and that his reward will be according to his works; but if it were possible to conceal his wrongdoing from human and divine inspection, the fact that he himself knows it is degrading to his mind and character. One act does not determine the character, but it breaks down the barrier, and the next temptation is more readily entertained, until finally a habit of prevarication and dishonesty in business is formed, and the man cannot be trusted.[3]

As we deal with our fellow men in petty dishonesty or in more daring fraud, so will we deal with God. Men who persist in a course of dishonesty will carry out their principles until they cheat their own souls and lose heaven and eternal life. They will sacrifice honor and religion for a small worldly advantage.[4]

Shun Debt—Many poor families are poor because they spend their money as soon as they receive it.[5]

You must see that one should not manage his affairs in a way that will incur debt.... When one becomes involved in debt, he is in one of Satan's nets, which he sets for souls....

[393] Abstracting and using money for any purpose, before it is earned, is a snare.[6]

Words to One Who Lived Beyond His Income—You ought not to allow yourself to become financially embarrassed, for the fact that you are in debt weakens your faith and tends to discourage you; and even the thought of it makes you nearly wild. You need to cut down your expenses and strive to supply this deficiency in your character. You can and should make determined efforts to bring under control your disposition to spend means beyond your income.[7]

The Cause of God May Be Reproached—The world has a right to expect strict integrity in those who profess to be Bible Christians. By one man's indifference in regard to paying his just dues all our people are in danger of being regarded as unreliable.[8]

Those who make any pretensions to godliness should adorn the doctrine they profess, and not give occasion for the truth to be reviled through their inconsiderate course of action. "Owe no man any thing," says the apostle.[9]

Counsel to One in Debt—Be determined never to incur another debt. Deny yourself a thousand things rather than run in debt. This has been the curse of your life, getting into debt. Avoid it as you would the smallpox.

Make a solemn covenant with God that by His blessing you will pay your debts and then owe no man anything if you live on porridge and bread. It is so easy in preparing your table to throw out of your pocket twenty-five cents for extras. Take care of the pennies, and the dollars will take care of themselves. It is the mites here and the mites there that are spent for this, that, and the other that soon run up into dollars. Deny self at least while you are walled in with debts.... Do not falter, be discouraged, or turn back. Deny your taste, deny the indulgence of appetite, save your pence, and pay your debts. [394] Work them off as fast as possible. When you can stand forth a free man again, owing no man anything, you will have achieved a great victory.[10]

Show Consideration for Unfortunate Debtors—If some are found to be in debt and really unable to meet their obligations, they should not be pressed to do that which is beyond their power. They should be given a favorable chance to discharge their indebtedness, and not be placed in a position where they are utterly unable to free themselves from debt. Though such a course might be considered justice, it is not mercy and the love of God.[11]

Danger in Extreme Positions—Some are not discreet and would incur debts that might be avoided. Others exercise a caution that savors of unbelief. By taking advantage of circumstances we may at times invest means to such advantage that the work of God will be strengthened and upbuilt, and yet keep strictly to right principles.[12] [395]

---

[1]Education, 135, 136.

[2]Patriarchs and Prophets, 309.

[3]Testimonies For The Church 5, 396.

[4]The Review and Herald, September 18, 1888.

[5]Counsels on Stewardship, 269.

[6]Letter 63, 1997.

[7]Letter 48, 1888.

[8]Testimonies For The Church 5, 179.

[9]Ibid., 5:181, 182.

[10]Counsels on Stewardship, 257.

[11]Manuscript 46, 1900.

[12]Manuscript 20, 1891.

Chapter 65—Provision for the Future

Home Ownership and Savings Versus Spendthrift Habits—Brother and Sister B have not learned the lesson of economy.... They would use all as they pass along, were it ever so much. They would enjoy as they go and then, when affliction draws upon them, would be wholly unprepared.... Had Brother and Sister B been economical managers, denying themselves, they could ere this have had a home of their own and besides this have had means to draw upon in case of adversity. But they will not economize as others have done, upon whom they have sometimes been dependent. If they neglect to learn these lessons, their characters will not be found perfect in the day of God.[1]

This Counsel May Help You—You have been in a business which would at times yield you large profits at once. After you have earned means, you have not studied to economize in reference to a time when means could not be earned so easily, but have expended much for imaginary wants. Had you and your wife understood it to be a duty that God enjoined upon you to deny your taste and your desires and make provision for the future instead of living merely for the present, you could now have had a competency and your family have had the comforts of life. You have a lesson to learn.... It is to make a little go the longest way.[2]

[396] **To a Family That Should Save Systematically**—You might today have had a capital of means to use in case of emergency and to aid the cause of God, if you had economized as you should. Every week a portion of your wages should be reserved and in no case touched unless suffering actual want, or to render back to the Giver in offerings to God....

The means you have earned has not been wisely and economically expended so as to leave a margin should you be sick and your family deprived of the means you bring to sustain them. Your family should have something to rely upon if you should be brought into straitened places.[3]

Another Family Advised Concerning a Savings Account—Every week you should lay by in some secure place five or ten dollars not to be used up unless in case of sickness. With economy you may place something at interest. With wise management you can save something after paying your debts.[4]

I have known a family receiving twenty dollars a week to spend every penny of this amount, while another family of the same size, receiving but twelve dollars a week, laid aside one or two dollars a week, managing to do this by refraining from purchasing things which seemed to be necessary but which could be dispensed with.[5]

Make Property Secure by Proper Will—Those who are faithful stewards of the Lord's means will know just how their business stands, and, like wise men, they will be prepared for any emergency. Should their probation close suddenly, they would not leave such great perplexity upon those who are called to settle their estate.

Many are not exercised upon the subject of making their wills while they are in apparent health. But this precaution should be taken by our brethren. They should know their financial standing and should not allow their business to become entangled. They should arrange their property in such a manner that they may leave it at any time.

[397]

Wills should be made in a manner to stand the test of law. After they are drawn, they may remain for years and do no harm, if donations continue to be made from time to time as the cause has need. Death will not come one day sooner, brethren, because you have made your will. In disposing of your property by will to your relatives, be sure that you do not forget God's cause. You are His agents, holding His property; and His claims should have your first consideration. Your wife and children, of course, should not be left destitute; provision should be made for them if they are needy. But do not, simply because it is customary, bring into your will a long line of relatives who are not needy.[6]

Remember God's Cause While Living—Let no one think that he will meet the mind of Christ in hoarding up property through life and then at death making a bequest of a portion of it to some benevolent cause.[7]

Some selfishly retain their means during their lifetime, trusting to make up for their neglect by remembering the cause in their wills.

But not half the means thus bestowed in legacies ever benefits the object specified. Brethren and sisters, invest in the bank of heaven yourselves, and do not leave your stewardship upon another.[8]

Stewardship Transferred to Children Is Often Unwise—Parents should have great fear in entrusting children with the talents of means that God has placed in their hands, unless they have the surest evidence that their children have greater interest in, love for, and devotion to the cause of God than they themselves possess, and that these children will be more earnest and zealous in forwarding the work of God and more benevolent in carrying forward the various enterprises connected with in which call for means. But many place their means in the hands of their children, thus throwing upon them the responsibility of their own stewardship because Satan prompts them to do it. In so doing they effectually place that means in the enemy's ranks. Satan works the matter to suit his own purpose and keeps from the cause of God the means which it needs, that it may be abundantly sustained.[9]

The Curse of Hoarded Wealth—Those who acquire wealth for the purpose of hoarding it leave the curse of wealth to their children. It is a sin, an awful, soul-periling sin for fathers and mothers to do this, and this sin extends to their posterity. Often the children spend their means in foolish extravagance, in riotous living, so that they become beggars. They know not the value of the inheritance they have squandered. Had their fathers and mothers set them a proper example, not in hoarding but in imparting their wealth, they would have laid up for themselves treasure in heaven and received a return even in this world of peace and happiness and in the future life eternal riches.[10]

[398]

[399]

[400]

---

[1]Testimonies For The Church 3, 30, 31.
[2]Testimonies For The Church 2, 432, 433.
[3]Letter 5, 1877.
[4]Uncopied Letter 49, 1884.
[5]Letter 156, 1901.
[6]Testimonies For The Church 4, 482.
[7]The Review and Herald, February 27, 1894.
[8]The Review and Herald, October 12, 1886.
[9]Testimonies For The Church 2, 655.
[10]Letter 20, 1897.

Section 14—Guarding the Avenues of the Soul

Chapter 66—The Portals We Must Watch

Why God Gave Us Eyes, Ears, and Speech—God gave men eyes, that they might behold wondrous things out of His law. He gave them the hearing ear, that they might listen to His message, spoken by the living preacher. He gave men the talent of speech, that they might present Christ as the sin-pardoning Saviour. With the heart man believeth unto righteousness, and with the mouth confession is made unto salvation.[1]

How Satan Gains Entrance to the Soul—All should guard the senses, lest Satan gain victory over them; for these are the avenues of the soul.[2]

You will have to become a faithful sentinel over your eyes, ears, and all your senses if you would control your mind and prevent vain and corrupt thoughts from staining your soul. The power of grace alone can accomplish this most desirable work.[3]

Satan and his angels are busy creating a paralyzed condition of the senses so that cautions, warnings, and reproofs shall not be heard; or, if heard, that they shall not take effect upon the heart and reform the life.[4]

My brethren, God calls upon you as His followers to walk in the light. You need to be alarmed. Sin is among us, and it is not seen to be exceedingly sinful. The senses of many are benumbed by the indulgence of appetite and by familiarity with sin. We need to advance nearer heaven.[5]

Satan's Strategy Is to Confuse the Senses—Satan's work is to

lead men to ignore God, to so engross and absorb the mind that God will not be in their thoughts. The education they have received has been of a character to confuse the mind and eclipse the true light. Satan does not wish the people to have a knowledge of God; and if he can set in operation games and theatrical performances that will so confuse the senses of the young that human beings will perish in darkness while light shines all about them, he is well pleased.[6]

Satan Cannot Enter the Mind Without Our Consent—We should present before the people the fact that God has provided that we shall not be tempted above what we are able to bear, but that with every temptation He will make a way of escape. If we live wholly for God, we shall not allow the mind to indulge in selfish imaginings.

If there is any way by which Satan can gain access to the mind, he will sow his tares and cause them to grow until they will yield an abundant harvest. In no case can Satan obtain dominion over the thoughts, words, and actions, unless we voluntarily open the door and invite him to enter. He will then come in and, by catching away the good seed sown in the heart, make of none effect the truth.[7]

Close Every Avenue to the Tempter—All who name the name of Christ need to watch and pray and guard the avenues of the soul, for Satan is at work to corrupt and destroy if the least advantage is given him.[8]

It is not safe for us to linger to contemplate the advantages to be reaped through yielding to Satan's suggestions. Sin means dishonor and disaster to every soul that indulges in it; but it is blinding and deceiving in its nature, and it will entice us with flattering presentations. If we venture on Satan's ground, we have no assurance of protection from his power. So far as in us lies, we should close every avenue by which the tempter may find access to us.[9]

[403]

Who can know, in the moment of temptation, the terrible consequences which will result from one wrong, hasty step! Our only safety is to be shielded by the grace of God every moment, and not put out our own spiritual eyesight so that we will call evil, good, and good, evil. Without hesitation or argument we must close and guard the avenues of the soul against evil.[10]

Every Christian must stand on guard continually, watching every avenue of the soul where Satan might find access. He must pray for divine help and at the same time resolutely resist every inclination to sin. By courage, by faith, by persevering toil, he can conquer. But let him remember that to gain the victory Christ must abide in him and he in Christ.[11]

Avoid Reading, Seeing, or Hearing Evil—The apostle [Peter] sought to teach the believers how important it is to keep the mind from wandering to forbidden themes or from spending its energies on trifling subjects. Those who would not fall a prey to Satan's devices must guard well the avenues of the soul; they must avoid reading, seeing, or hearing that which will suggest impure thoughts. The mind must not be left to dwell at random upon every subject that the enemy of souls may suggest. The heart must be faithfully sentineled, or evils without will awaken evils within, and the soul will wander in darkness.[12]

[404]   Everything that can be done should be done to place ourselves and our children where we shall not see the iniquity that is practiced in the world. We should carefully guard the sight of our eyes and the hearing of our ears so that these awful things shall not enter our minds. When the daily newspaper comes into the house, I feel as if I want to hide it, that the ridiculous, sensational things in it may not be seen. It seems as if the enemy is at the foundation of the publishing of many things that appear in newspapers. Every sinful thing that can be found is uncovered and laid bare before the world.[13]

Those who would have that wisdom which is from God must become fools in the sinful knowledge of this age, in order to be wise. They should shut their eyes, that they may see and learn no evil. They should close their ears, lest they hear that which is evil and obtain that knowledge which would stain their purity of thoughts and acts. And they should guard their tongues, lest they utter corrupt communications and guile be found in their mouths.[14]

Resistance Is Weakened by Opening the Door—Do not see how close you can walk upon the brink of a precipice and be safe. Avoid the first approach to danger. The soul's interests cannot be trifled with. Your capital is your character. Cherish it as you would a golden treasure. Moral purity, self-respect, a strong power of resistance, must be firmly and constantly cherished. There should not be one departure from reserve; one act of familiarity, one indiscretion, may jeopardize the soul in opening the door to temptation, and the power of resistance becomes weakened.[15]

Satan Would Eclipse the Future Glories—Satan has worked continually to eclipse the glories of the future world and to attract the whole attention to the things of this life. He has striven so to
[405]   arrange matters that our thought, our anxiety, our labor might be so fully employed in temporal things that we should not see or realize the value of eternal realities. The world and its cares have too large

a place, while Jesus and heavenly things have altogether too small a share in our thoughts and affections. We should conscientiously discharge all the duties of everyday life, but it is also essential that we should cultivate, above everything else, holy affection for our Lord Jesus Christ.[16]

Heavenly Angels Will Help Us—We should ever keep in mind that unseen agencies are at work, both evil and good, to take the control of the mind. They act with unseen yet effectual power. Good angels are ministering spirits, exerting a heavenly influence upon heart and mind; while the great adversary of souls, the devil, and his angels are continually laboring to accomplish our destruction....

While we should be keenly alive to our exposure to the assaults of unseen and invisible foes, we are to be sure that they cannot harm us without gaining our consent.[17]

[406]

[1] Letter 21, 1899.

[2] Testimonies For The Church 3, 507.

[3] Testimonies For The Church 2, 561.

[4] Ibid., 5:493.

[5] Ibid., 3:476.

[6] The Review and Herald, March 13, 1900.

[7] The Review and Herald, July 11, 1893.

[8] Testimonies For The Church 3, 476.

[9] Thoughts from the Mount of Blessing, 118.

[10] Testimonies For The Church 3, 324.

[11] Ibid., 5:47.

[12] The Acts of the Apostols, 518, 519.

[13] Notebook Leaflets from the Elmshaven Library, Education, Volume 1 (1845).

[14] A Solemn Appeal, 76.

[15] Medical Ministry, 143.

[16] The Review and Herald, January 7, 1890.

[17] The Review and Herald, July 19, 1887.

Chapter 67—Enticing Sights and Sounds

Evil Sights and Sounds All About Us—There is reason for deep solicitude on your part for your children, who have temptations to encounter at every advance step. It is impossible for them to avoid contact with evil associates.... They will see sights, hear sounds, and be subjected to influences which are demoralizing and which, unless they are thoroughly guarded, will imperceptibly but surely corrupt the heart and deform the character.[1]

All Need a Bulwark Against Temptation—In Christian homes a bulwark should be built against temptation. Satan is using every means to make crime and degrading vice popular. We cannot walk the streets of our cities without encountering flaring notices of crime presented in some novel or to be acted at some theater. The mind is educated to familiarity with sin. The course pursued by the base and vile is kept before the people in the periodicals of the day, and everything that can arouse passion is brought before them in exciting stories.[2]

Some fathers and mothers are so indifferent, so careless, that they think it makes no difference whether their children attend a church school or a public school. "We are in the world," they say, "and we cannot get out of it." But, parents, we can get a good way out of the world, if we choose to do so. We can avoid seeing many of the evils that are multiplying so fast in these last days. We can [407] avoid hearing about much of the wickedness and crime that exist.[3]

Sow Lawlessness, Reap a Harvest of Crime—Many of the popular publications of the day are filled with sensational stories that are educating the youth in wickedness and leading them in the path to perdition. Mere children in years are old in a knowledge of crime. They are incited to evil by the tales they read. In imagination they act over the deeds portrayed, until their ambition is aroused to see what they can do in committing crime and evading punishment.

To the active minds of children and youth the scenes pictured in imaginary revelations of the future are realities. As revolutions

318

are predicted and all manner of proceedings described that break down the barriers of law and self-restraint, many catch the spirit of these representations. They are led to the commission of crimes even worse, if possible, than these sensational writers depict. Through such influences as these society is becoming demoralized. The seeds of lawlessness are sown broadcast. None need marvel that a harvest of crime is the result.[4]

The Lure of Popular Music—I feel alarmed as I witness everywhere the frivolity of young men and young women who profess to believe the truth. God does not seem to be in their thoughts. Their minds are filled with nonsense. Their conversation is only empty, vain talk. They have a keen ear for music, and Satan knows what organs to excite to animate, engross, and charm the mind so that Christ is not desired. The spiritual longings of the soul for divine knowledge, for a growth in grace, are wanting.

I was shown that the youth must take a higher stand and make the word of God the man of their counsel and their guide. Solemn responsibilities rest upon the young, which they lightly regard. The introduction of music into their homes, instead of inciting to holiness and spirituality, has been the means of diverting their minds from the truth. Frivolous songs and the popular sheet music of the day seem congenial to their taste. The instruments of music have taken time which should have been devoted to prayer. Music, when not abused, is a great blessing; but when put to a wrong use, it is a terrible curse. It excites, but does not impart that strength and courage which the Christian can find only at the throne of grace while humbly making known his wants and, with strong cries and tears, pleading for heavenly strength to be fortified against the powerful temptations of the evil one. Satan is leading the young captive. Oh, what can I say to lead them to break his power of infatuation! He is a skillful charmer luring them on to perdition.[5]

Impure Thoughts Lead to Impure Actions—This is an age when corruption is teeming everywhere. The lust of the eye and corrupt passions are aroused by beholding and by reading. The heart is corrupted through the imagination. The mind takes pleasure in contemplating scenes which awaken the lower and baser passions. These vile images, seen through defiled imagination, corrupt the morals and prepare the deluded, infatuated beings to give loose rein

[408]

to lustful passions. Then follow sins and crimes which drag beings formed in the image of God down to a level with the beasts, sinking them at last in perdition.[6]

I Will See No Wicked Thing—Parents must exercise unceasing watchfulness, that their children be not lost to God. The vows of David, recorded in the 101st Psalm, should be the vows of all upon whom rest the responsibilities of guarding the influences of the home. The psalmist declares: "I will set no wicked thing before mine eyes: I hate the work of them that turn aside; it shall not cleave to me. A froward heart shall depart from me: I will not know a wicked person. Whoso privily slandereth his neighbour, him will I cut off: him that hath an high look and a proud heart will not I suffer. Mine eyes shall be upon the faithful of the land, that they may dwell with me: he that walketh in a perfect way, he shall serve me. He that worketh deceit shall not dwell within my house: he that telleth lies shall not tarry in my sight."[7]

[409]

Say firmly: "I will not spend precious moments in reading that which will be of no profit to me, and which only unfits me to be of service to others. I will devote my time and my thoughts to acquiring a fitness for God's service. I will close my eyes to frivolous and sinful things. My ears are the Lord's, and I will not listen to the subtle reasoning of the enemy. My voice shall not in any way be subject to a will that is not under the influence of the Spirit of God. My body is the temple of the Holy Spirit, and every power of my being shall be consecrated to worthy pursuits."[8]

[410]

---

[1] Pacific Health Journal, June, 1890.

[2] Bible Echo, October 15, 1894, par.4.

[3] Notebook Leaflets from the Elmshaven Library, Education, Volume 1 (1845).

[4] The Ministry of Healing, 444, 445.

[5] Testimonies For The Church 1, 496, 497.

[6] Testimonies For The Church 2, 410.

[7] Counsels to Teachers, Parents, and Students, 119.

[8] Testimonies For The Church 7, 64.

Chapter 68—Reading and its Influence

Feed the Child's Mind With Proper Food—The susceptible, expanding mind of the child longs for knowledge. Parents should keep themselves well informed, that they may give the minds of their children proper food. Like the body, the mind derives its strength from the food it receives. It is broadened and elevated by pure, strengthening thoughts; but it is narrowed and debased by thoughts that are of the earth earthy.

Parents, you are the ones to decide whether the minds of your children shall be filled with ennobling thoughts or with vicious sentiments. You cannot keep their active minds unoccupied; neither can you frown away evil. Only by the inculcation of right principles can you exclude wrong thoughts. Unless parents plant the seeds of truth in the hearts of their children, the enemy will sow tares. Good, sound instruction is the only preventive of the evil communications that corrupt good manners. Truth will protect the soul from the endless temptations that must be encountered.[1]

Parents to Control Reading Habits—Many youth are eager for books. They read anything that they can obtain. I appeal to the parents of such children to control their desire for reading. Do not permit upon your tables the magazines and newspapers in which are found love stories. Supply their place with books that will help the youth to put into their character-building the very best material—the love and fear of God, the knowledge of Christ. Encourage your children to store the mind with valuable knowledge, to let that which is good occupy the soul and control its powers, leaving no place for [411] low, debasing thoughts. Restrict the desire for reading matter that does not furnish good food for the mind.[2]

Parents should endeavor to keep out of the home every influence that is not productive of good. In this matter some parents have much to learn. To those who feel free to read story magazines and novels I would say: You are sowing seed the harvest of which you will not care to garner. From such reading there is no spiritual

321

strength to be gained. Rather it destroys love for the pure truth of the word. Through the agency of novels and story magazines, Satan is working to fill with unreal and trivial thoughts minds that should be diligently studying the word of God. Thus he is robbing thousands upon thousands of the time and energy and self-discipline demanded by the stern problems of life.[3]

Children need proper reading which will afford amusement and recreation and not demoralize the mind or weary the body. If they are taught to love romance and newspaper tales, instructive books and papers will become distasteful to them. Most children and young people will have reading matter; and if it is not selected for them, they will select it for themselves. They can find a ruinous quality of reading anywhere, and they soon learn to love it; but if pure and good reading is furnished them, they will cultivate a taste for that.[4]

Discipline and Educate Mental Tastes—The mental tastes must be disciplined and educated with the greatest care. Parents must begin early to unfold the Scriptures to the expanding minds of their children, that proper habits of thought may be formed.

[412]
No effort should be spared to establish right habits of study. If the mind wanders, bring it back. If the intellectual and moral tastes have been perverted by over-wrought and exciting tales of fiction so that there is a disinclination to apply the mind, there is a battle to be fought to overcome this habit. A love for fictitious reading should be overcome at once. Rigid rules should be enforced to hold the mind in the proper channel.[5]

Avoid Cultivating Taste for Fiction—What shall our children read? This is a serious question and one that demands a serious answer. It troubles me to see in Sabbathkeeping families periodicals and newspapers containing continued stories which leave no impressions for good on the minds of children and youth. I have watched those whose taste for fiction was thus cultivated. They have had the privilege of listening to the truth, of becoming acquainted with the reasons of our faith; but they have grown to maturer years destitute of true piety and practical godliness.[6]

The readers of fiction are indulging an evil that destroys spirituality, eclipsing the beauty of the sacred page.[7]

Prevalence of Harmful Books—The world is deluged with books that might better be consumed than circulated. Books on sensational topics, published and circulated as a money-making scheme, might better never be read by the youth. There is a satanic fascination in such books....

The practice of story reading is one of the means employed by Satan to destroy souls. It produces a false, unhealthy excitement, fevers the imagination, unfits the mind for usefulness, and disqualifies it for any spiritual exercise. It weans the soul from prayer and from the love of spiritual things.[8]

[413]

Works of romance, frivolous, exciting tales, are, in hardly less degree, a curse to the reader. The author may profess to teach a moral lesson; throughout his work he may interweave religious sentiments, but often these serve only to veil the folly and worthlessness beneath.[9]

Infidel Authors—Another source of danger against which we should be constantly on guard is the reading of infidel authors. Such works are inspired by the enemy of truth, and no one can read them without imperiling the soul. It is true that some who are affected by them may finally recover; but all who tamper with their evil influence place themselves on Satan's ground, and he makes the most of his advantage. As they invite his temptations, they have not wisdom to discern or strength to resist them. With a fascinating, bewitching power unbelief and infidelity fasten themselves upon the mind.[10]

Myths and Fairy Tales—In the education of children and youth fairy tales, myths, and fictitious stories are now given a large place. Books of this character are used in schools, and they are to be found in many homes. How can Christian parents permit their children to use books so filled with falsehood? When the children ask the meaning of stories so contrary to the teaching of their parents, the answer is that the stories are not true; but this does not do away with the evil results of their use. The ideas presented in these books mislead the children. They impart false views of life and beget and foster a desire for the unreal....

Never should books containing a perversion of truth be placed in the hands of children or youth. Let not our children, in the very process of obtaining an education, receive ideas that will prove to be seeds of sin.[11]

[414]

How Mental Vigor Is Destroyed—There are few well-balanced minds because parents are wickedly negligent of their duty to stimulate weak traits and repress wrong ones. They do not remember that they are under the most solemn obligation to watch the tendencies of each child, that it is their duty to train their children to right habits and right ways of thinking.[12]

Cultivate the moral and intellectual powers. Let not these noble powers become enfeebled and perverted by much reading of even storybooks. I know of strong minds that have been unbalanced and partially benumbed, or paralyzed, by intemperance in reading.[13]

Exciting Reading Makes Restless, Dreamy Child—Readers of frivolous, exciting tales become unfitted for the duties of practical life. They live in an unreal world. I have watched children who have been allowed to make a practice of reading such stories. Whether at home or abroad, they were restless, dreamy, unable to converse except upon the most commonplace subjects. Religious thought and conversation was entirely foreign to their minds. With the cultivation of an appetite for sensational stories the mental taste is perverted, and the mind is not satisfied unless fed upon this unwholesome food. I can think of no more fitting name for those who indulge in such reading than mental inebriates. Intemperate habits of reading have an effect upon the brain similar to that which intemperate habits of eating and drinking have upon the body.[14]

[415] Before accepting the present truth, some had formed the habit of novel reading. Upon uniting with the church, they made an effort to overcome this habit. To place before this class reading similar to that which they have discarded is like offering intoxicants to the inebriate. Yielding to the temptation continually before them, they soon lose their relish for solid reading. They have no interest in Bible study. Their moral power becomes enfeebled. Sin appears less and less repulsive. There is manifest an increasing unfaithfulness, a growing distaste for life's practical duties. As the mind becomes perverted, it is ready to grasp any reading of a stimulating character. Thus the way is open for Satan to bring the soul fully under his domination.[15]

Hasty, Superficial Reading Weakens Power of Concentration—With the immense tide of printed matter constantly pouring from the press, old and young form the habit of reading hastily and superficially, and the mind loses its power of connected and vigorous thought. Furthermore, a large share of the periodicals and books that, like the frogs of Egypt, are overspreading the land are not merely commonplace, idle, and enervating, but unclean and degrading. Their effect is not merely to intoxicate and ruin the mind, but to corrupt and destroy the soul.[16]

"I Cannot Afford Our Church Papers."—There are those who profess to be brethren who do not take the *Review, Signs, Instructor,* or *Good Health,* but take one or more secular papers. Their children are deeply interested in reading the fictitious tales and love stories which are found in these papers, and which their father can afford to pay for, although claiming that he cannot afford to pay for our periodicals and publications on present truth....

Parents should guard their children and teach them to cultivate a pure imagination and to shun, as they would a leper, the lovesick pen pictures presented in newspapers. Let publications upon moral and religious subjects be found on your tables and in your libraries, that your children may cultivate a taste for elevated reading.[17]

[416]

Messages to Youth on Objectives in Reading—As I see the danger that threatens the youth from improper reading, I cannot forbear to present still further the warnings given me in regard to this great evil.

The harm that results to the workers from handling matter of an objectionable character is too little realized. Their attention is arrested and their interest aroused by the subject matter with which they are dealing. Sentences are imprinted in the memory. Thoughts are suggested. Almost unconsciously the reader is influenced by the spirit of the writer, and mind and character receive an impress for evil. There are some who have little faith and little power of self-control, and it is difficult for them to banish the thoughts suggested by such literature.[18]

Oh, that the young would reflect upon the influence which exciting stories have upon the mind! Can you, after such reading, open the word of God and read the words of life with interest? Do you not find the book of God uninteresting? The charm of that love story is upon the mind, destroying its healthy tone and making it impossible for you to fix your mind upon the important, solemn truths which concern your eternal interest. You sin against your parents in devoting to such a poor purpose the time which belongs to them, and you sin against God in thus using the time which should be spent in devotion to Him.[19]

Children, I have a message for you. You are now deciding your future destiny, and your character building is of that kind which will exclude you from the Paradise of God.... How sad it is for Jesus, the [417] world's Redeemer, to look upon a family where the children have no love for God, no respect for the word of God, but are all absorbed in reading storybooks. The time occupied in this way robs you of a desire to become effective in household duties; it disqualifies you to stand at the head of a family, and if continued it will entangle you more and more closely in Satan's snare.... Some of the books you read contain excellent principles, but you read only to get the story. If you would gather from the books you read that which would help you in the formation of your character, your reading would do you some good. But as you take up your books and peruse page after page of them, do you ask yourself, What is my object in reading? Am I seeking to gain substantial knowledge? You cannot build a right character by bringing to the foundation wood, hay, and stubble.[20]

Sow in the Mind Seeds of Bible Truth—Between an uncultivated field and an untrained mind there is a striking similarity. In the minds of children and youth the enemy sows tares, and unless parents keep watchful guard, these will spring up to bear their evil fruit. Unceasing care is needed in cultivating the soil of the mind and sowing it with the precious seed of Bible truth. Children should be taught to reject trashy, exciting tales and to turn to sensible reading, which will lead the mind to take an interest in Bible story, history, and argument. Reading that will throw light upon the Sacred Volume and quicken the desire to study it is not dangerous, but beneficial.[21]

It is impossible for the youth to possess a healthy tone of mind and correct religious principles unless they enjoy the perusal of the word of God. This book contains the most interesting history, points [418] out the way of salvation through Christ, and is their guide to a higher and better life.[22]

[419]

[420]

---

[1]Counsels to Teachers, Parents, and Students, 121.
[2]Ibid., 133.
[3]Ibid., 120, 121.
[4]The Review and Herald, December 11, 1879.

[5]Counsels to Teachers, Parents, and Students, 136.

[6]Ibid., 132.

[7]The Youth's Instructor, October 9, 1902.

[8]Counsels to Teachers, Parents, and Students, 133, 134.

[9]The Ministry of Healing, 445.

[10]Counsels to Teachers, Parents, and Students, 135, 136.

[11]Ibid., 384, 385.

[12]The Review and Herald, November 12, 1908.

[13]Testimonies For The Church 2, 410.

[14]Counsels to Teachers, Parents, and Students, 134, 135.

[15]Testimonies For The Church 7, 203.

[16]Education, 189, 190.

[17]The Review and Herald, December 11, 1879.

[18]Testimonies For The Church 7, 203.

[19]Testimonies For The Church 2, 236.

[20]Letter 32, 1896.

[21]Counsels to Teachers, Parents, and Students, 136, 137.

[22]Testimonies For The Church 2, 410, 411.

Section 15—Graces that Brighten Family Life

Chapter 69—Courtesy and Kindness

Courtesy Will Banish Half Life's Ills—The principle inculcated by the injunction, "Be kindly affectioned one to another," lies at the very foundation of domestic happiness. Christian courtesy should reign in every household. It is cheap, but it has power to soften natures which would grow hard and rough without it. The cultivation of a uniform courtesy, a willingness to do by others as we would like them to do by us, would banish half the ills of life.[1]

Courtesy Begins in the Home—If we would have our children practice kindness, courtesy, and love, we ourselves must set them the example.[2]

Courtesy, even in little things, should be manifested by the parents toward each other. Universal kindness should be the law of the house. No rude language should be indulged; no bitter words should be spoken.[3]

All may possess a cheerful countenance, a gentle voice, a courteous manner; and these are elements of power. Children are attracted by a cheerful, sunny demeanor. Show them kindness and courtesy, and they will manifest the same spirit toward you and toward one another.[4]

Your courtesy and self-control will have greater influence upon the characters of your children than mere words could have.[5]

Mutual Kindness Makes Home a Paradise—By speaking kindly to their children and praising them when they try to do right, parents may encourage their efforts, make them very happy, and throw around the family circle a charm which will chase away very dark shadow and bring cheerful sunlight in. Mutual kindness and forbearance will make home a Paradise and attract holy angels into the family circle; but they will flee from a house where there are unpleasant words, fretfulness, and strife. Unkindness, complaining, and anger shut Jesus from the dwelling.[6]

The courtesies of everyday life and the affection that should exist between members of the same family do not depend upon outward circumstances.[7]

Pleasant voices, gentle manners, and sincere affection that finds expression in all the actions, together with industry, neatness, and economy, make even a hovel the happiest of homes. The Creator regards such a home with approbation.[8]

There are many who should live less for the outside world and more for the members of their own family circle. There should be less display of superficial politeness and affection toward strangers and visitors and more of the courtesy that springs from genuine love and sympathy toward the dear ones of our own firesides.[9]

True Politeness Defined—There is great need of the cultivation of true refinement in the home. This is a powerful witness in favor of the truth. In whomsoever they may appear, vulgarity of language and of demeanor indicate a vitiated heart. Truth of heavenly origin never degrades the receiver, never makes him coarse or rough. Truth is softening and refining in its influence. When received into the heart, it makes the youth respectful and polite. Christian politeness is received only under the working of the Holy Spirit. It does not consist in affection or artificial polish, in bowing and simpering. This is the class of politeness possessed by those of the world, but they are destitute of true Christian politeness. True polish, true politeness, is obtained only from a practical knowledge of the gospel of Christ. True politeness, true courtesy, is a kindness shown to all, high or low, rich or poor.[10]

[423]

The essence of true politeness is consideration for others. The essential, enduring education is that which broadens the sympathies and encourages universal kindliness. That so-called culture which does not make a youth deferential toward his parents, appreciative of their excellences, forbearing toward their defects, and helpful to their necessities; which does not make him considerate and tender, generous and helpful toward the young, the old, and the unfortunate, and courteous toward all is a failure.[11]

Christian courtesy is the golden clasp which unites the members of the family in bonds of love, becoming closer and stronger every day.[12]

Make the Golden Rule the Law for the Family—The most valuable rules for social and family intercourse are to be found in the Bible. There is not only the best and purest standard of morality but the most valuable code of politeness. Our Saviour's Sermon on the Mount contains instruction of priceless worth to old and young. It should be often read in the family circle and its precious teachings exemplified in the daily life. The golden rule, "Whatsoever ye would that men should do to you, do ye even so to them," as well as the apostolic injunction, "In honour preferring one another," should be made the law of the family. Those who cherish the spirit of Christ will manifest politeness at home, a spirit of benevolence even in little things. They will be constantly seeking to make all around them happy, forgetting self in their kind attentions to others. This is the fruit which grows upon the Christian tree.[13]

[424]

The golden rule is the principle of true courtesy, and its truest illustration is seen in the life and character of Jesus. Oh, what rays of softness and beauty shone forth in the daily life of our Saviour! What sweetness flowed from His very presence! The same spirit will be revealed in His children. Those with whom Christ dwells will be surrounded with a divine atmosphere. Their white robes of purity will be fragrant with perfume from the garden of the Lord. Their faces will reflect light from His, brightening the path for stumbling and weary feet.[14]

The Best Treatise on Etiquette—The most valuable treatise on etiquette ever penned is the precious instruction given by the Saviour, with the utterance of the Holy Spirit through the Apostle Paul—words that should be ineffaceably written in the memory of every human being, young or old:

"As I have loved you, that ye also love one another."

"Love suffereth long, and is kind;
    Love envieth not;
Love vaunteth not itself,
    Is not puffed up,
Doth not behave itself unseemly,
    Seeketh not its own,
Is not provoked,
    Taketh not account of evil;

Rejoiceth not in unrighteousness,
  But rejoiceth with the truth;
Beareth all things, believeth all things,
  Hopeth all things, endureth all things.
Love never faileth."[15]

[425]

The Bible enjoins courtesy; and it presents many illustrations of the unselfish spirit, the gentle grace, the winsome temper, that characterize true politeness. These are but reflections of the character of Christ. All the real tenderness and courtesy in the world, even among those who do not acknowledge His name, is from Him. And He desires these characteristics to be perfectly reflected in His children. It is His purpose that in us men shall behold His beauty.[16]

Christianity will make a man a gentleman. Christ was courteous, even to His persecutors; and His true followers will manifest the same spirit. Look at Paul when brought before rulers. His speech before Agrippa is an illustration of true courtesy as well as persuasive eloquence. The gospel does not encourage the formal politeness current with the world, but the courtesy that springs from real kindness of heart.[17]

We do not plead for a manifestation of what the world calls courtesy, but for that courtesy which everyone will take with him to the mansions of the blessed.[18]

True Courtesy Must Be Motivated by Love—The most careful cultivation of the outward proprieties of life is not sufficient to shut out all fretfulness, harsh judgment, and unbecoming speech. True refinement will never be revealed so long as self is considered as the supreme object. Love must dwell in the heart. A thoroughgoing Christian draws his motives of action from his deep heart-love for his Master. Up through the roots of his affection for Christ springs an unselfish interest in his brethren.[19]

Of all things that are sought, cherished, and cultivated, there is nothing so valuable in the sight of God as a pure heart, a disposition imbued with thankfulness and peace.

[426]

If the divine harmony of truth and love exists in the heart, it will shine forth in words and actions.... The spirit of genuine benevolence must dwell in the heart. Love imparts to its possessor grace, propriety, and comeliness of deportment. Love illuminates the countenance and subdues the voice; it refines and elevates the entire man. It brings him into harmony with God, for it is a heavenly attribute.[20]

True courtesy is not learned by the mere practice of rules of etiquette. Propriety of deportment is at all times to be observed; wherever principle is not compromised, consideration of others will lead to compliance with accepted customs; but true courtesy requires no sacrifice of principle to conventionality. It ignores caste. It teaches self-respect, respect for the dignity of man as man, a regard for every member of the great human brotherhood.[21]

Love Is Expressed in Looks, Words, and Acts—Above all things, parents should surround their children with an atmosphere of cheerfulness, courtesy, and love. A home where love dwells and where it finds expression in looks, in words, in acts, is a place where angels delight to dwell. Parents, let the sunshine of love, cheer, and happy content enter your own hearts, and let its sweet influence pervade the home. Manifest a kindly, forbearing spirit, and encourage the same in your children, cultivating all those graces that will brighten the home life. The atmosphere thus created will be to the children what air and sunshine are to the vegetable world, promoting health and vigor of mind and body.[22]

Gentle manners, cheerful conversation, and loving acts will bind the hearts of children to their parents by the silken cords of affection and will do more to make home attractive than the rarest ornaments that can be bought for gold.[23]

[427]

Varied Temperaments Must Blend—It is in the order of God that persons of varied temperament should associate together. When this is the case, each member of the household should sacredly regard the feelings and respect the rights of the others. By this means mutual consideration and forbearance will be cultivated, prejudices will be softened, and rough points of character smoothed. Harmony may be secured, and the blending of the varied temperaments may be a benefit to each.[24]

Nothing Will Atone for Lack of Courtesy—Those who profess to be followers of Christ and are at the same time rough, unkind, and uncourteous in words and deportment have not learned of Jesus. A blustering, overbearing, faultfinding man is not a Christian; for to be a Christian is to be Christlike. The conduct of some professed Christians is so lacking in kindness and courtesy that their good is evil spoken of. Their sincerity may not be doubted; their uprightness may not be questioned, but sincerity and uprightness will not atone for a lack of kindness and courtesy. The Christian is to be sympathetic as well as true, pitiful and courteous as well as upright and honest.[25]

Any negligence of acts of politeness and tender regard on the part of brother for brother, any neglect of kind, encouraging words in the family circle, parents with children and children with parents, confirms habits which make the character unchristlike. But if these little things are performed, they become great things. They increase to large proportions. They breathe a sweet perfume in the life which ascends to God as holy incense.[26]

[428]

Many Are Longing for Thoughtfulness—Many long intensely for friendly sympathy.... We should be self-forgetful, ever looking out for opportunities, even in little things, to show gratitude for the favors we have received of others, and watching for opportunities to cheer others and lighten and relieve their sorrows and burdens by acts of tender kindness and little deeds of love. These thoughtful courtesies that, commencing in our families, extend outside the family circle help make up the sum of life's happiness; and the neglect of these little things makes up the sum of life's bitterness and sorrow.[27]

Through Social Relations Contact Is Made With the World—It is through the social relations that Christianity comes in contact with the world. Every man or woman who has tasted of the love of Christ and has received into the heart the divine illumination is required of God to shed light on the dark pathway of those who are unacquainted with the better way.[28]

We can manifest a thousand little attentions in friendly words and pleasant looks, which will be reflected upon us again. Thoughtless Christians manifest by their neglect of others that they are not in union with Christ. It is impossible to be in union with Christ and yet be unkind to others and forgetful of their rights.[29]

We should all become witnesses for Jesus. Social power, sanctified by the grace of Christ, must be improved in winning souls to the Saviour. Let the world see that we are not selfishly absorbed in our own interests, but that we desire others to share our blessings and privileges. Let them see that our religion does not make us unsympathetic or exacting. Let all who profess to have found Christ [429] minister as He did for the benefit of men. We should never give to the world the false impression that Christians are a gloomy, unhappy people.[30]

If we are courteous and gentle at home, we shall carry the savor of a pleasant disposition when away from home. If we manifest forbearance, patience, meekness, and fortitude in the home, we shall [430] be able to be a light to the world.[31]

[1] The Signs of the Times, September 9, 1886.

[2] The Signs of the Times, May 25, 1882.

[3] The Good Health, January 1, 1880, par. 6.

[4] Education, 240.

[5] The Review and Herald, June 13, 1882.

[6] The Signs of the Times, April 17, 1884.

[7] The Signs of the Times, August 23, 1877.

[8] The Signs of the Times, October 2, 1884.

[9] Ibid.

[10] Manuscript 74, 1900.

[11] Education, 241.

[12] The Signs of the Times, November 29, 1877.

[13] The Signs of the Times, July 1, 1886.

[14] Thoughts from the Mount of Blessing, 100, 101.

[15] Education, 242.

[16] Ibid., 241, 242.

[17] The Ministry of Healing, 489, 490.

[18] The Signs of the Times, August 13, 1912.

[19] The Ministry of Healing, 490.

[20] Testimonies For The Church 4, 559, 560.

[21] Education, 240.

[22] Counsels to Teachers, Parents, and Students, 115.

[23] The Signs of the Times, October 2, 1884.

[24] The Signs of the Times, April 4, 1911.

[25] The Youth's Instructor, March 31, 1908.

[26] Manuscript 107, 1898.

[27] Testimonies For The Church 3, 539, 540.

[28] Testimonies For The Church 4, 555.

[29] Testimonies For The Church 3, 539.

[30] The Desire of Ages, 152.

[31] The Signs of the Times, November 14, 1892.

Chapter 70—Cheerfulness

The True Christian Will Be Cheerful—Do not allow the perplexities and worries of everyday life to fret your mind and cloud your brow. If you do, you will always have something to vex and annoy. Life is what we make it, and we shall find what we look for. If we look for sadness and trouble, if we are in a frame of mind to magnify little difficulties, we shall find plenty of them to engross our thoughts and our conversation. But if we look on the bright side of things, we shall find enough to make us cheerful and happy. If we give smiles, they will be returned to us; if we speak pleasant, cheerful words, they will be spoken to us again.

When Christians appear as gloomy and depressed as though they thought themselves friendless, they give a wrong impression of religion. In some cases the idea has been entertained that cheerfulness is inconsistent with the dignity of the Christian character, but this is a mistake. Heaven is all joy; and if we gather to our souls the joys of heaven and, as far as possible, express them in our words and deportment, we shall be more pleasing to our heavenly Father than if we were gloomy and sad.

It is the duty of everyone to cultivate cheerfulness instead of brooding over sorrow and troubles. Many not only make themselves wretched in this way, but they sacrifice health and happiness to a morbid imagination. There are things in their surroundings that are not agreeable, and their countenances wear a continual frown that, more plainly than words, expresses discontent. These depressing [431] emotions are a great injury to them healthwise; for by hindering the process of digestion, they interfere with nutrition. While grief and anxiety cannot remedy a single evil, they can do great harm; but cheerfulness and hope, while they brighten the pathway of others, "are life unto those that find them, and health to all their flesh."[1]

Mrs. White Was Cheerful in Adversity [Note: in 1867 Elder James White, who was in a critical condition following a paralytic stroke, was a patient at "Our Home," in Dansville, New York. The

337

doctor in charge of the institution regarded religion as a depressing influence and encouraged his patients to participate in various amusements for the purpose of making them cheerful. Mrs. White was solicited by one of the attendants to make a subscription for a dance and invited to bury her sorrows by attending. The words above indicate the nature of her reply to the suggestion.]—Do you ever see me gloomy, desponding, complaining? I have a faith which forbids this. It is a misconception of the true ideal of Christian character and Christian service that leads to these conclusions. It is the want of genuine religion that produces gloom, despondency, and sadness. Earnest Christians seek to imitate Jesus, for to be Christians is to be Christlike. It will be really essential to have correct conceptions of Christ's life, Christ's habits, that His principles may be reproduced in us who would be Christlike.

A half service, loving the world, loving self, loving frivolous amusements, makes a timid, cowardly servant; he follows Christ a great way off. A hearty, willing service to Jesus produces a sunny religion. Those who follow Christ the most closely have not been gloomy. In Christ is light and peace and joy forevermore. We need [432] more Christ and less worldliness, more Christ and less selfishness.[2]

Walk as Children of Light—It is not the will of God that we should be gloomy or impatient, nor that we should be light and trifling. It is Satan's studied plan to push persons from one extreme to the other. As children of the light, God would have us cultivate a cheerful, happy spirit, that we may show forth the praises of Him who hath called us out of darkness into His marvelous light.[3]

Winning the Affection of Children—Smile, parents; smile, teachers. If your heart is sad, let not your face reveal the fact. Let the sunshine from a loving, grateful heart light up the countenance. Unbend from your iron dignity, adapt yourselves to the children's needs, and make them love you. You must win their affection, if you would impress religious truth upon their heart.[4]

Keep a Pleasant Countenance and Melodious Voice—Parents, be cheerful, not common and cheap, but be thankful and obedient and submissive to your heavenly Father. You are not at liberty to act out your feelings if things should arise that irritate. Winning love is to be like deep waters, ever flowing forth in the management of your children. They are the lambs of the flock of God. Bring your little ones to Christ. If parents would educate their children to be pleasant, they should never speak in a scolding manner to them. Educate yourself to carry a pleasant countenance, and bring all the sweetness and melody possible into your voice. The angels of God are ever near your little ones, and your harsh loud tones of fretfulness are not pleasant to their ears.[5]

The mother should cultivate a cheerful, contented, happy disposition. Every effort in this direction will be abundantly repaid in both the physical well-being and the moral character of her children. A cheerful spirit will promote the happiness of her family and in a very great degree improve her own health.[6]

[433]

Lift the Shadows and Lighten the Task—Look upon matters in a cheerful light, seeking to lift the shadows that, if cherished, will envelop the soul. Cultivate sympathy for others. Let cheerfulness, kindness, and love pervade the home. This will increase a love for religious exercises, and duties large and small will be performed with a light heart.[7]

Cheerfulness Without Levity Is Christian Grace—We may have true Christian dignity and at the same time be cheerful and pleasant in our deportment. Cheerfulness without levity is one of the Christian graces.[8]

[434]

---

[1] The Signs of the Times, February 12, 1885.

[2] Manuscript 1, 1867.

[3] Australasian Union Conference Record, November 1, 1904.

[4] Fundamentals of Christian Education, 68.

[5] Manuscript 126, 1897.

[6] The Ministry of Healing, 374.

[7] The Signs of the Times, September 1, 1898.

[8] Testimonies For The Church 4, 62.

Chapter 71—Speech

The Voice Is a Talent—The voice is an entrusted talent, and it should be used to help and encourage and strengthen our fellow men. If parents will love God and keep the way of the Lord to do justice and judgment, their language will not savor of sickly sentimentalism. It will be of a sound, pure, edifying character. Whether they are at home or abroad, their words will be well chosen. They will descend to no cheapness.[1]

Every Word Has an Influence—Every word spoken by fathers and mothers has its influence over the children, for good or for evil. If the parents speak passionately, if they show the spirit shown by the children of this world, God counts them as the children of this world, not as His sons and daughters.[2]

A word spoken in due season may be as good seed in youthful minds and may result in leading little feet in the right path. But a wrong word may lead their feet in the path of ruin.[3]

Angels hear the words that are spoken in the home. Therefore, never scold; but let the influence of your words be such that it will ascend to heaven as fragrant incense.[4]

Parents should keep the atmosphere of the home pure and fragrant with kind words, with tender sympathy and love; but at the same time they are to be firm and unyielding in principle. If you are firm with your children, they may think that you do not love them. This you may expect, but never manifest harshness. Justice and mercy must clasp hands; there must be no wavering or impulsive [435] movements.[5]

Language to Be an Outward Expression of Inward Grace—The chief requisite of language is that it be pure and kind and true—"the outward expression of an inward grace." ... The best school for this language study is the home.[6]

Kind words are as dew and gentle showers to the soul. The Scripture says of Christ that grace was poured into His lips, that He might "know how to speak a word in season to him that is weary."

And the Lord bids us, "Let your speech be alway with grace," "that it may minister grace unto the hearers."[7]

Voice Culture Should Be Given in the Home—Instruction in vocal culture should be given in the home circle. Parents should teach their children to speak so plainly that those who are listening can understand every word that is said. They should teach them to read the Bible in clear, distinct utterance, in a way that will honor God. And let not those who kneel round the family altar put their faces in their hands and in their chair when they address God. Let them lift up their heads and, with holy awe and boldness, come to the throne of grace.[8]

Be pure in speech. Cultivate a soft and persuasive, not a harsh and dictatorial, tone of voice. Give the children lessons in voice culture. Train their habits of speech, until no coarse or rough words will come spontaneously from their lips when any trial comes to them.[9]

Voice culture is a subject that has much to do with the health of students. The youth should be taught how to breathe properly and how to read in such a way that no unnatural strain shall come on the throat and lungs, but that the work shall be shared by the abdominal muscles. Speaking from the throat, letting the sound come from the upper part of the vocal organs, impairs the health of these organs [436] and decreases their efficiency. The abdominal muscles are to do the heaviest part of the labor, the throat being used as a channel. Many have died who might have lived had they been taught how to use the voice correctly. The right use of the abdominal muscles in reading and speaking will prove a remedy for many voice and chest difficulties and the means of prolonging life.[10]

The Effect of Harsh, Scolding Words—In a home where harsh, fretful, scolding words are spoken, a child cries much; and upon its tender sensibilities are impressed the marks of unhappiness and discord. Then, mothers, let your countenance be full of sunshine. Smile, if you can, and the infant's mind and heart will reflect the light of your countenance as the polished plate of an artist portrays the human features. Be sure, mothers, to have an indwelling Christ so that on your child's plastic mind may be impressed the divine likeness.[11]

Let There Be No Jarring Note—Allow nothing like strife or dissension to come into the home. Speak gently. Never raise your voice to harshness. Keep yourselves calm. Put away faultfinding and all untruthfulness. Tell the children that you want to help them to prepare for a holy heaven, where all is peace, where not one jarring note is heard. Be patient with them in their trials, which may look small to you but which are large to them.[12]

When fathers and mothers are converted, there will be a thorough conversion of their principles of management. Their thoughts will be converted; their tongues will be converted....

There will be no loud, angry talking in the home. The words will be of a character to soothe and bless the hearer.... Take all the

[437]   ugly features out of the voice.[13]

We must subdue a hasty temper and control our words, and in this we shall gain great victories. Unless we control our words and temper, we are slaves to Satan. We are in subjection to him. He leads us captive. All jangling and unpleasant, impatient, fretful words are an offering presented to his satanic majesty. And it is a costly offering, more costly than any sacrifice we can make for God; for it destroys the peace and happiness of whole families, destroys health, and is eventually the cause of forfeiting an eternal life of happiness.[14]

Shall the Words Cause Sunshine or Shadow?—It is important that children and youth should be trained to guard their words and deeds; for their course of action causes sunshine or shadow, not only in their own home, but also with all with whom they come in contact.[15]

Unhappiness is often caused by an unwise use of the talent of speech. The word of God does not authorize anyone to speak harshly, thereby creating disagreeable feelings and unhappiness in the family. The other members of the family lose their respect for the one who speaks thus, when if he would restrain his feelings, he might win the confidence and affection of all.[16]

Pleasant Words to Children; Respectful Words to Parents—Let only pleasant words be spoken by parents to their children, and respectful words by children to their parents. Attention must be given to these things in the home life; for if, in their character building, children form right habits, it will be much easier for them to be taught by God and to be obedient to His requirements.[17]

Shun Vulgarity in Every Form—Fathers and mothers, husbands and wives, brothers and sisters, do not educate yourselves in the line of vulgarity of action, word, or thought. Coarse sayings, low jests, lack of politeness and true courtesy in the home life, will become as second nature to you and will unfit you for the society of those who are becoming sanctified through the truth. The home is too sacred a place to be polluted by vulgarity, sensuality, recrimination, and scandal. Silence the evil word; put away the unholy thought, for the True Witness weighs every word, sets a value on every action, and declares, "I know thy works."[18]

[438]

Low, cheap, common talk should find no place in the family. When the heart is pure, rich treasures of wisdom will flow forth.[19]

Indulge in no foolish talking in your house. Even very young children will be benefited by "the form of sound words." But idle and foolish words exchanged between father and mother will lead to the same kind of words among the children; while right, candid, truthful, and serious words will lead to the same in all the household and will lead to right actions also.[20]

The Evils of Angry, Hasty Words—When you speak angry words to your children, you are helping the cause of the enemy of all righteousness. Let every child have a fair chance from babyhood up. The work of teaching should begin in childhood, not accompanied by harshness and fretting, but in kindness and patience; and this instruction should be continued through all their years to manhood and womanhood.[21]

Let every family seek the Lord in earnest prayer for help to do the work of God. Let them overcome the habits of hasty speech and the desire to blame others. Let them study to be kind and courteous in the home, to form habits of thoughtfulness and care.[22]

[439]

What harm is wrought in the family circle by the utterance of impatient words, for the impatient utterance of one leads another to retort in the same spirit and manner. Then come words of retaliation, words of self-justification, and it is by such words that a heavy, galling yoke is manufactured for your neck; for all these bitter words will come back in a baleful harvest to your soul.[23]

Hard words beat upon the heart through the ear, awakening to life the worst passions of the soul and tempting men and women to break God's commandments .... Words are as seeds which are planted.[24]

Passionate Words a Species of Swearing—Among the members of many families there is practiced the habit of saying loose, careless things; and the habit of tantalizing, of speaking harsh words, becomes stronger and stronger as it is indulged, and thus many objectionable words are spoken that are after Satan's order and not after the order of God.... Burning words of passion should never be spoken, for in the sight of God and holy angels they are as a species of swearing.[25]

How a Father Lost His Children's Confidence—My brother, your overbearing words hurt your children. As they advance in years, their tendency to criticize will grow. Faultfinding is corrupting your life and is extending to your wife and to your children. Your children are not encouraged to give you their confidence or to acknowledge their faults, because they know that your stern rebuke is sure to follow. Your words are often as a desolating hail which breaks down tender plants. It is impossible to estimate the harm thus done. Your children practice deception in order to avoid the hard words you [440] speak. They will evade the truth to escape censure and punishment. A hard, cold command will do them no good.[26]

A Suggestive Pledge—It would be well for every man to sign a pledge to speak kindly in his home, to let the law of love rule his speech. Parents, never speak hastily. If your children do wrong, correct them, but let your words be full of tenderness and love. Every time you scold, you lose a precious opportunity of giving a lesson in forbearance and patience. Let love be the most prominent feature in your correction of wrong.[27]

Table Conversation—How many families season their daily meals with doubt and questionings! They dissect the characters of their friends and serve them up as a dainty dessert. A precious bit of slander is passed around the board to be commented upon, not only by adults, but by children. In this God is dishonored.[28]

In the home the spirit of criticism and faultfinding should have no place. The peace of the home is too sacred to be marred by this spirit. But how often, when seated at the meal table, the members of the family pass round a dish of criticism, faultfinding, and scandal. Were Christ to come today, would He not find many of the families who profess to be Christians cherishing the spirit of criticism and unkindness? The members of such families are unready to unite with the family above.[29]

Let the conversation at the family board be such as is calculated to leave a fragrant influence on the minds of the children.[30]

Gossip and Talebearing—We think with horror of the cannibal who feasts on the still warm and trembling flesh of his victim; but are the results of even this practice more terrible than are the agony and ruin caused by misrepresenting motive, blackening reputation, dissecting character? Let the children, and the youth as well, learn what God says about these things: "Death and life are in the power of the tongue."[31] [441]

The spirit of gossip and talebearing is one of Satan's special agencies to sow discord and strife, to separate friends, and to undermine the faith of many in the truthfulness of our positions.[32]

Sowing Seeds of Distrust Is an Aid to the Enemy—It is natural for human beings to speak sharp words. Those who yield to this inclination open the door for Satan to enter their hearts and to make them quick to remember the mistakes and errors of others. Their failings are dwelt upon, their deficiencies noted, and words are spoken that cause a lack of confidence in one who is doing his best to fulfill his duty as a laborer together with God. Often the seeds of distrust are sown because one thinks that he ought to have been favored but was not.[33]

God calls upon believers to cease finding fault, to cease making hasty, unkind speeches. Parents, let the words that you speak to your children be kind and pleasant, that angels may have your help in drawing them to Christ. A thorough reformation is needed in the home church. Let it begin at once. Let all grumbling and fretting and scolding cease. Those who fret and scold shut out the angels of heaven and open the door to evil angels.[34]

A Plea for Parental Forbearance and Restraint—Parents, when you feel fretful, you should not commit so great a sin as to poison the whole family with this dangerous irritability. At such times set a double watch over yourselves, and resolve in your heart [442] not to offend with your lips, that you will utter only pleasant, cheerful words. Say to yourselves: "I will not mar the happiness of my children by a fretful word." By thus controlling yourselves, you will grow stronger. Your nervous system will not be so sensitive. You will be strengthened by the principles of right. The consciousness that you are faithfully discharging your duty will strengthen you. Angels of God will smile upon your efforts and help you.[35]

Fathers and mothers, speak kindly to your children; remember how sensitive you are, how little you can bear to be blamed; reflect, and know that your children are like you. That which you cannot bear do not lay upon them. If you cannot bear censure and blame, neither can your children, who are weaker than you and cannot endure as much. Let your pleasant, cheerful words ever be like sunbeams in your family. The fruits of self-control, thoughtfulness, and painstaking on your part will be a hundredfold.[36]

A Time for Silence or Song—Trials will come, it is true, even to those who are fully consecrated. The patience of the most patient will be severely tested. The husband or the wife may utter words that are liable to provoke a hasty reply, but let the one who is spoken to keep silent. In silence there is safety. Often silence is the severest rebuke that could be given to the one who has sinned with his lips.[37]

When they [the children and youth] lose self-control and speak words that are passionate, an attitude of silence is often the best course to pursue, not taking up a line of reproof or argument or condemnation. Repentance will come very soon. The silence that is golden will often do more than all the words that can be uttered.[38]

[443]

When others are impatient, fretful, and complaining because self is not subdued, begin to sing some of the songs of Zion. While Christ was working at the carpenter's bench, others would sometimes surround Him, trying to cause Him to be impatient; but He would begin singing some of the beautiful psalms, and before they realized what they were doing, they had joined with Him in singing, influenced, as it were, by the power of the Holy Spirit which was there.[39]

The Battle for Self-control in Speech—God requires parents, by self-control, by an example of solid character building, to disseminate light within the immediate circle of their own little flock. No trifling, common conversation is to be indulged. God looks into every secret thing of life. By some a constant battle is maintained for self-control. Daily they strive silently and prayerfully against harshness of speech and temper. These strivings may never be appreciated by human beings. They may get no praise from human lips for keeping back the hasty words which sought for utterance. The world will never see these conquests, and if it could, it would only despise the conquerors. But in heaven's record they are registered as overcomers. There is One who witnesses every secret combat and every silent victory, and He says, "He that is slow to anger is better than the mighty; and he that ruleth his spirit than he that taketh a city."[40]

If you refuse to storm or fret or scold, the Lord will show you the way through. He will help you to use the talent of speech in such a Christlike way that the precious attributes of patience, comfort, and love will be brought into the home.[41]

[444]

[445]

[1] Manuscript 36, 1899.

[2] Manuscript 100, 1902.

[3] The Review and Herald, June 24, 1890.

[4] Letter 10, 1912.

[5] The Review and Herald, March 30, 1897.

[6] Education, 235.

[7] The Youth's Instructor, March 31, 1908.

[8] Manuscript 4, 1901.

[9] Manuscript 60, 1903.

[10] Counsels to Teachers, Parents, and Students, 297.

[11] The Review and Herald, September 8, 1904.

[12] Manuscript 14, 1905.

[13] Letter 75, 1898.

[14] Testimonies For The Church 1, 310.

[15] The Youth's Instructor, November 5, 1896.

[16] Manuscript 60, 1903.

[17] The Review and Herald, November 17, 1896.

[18] The Signs of the Times, November 14, 1892.

[19] The Review and Herald, May 17, 1898.

[20] The Review and Herald, April 14, 1885.

[21] Manuscript 53, 1912.

[22] Manuscript 31, 1907.

[23] The Review and Herald, February 27, 1913.

[24] Letter 105, 1893.

[25] The Youth's Instructor, September 20, 1894.

[26] Letter 8a, 1896.

[27] Letter 29, 1902.

[28] Testimonies For The Church 4, 195.

[29] The Signs of the Times, February 17. 1904.

[30] Manuscript 49, 1898.

[31] Education, 235.

[32] Testimonies For The Church 4, 195.

[33] Letter 169. 1904.

[34] Letter 133. 1904.

[35] Testimonies For The Church 1, 386, 387.

[36] Ibid., 1:401.

[37] Manuscript 70, 1903.

[38] Manuscript 59, 1900.

[39] Manuscript 102, 1901.

[40] The Signs of the Times, August 23. 1899.

[41] Manuscript 67, 1901.

Chapter 72—Hospitality

Angels May Be Entertained Today—The Bible lays much stress upon the practice of hospitality. Not only does it enjoin hospitality as a duty, but it presents many beautiful pictures of the exercise of this grace and the blessings which it brings. Foremost among these is the experience of Abraham....

These acts of courtesy God thought of sufficient importance to record in His word; and more than a thousand years later they were referred to by an inspired apostle: "Be not forgetful to entertain strangers: for thereby some have entertained angels unawares."

The privilege granted Abraham and Lot is not denied to us. By showing hospitality to God's children we, too, may receive His angels into our dwellings. Even in our day angels in human form enter the homes of men and are entertained by them. And Christians who live in the light of God's countenance are always accompanied by unseen angels, and these holy beings leave behind them a blessing in our homes.[1]

Neglected Opportunities and Privileges—"A lover of hospitality" is among the specifications given by the Holy Spirit as marking one who is to bear responsibility in the church. And to the whole church is given the injunction: "Use hospitality one to another without grudging. As every man hath received the gift, even so minister the same one to another, as good stewards of the manifold grace of God."

These admonitions have been strangely neglected. Even among those who profess to be Christians true hospitality is little exercised. [446] Among our own people the opportunity of showing hospitality is not regarded as it should be, as a privilege and blessing. There is altogether too little sociability, too little of a disposition to make room for two or three more at the family board without embarrassment or parade.[2]

Inadequate Excuses—I have heard many excuse themselves from inviting to their homes and hearts the saints of God: "Why, I have nothing prepared; I have nothing cooked; they must go to some other place." And at that place there may be some other excuse invented for not receiving those who need hospitality, and the feelings of the visitors are deeply grieved, and they leave with unpleasant impressions in regard to the hospitality of these professed brethren and sisters. If you have no bread, sister, imitate the case brought to view in the Bible. Go to your neighbor and say: "Friend, lend me three loaves; for a friend of mine in his journey is come to me, and I have nothing to set before him."

We have not an example of this lack of bread ever being made an excuse to refuse entrance to an applicant. When Elijah came to the widow of Sarepta, she shared her morsel with the prophet of God, and he wrought a miracle and caused that in that act of making a home for his servant and sharing her morsel with him, she herself was sustained, and her life and that of her son preserved. Thus will it prove in the case of many, if they do this cheerfully, for the glory of God.

[447] Some plead their poor health—they would love to do if they had strength. Such have so long shut themselves up to themselves and thought so much of their own poor feelings and talked so much of their sufferings, trials, and afflictions that it is their present truth. They can think of no one but self, however much others may be in need of sympathy and assistance. You who are suffering with poor health, there is a remedy for you. If thou clothe the naked and bring the poor that are cast out to thy house and deal thy bread to the hungry, "then shall thy light break forth as the morning, and thine health shall spring forth speedily." Doing good is an excellent remedy for disease. Those who engage in the work are invited to call upon God, and He has pledged Himself to answer them. Their soul shall be satisfied in drought, and they shall be like a watered garden, whose waters fail not.[3]

Blessings Lost by Selfish Exclusiveness—God is displeased with the selfish interest so often manifested for "me and my family." Every family that cherishes this spirit needs to be converted by the pure principles exemplified in the life of Christ. Those who shut themselves up within themselves, who are unwilling to drawn upon to entertain visitors, lose many blessings.[4]

Angels are waiting to see if we embrace opportunities within our reach of doing good—waiting to see if we will bless others, that they in their turn may bless us. The Lord Himself has made us to differ—some poor, some rich, some afflicted—that all may have an opportunity to develop character. The poor are purposely permitted to be thus of God, that we may be tested and proved and develop what is in our hearts.[5]

When the spirit of hospitality dies, the heart becomes palsied with selfishness.[6]

To Whom Should Hospitality Be Extended?—Our social entertainments should not be governed by the dictates of worldly custom, but by the Spirit of Christ and the teaching of His word. The Israelites, in all their festivities, included the poor, the stranger, and the Levite, who was both the assistant of the priest in the sanctuary and a religious teacher and missionary. These were regarded as the guests of the people, to share their hospitality on all occasions of social and religious rejoicing, and to be tenderly cared for in sickness or in need. It is such as these whom we should make welcome to our homes. How much such a welcome might do to cheer and encourage the missionary nurse or the teacher, the care-burdened, hard-working mother, or the feeble and aged, so often without a home and struggling with poverty and many discouragements.

[448]

"When thou makest a dinner or a supper," Christ says, "call not thy friends, nor thy brethren, neither thy kinsmen, nor thy rich neighbours; lest they also bid thee again, and a recompence be made thee. But when thou makest a feast, call the poor, the maimed, the lame, the blind: and thou shalt be blessed; for they cannot recompense thee: for thou shalt be recompensed at the resurrection of the just."

These are guests whom it will lay on you no great burden to receive. You will not need to provide for them elaborate or expensive entertainment. You will need to make no effort at display. The warmth of a genial welcome, a place at your fireside, a seat at your home table, the privilege of sharing the blessing of the hour of prayer, would to many of these be like a glimpse of heaven.

Our sympathies are to overflow the boundaries of self and the enclosure of family walls. There are precious opportunities for those who will make their homes a blessing to others. Social influence is

[449]

a wonderful power. We can use it, if we will, as a means of helping those about us.[7]

A Refuge for Tempted Youth—Our homes should be a place of refuge for the tempted youth. Many there are who stand at the parting of the ways. Every influence, every impression, is determining the choice that shapes their destiny both here and hereafter. Evil invites them. Its resorts are made bright and attractive. They have a welcome for every comer. All about us are youth who have no home and many whose homes have no helpful, uplifting power, and the youth drift into evil. They are going down to ruin within the very shadow of our own doors.

These youth need a hand stretched out to them in sympathy. Kind words simply spoken, little attentions simply bestowed, will sweep away the clouds of temptations which gather over the soul. The true expression of heaven-born sympathy has power to open the door of hearts that need the fragrance of Christlike words and the simple, delicate touch of the spirit of Christ's love. If we would show an interest in the youth, invite them to our homes, and surround them with cheering, helpful influences, there are many who would gladly turn their steps into the upward path.[8]

Preserve Family Simplicity—When visitors come, as they frequently will, they should not be allowed to absorb all the time and attention of the mother; her children's temporal and spiritual welfare should come first. Time should not be used in preparing rich cakes, pies, and unhealthful viands for the table. These are an extra expense, and many cannot afford it. But the greater evil is in the example. Let the simplicity of the family be preserved. Do not try to give the impression that you can sustain a style of living which is

[450]

really beyond your means. Do not try to appear what you are not, either in your table preparations or in your manners.

While you should treat your visitors kindly and make them feel at home, you should ever remember that you are a teacher to the little ones God has given you. They are watching you, and no course of yours should direct their feet in the wrong way. Be to your visitors just what you are to your family every day—pleasant, considerate, and courteous. In this way all can be educators, an example of good works. They testify that there is something more essential than to keep the mind on what they shall eat and drink and wherewithal they shall be clothed.[9]

Maintain a Peaceful, Restful Atmosphere—We would be much happier and more useful if our home life and social intercourse were governed by the meekness and simplicity of Christ. Instead of toiling for display to excite the admiration or the envy of visitors, we should endeavor to make all around us happy by our cheerfulness, sympathy, and love. Let visitors see that we are striving to conform to the will of Christ. Let them see in us, even though our lot is humble, a spirit of content and gratitude. The very atmosphere of a truly Christian home is that of peace and restfulness. Such an example will not be without effect.[10]

An Expense Account Is Kept in Heaven—Christ keeps an account of every expense incurred in entertaining for His sake. He supplies all that is necessary for this work. Those who for Christ's sake entertain their brethren, doing their best to make the visit profitable both to their guests and to themselves, are recorded in heaven as worthy of special blessings....

[451]

Christ has given in His own life a lesson of hospitality. When surrounded by the hungry multitude beside the sea, He did not send them unrefreshed to their homes. He said to His disciples: "Give ye them to eat." Matthew 14:16. And by an act of creative power He supplied food sufficient to satisfy their need. Yet how simple was the food provided! There were no luxuries. He who had all the resources of heaven at His command could have spread for the people a rich repast. But He supplied only that which would suffice for their need, that which was the daily food of the fisherfolk about the sea.

If men were today simple in their habits, living in harmony with nature's laws, there would be an abundant supply for all the needs of the human family. There would be fewer imaginary wants and more opportunity to work in God's ways....

Poverty need not shut us out from showing hospitality. We are to impart what we have. There are those who struggle for a livelihood and who have great difficulty in making their income meet their necessities; but they love Jesus in the person of His saints and are ready to show hospitality to believers and unbelievers, trying to make their visits profitable. At the family board and the family altar the guests are made welcome. The season of prayer makes its impression on those who receive entertainment, and even one visit may mean the saving of a soul from death. For this work the Lord makes a reckoning, saying: "I will repay."[11]

Awake to Opportunities—Wake up, brethren and sisters. Do not be afraid of good works. "Let us not be weary in well doing: for in due season we shall reap, if we faint not." Do not wait to be [452] told your duty. Open your eyes and see who are around you; make yourselves acquainted with the helpless, afflicted, and needy. Hide not yourselves from them, and seek not to shut out their needs. Who gives the proofs mentioned in James, of possessing pure religion, untainted with selfishness or corruption? Who are anxious to do all [453] in their power to aid in the great plan of salvation?[12]

[454]

[1]Testimonies For The Church 6. 341, 342.

[2]Ibid., 6:342, 343.

[3]Ibid., 2:28, 29.

[4]Ibid., 6:344.

[5]Ibid., 2:28.

[6]Manuscript 41, 1903.

[7]The Ministry of Healing, 352-354.

[8]Ibid., 354.

[9]Christian Temperance and Bible Hygiene, 143.

[10]The Review and Herald, November 29, 1887.

[11]Testimonies For The Church 6. 344, 345, 347.

[12]Ibid., 2:29.

Section 16—The Home and its Social Relationships

Chapter 73—Our Social Needs

God Made Provision for Our Social Needs—In the arrangements for the education of the chosen people it is made manifest that a life centered in God is a life of completeness. Every want He has implanted He provides to satisfy; every faculty imparted He seeks to develop.

The Author of all beauty, Himself a lover of the beautiful, God provided to gratify in His children the love of beauty. He made provision also for their social needs, for the kindly and helpful associations that do so much to cultivate sympathy and to brighten and sweeten life.[1]

The Influence of Association—Everyone will find companions or make them. And just in proportion to the strength of the friendship will be the amount of influence which friends will exert over one another for good or for evil. All will have associates and will influence and be influenced in their turn.[2]

God's word places great stress upon the influence of association, even on men and women. How much greater is its power on the developing mind and character of children and youth! The company they keep, the principles they adopt, the habits they form, will decide the question of their usefulness here and of their future destiny....

It is inevitable that the youth will have associates, and they will necessarily feel their influence. There are mysterious links that bind souls together so that the heart of one answers to the heart of another. One catches the ideas, the sentiments, the spirit, of another. This

association may be a blessing or a curse. The youth may help and strengthen one another, improving in deportment, in disposition, in knowledge; or, by permitting themselves to become careless and unfaithful, they may exert an influence that is demoralizing.[3]

It has been truly said, "Show me your company, and I will show you your character." The youth fail to realize how sensibly both their character and their reputation are affected by their choice of associates. One seeks the company of those whose tastes and habits and practices are congenial. He who prefers the society of the ignorant and vicious to that of the wise and good shows that his own character is defective. His tastes and habits may at first be altogether dissimilar to the tastes and habits of those whose company he seeks; but as he mingles with this class, his thoughts and feelings change; he sacrifices right principles and insensibly yet unavoidably sinks to the level of his companions. As a stream always partakes of the property of the soil through which it runs, so the principles and habits of youth invariably become tinctured with the character of the company in which they mingle.[4]

Natural Tendencies Are Downward—If the youth could be persuaded to associate with the pure, the thoughtful, and the amiable, the effect would be most salutary. If choice is made of companions who fear the Lord, the influence will lead to truth, to duty, and to holiness. A truly Christian life is a power for good. But, on the other hand, those who associate with men and women of questionable morals, of bad principles and practices, will soon be walking in the same path. The tendencies of the natural heart are downward. He who associates with the skeptic will soon become skeptical; he who chooses the companionship of the vile will most assuredly become vile. To walk in the counsel of the ungodly is the first step toward standing in the way of sinners and sitting in the seat of the scornful.[5]

[457]

With worldly youth the love of society and pleasure becomes an absorbing passion. To dress, to visit, to indulge the appetite and passions, and to whirl through the round of social dissipation appear to be the great end of existence. They are unhappy if left in solitude. Their chief desire is to be admired and flattered and to make a sensation in society; and when this desire is not gratified, life seems unendurable.[6]

Those who love society frequently indulge this trait until it becomes an overruling passion.... They cannot endure to read the Bible and contemplate heavenly things. They are miserable unless there is something to excite. They have not within them the power to be happy, but they depend for happiness upon the company of other youth as thoughtless and reckless as themselves. The powers which might be turned to noble purposes they give to folly and mental dissipation.[7]

The Blessings of Christian Sociability—Christian sociability is altogether too little cultivated by God's people.... Those who shut themselves up within themselves, who are unwilling to be drawn upon to bless others by friendly associations, lose many blessings; for by mutual contact minds receive polish and refinement; by social intercourse acquaintances are formed and friendships contracted which result in a unity of heart and an atmosphere of love which is pleasing in the sight of heaven.

Especially should those who have tasted the love of Christ develop their social powers, for in this way they may win souls to the [458] Saviour. Christ should not be hid away in their hearts, shut in as a coveted treasure, sacred and sweet, to be enjoyed solely by themselves; nor should the love of Christ be manifested toward those only who please their fancy. Students are to be taught the Christlikeness of exhibiting a kindly interest, a social disposition, toward those who are in the greatest need, even though these may not be their own chosen companions. At all times and in all places Jesus manifested a loving interest in the human family and shed about Him the light [459] of a cheerful piety.[8]

[1]Education, 41.

[2]Testimonies For The Church 4, 587.

[3]Counsels to Teachers, Parents, and Students, 220.

[4]Ibid., 221.

[5]Testimonies For The Church 4, 587.

[6]Testimonies For The Church 5, 112.

[7]Testimonies For The Church 4, 624.

[8]Testimonies For The Church 6, 172, 173.

Chapter 74—Safe And Unsafe Associations

Things Which Influence Us and Our Children—Every association we form, however limited, exerts some influence upon us. The extent to which we yield to that influence will be determined by the degree of intimacy, the constancy of the intercourse, and our love and veneration for the one with whom we associate.[1]

If we place ourselves among associates whose influence has a tendency to make us forgetful of the high claims the Lord has upon us, we invite temptation and become too weak in moral power to resist it. We come to partake of the spirit and cherish the ideas of our associates and to place sacred and eternal things lower than the ideas of our friends. We are, in short, leavened just as the enemy of all righteousness designed we should be.

The young, if brought under this influence, are more easily affected by it than those who are older. Everything leaves its impress upon their minds—the countenances they look upon, the voices they hear, the places they visit, the company they keep, and the books they read. It is impossible to overestimate the importance for this world and the next of the associations we choose for ourselves and, more especially, for our children.[2]

Dangers of Associating With the Ungodly—The world is not to be our criterion. We are not to associate with the ungodly and partake of their spirit, for they will lead the heart away from God to the worship of false gods. The steadfast soul, firm in the faith, can do much good; he can impart blessings of the highest order to those with whom he associates, for the law of the Lord is in his heart. But [460] we cannot willingly associate with those who are trampling upon the law of God, and preserve our faith pure and untarnished. We shall catch the spirit, and unless we separate from them, we shall be bound up with them at last, to share their doom.[3]

It was by associating with idolaters and joining in their festivities that the Hebrews were led to transgress God's law and bring His judgments upon the nation. So now it is by leading the followers of

Christ to associate with the ungodly and unite in their amusements that Satan is most successful in alluring them into sin. "Come out from among them, and be ye separate, saith the Lord, and touch not the unclean." God requires of His people now as great a distinction from the world, in customs, habits, and principles, as He required of Israel anciently.[4]

Samson's Willful Choice—God's providential care had been over Samson, that he might be prepared to accomplish the work which he was called to do. At the very outset of life he was surrounded with favorable conditions for physical strength, intellectual vigor, and moral purity. But under the influence of wicked associates he let go that hold upon God which is man's only safeguard, and he was swept away by the tide of evil. Those who in the way of duty are brought into trial may be sure that God will preserve them; but if men willfully place themselves under the power of temptation, they will fall sooner or later.[5]

The Insidious Leaven of Wickedness—Dear students, day and night the prayers of your parents will follow you. Listen to their entreaties and warnings, and do not choose reckless associates. You [461] cannot discern how the leaven of wickedness will insidiously corrupt your mind and impair your habits and, by leading you to repeat evil habits, cause you to develop an unsound character. You may see no real danger and think that you will be able to do right as easily as before you yielded to temptation to do wrong, but this is a mistake. Parents and teachers who love and fear God may warn and entreat and counsel, but it may all be in vain if you do not yield yourself to God and improve the talents which He has given you to His glory.[6]

Beware of Those Indifferent to Religion—If children are with those whose conversation is upon unimportant, earthly things, their minds will come to the same level. If they hear the principles of religion slurred and our faith belittled, if sly objections to the truth are dropped in their hearing, these things will fasten in their minds and mold their characters.[7]

Nothing can more effectually prevent or banish serious impressions and good desires than association with vain, careless, and corrupt-minded persons. Whatever attractions such persons may possess by their wit, sarcasm, and fun, the fact that they treat religion with levity and indifference is sufficient reason why they should not be associated with. The more engaging they are in other respects, the more should their influence be dreaded as companions because they throw around an irreligious life so many dangerous attractions.[8]

Worldly associations attract and dazzle the senses so that piety, the fear of God, faithfulness, and loyalty have not power to keep men steadfast. The humble, unassuming life of Christ seems altogether unattractive. To many who claim to be sons and daughters of God, Jesus, the Majesty of heaven, is "as a root out of a dry ground: He hath no form nor comeliness."[9]

[462]

Do Not Center Affections on Worldly Relatives—We cannot serve God and the world at the same time. We must not center our affections on worldly relatives, who have no desire to learn the truth. We may seek in every way, while associated with them, to let our light shine; but our words, our deportment, our customs and practices, should not in any sense be molded by their ideas and customs. We are to show forth the truth in all our intercourse with them. If we cannot do this, the less association we have with them the better it will be for our spirituality.[10]

Shun Those With Low Standards, Loose Morals—It is wrong for Christians to associate with those whose morals are loose. An intimate, daily intercourse which occupies time without contributing in any degree to the strength of the intellect or morals is dangerous. If the moral atmosphere surrounding persons is not pure and sanctified, but is tainted with corruption, those who breathe this atmosphere will find that it operates almost insensibly upon the intellect and heart to poison and to ruin. It is dangerous to be conversant with those whose minds naturally take a low level. Gradually and imperceptibly those who are naturally conscientious and love purity will come to the same level and partake of and sympathize with the imbecility and moral barrenness with which they are so constantly brought in contact.[11]

A good name is more precious than gold. There is an inclination with the youth to associate with those who are inferior in mind and morals. What real happiness can a young person expect from a voluntary connection with persons who have a low standard of thoughts, feelings, and deportment? Some are debased in taste and depraved in habits, and all who choose such companions will follow

[463]

their example. We are living in times of peril that should cause the hearts of all to fear.[12]

Many Yield to Temptation Through Fear of Ridicule—Children ... should have companions who will not ridicule what is pure and worthy, but will rather advocate what is right. The fear of ridicule leads many a youth to yield to temptation and to walk in the way of the ungodly. Mothers may do much by example as well as by precept to show their children how to be upright amid scorn and ridicule.[13]

Why do our youth not consider that those who are ready to lead others into forbidden paths are easily overcome by temptation and are Satan's agents to encourage disorderly habits, to laugh at those who are conscientious and who would preserve their integrity of character?[14]

Live Before Strangers As You Would Before God—Young friends, do not spend an hour in the company of those who would unfit you for the pure and sacred work of God. Do nothing before strangers that you would not do before your father and mother, or that you would be ashamed of before Christ and the holy angels.

Some may think these cautions are not needed by Sabbathkeepers, but those to whom they apply know what I mean. I tell you, young men, to beware; for you can do nothing that is not open to the eyes of angels and of God. You cannot do an evil work and others not be affected by it. While your course of action reveals what kind of material is used in your own character building, it also has a powerful influence over others. Never lose sight of the fact that you belong to God, that He has bought you with a price, and [464] you must render an account to Him for all His entrusted talents.[15]

Special Help Is Promised When Needed—We are not to place our children where they must associate with the depraved and degraded. Sometimes God in His providence may bring our youth into association with those who are impure and intemperate. He will give them strength of purpose and power to resist temptation, even as He did Daniel and his associates in Babylon, if they will co-operate with Him. They must constantly commune with God. They must keep themselves pure, refusing to do anything that would dishonor God, living always with an eye single to His glory. They must watch for souls, laboring earnestly for those in whom the image of God has been defaced, seeking to reform, to elevate, and to ennoble them.[16]

Choose Thoughtful, Serious Companions—The youth who are in harmony with Christ will choose companions who will help them in right doing, and will shun society that gives no aid in the development of right principles and noble purposes. In every place are to be found youth whose minds are cast in an inferior mold. When brought into association with this class, those who have placed themselves without reserve on the side of Christ will stand firmly by that which reason and conscience tell them is right.[17]

Let all who would form a right character choose associates who are of a serious, thoughtful turn of mind and who are religiously inclined. Those who have counted the cost and wish to build for eternity must put good material into their building. If they accept of rotten timbers, if they are content with deficiencies of character, the building is doomed to ruin. Let all take heed how they build. The storm of temptation will sweep over the building, and unless it is [465] firmly and faithfully constructed, it will not stand the test.[18]

By association with those who walk according to principle, even the careless will learn to love righteousness. And by the practice of right doing there will be created in the heart a distaste for that which is cheap and common and at variance with the principles of God's word.[19] [466]

---

[1]Testimonies For The Church 5, 222, 223.

[2]Ibid., 543.

[3]Manuscript 6, 1892.

[4]Patriarchs and Prophets, 458.

[5]Ibid., 568.

[6]The Youth's Instructor, January 18, 1894.

[7]Testimonies For The Church 5, 545.

[8]Ibid., 3:125.

[9]Manuscript 6, 1892.

[10]Testimonies For The Church 5, 543.

[11]Testimonies For The Church 3, 125.

[12]Testimonies For The Church 4, 558.

[13]The Review and Herald, March 31, 1891.

[14]The Youth's Instructor, January 18, 1894.

[15]Testimonies For The Church 5, 398, 399.

[16]Manuscript 18, 1892.

[17]Counsels to Teachers, Parents, and Students, 226.

[18]Testimonies For The Church 4, 588.

[19]Counsels to Teachers, Parents, and Students, 222.

Chapter 75—Parental Guidance In Social Affairs

Evil Influences Almost Overpowering—The evil influence around our children is almost overpowering; it is corrupting their minds and leading them down to perdition. The minds of youth are naturally given to folly; and at an early age, before their characters are formed and their judgment matured, they frequently manifest a preference for associates who will have an injurious influence over them.[1]

Could my voice reach the parents all through the land, I would warn them not to yield to the desires of their children in choosing their companions or associates. Little do parents consider that injurious impressions are far more readily received by the young than are divine impressions; therefore their associations should be the most favorable for the growth of grace and for the truth revealed in the word of God to be established in the heart.[2]

Let the youth be placed in the most favorable circumstances possible; for the company they keep, the principles they adopt, the habits they form, will settle the question of their usefulness here and of their future, eternal interests with a certainty that is infallible.[3]

The Peril of Unlimited Freedom—Parents, your sons and daughters are not properly guarded. They should never be permitted to go and come when they please, without your knowledge and consent. The unbounded freedom granted to children at this age has proved the ruin of thousands. How many are allowed to be in the streets at night, and parents are content to be ignorant of the associates of their children. Too often companions are chosen whose influence tends only to demoralize.

Under the cover of darkness boys collect in groups to learn their first lessons in card playing, gambling, smoking, and wine or beer sipping. The sons of religious parents venture into the saloons for an oyster supper or some similar indulgence, and thus place themselves in the way of temptation. The very atmosphere of these resorts is redolent with blasphemy and pollution. No one can long remain

365

in it without becoming corrupted. It is by such associations that promising youth are becoming inebriates and criminals. The very beginnings of the evil should be guarded against. Parents, unless you know that their surroundings are unexceptionable, do not permit your children to go into the streets after nightfall to engage in outdoor sports or to meet other boys for amusement. If this rule be rigidly enforced, obedience to it will become habitual, and the desire to transgress will soon cease.[4]

Parents Must Choose the Child's Associates—Parents should remember that association with those of lax morals and coarseness of character will have a detrimental influence upon the youth. If they fail to choose proper society for their children, if they allow them to associate with youth of questionable morals, they place them, or permit them to place themselves, in a school where lessons of depravity are taught and practiced. They may feel that their children are strong enough to withstand temptation, but how can they be sure of this? It is far easier to yield to evil influences than to resist them. [468] Ere they are aware of it, their children may become imbued with the spirit of their associates and may be degraded or ruined.[5]

The dangers of the young are greatly increased as they are thrown into the society of a large number of their own age, of varied character and habits of life. Under these circumstances many parents are inclined to relax rather than redouble their own efforts to guard and control their children.[6]

Prayerfully, unitedly, the father and the mother should bear the grave responsibility of guiding their children aright. Whatever else they neglect, they should never leave their children free to wander in paths of sin. Many parents allow children to go and do as they please, amusing themselves and choosing evil associates. In the judgment such parents will learn that their children have lost heaven because they have not been kept under home restraint.[7]

Where Are the Evenings Spent?—Every son and daughter should be called to account if absent from home at night. Parents should know what company their children are in and at whose house they spend their evenings. Some children deceive their parents with falsehoods to avoid exposure of their wrong course.[8]

Weeds Predominate in an Uncultivated Field—Fathers and mothers too often leave their children to choose for themselves their amusements, their companions, and their occupation. The result is such as might reasonably be expected. Leave a field uncultivated, and it will grow up to thorns and briers. You will never see a lovely flower or a choice shrub peering above the unsightly, poisonous weeds. The worthless bramble will grow luxuriantly without thought or care, while plants that are valued for use or beauty require [469] thorough culture. Thus it is with our youth. If right habits are formed and right principles established, there is earnest work to be done. If wrong habits are corrected, diligence and perseverance are required to accomplish the task.[9]

Accustom Child to Trust Parents' Judgment—Parents, guard the principles and habits of your children as the apple of the eye. Allow them to associate with no one with whose character you are not well acquainted. Permit them to form no intimacy until you are assured that it will do them no harm. Accustom your children to trust your judgment and experience. Teach them that you have clearer perception of character than they in their inexperience can have, and that your decisions must not be disregarded.[10]

The Restraint to Be Firm, but Kind—The parents should not concede to the inclinations of their children, but should follow the plain path of duty which God has marked out, restraining them in kindness, denying with firmness and determination, yet with love, their wrong desires, and with earnest, prayerful, persevering effort leading their steps away from the world upward to heaven. Children should not be left to drift into whatever way they are inclined, and to go into avenues which are open on every side, leading away from the right path. None are in so great danger as those who apprehend no danger and are impatient of caution and counsel.[11]

Guard your children from every objectionable influence possible; for in childhood they are more ready to receive impressions, either of moral dignity, purity, and loveliness of character, or of selfishness, impurity, and disobedience. Once let them become influenced by the spirit of murmuring, pride, vanity, and impurity, and the taint [470] may be as indelible as life itself.[12]

It is because the home training is defective that the youth are so unwilling to submit to proper authority. I am a mother; I know whereof I speak when I say that youth and children are not only safer but happier under wholesome restraint than when following their own inclination.[13]

Unaccompanied Visits Inadvisable—Some parents mistake in giving their children too much liberty. They sometimes have so much confidence in them that they do not see their faults. It is wrong to allow children, at some expense, to visit at a distance, unaccompanied by their parents or guardians. It has a wrong influence upon the children. They come to feel that they are of considerable consequence and that certain privileges belong to them, and if these are not granted, they think themselves abused. They refer to children who go and come and have many privileges, while they have so few.

And the mother, fearing that her children will think her unjust, gratifies their wishes, which in the end proves a great injury to them. Young visitors, who have not a parent's watchful eye over them to see and correct their faults, often receive impressions which it will take months to remove.[14]

Unwise Advice and How to Meet It—Keep your children at their home; and if people say to you, "Your children will not know how to conduct themselves in the world," tell your friends that you are not so concerned about that matter, but that you do want to take them to the Master for His blessing, even as the mothers of old [471] took their children to Jesus. Say to your advisers: Children are the heritage of the Lord, and I want to prove faithful to my trust.... My children must be brought up in such a way that they shall not be swayed by the influences of the world, but where, when tempted to sin, they may be able to say a square, hearty *no*." ...Tell your friends and neighbors that you want to see your family inside the gates of the beautiful city.[15]

Powerful Tests Are Before Our Youth—Children should be trained and educated so that they may calculate to meet with difficulties and expect temptations and dangers. They should be taught to have control over themselves and to nobly overcome difficulties; and if they do not willfully rush into danger and needlessly place themselves in the way of temptation, if they avoid evil influences and vicious society, and then are unavoidably compelled to be in dangerous company, they will have strength of character to stand for the right and preserve principle and will come forth in the strength of God with their morals untainted. The moral powers of youth who have been properly educated, if they make God their trust, will be equal to stand the most powerful test.[16]

[1] Testimonies For The Church 1, 400, 401.

[2] Ibid., 5:544, 545.

[3] Ibid., 5:545.

[4] Fundamentals of Christian Education, 63.

[5] Counsels to Teachers, Parents, and Students, 120.

[6] Ibid., 332.

[7] The Review and Herald, September 8. 1904.

[8] Counsels to Teachers. Parents. and Students. 332. 333.

[9] The Review and Herald, September 13. 1881.

[10] Counsels to Teachers, Parents, and Students, 120.

[11] Testimonies For The Church 5, 545, 546.

[12] The Signs of the Times, April 16, 1896.

[13] Fundamentals of Christian Education, 62, 63.

[14] Testimonies For The Church 1: 401, 402.

[15] The Signs of the Times. April 23. 1894.

[16] The Health Reformer, December. 1872.

Chapter 76—Holidays And Anniversaries

The Need of Guidance in Holiday Observance—I saw that our holidays should not be spent in patterning after the world, yet they should not be passed by unnoticed, for this will bring dissatisfaction to our children. On these days when there is danger that our children will be exposed to evil influences and become corrupted by the pleasures and excitement of the world, let the parents study to get up something to take the place of more dangerous amusements. Give your children to understand that you have their good and happiness in view.[1]

Through the observance of holidays the people both of the world and of the churches have been educated to believe that these lazy days are essential to health and happiness, but the results reveal that they are full of evil.[2]

We have tried earnestly to make the holidays as interesting as possible to the youth and children, while changing this order of things. Our object has been to keep them away from scenes of amusement among unbelievers.[3]

Shall the Angel Record, "A Day Lost?"—After a day of pleasure seeking is ended, where is the satisfaction to the pleasure seeker? As Christian workers, whom have they helped to a better, higher, and purer life? What would they see if they should look over the record the angel wrote? A day lost! To their own souls a day lost, a day lost in the service of Christ, because no good was accomplished. They may have other days but never that day which was idled away in cheap, foolish talk, of girls with boys, and boys with girls.

[473] Never will these same opportunities offer themselves again. They had better been doing the hardest kind of labor on that holiday. They did not make the right use of their holiday, and it passed into eternity to confront them in the judgment as a day misspent.[4]

Birthdays—a Time to Praise God—Under the Jewish economy on the birth of children an offering was made to God, by

370

His own appointment. Now we see parents taking special pains to present gifts to their children upon their birthdays; they make this an occasion of honoring the child, as though honor were due to the human being. Satan has had his own way in these things; he has diverted the minds and the gifts to human beings; thus the thoughts of the children are turned to themselves, as if they were to be made the objects of special favor....

On birthday occasions the children should be taught that they have reason for gratitude to God for His loving-kindness in preserving their lives for another year. Precious lessons might thus be given. For life, health, food, and clothing, no less than for the hope of eternal life, we are indebted to the Giver of all mercies; and it is due to God to recognize His gifts and to present our offerings of gratitude to our greatest benefactor. These birthday gifts are recognized of Heaven.[5]

A Time to Review the Year's Record—Teach them to review the past year of their life, to consider whether they would be glad to meet its record just as it stands in the books of heaven. Encourage in them serious thoughts, whether their deportment, their words, their works, are of a character pleasing to God. Have they been making their lives more like Jesus, beautiful and lovely in the sight of God? Teach them the knowledge of the Lord, His ways, His precepts.[6]

[474]

Making God's Cause First—I have said to my family and my friends, I desire that no one shall make me a birthday or Christmas gift, unless it be with permission to pass it on into the Lord's treasury, to be appropriated in the establishment of missions.[7]

How Shall We Observe Thanksgiving?—Our Thanksgiving is approaching. Will it be, as it has been in many instances, a thanksgiving to ourselves? Or will it be a thanksgiving to God? Our Thanksgivings may be made seasons of great profit to our own souls as well as to others if we improve this opportunity to remember the poor among us....

There are a hundred ways that can be devised to help the poor in so delicate a manner as to make them feel that they are doing us a favor by receiving our gifts and sympathy. We are to remember that it is more blessed to give than to receive. The attentions of our brethren are most liberal to those whom they wish to honor, and whose respect they desire, but who do not need their help at all.

Custom and fashion say, Give to those who will give to you; but this is not the Bible rule of giving. The word of God declares against this way of gratifying self in thus bestowing our gifts, and says, "He that giveth to the rich, shall surely come to want."

Now a season is coming when we shall have our principles tested. Let us begin to think what we can do for God's needy ones. We can make them through ourselves the recipients of God's blessings. Think what widow, what orphan, what poor family you can relieve, [475] not in a way to make a great parade about the matter, but be as a channel through which the Lord's substance shall flow as a blessing to His poor....

But this does not embrace all your duty. Make an offering to your best Friend; acknowledge His bounties; show your gratitude for His favors; bring a thank offering to God.... Brethren and sisters, eat a plain dinner on Thanksgiving Day, and with the money you would spend in extras with which to indulge the appetite, make a thank offering to God.[8]

Let not any more Thanksgiving days be observed to please and gratify the appetite and glorify self. We have reason for coming into the courts of the Lord with offerings of gratitude that He has preserved our lives another year.... If a feast is to be made, let it be for those who are in need.[9]

A Day to Give Thanks [Note: part of a thanksgiving sermon delivered at the Battle Creek Tabernacle, Nov. 27, 1884.]—I think we have something to be thankful for. We ought to be glad and rejoice in God, for He has given us many mercies.... We want this Thanksgiving to be all that it implies. Do not let it be perverted, mingled with dross; but let it be what its name implies—giving thanks. Let our voices ascend in praise.[10]

Why Not Holidays Unto God?—Would it not be well for us to observe holidays unto God, when we could revive in our minds the memory of His dealing with us? Would it not be well to consider His past blessings, to remember the impressive warnings that have come home to our souls so that we shall not forget God?

[476]   The world has many holidays, and men become engrossed with games, with horse races, with gambling, smoking, and drunkenness....

Shall not the people of God more frequently have holy convocations in which to thank God for His rich blessings?[11]

Holidays Afford Opportunity for Missionary Service—We want men in the church who have ability to develop in the line of organizing and giving practical work to young men and women in the line of relieving the wants of humanity and working for the salvation of the souls of men, women, youth, and children. It will not be possible for all to give their whole time to the work because of the labor they must do to earn their daily living. Yet these have their holidays and times that they can devote to Christian work and do good in this way if they cannot give much of their means.[12]

When you have a holiday, make it a pleasant and happy day for your children, and make it also a pleasant day for the poor and the afflicted. Do not let the day pass without bringing thanksgiving and thank offerings to Jesus.[13]

[477]

[1] Testimonies For The Church 1, 514, 515.

[2] Fundamentals of Christian Education, 317.

[3] The Review and Herald, January 29, 1884.

[4] Letter 12, 1892.

[5] The Review and Herald, December 9, 1890.

[6] The Review and Herald, December 23, 1884.

[7] The Review and Herald, December 27, 1906.

[8] The Review and Herald, November 18, 1884.

[9] The Review and Herald, December 23, 1884.

[10] Ibid.

[11] Counsels to Teachers, Parents, and Students, 343.

[12] Letter 12, 1892.

[13] The Review and Herald, November 13, 1894.

Chapter 77—Christmas

Christmas as a Holiday—"Christmas is coming," is the note that is sounded throughout our world from east to west and from north to south. With youth, those of mature age, and even the aged, it is a period of general rejoicing, of great gladness. But what is Christmas, that it should demand so much attention? ...

The twenty-fifth of December is supposed to be the day of the birth of Jesus Christ, and its observance has become customary and popular. But yet there is no certainty that we are keeping the veritable day of our Saviour's birth. History gives us no certain assurance of this. The Bible does not give us the precise time. Had the Lord deemed this knowledge essential to our salvation, He would have spoken through His prophets and apostles, that we might know all about the matter. But the silence of the Scriptures upon this point evidences to us that it is hidden from us for the wisest purposes.

In His wisdom the Lord concealed the place where He buried Moses. God buried him, and God resurrected him and took him to heaven. This secrecy was to prevent idolatry. He against whom they rebelled while he was in active service, whom they provoked almost beyond human endurance, was almost worshiped as God after his separation from them by death. For the very same purpose He has concealed the precise day of Christ's birth, that the day should not receive the honor that should be given to Christ as the Redeemer of the world—one to be received, to be trusted, to be relied on as He [478] who could save to the uttermost all who come unto Him. The soul's adoration should be given to Jesus as the Son of the infinite God.[1]

The Day Not to Be Ignored—As the twenty-fifth of December is observed to commemorate the birth of Christ, as the children have been instructed by precept and example that this was indeed a day of gladness and rejoicing, you will find it a difficult matter to pass over this period without giving it some attention. It can be made to serve a very good purpose.

374

The youth should be treated very carefully. They should not be left on Christmas to find their own amusement in vanity and pleasure seeking, in amusements which will be detrimental to their spirituality. Parents can control this matter by turning the minds and the offerings of their children to God and His cause and the salvation of souls.

The desire for amusement, instead of being quenched and arbitrarily ruled down, should be controlled and directed by painstaking effort upon the part of the parents. Their desire to make gifts may be turned into pure and holy channels and made to result in good to our fellow men by supplying the treasury in the great, grand work for which Christ came into our world. Self-denial and self-sacrifice marked His course of action. Let it mark ours who profess to love Jesus because in Him is centered our hope of eternal life.[2]

The Interchange of Gifts as Tokens of Affection—The holiday season is fast approaching with its interchange of gifts, and old and young are intently studying what they can bestow upon their friends as a token of affectionate remembrance. It is pleasant to receive a gift, however small, from those we love. It is an assurance that we are not forgotten, and seems to bind us to them a little closer....

[479]

It is right to bestow upon one another tokens of love and remembrance if we do not in this forget God, our best friend. We should make our gifts such as will prove a real benefit to the receiver. I would recommend such books as will be an aid in understanding the word of God or that will increase our love for its precepts. Provide something to be read during these long winter evenings.[3]

Books for Children Are Recommended—There are many who have not books and publications upon present truth. Here is a large field where money can be safely invested. There are large numbers of little ones who should be supplied with reading. *The Sunshine Series, Golden Grains Series, Poems, Sabbath Readings,* [Note: reference is made in this article to noncurrent publications. As the principles set forth in this connection are applicable today, these specific references are left in the article.] etc., are all precious books and may be introduced safely into every family. The many trifles usually spent on candies and useless toys may be treasured up with which to buy these volumes....

Let those who wish to make valuable presents to their children, grandchildren, nephews, and nieces procure for them the children's books mentioned above. For young people the *Life of Joseph Bates* is a treasure; also the three volumes of *The Spirit of Prophecy*. [Note: early E. G. White books preceding the present "Conflict Of The Ages Series."] These volumes should be placed in every family in the land. God is giving light from heaven, and not a family should be without it. Let the presents you shall make be of that order which will shed beams of light upon the pathway to heaven.[4]

[480]

Jesus Not to Be Forgotten—Brethren and sisters, while you are devising gifts for one another, I would remind you of our heavenly Friend, lest you should be unmindful of His claims. Will He not be pleased if we show that we have not forgotten Him? Jesus, the Prince of life, gave all to bring salvation within our reach.... He suffered even unto death, that He might give us eternal life.

It is through Christ that we receive every blessing.... Shall not our heavenly Benefactor share in the tokens of our gratitude and love? Come, brethren and sisters, come with your children, even the babes in your arms, and bring your offerings to God according to your ability. Make melody to Him in your hearts, and let His praise be upon your lips.[5]

Christmas—a Time to Honor God—By the world the holidays are spent in frivolity and extravagance, gluttony and display.... Thousands of dollars will be worse than thrown away upon the coming Christmas and New Year's in needless indulgences. But it is our privilege to depart from the customs and practices of this degenerate age; and instead of expending means merely for the gratification of the appetite or for needless ornaments or articles of clothing, we may make the coming holidays an occasion in which to honor and glorify God.[6]

Christ should be the supreme object; but as Christmas has been observed, the glory is turned from Him to mortal man, whose sinful, defective character made it necessary for Him to come to our world.

[481]

Jesus, the Majesty of heaven, the royal King of heaven, laid aside His royalty, left His throne of glory, His high command, and came into our world to bring to fallen man, weakened in moral power and corrupted by sin, aid divine....

Parents should keep these things before their children and instruct them, line upon line, precept upon precept, in their obligation to God—not their obligation to each other, to honor and glorify one another by gifts and offerings.[7]

Turn Thoughts of the Children Into a New Channel—There are many things which can be devised with taste and cost far less than the unnecessary presents that are so frequently bestowed upon our children and relatives, and thus courtesy can be shown and happiness brought into the home.

You can teach your children a lesson while you explain to them the reason why you have made a change in the value of their presents, telling them that you are convinced that you have hitherto considered their pleasure more than the glory of God. Tell them that you have thought more of your own pleasure and of their gratification and of keeping in harmony with the customs and traditions of the world, in making presents to those who did not need them, than you have of advancing the cause of God. Like the wise men of old, you may offer to God your best gifts and show by your offerings to Him that you appreciate His Gift to a sinful world. Set your children's thoughts running in a new, unselfish channel by inciting them to present offerings to God for the gift of His only-begotten Son.[8]

[482]

"Shall We Have a Christmas Tree?"—God would be well pleased if on Christmas each church would have a Christmas tree on which shall be hung offerings, great and small, for these houses of worship. [Note: reference is made in this article to current building projects. As the principles set forth in this connection are applicable today, these specific references are left in the article.] Letters of inquiry have come to us asking, Shall we have a Christmas tree? Will it not be like the world? We answer, You can make it like the world if you have a disposition to do so, or you can make it as unlike the world as possible. There is no particular sin in selecting a fragrant evergreen and placing it in our churches, but the sin lies in the motive which prompts to action and the use which is made of the gifts placed upon the tree.

The tree may be as tall and its branches as wide as shall best suit the occasion; but let its boughs be laden with the golden and silver fruit of your beneficence, and present this to Him as your Christmas gift. Let your donations be sanctified by prayer.[9]

Christmas and New Year celebrations can and should be held in behalf of those who are helpless. God is glorified when we give to help those who have large families to support.[10]

A Tree Laden With Offerings Is Not Sinful—Let not the parents take the position that an evergreen placed in the church for the amusement of the Sabbath school scholars is a sin, for it may be made a great blessing. Keep before their minds benevolent objects. In no case should mere amusement be the object of these gatherings. While there may be some who will turn these occasions into seasons of careless levity, and whose minds will not receive the [483] divine impress, to other minds and characters these seasons will be highly beneficial. I am fully satisfied that innocent substitutes can be devised for many gatherings that demoralize.[11]

Provide Innocent Enjoyment for the Day—Will you not arise, my Christian brethren and sisters, and gird yourselves for duty in the fear of God, so arranging this matter that it shall not be dry and uninteresting, but full of innocent enjoyment that shall bear the signet of Heaven? I know the poorer class will respond to these suggestions. The most wealthy should also show an interest and bestow their gifts and offerings proportionate to the means with which God has entrusted them. Let there be recorded in the heavenly books such a Christmas as has never yet been seen because of the donations which shall be given for the sustaining of the work of God [484] and the upbuilding of His kingdom.[12]

---

[1] The Review and Herald, December 9, 1884.

[2] Ibid.

[3] The Review and Herald, December 26, 1882.

[4] The Review and Herald, December 11, 1879.

[5] The Review and Herald, December 26, 1882.

[6] The Review and Herald, December 11, 1879.

[7] The Review and Herald, December 9, 1884.

[8] The Review and Herald, November 13, 1894.

[9] The Review and Herald, December 11, 1879.

[10] Manuscript 13, 1896.

[11] The Review and Herald, December 9, 1884.

[12] Ibid.

Chapter 78—The Family a Missionary Center

Parents Should Give Children Right Direction—With us as parents and as Christians it rests to give our children right direction. They are to be carefully, wisely, tenderly guided into paths of Christlike ministry. We are under sacred covenant with God to rear our children for His service. To surround them with such influences as shall lead them to choose a life of service, and to give them the training needed, is our first duty.[1]

Children May Be Daniels and Esthers Today—God's purpose for the children growing up beside our hearths is wider, deeper, higher, than our restricted vision has comprehended. From the humblest lot those whom He has seen faithful have in time past been called to witness for Him in the world's highest places. And many a lad of today, growing up as did Daniel in his Judean home, studying God's word and His works, and learning the lessons of faithful service, will yet stand in legislative assemblies, in halls of justice, or in royal courts as a witness for the King of kings. Multitudes will be called to a wider ministry. The whole world is opening to the gospel.... From every quarter of this world of ours comes the cry of sin-stricken hearts for a knowledge of the God of love.... It rests with us who have received the knowledge, with our children to whom we may impart it, to answer their cry. To every household and every school, to every parent, teacher, and child upon whom has shone the light of the gospel, comes at this crisis the question put to Esther the queen at that momentous crisis in Israel's history, "Who [485] knoweth whether *thou* art come to the kingdom for such a time as this?"[2]

Successful Ways of Witnessing for Christ—Not all can go as missionaries to foreign lands, but all can be home missionaries in their families and neighborhoods. There are many ways in which church members may give the message to those around them. One of the most successful is by living helpful, unselfish Christian lives. Those who are fighting the battle of life at great odds may be refreshed and strengthened by little attentions which cost nothing. Kindly words simply spoken, little attentions simply bestowed, will sweep away the clouds of temptation and doubt that gather over the soul. The true heart expression of Christlike sympathy, given in simplicity, has power to open the door of hearts that need the simple, delicate touch of the spirit of Christ.[3]

There is a wide field of service for women as well as for men. The efficient cook, the seamstress, the nurse—the help of all is needed. Let the members of poor households be taught how to cook, how to make and mend their own clothing, how to nurse the sick, how to care properly for the home. Even the children should be taught to do some little errand of love and mercy for those less fortunate than themselves.[4]

Children and Youth to Join in Service for Others—In an effort to excuse themselves some say: "My home duties, my children, claim my time and my means." Parents, your children should be your helping hand, increasing your power and ability to work for the Master. Children are the younger members of the Lord's family. They should be led to consecrate themselves to God, whose they are by creation and by redemption. They should be taught that all their powers of body, mind, and soul are His. They should be trained to help in various lines of unselfish service. Do not allow your children to be hindrances. With you the children should share spiritual as well as physical burdens. By helping others they increase their own happiness and usefulness.[5]

[486]

If in every church the young men and the young women would solemnly consecrate themselves to God, if they would practice self-denial in the home life, relieving their tired, careworn mothers, what a change would take place in our churches! The mother could find time to make neighborly visits. When opportunity offered, the children could give assistance by doing, when quite young, little errands of mercy and love to bless others. Thus thousands of the homes of the poor and needy not of our faith could be entered. Books relating to health and temperance could be placed in many homes. The circulation of these books is an important work; for they contain precious knowledge in regard to the treatment of disease—knowledge that would be a great blessing to those who cannot afford to pay for the physician's visits.[6]

God Wants Children as Little Missionaries—God wants every child of tender age to be His child, to be adopted into His family. Young though they may be, the youth may be members of the household of faith and have a most precious experience.[7]

In their early years children may be useful in God's work.... He will give them His grace and His Holy Spirit, that they may overcome impatience, fretfulness, and all sin. Jesus loves the children. He has blessings for them, and He loves to see them obedient to their parents. He desires them to be His little missionaries, denying their own inclinations and desires for selfish pleasure to do service for Him; and this service is just as acceptable to God as is the service of grown-up children.[8]

[487]

By precept and example parents are to teach their children to labor for the unconverted. The children should be so educated that they will sympathize with the aged and afflicted and will seek to alleviate the sufferings of the poor and distressed. They should be taught to be diligent in missionary work; and from their earliest years self-denial and sacrifice for the good of others and the advancement of Christ's cause should be inculcated, that they may be laborers together with God.[9]

Let parents teach their little ones the truth as it is in Jesus. The children in their simplicity will repeat to their associates that which they have learned.[10]

The Church Has Work for the Youth—Let the overseers of the church devise plans whereby young men and women may be trained to put to use their entrusted talents. Let the older members of the church seek to do earnest, compassionate work for the children and youth. Let ministers put to use all their ingenuity in devising plans whereby the younger members of the church may be led to co-operate with them in missionary work. But do not imagine that you can arouse their interest merely by preaching a long sermon at the missionary meeting. Plan ways whereby a live interest may be kindled. Let all have a part to act. Train the young to do what is appointed them, and from week to week let them bring their reports to the missionary meeting, telling what they have experienced and through the grace of Christ what success has been theirs. If such reports were brought in by consecrated workers, the missionary meetings would not be dull and tedious. They would be full of

[488]

interest, and there would be no lack in attendance.[11]

Seek Opportunities in the Neighborhood—Opportunities are within the reach of everyone. Take up the work that should be done in your neighborhood, for which you are held responsible. [Note: for detailed counsel on the methods and effectiveness of neighborhood ministry of kindness, see *Welfare Ministry.—Compilers.*] Wait not for others to urge you to take advance steps. Move without delay, bearing in mind your individual responsibility to Him who gave His life for you. Move as if you heard Christ calling upon you personally to awake out of sleep and to exert every God-given faculty in doing the utmost in His service. Look not to see who else is ready to catch inspiration from the word of the living God. If you are thoroughly consecrated, through your instrumentality He will bring into the truth others whom He can use as channels to convey light to many souls in darkness.[12]

Let Christian Families Enter Dark Counties.—God calls for Christian families to go into communities that are in darkness and error, and work wisely and perseveringly for the Master. To answer this call requires self-sacrifice. While many are waiting to have every obstacle removed, souls are dying without hope and without God in the world. Many, very many, for the sake of worldly advantage, for the sake of acquiring scientific knowledge, will venture into pestilential regions and endure hardship and privation. Where are those who are willing to do this for the sake of telling others of the

[489] Saviour? Where are the men and women who will move into regions that are in need of the gospel, that they may point those in darkness to the Redeemer?[13]

If families would locate in the dark places of the earth, places where the people are enshrouded in spiritual gloom, and let the light of Christ's life shine out through them, a great work might be accomplished. Let them begin their work in a quiet, unobtrusive way, not drawing on the funds of the conference until the interest becomes so extensive that they cannot manage it without ministerial help.[14]

Children Will Work When Others Cannot—When heavenly intelligences see that men are no longer permitted to present the truth, the Spirit of God will come upon the children, and they will do a work in the proclamation of the truth which the older workers cannot do because their way will be hedged up.[15]

In the closing scenes of this earth's history many of these children and youth will astonish people by their witness to the truth, which will be borne in simplicity, yet with spirit and power. They have been taught the fear of the Lord, and their hearts have been softened by a careful and prayerful study of the Bible. In the near future many children will be endued with the Spirit of God and will do a work in proclaiming the truth to the world that at that time cannot well be done by the older members of the church.[16]

Our church schools are ordained by God to prepare the children for this great work. Here children are to be instructed in the special truths for this time and in practical missionary work. They are to enlist in the army of workers to help the sick and the suffering. Children can take part in the medical missionary work and by their jots and tittles can help to carry it forward.... By them God's message [490] will be made known and His saving health to all nations. Then let the church carry a burden for the lambs of the flock. Let the children be educated and trained to do service for God.[17]

Learn to Do by Doing—Love and loyalty to Christ are the spring of all true service. In the heart touched by His love there is begotten a desire to work for Him. Let this desire be encouraged and rightly guided. Whether in the home, the neighborhood, or the school, the presence of the poor, the afflicted, the ignorant, or the unfortunate should be regarded, not as a misfortune, but as affording precious opportunity for service.

In this work, as in every other, skill is gained in the work itself. It is by training in the common duties of life and in ministry to the needy and suffering that efficiency is assured. Without this the best-meant efforts are often useless and even harmful. It is in the water, not on the land, that men learn to swim.[18] [491]

[492]

[1]The Ministry of Healing, 396.

[2]Education, 262, 263.

[3]Testimonies For The Church 9, 30.

[4]Ibid., 9:36, 37.

[5]Ibid., 7:63.

[6]Manuscript 119, 1901.

[7]Letter 104, 1897.

[8]The Review and Herald, November 17, 1896.

[9]Testimonies For The Church 6: 429.

[10]Manuscript 19, 1900.

[11]Testimonies For The Church 6, 435, 436.

[12]Manuscript 128, 1901.

[13]Testimonies For The Church 9, 33.

[14]Ibid., 6:442.

[15]Ibid., 202.

[16]Counsels to Teachers, Parents, and Students, 166, 167.

[17]Testimonies For The Church 6, 203.

[18]Education, 268.

Section 17—Relaxation and Recreation

Chapter 79—Recreation is Essential

Extreme Views Regarding Recreation—There are persons with a diseased imagination to whom religion is a tyrant, ruling them as with a rod of iron. Such are constantly mourning over their depravity and groaning over supposed evil. Love does not exist in their hearts; a frown is ever upon their countenances. They are chilled by the innocent laugh from the youth or from anyone. They consider all recreation or amusement a sin and think that the mind must be constantly wrought up to just such a stern, severe pitch. This is one extreme. Others think that the mind must be ever on the stretch to invent new amusements and diversions in order to gain health. They learn to depend on excitement and are uneasy without it. Such are not true Christians. They go to another extreme. The true principles of Christianity open before all a source of happiness, the height and depth, the length and breadth of which are immeasurable.[1]

To Refresh the Spirits and Invigorate the Body—It is the privilege and duty of Christians to seek to refresh their spirits and invigorate their bodies by innocent recreation, with the purpose of using their physical and mental powers to the glory of God. Our recreations should not be scenes of senseless mirth, taking the form of the nonsensical. We can conduct them in such a manner as will benefit and elevate those with whom we associate, and better qualify us and them to more successfully attend to the duties devolving upon
us as Christians.[2]

I was shown that Sabbathkeepers as a people labor too hard without allowing themselves change or periods of rest. Recreation is needful to those who are engaged in physical labor and is still more essential for those whose labor is principally mental. It is not essential to our salvation, nor for the glory of God, to keep the mind laboring constantly and excessively, even upon religious themes.[3]

With the question of recreation the surroundings of the home and the school have much to do. In the choice of a home or the location of a school these things should be considered. Those with whom mental and physical well-being is of greater moment than money or the claims and customs of society should seek for their children the benefit of nature's teaching and recreation amidst her surroundings.[4]

Recreation Is Essential to Best Work—The time spent in physical exercise is not lost.... A proportionate exercise of all the organs and faculties of the body is essential to the best work of each. When the brain is constantly taxed while the other organs of the living machinery are inactive, there is a loss of strength, physical and mental. The physical system is robbed of its healthful tone, the mind loses its freshness and vigor, and a morbid excitability is the result.[5]

Care needs to be exercised in regard to the regulation of hours for sleeping and laboring. We must take periods of rest, periods of recreation, periods for contemplation.... The principles of temperance have a wider range than many think.[6]

Students Need Relaxation—Those who are engaged in study should have relaxation. The mind must not be constantly confined to close thought, for the delicate mental machinery becomes worn. The body as well as the mind must have exercise.[7]

[495]

Attention to recreation and physical culture will at times, no doubt, interrupt the regular routine of schoolwork; but the interruption will prove no real hindrance. In the invigoration of mind and body, the fostering of an unselfish spirit, and the binding together of pupil and teacher by the ties of common interest and friendly association, the expenditure of time and effort will be repaid a hundredfold. A blessed outlet will be afforded for that restless energy which is so often a source of danger to the young. As a safeguard against evil, the preoccupation of the mind with good is worth more than unnumbered barriers of law and discipline.[8]

Office Workers Who Needed Days for Recreation—I saw that but few realize the constant, wearing labor of those who are bearing the responsibilities of the work in the office. They are confined within doors day after day and week after week, while a constant strain upon the mental powers is surely undermining their constitutions and lessening their hold on life. These brethren are in danger of breaking suddenly. They are not immortal, and without a change they must wear out and be lost to the work.

We have precious gifts in Brethren A, B, and C. We cannot afford to have them ruin their health through close confinement and incessant toil....

They have had scarcely any variation except what fevers and other sickness have given them. They should have a change frequently, should often devote a day wholly to recreation with their families, who are almost entirely deprived of their society. All may [496] not be able to leave the work at the same time; but they should so arrange their work that one or two may go, leaving others to supply their places, and then let these in their turn have the same opportunity.

I saw that these brethren, A, B, and C, should as a religious duty take care of the health and strength which God has given them. The Lord does not require them just now to become martyrs to His cause. They will obtain no reward for making this sacrifice, for God wants them to live.[9]

Seek Means for Innocent, Instructive Recreation—There are modes of recreation which are highly beneficial to both mind and body. An enlightened, discriminating mind will find abundant means for entertainment and diversion, from sources not only innocent, but instructive. Recreation in the open air, the contemplation of the works of God in nature, will be of the highest benefit.[10]

I believe that, while we are seeking to refresh our spirits and invigorate our bodies, we *are required of God* to use all our powers at all times to the best purpose. We may associate together as we do here today, [Note: portion of an address to a company of about two hundred, enjoying a season of recreation at Lake Goguac, near Battle Creek, Michigan, in May, 1870.] and do all to the glory of God. We can and should conduct our recreations in such a manner that we shall be fitted for the more successful discharge of the duties devolving upon us, and that our influence shall be more beneficial upon those with whom we associate. Especially should it be the case upon an occasion like this, which should be of good cheer to us all. We can return to our homes improved in mind and refreshed in body, and prepared to engage in the work anew, with better hope [497] and better courage.[11]

God's Invitation to Youth—God's invitation comes to each youth, "My son, give Me thine heart; I will keep it pure; I will satisfy its longings with true happiness." God loves to make the youth happy, and that is why He would have them give their hearts into His keeping, that all the God-given faculties of the being may be kept in a vigorous, healthful condition. They are holding God's gift of life. He makes the heart beat; He gives strength to every faculty. Pure enjoyment will not debase one of God's gifts.[12]   [498]

[1]Testimonies For The Church 1, 565.

[2]The Health Reformer, July, 1871.

[3]Testimonies For The Church 1, 514.

[4]Education, 211, 212.

[5]Fundamentals of Christian Education, 418.

[6]Manuscript 60, 1894.

[7]Counsels to Teachers, Parents, and Students, 333.

[8]Education, 213.

[9]Testimonies For The Church 1, 515, 516.

[10]Testimonies For The Church 4, 653.

[11]Testimonies For The Church 2, 586.

[12]The Youth's Instructor, January 5, 1887.

Chapter 80—What Shall We Play?

Substitute the Innocent for the Sinful—Youth cannot be made as sedate and grave as old age, the child as sober as the sire. While sinful amusements are condemned, as they should be, let parents, teachers, and guardians of youth provide in their stead innocent pleasures which will not taint or corrupt the morals. Do not bind down the young to rigid rules and restraints that will lead them to feel themselves oppressed and to break over and rush into paths of folly and destruction. With a firm, kind, considerate hand hold the lines of government, guiding and controlling their minds and purposes, yet so gently, so wisely, so lovingly, that they will still know that you have their best good in view.[1]

There are amusements, such as dancing, card playing, chess, checkers, etc., which we cannot approve because Heaven condemns them. These amusements open the door for great evil. They are not beneficial in their tendency, but have an exciting influence, producing in some minds a passion for those plays which lead to gambling and dissipation. All such plays should be condemned by Christians, and something perfectly harmless should be substituted in their place.[2]

While we restrain our children from worldly pleasures that have a tendency to corrupt and mislead, we ought to provide them innocent recreation, to lead them in pleasant paths where there is no danger. No child of God need have a sad or mournful experience. Divine commands, divine promises, show that this is so. Wisdom's ways [499] "are ways of pleasantness, and all her paths are peace."[3]

While we shun the false and artificial, discarding horse racing, card playing, lotteries, prize fights, liquor drinking, and tobacco using, we must supply sources of pleasure that are pure and noble and elevating.[4]

The Useful Place of the Gymnasium—Gymnastic exercises fill a useful place in many schools, but without careful supervision they are often carried to excess. In the gymnasium many youth,

390

by their attempted feats of strength, have done themselves lifelong injury.

Exercise in a gymnasium, however well conducted, cannot supply the place of recreation in the open air, and for this our schools should afford better opportunity.[5]

Games With a Ball—Basic Guiding Principles—I do not condemn the simple exercise of playing ball; but this, even in its simplicity, may be overdone.

I shrink always from the almost sure result which follows in the wake of these amusements. It leads to an outlay of means that should be expended in bringing the light of truth to souls that are perishing out of Christ. The amusements and expenditures of means for self-pleasing, which lead on step by step to self-glorifying, and the educating in these games for pleasure produce a love and passion for such things that is not favorable to the perfection of Christian character.

The way that they have been conducted at the college does not bear the impress of heaven. It does not strengthen the intellect. It does not refine and purify the character. There are threads leading out through the habits and customs and worldly practices, and the actors become so engrossed and infatuated that they are pronounced in heaven lovers of pleasure more than lovers of God. In the place of the intellect becoming strengthened to do better work as students, to be better qualified as Christians to perform the Christian duties, the exercise in these games is filling their brains with thoughts that distract the mind from their studies....

[500]

Is the eye single to the glory of God in these games? I know that this is not so. There is a losing sight of God's way and His purpose. The employment of intelligent beings, in probationary time, is superseding God's revealed will and substituting for it the speculations and inventions of the human agent, with Satan by his side to imbue with his spirit.... The Lord God of heaven protests against the burning passion cultivated for supremacy in the games that are so engrossing.[6]

The Problem of Many Athletic Sports—Vigorous exercise the pupils must have. Few evils are more to be dreaded than indolence and aimlessness. Yet the tendency of most athletic sports is a subject of anxious thought to those who have at heart the well-being of the youth. Teachers are troubled as they consider the influence of these sports both on the student's progress in school and on his success in afterlife. The games that occupy so much of his time are diverting the mind from study. They are not helping to prepare the youth for practical, earnest work in life. Their influence does not tend toward refinement, generosity, or real manliness.

Some of the most popular amusements, such as football and boxing, have become schools of brutality. They are developing the same characteristics as did the games of ancient Rome. The love of domination, the pride in mere brute force, the reckless disregard of life, are exerting upon the youth a power to demoralize that is appalling.

[501] Other athletic games, though not so brutalizing, are scarcely less objectionable because of the excess to which they are carried. They stimulate the love of pleasure and excitement, thus fostering a distaste for useful labor, a disposition to shun practical duties and responsibilities. They tend to destroy a relish for life's sober realities and its tranquil enjoyments. Thus the door is opened to dissipation and lawlessness with their terrible results.[7]

When Life Was Less Complex—In early ages, with the people who were under God's direction, life was simple. They lived close to the heart of nature. Their children shared in the labor of the parents and studied the beauties and mysteries of nature's treasure house. And in the quiet of field and wood they pondered those mighty truths handed down as a sacred trust from generation to generation. Such training produced strong men.

In this age life has become artificial, and men have degenerated. While we may not return fully to the simple habits of those early times, we may learn from them lessons that will make our seasons of recreation what the name implies—seasons of true upbuilding for body and mind and soul.[8]

Family Outings—Let several families living in a city or village unite and leave the occupations which have taxed them physically and mentally, and make an excursion into the country, to the side of a fine lake, or to a nice grove where the scenery of nature is beautiful. They should provide themselves with plain, hygienic food, the very best fruits and grains, and spread their table under the shade of some tree or under the canopy of heaven. The ride, the exercise, and the scenery will quicken the appetite, and they can enjoy a repast which kings might envy.

[502]

On such occasions parents and children should feel free from care, labor, and perplexity. Parents should become children with their children, making everything as pleasant for them as possible. Let the whole day be given to recreation. Exercise in the open air for those whose employment has been within doors and sedentary will be beneficial to health. All who can should feel it a duty to pursue this course. Nothing will be lost, but much gained. They can return to their occupations with new life and new courage to engage in their labor with zeal, and they are better prepared to resist disease.[9]

Find Happiness in the Charms of Nature—Do not think that God wishes us to yield up everything which it is for our happiness here to retain. All He requires us to give up is that which would not be for our good and happiness to retain.

That God who has planted the noble trees and clothed them with their rich foliage, and given us the brilliant and beautiful shades of the flowers, and whose handy and lovely work we see in all the realm of nature, does not design to make us unhappy; He does not design that we shall have no taste and take no pleasure in these things. It is His design that we shall enjoy them. It is His design that we shall be happy in the charms of nature, which are of His own creating.[10]

Profitable Social Gatherings—Gatherings for social intercourse are made in the highest degree profitable and instructive when those who meet together have the love of God glowing in their hearts, when they meet to exchange thoughts in regard to the word of God or to consider methods for advancing His work and doing good to their fellow men. When the Holy Spirit is regarded as a welcome guest at these gatherings, when nothing is said or done to grieve Him away, God is honored, and those who meet together are refreshed and strengthened.[11]

[503]

Our gatherings should be so conducted, and we should so conduct ourselves, that when we return to our homes, we can have a conscience void of offense toward God and man, a consciousness that we have not wounded or injured in any manner those with whom we have been associated, or had an injurious influence over them.[12]

Jesus Found Pleasure in Scenes of Innocent Happiness—Jesus reproved self-indulgence in all its forms, yet He was social in

His nature. He accepted the hospitality of all classes, visiting the homes of the rich and the poor, the learned and the ignorant, and seeking to elevate their thoughts from questions of commonplace life to those things that are spiritual and eternal. He gave no license to dissipation, and no shadow of worldly levity marred His conduct; yet He found pleasure in scenes of innocent happiness and by His presence sanctioned the social gathering. A Jewish marriage was an impressive occasion, and its joy was not displeasing to the Son of man.... To the mind of Jesus the gladness of the wedding festivities pointed forward to the rejoicing of that day when He shall bring home His bride to the Father's house, and the redeemed with the Redeemer shall sit down to the marriage supper of the Lamb.[13]

His Example in Conversation and Conduct—When invited, as His work commenced, to a dinner or feast by Pharisee or publican, He accepted the invitation.... On such occasions Christ controlled the table talk and gave many precious lessons. Those present listened to Him; for had He not healed their sick, comforted their sorrowing, taken their children in His arms and blessed them? Publicans and sinners were drawn to Him, and when He opened His lips to speak, their attention was riveted on Him.

[504]

Christ taught His disciples how to conduct themselves when in the company of those who were not religious and those who were. He taught them by example that when attending any public gathering, they need not want for something to say. But His conversation differed most decidedly from that which had been listened to at feasts in the past. Every word He uttered was a savor of life unto life to His hearers, and they listened with subdued attention as though desirous of hearing to a purpose.[14]

Ellen G. White and a Pleasant Social Gathering—At the close of my long journey east, I reached my home in time to spend New Year's Eve in Healdsburg. The college hall had been fitted up for a Sabbath school reunion. Cypress wreaths, autumn leaves, evergreens, and flowers were tastefully arranged; and a large bell of evergreens hung from the arched doorway at the entrance to the room. The tree was well loaded with donations, which were to be used for the benefit of the poor and to help purchase a bell.... On this occasion nothing was said or done that need burden the conscience of anyone.

Some have said to me, "Sister White, what do you think of this? Is it in accordance with our faith?" I answer them, "It is with *my* faith."[15]

Draw Youth With a Winning Power—God would have every household and every church exert a winning power to draw the children away from the seducing pleasures of the world and from association with those whose influence would have a corrupting [505] tendency. Study to win the youth to Jesus.[16]   [506]

[1]Counsels to Teachers, Parents, and Students, 335.

[2]Testimonies For The Church 1, 514.

[3]The Review and Herald, January 29, 1884.

[4]Special Testimonies on Education "Living by Principle", 1898, 19, 20.

[5]Education, 210.

[6]Notebook Leaflets from the Elmshaven Library, Vol. 1 (1945).

[7]Education, 210, 211.

[8]Ibid., 211.

[9]Testimonies For The Church 1, 514, 515.

[10]The Review and Herald, May 25, 1886.

[11]The Youth's Instructor, February 4, 1897.

[12]Counsels to Teachers, Parents, and Students, 337.

[13]The Desire of Ages, 150, 151.

[14]Welfare Ministry, 287.

[15]The Review and Herald, January 29, 1884.

[16]Ibid.

Chapter 81—Recreation that Yields Enduring Satisfactions

Exercise That Develops Hand, Mind, and Character—The greatest benefit is not gained from exercise that is taken as play or exercise merely. There is some benefit derived from being in the fresh air and also from the exercise of the muscles; but let the same amount of energy be given to the performance of helpful duties, and the benefit will be greater, and a feeling of satisfaction will be realized; for such exercise carries with it the sense of helpfulness and the approval of conscience for duty well done.[1]

In the children and youth an ambition should be awakened to take their exercise in doing something that will be beneficial to themselves and helpful to others. The exercise that develops mind and character, that teaches the hands to be useful and trains the young to bear their share of life's burdens, is that which gives physical strength and quickens every faculty. And there is a reward in virtuous industry, in the cultivation of the habit of living to do good.[2]

No recreation helpful only to themselves will prove so great a blessing to the children and youth as that which makes them helpful to others. Naturally enthusiastic and impressible, the young are quick to respond to suggestion.[3]

Jesus' Example as a Youth—The life of Jesus was filled with industry, and He took exercise in performing varied tasks in harmony with His developing physical strength. In doing the work that was marked out for Him, He had no time for indulgence in exciting, useless amusements. He took no part in that which would poison the moral and lower the physical tone, but was trained in useful labor and even for the endurance of hardship.[4]

In His earth life Christ was an example to all the human family, and He was obedient and helpful in the home. He learned the carpenter's trade and worked with His own hands in the little shop at Nazareth....

[507]

The Bible says of Jesus, "And the child grew, and waxed strong in spirit, filled with wisdom: and the grace of God was upon Him." As He worked in childhood and youth, mind and body were developed. He did not use His physical powers recklessly, but gave them such exercise as would keep them in health, that He might do the best work in every line. He was not willing to be defective, even in the handling of tools. He was perfect as a workman, as He was perfect in character. By precept and example Christ has dignified useful labor.[5]

Refreshment Through Variation of Labor—Young men should remember that they are accountable for all the privileges they have enjoyed, for the improvement of their time, and for the right use of their abilities. They may inquire, Shall we have no amusement or recreation? Shall we work, work, work, without any variation?[6]

A change from physical labor that has taxed the strength severely may be very necessary for a time, that they may again engage in labor, putting forth exertion with greater success. But entire rest may not be necessary or even be attended with the best results so far as their physical strength is concerned. They need not, even when weary with one kind of labor, trifle away their precious moments. They may then seek to do something not so exhausting but which will be a blessing to their mother and sisters. In lightening their cares by taking upon themselves the roughest burdens they have to bear, they can find that amusement which springs from principle and which will yield them true happiness, and their time will not be spent in trifling or in selfish indulgence. Their time may be ever employed to advantage, and they be constantly refreshed with variation, and yet be redeeming the time so that every moment will tell with good account to someone.[7]

[508]

Many claim that it is necessary for the preservation of physical health to indulge in selfish amusement. It is true that change is required for the best development of the body, for mind and body are refreshed and invigorated by change; but this object is not gained by indulgence in foolish amusements, to the neglect of daily duties which the youth should be required to do.[8]

A Program for Students That God Blessed—We are to educate the youth to exercise equally the mental and the physical powers.

The healthful exercise of the whole being will give an education that is broad and comprehensive.

We had stern work to do in Australia in educating parents and youth along these lines; but we persevered in our efforts until the lesson was learned that in order to have an education that was complete, the time of study must be divided between the gaining of book knowledge and the securing of a knowledge of practical work.

Part of each day was spent in useful work, the students learning how to clear the land, how to cultivate the soil and to build houses in time that would otherwise have been spent in playing games and seeking amusement. And the Lord blessed the students who thus devoted their time to learning lessons of usefulness.[9]

[509]

God has provided useful employments for the development of health, and these useful employments will also qualify students to be a help to themselves and to others.[10]

In the place of providing diversions that merely amuse, arrangements should be made for exercises that will be productive of good.[11]

Missionary Activity Is an Ideal Exercise—There are plenty of necessary, useful things to do in our world that would make the pleasure amusement exercise almost wholly unnecessary. Brain, bone, and muscle will acquire solidity and strength in using them to a purpose, doing good, hard thinking, and devising plans which shall train them to develop powers of intellect and strength of the physical organs, which will be putting into practical use their God-given talents with which they may glorify God.[12]

It is our duty ever to seek to do good in the use of the muscles and brain God has given to youth, that they may be useful to others, making their labors lighter, soothing the sorrowing, lifting up the discouraged, speaking words of comfort to the hopeless, turning the minds of the students from fun and frolic which often carries them beyond the dignity of manhood and womanhood to shame and disgrace. The Lord would have the mind elevated, seeking higher, nobler channels of usefulness.[13]

The same power of exercise of mind and muscle might invent ways and means of altogether a higher class of exercise, in doing missionary work which would make them laborers together with God, and would be educating for higher usefulness in the present life, in doing useful work, which is a most essential branch in education....

[510]

Is not this the work that every youth should be seeking to do, working in Christ's lines? You have Christ's help. The ideas of the students will broaden. They will be far reaching, and the powers of usefulness, even in your student's life, will be continually growing. The arms, the hands, which God has given, are to be used in doing good which shall bear the signet of heaven, that you can at last hear the "Well done, thou good and faithful servant."[14]

A Prescription for Invalids—I have been instructed that as the sick are encouraged to leave their rooms and spend time in the open air, tending the flowers or doing some other light, pleasant work, their minds will be called from self to something more health giving. Open-air exercise should be prescribed as a beneficial, life-giving necessity.[15]

We can but be cheerful as we listen to the music of the happy birds and feast our eyes upon flourishing fields and gardens. We should invite our minds to be interested in all the glorious things God has provided for us with a liberal hand. And in reflecting upon these rich tokens of His love and care, we may forget infirmities, be cheerful, and make melody in our hearts unto the Lord.[16]

For years I have from time to time been shown that the sick should be taught that it is wrong to suspend all physical labor in order to regain health. In thus doing the will becomes dormant, the blood moves sluggishly through the system and constantly grows more impure. Where the patient is in danger of imagining his case worse than it really is, indolence will be sure to produce the most unhappy results. Well-regulated labor gives the invalid the idea that he is not totally useless in the world, that he is at least of some benefit. This will afford him satisfaction, give him courage, and impart to him vigor, which vain mental amusements can never do.[17]

[511]

God's Provision for Finding True Pleasures—God has provided for everyone pleasure that may be enjoyed by rich and poor alike—the pleasure found in cultivating pureness of thought and unselfishness of action, the pleasure that comes from speaking sympathizing words and doing kindly deeds. From those who perform such service, the light of Christ shines to brighten lives darkened by many sorrows.[18]

[512]

[1] Fundamentals of Christian Education, 418.

[2] Ibid., 418, 419.

[3] Education, 212.

[4] The Youth's Instructor, July 27, 1893.

[5] Fundamentals of Christian Education, 417, 418.

[6] Counsels to Teachers, Parents, and Students, 337.

[7] Testimonies For The Church 3, 223.

[8] The Youth's Instructor, July 27, 1893.

[9] Letter 84, 1909.

[10] The Review and Herald, October 25, 1898.

[11] Pamphlet Recreation, 47.

[12] Notebook Leaflets from the Elmshaven Library Vol. 1, Education, 97.

[13] Ibid., 98.

[14] Ibid., 98, 99.

[15] Medical Ministry, 234.

[16] The Health Reformer, July, 1871.

[17] Testimonies For The Church 1, 555.

[18] Testimonies For The Church 9, 57.

Chapter 82—How the Christian Chooses His Recreation

Christian Recreation Versus Worldly Amusement—There is a distinction between recreation and amusement. Recreation, when true to its name, re-creation, tends to strengthen and build up. Calling us aside from our ordinary cares and occupations, it affords refreshment for mind and body and thus enables us to return with new vigor to the earnest work of life.

Amusement, on the other hand, is sought for the sake of pleasure and is often carried to excess; it absorbs the energies that are required for useful work and thus proves a hindrance to life's true success.[1]

Between the associations of the followers of Christ for Christian recreation and worldly gatherings for pleasure and amusement will exist a marked contrast. Instead of prayer and the mentioning of Christ and sacred things will be heard from the lips of worldlings the silly laugh and the trifling conversation. Their idea is to have a general high time. Their amusements commence in folly and end in vanity.[2]

There is great need of temperance in amusements, as in every other pursuit. And the character of these amusements should be carefully and thoroughly considered. Every youth should ask himself, What influence will these amusements have on physical, mental, and moral health? Will my mind become so infatuated as to forget God? Shall I cease to have His glory before me?[3]

[513]

A Rule by Which Lawful Pleasures May Be Recognized—Let us never lose sight of the fact that Jesus is a wellspring of joy. He does not delight in the misery of human beings, but loves to see them happy.

Christians have many sources of happiness at their command, and they may tell with unerring accuracy what pleasures are lawful and right. They may enjoy such recreations as will not dissipate the mind or debase the soul, such as will not disappoint and leave a sad after-influence to destroy self-respect or bar the way to usefulness.

If they can take Jesus with them and maintain a prayerful spirit, they are perfectly safe.[4]

Any amusement in which you can engage asking the blessing of God upon it in faith will not be dangerous. But any amusement which disqualifies you for secret prayer, for devotion at the altar of prayer, or for taking part in the prayer meeting is not safe, but dangerous.[5]

Amusements That Unfit for Ordinary Duties—We are of that class who believe that it is our privilege every day of our lives to glorify God upon the earth, that we are not to live in this world merely for our own amusement, merely to please ourselves. We are here to benefit humanity and to be a blessing to society; and if we let our minds run in that low channel that many who are seeking only vanity and folly permit their minds to run in, how can we be a benefit to our race and generation? How can we be a blessing to society around us? We cannot innocently indulge in any amusement which will unfit us for the more faithful discharge of ordinary duties.[6]

The welfare of the soul should not be endangered by the gratification of any selfish desire, and we should shun any amusement which so fascinates the mind that the ordinary duties of life seem [514] tame and uninteresting. By indulgence in such pleasure the mind becomes confirmed in a wrong direction, and Satan so perverts the thoughts that wrong is made to appear as right. Then restraint and submission to parents, such as Christ rendered to His parents, seem unbearable.[7]

Objectionable Social Gatherings Depicted—There are many things which are right in themselves, but which, perverted by Satan, prove a snare to the unwary.[8]

As ordinarily conducted, parties of pleasure ... are a hindrance to real growth, either of mind or of character. Frivolous associations, habits of extravagance, of pleasure seeking, and too often of dissipation are formed that shape the whole life for evil. In place of such amusements parents and teachers can do much to supply diversions wholesome and life giving.[9]

There has been a class of social gatherings in——, ... parties of pleasure that have been a disgrace to our institutions and to the church. They encourage pride of dress, pride of appearance, self-gratification, hilarity, and trifling. Satan is entertained as an honored guest, and he takes possession of those who patronize these gatherings.

A view of one such company was presented to me, where were assembled those who profess to believe the truth. One was seated at the instrument of music, and such songs were poured forth as made the watching angels weep. There was mirth, there was coarse laughter, there was abundance of enthusiasm and a kind of inspiration; but the joy was such as Satan only is able to create. This is an enthusiasm and infatuation of which all who love God will be ashamed. It prepares the participants for unholy thought and action. I have reason to think that some who were engaged in that scene heartily repented of the shameful performance.

[515]

Many such gatherings have been presented to me. I have seen the gaiety, the display in dress, the personal adornment. All want to be thought brilliant, and give themselves up to hilarity, foolish jesting, cheap, coarse flattery, and uproarious laughter. The eyes sparkle, the cheek is flushed, conscience sleeps. With eating and drinking and merrymaking, they do their best to forget God. The scene of pleasure is their paradise. And Heaven is looking on, seeing and hearing all.[10]

Gatherings for amusement confuse faith and make the motive mixed and uncertain. The Lord accepts no divided heart. He wants the whole man.[11]

Few Popular Amusements Are Safe—Many of the amusements popular in the world today, even with those who claim to be Christians, tend to the same end as did those of the heathen. There are indeed few among them that Satan does not turn to account in destroying souls. Through the drama he has worked for ages to excite passion and glorify vice. The opera, with its fascinating display and bewildering music, the masquerade, the dance, the card table, Satan employs to break down the barriers of principle and open the door to sensual indulgence. In every gathering for pleasure where pride is fostered or appetite indulged, where one is led to forget God and lose sight of eternal interests, there Satan is binding his chains about the soul.[12]

The true Christian will not desire to enter any place of amusement or engage in any diversion upon which he cannot ask the blessing of God. He will not be found at the theater, the billiard hall, or the bowling saloon. He will not unite with the gay waltzers or indulge in any other bewitching pleasure that will banish Christ from the mind.

To those who plead for these diversions we answer, We cannot indulge in them in the name of Jesus of Nazareth. The blessing of God would not be invoked upon the hour spent at the theater or in the dance. No Christian would wish to meet death in such a place. No one would wish to be found there when Christ shall come.[13]

The Theater the Hotbed of Immorality—Among the most dangerous resorts for pleasure is the theater. Instead of being a school for morality and virtue, as is so often claimed, it is the very hotbed of immorality. Vicious habits and sinful propensities are strengthened and confirmed by these entertainments. Low songs, lewd gestures, expressions, and attitudes deprave the imagination and debase the morals. Every youth who habitually attends such exhibitions will be corrupted in principle. There is no influence in our land more powerful to poison the imagination, to destroy religious impressions, and to blunt the relish for the tranquil pleasures and sober realities of life than theatrical amusements. The love for these scenes increases with every indulgence as the desire for intoxicating drink strengthens with its use. The only safe course is to shun the theater, the circus, and every other questionable place of amusement.[14]

Dancing—a School of Depravity—In many religious families dancing and card playing are made a parlor pastime. It is urged that these are quiet home amusements, which may be safely enjoyed under the parental eye. But a love for these exciting pleasures is thus cultivated, and that which was considered harmless at home will not long be regarded dangerous abroad. It is yet to be ascertained that there is any good to be obtained from these amusements. They do not give vigor to the body nor rest to the mind. They do not implant in the soul one virtuous or holy sentiment. On the contrary, they destroy all relish for serious thought and for religious services. It is true that there is a wide contrast between the better class of select parties and the promiscuous and degraded assemblies of the low dance house. Yet all are steps in the path of dissipation.[15]

David's Dancing Not a Precedent—David's dancing in reverent joy before God has been cited by pleasure lovers in justification of the fashionable modern dance, but there is no ground for such

[516]

[517]

an argument. In our day dancing is associated with folly and midnight reveling. Health and morals are sacrificed to pleasure. By the frequenters of the ballroom God is not an object of thought and reverence; prayer or the song of praise would be felt to be out of place in their assemblies. This test should be decisive. Amusements that have a tendency to weaken the love for sacred things and lessen our joy in the service of God are not to be sought by Christians. The music and dancing in joyful praise to God at the removal of the ark had not the faintest resemblance to the dissipation of modern dancing. The one tended to the remembrance of God and exalted His holy name. The other is a device of Satan to cause men to forget God and to dishonor Him.[16]

Card Playing—a Prelude to Crime—Card playing should be prohibited. The associations and tendencies are dangerous. The prince of the powers of darkness presides in the gaming room and wherever there is card playing. Evil angels are familiar guests in these places. There is nothing in such amusements beneficial to soul or body. There is nothing to strengthen the intellect, nothing to store it with valuable ideas for future use. The conversation is upon trivial and degrading subjects.... Expertness in handling cards will soon lead to a desire to put this knowledge and tact to some use for personal benefit. A small sum is staked, and then a larger, until a thirst for gaming is acquired, which leads to certain ruin. How many has this pernicious amusement led to every sinful practice, to poverty, to prison, to murder, and to the gallows! And yet many parents do not see the terrible gulf of ruin that is yawning for our youth.[17]

[518]

The Fear of Being Singular—Professed Christians who are superficial in character and religious experience are used by the tempter as his decoys. This class are always ready for the gatherings for pleasure or sport, and their influence attracts others. Young men and women who have tried to be Bible Christians are persuaded to join the party, and they are drawn into the ring. They do not prayerfully consult the divine standard to learn what Christ has said in regard to the fruit to be borne on the Christian tree. They do not discern that these entertainments are really Satan's banquet, prepared to keep souls from accepting the call to the marriage supper of the Lamb and preventing them from receiving the white robe of character, which is the righteousness of Christ. They become confused as to what it is right for them as Christians to do. They do not want to be thought singular, and naturally incline to follow the example of others. Thus they come under the influence of those who have never had the divine touch on heart or mind.[18]

Avoid the First Step Toward Indulgence—You may see no real danger in taking the first step in frivolity and pleasure seeking and think that when you desire to change your course, you will be able to do right as easily as before you yielded yourselves to do wrong. But this is a mistake. By the choice of evil companions many have been led step by step from the path of virtue into depths of disobedience and dissipation to which at one time they would have thought it impossible for them to sink.[19]

A Clear Declaration of Christian Principles—If you truly belong to Christ, you will have opportunities for witnessing for Him. You will be invited to attend places of amusement, and then it will be that you will have an opportunity to testify to your Lord. If you are true to Christ then, you will not try to form excuses for your nonattendance, but will plainly and modestly declare that you are a child of God, and your principles would not allow you to be in a place, even for one occasion, where you could not invite the presence of your Lord.[20]

It is God's purpose to manifest through His people the principles of His kingdom. That in life and character they may reveal these principles, He desires to separate them from the customs, habits, and practices of the world....

Wonderful scenes are opening before us; and at this time a living testimony is to be borne in the lives of God's professed people so that the world may see that in this age, when evil reigns on every side, there is yet a people who are laying aside their will and are seeking to do God's will—a people in whose hearts and lives God's law is written.

God expects those who bear the name of Christ to represent Him. Their thoughts are to be pure, their words noble and uplifting. The religion of Christ is to be interwoven with all that they do and say.... God desires His people to show by their lives the advantage of Christianity over worldliness, to show that they are working on a high, holy plane.[21]

[1] Education, 207.

[2] The Review and Herald, May 25, 1886.

[3] Counsels to Teachers, Parents, and Students, 333, 334.

[4] The Review and Herald, August 19, 1884.

[5] Counsels to Teachers, Parents, and Students, 337.

[6] Ibid., 336.

[7] The Youth's Instructor, July 27, 1893.

[8] Letter 144, 1906.

[9] Education, 211.

[10] Counsels to Teachers, Parents, and Students, 339, 340.

[11] Ibid., 345.

[12] Patriarchs and Prophets, 459, 460.

[13] The Review and Herald, February 28, 1882.

[14] Counsels to Teachers, Parents, and Students, 334, 335.

[15] The Review and Herald, February 28, 1882.

[16] Patriarchs and Prophets, 707.

[17] Testimonies For The Church 4, 652.

[18] Counsels to Teachers, Parents, and Students, 340, 341.

[19] Ibid., 224.

[20] The Youth's Instructor, May 4, 1893.

[21] Counsels to Teachers, Parents, and Students, 321-324.

Chapter 83—The Lure of Pleasure

The Natural Heart Seeks Pleasure—The natural mind leans toward pleasure and self-gratification. It is Satan's policy to manufacture an abundance of this. He seeks to fill the minds of men with a desire for worldly amusement, that they may have no time to ask themselves the question, How is it with my soul? The love of pleasure is infectious. Given up to this, the mind hurries from one point to another, ever seeking for some amusement.[1]

Worldly pleasures are infatuating; and for their momentary enjoyment many sacrifice the friendship of Heaven, with the peace, love, and joy that it affords. But these chosen objects of delight soon become disgusting, unsatisfying.[2]

Millions Flock to Places of Amusement—In this age of the world there is an unprecedented rage for pleasure. Dissipation and reckless extravagance everywhere prevail. The multitudes are eager for amusement. The mind becomes trifling and frivolous because it is not accustomed to meditation or disciplined to study. Ignorant sentimentalism is current. God requires that every soul shall be cultivated, refined, elevated, and ennobled. But too often every valuable attainment is neglected for fashionable display and superficial pleasure.[3]

The exciting amusements of our time keep the minds of men and women, but more especially the youth, in a fever of excitement, which is telling upon their stock of vitality in a far greater degree than all their studies and physical labors, and have a tendency to [522] dwarf the intellect and corrupt the morals.[4]

The youth are swept away by the popular current. Those who learn to love amusement for its own sake open the door to a flood of temptations. They give themselves up to social gaiety and thoughtless mirth. They are led on from one form of dissipation to another, until they lose both the desire and the capacity for a life of usefulness. Their religious aspirations are chilled; their spiritual life is darkened. All the nobler faculties of the soul, all that link man with the spiritual world, are debased.[5]

Among Pleasure Lovers Are Many Church Members— Many are eagerly participating in worldly, demoralizing amusements which God's word forbids. Thus they sever their connection with God and rank themselves with the pleasure lovers of the world. The sins that destroyed the antediluvians and the cities of the plain exist today—not merely in heathen lands, not only among popular professors of Christianity, but with some who profess to be looking for the coming of the Son of man. If God should present these sins before you as they appear in His sight, you would be filled with shame and terror.[6]

The desire for excitement and pleasing entertainment is a temptation and a snare to God's people and especially to the young. Satan is constantly preparing inducements to attract minds from the solemn work of preparation for scenes just in the future. Through the agency of worldlings he keeps up a continual excitement to induce the unwary to join in worldly pleasures. There are shows, lectures, and an endless variety of entertainments that are calculated to lead to a love of the world; and through this union with the world, faith is weakened.[7]

[523]

Satan, a Skillful Charmer—The young generally conduct themselves as though the precious hours of probation, while mercy lingers, were one grand holiday and they were placed in this world merely for their own amusement, to be gratified with a continued round of excitement. Satan has been making special efforts to lead them to find happiness in worldly amusements and to justify themselves by endeavoring to show that these amusements are harmless, innocent, and even important for health.[8]

He [Satan] presents the path of holiness as difficult, while the paths of worldly pleasure are strewn with flowers. In false and flattering colors he arrays the world with its pleasures before the youth. But the pleasures of earth will soon come to an end, and that which is sown must also be reaped.[9]

He is in every sense of the word a deceiver, a skillful charmer. He has many finely woven nets, which appear innocent, but which are skillfully prepared to entangle the young and unwary.[10]

Education Is Dwarfed by the Love of Pleasure—Parents make a mistake in rushing their children into society at an early age, fearing that they will not know anything unless they attend parties and mingle with those who are lovers of pleasure. Even while they are at school, they allow their children to attend parties and mingle in society. This is a great mistake. In this way children learn evil much faster than they do the sciences, and their minds are filled with useless things, while their passion for amusement is developed to such an extent that it is impossible for them to obtain a knowledge of even the common branches of education. Their attention is divided between education and a love of pleasure, and as the love of pleasure predominates, their intellectual advancement is slow.[11]

[524]

Like Israel of old, the pleasure lovers eat and drink and rise up to play. There is mirth and carousing, hilarity and glee. In all this the youth follow the example of the authors of the books placed in their hands for study. The greatest evil of it all is the permanent effect that these things have upon the character.[12]

God's Last Message Regarded With Indifference—As the time of their probation was closing, the antediluvians gave themselves up to exciting amusements and festivities. Those who possessed influence and power were bent on keeping the minds of the people engrossed with mirth and pleasure, lest any should be impressed by the last solemn warning. Do we not see the same repeated in our day? While God's servants are giving the message that the end of all things is at hand, the world is absorbed in amusements and pleasure seeking. There is a constant round of excitement that causes indifference to God and prevents the people from being impressed by the truths which alone can save them from the coming destruction.[13]

Sabbathkeepers Will Be Tested and Proved—Young Sabbathkeepers who have yielded to the influence of the world will have to be tested and proved. The perils of the last days are upon us, and a trial is before the young which many have not anticipated. They will be brought into distressing perplexity, and the genuineness of their faith will be proved. They profess to be looking for the Son of man, yet some of them have been a miserable example to unbelievers. They have not been willing to give up the world, but have united with the world in attending picnics [Note: the simple outdoor gathering [525] of families or church members is not referred to here, but that in which church members "united with the world" in a carnival type of community gathering quite common then.] and other gatherings for pleasure, flattering themselves that they were engaging in innocent amusement. Yet it is just such indulgences that separate them from God and make them children of the world....

God does not own the pleasure seeker as His follower. Those only who are self-denying and who live lives of sobriety, humility, and holiness are true followers of Jesus. And such cannot enjoy the frivolous, empty conversation of the lover of the world.[14]

The All-Important Consideration—Let none begin to believe that amusements are essential and that a careless disregard of the Holy Spirit during hours of selfish pleasure is to be looked upon as a light matter. God will not be mocked. Let every young man, every young woman, consider: "Am I prepared today for my life to close? Have I the heart preparation that fits me to do the work which the Lord has given me to do?"[15] [526]

[1] Counsels to Teachers, Parents, and Students, 337.

[2] The Review and Herald, January 29, 1884.

[3] The Review and Herald, December 6, 1881.

[4] The Health Reformer, December, 1872.

[5] Testimonies For The Church 90.

[6] Ibid., 5:218.

[7] Counsels to Teachers, Parents, and Students, 325.

[8] Testimonies For The Church 1: 501.

[9] The Youth's Instructor, January 1, 1907.

[10] Counsels to Teachers, Parents, and Students, 325.

[11] The Youth's Instructor, July 27, 1893.

[12] Testimonies For The Church 8, 66.

[13] Patriarchs and Prophets, 103.

[14] Counsels to Teachers, Parents, and Students, 327, 328.

[15] The Youth's Instructor, August 14, 1906.

Chapter 84—Directing Juvenile Thinking Regarding Recreation

Standards Are Being Lowered—Christian parents are giving way to the world-loving propensities of their children. They open the door to amusements which from principle they once prohibited.[1]

Even among Christian parents there has been too much sanctioning of the love of amusements. Parents have received the world's maxim, have conformed to the general opinion that it was necessary that the early life of children and youth should be frittered away in idleness, in selfish amusements, and in foolish indulgences. In this way a taste has been created for exciting pleasure, and children and youth have trained their minds so that they delight in exciting displays; and they have a positive dislike for the sober, useful duties of life. They live lives more after the order of the brute creation. They have no thoughts of God or of eternal realities, but flit like butterflies in their season. They do not act like sensible beings whose lives are capable of measuring with the life of God, and who are accountable to Him for every hour of their time.[2]

Mothers to Invent and Direct Amusements—Instead of sending her children from her presence, that she may not be troubled with their noise and be annoyed with the numerous attentions they would desire, she will feel that her time cannot be better employed than in soothing and diverting their restless, active minds with some [527] amusement or light, happy employment. The mother will be amply repaid for the efforts she may make and the time she may spend to invent amusement for her children.

Young children love society. They cannot, as a general thing, enjoy themselves alone; and the mother should feel that, in most cases, the place for her children when they are in the house is in the room she occupies. She can then have a general oversight of them and be prepared to set little differences right, when appealed to by them, and correct wrong habits or the manifestation of selfishness or passion, and can give their minds a turn in the right direction.

That which children enjoy they think mother can be pleased with, and it is perfectly natural for them to consult mother in little matters of perplexity. And the mother should not wound the heart of her sensitive child by treating the matter with indifference or by refusing to be troubled with such small matters. That which may be small to the mother is large to them. And a word of direction or caution, at the right time, will often prove of great value.[3]

Do Not Deny Innocent Pleasures—For lack of time and thought many a mother refuses her children some innocent pleasure, while busy fingers and weary eyes are diligently engaged on work designed only for adornment, something that, at best, will serve only to encourage vanity and extravagance in their young hearts. As the children approach manhood and womanhood, these lessons bear fruit in pride and moral worthlessness. The mother grieves over her children's faults but does not realize that the harvest she is reaping is from seed which she herself planted.

Some mothers are not uniform in the treatment of their children. At times they indulge them to their injury, and again they refuse some innocent gratification that would make the childish heart very happy. In this they do not imitate Christ; He loved the children; He comprehended their feelings and sympathized with them in their pleasures and their trials.[4]

[528]

How Mrs. White Restrained Her Children—When the children will beg that they may go to this company or join that party of amusement, say to them: "I cannot let you go, children; sit right down here, and I will tell you why. I am doing up work for eternity and for God. God has given you to me and entrusted you to my care. I am standing in the place of God to you, my children; therefore I must watch you as one who must give an account in the day of God. Do you want your mother's name written in the books of heaven as one who failed to do her duty to her children, as one who let the enemy come in and preoccupy the ground that I ought to have occupied? Children, I am going to tell you which is the right way, and then if you choose to turn away from your mother and go into the paths of wickedness, your mother will stand clear, but you will have to suffer for your own sins."

This is the way I did with my children, and before I would get through, they would be weeping, and they would say, "Won't you pray for us?" Well, I never refused to pray for them. I knelt by their side and prayed with them. Then I have gone away and have pleaded with God until the sun was up in the heavens, the whole night long, that the spell of the enemy might be broken, and I have had the victory. Although it cost me a night's labor, yet I felt richly paid when my children would hang about my neck and say, "Oh, Mother, we are so glad that you did not let us go when we wanted to. Now [529] we see that it would have been wrong."

Parents, this is the way you must work, as though you meant it. You must make a business of this work if you expect to save your children in the kingdom of God.[5]

Problems of the Perplexing Teen Ages—In the present state of society it is no easy task for parents to restrain their children and instruct them according to the Bible rule of right. Children often become impatient under restraint and wish to have their own way and to go and come as they please. Especially from the age of ten to eighteen they are inclined to feel that there can be no harm in going to worldly gatherings of young associates. But the experienced Christian parents can see danger. They are acquainted with the peculiar temperaments of their children and know the influence of these things upon their minds; and from a desire for their salvation, they should keep them back from these exciting amusements.[6]

Vigilance Is Especially Needed After Conversion—When the children decide for themselves to leave the pleasures of the world and to become Christ's disciples, what a burden is lifted from the hearts of careful, faithful parents! Yet even then the labors of the parents must not cease. These youth have just commenced in earnest the warfare against sin and against the evils of the natural heart, and they need in a special sense the counsel and watchcare of their parents.[7]

The Secret of Guarding the Children From Worldly Attractions—How many parents are lamenting the fact that they cannot keep their children at home, that they have no love for home! At an early age they have a desire for the company of strangers; and [530] as soon as they are old enough, they break away from that which appears to them to be bondage and unreasonable restraint and will neither heed a mother's prayers nor a father's counsels. Investigation would generally reveal that the sin lay at the door of the parents.

They have not made home what it ought to be—attractive, pleasant, radiant with the sunshine of kind words, pleasant looks, and true love.

The secret of saving your children lies in making your home lovely and attractive. Indulgence in parents will not bind the children to God nor to home; but a firm, godly influence to properly train and educate the mind would save many children from ruin.[8]

It is the duty of parents to watch the going out and the coming in of their children. They should encourage them and present inducements before them which will attract them at home and lead them to see that their parents are interested for them. They should make home pleasant and cheerful.[9]

[531]

[532]

---

[1]Manuscript 119, 1899.

[2]The Youth's Instructor, January July 20, 1893.

[3]A Solemn Appeal. 136, 137.

[4]The Ministry of Healing, 389, 390.

[5]Undated Manuscript 70.

[6]Counsels to Teachers, Parents, and Students, 327.

[7]Ibid.

[8]The Review and Herald, December 9, 1884.

[9]Testimonies For The Church 1, 400, 401.

Section 18—Thou Shalt be Recompensed

Chapter 85—The Reward Here and Hereafter

A Rich Reward Awaits Faithful Parents—If parents give their children the proper education, they themselves will be made happy by seeing the fruit of their careful training in the Christlike character of their children. They are doing God the highest service by presenting to the world well-ordered, well-disciplined families, who not only fear the Lord, but honor and glorify Him by their influence upon other families; and they will receive their reward.[1]

Believing parents, you have a responsible work before you to guide the footsteps of your children, even in their religious experience. When they truly love God, they will bless and reverence you for the care which you have manifested for them, and for your faithfulness in restraining their desires and subduing their wills.[2]

There is a reward when the seed of truth is early sown in the heart and carefully tended.[3]

Parents should labor with reference to the future harvest. While they sow in tears, amid many discouragements, it should be with earnest prayer. They may see the promise of but a late and scanty harvest, yet that should not prevent the sowing. They should sow beside all waters, embracing every opportunity both to improve themselves and to benefit their children. Such seed sowing will not be in vain. At the harvest time many faithful parents will return with [534] joy, bringing their sheaves with them.[4]

Give your children intellectual culture and moral training. Fortify their young minds with firm, pure principles. While you have opportunity, lay the foundation for a noble manhood and womanhood. Your labor will be rewarded a thousandfold.[5]

Parents Will Be Revered by Children Fitted for Heaven—In the word of God we find a beautiful description of a happy home and the woman who presides over it: "Her children arise up, and call her blessed; her husband also, and he praiseth her." What greater commendation can be desired by the mistress of a home than that which is here expressed?[6]

If she [the true wife and mother] looks to God for her strength and comfort, and in His wisdom and fear seeks to do her daily duty, she will bind her husband to her heart and see her children coming to maturity honorable men and women, having moral stamina to follow the example of their mother.[7]

The great stimulus to the toiling, burdened mother should be that every child who is trained aright, and who has the inward adorning, the ornament of a meek and quiet spirit, will have a fitness for heaven and will shine in the courts of the Lord.[8]

The Joys of Heaven to Begin in the Home—Heaven and earth are no wider apart today than when shepherds listened to the angels' song. Humanity is still as much the object of heaven's solicitude as when common men of common occupations met angels at noonday and talked with the heavenly messengers in the vineyards and the fields. To us in the common walks of life heaven may be very near. Angels from the courts above will attend the steps of those who come and go at God's command.[9]

[535]

The life on earth is the beginning of the life in heaven; education on earth is an initiation into the principles of heaven; the lifework here is a training for the lifework there. What we now are, in character and holy service is the sure foreshadowing of what we shall be.[10]

The service rendered in sincerity of heart has great recompense. "Thy Father which seeth in secret Himself shall reward thee openly." By the life we live through the grace of Christ, the character is formed. The original loveliness begins to be restored to the soul. The attributes of the character of Christ are imparted, and the image of the Divine begins to shine forth. The faces of men and women who walk and work with God express the peace of heaven. They are surrounded with the atmosphere of heaven. For these souls the kingdom of God has begun. They have Christ's joy, the joy of being a blessing to humanity. They have the honor of being accepted for the Master's use; they are trusted to do His work in His name.[11]

All to Be Fitted for the Society of Heaven—God desires that heaven's plan shall be carried out, and heaven's divine order and harmony prevail, in every family, in every church, in every institution. Did this love leaven society, we should see the outworking of noble principles in Christian refinement and courtesy and in Christian charity toward the purchase of the blood of Christ. Spiritual transformation would be seen in all our families, in our institutions, in our churches. When this transformation takes place, these agencies will become instrumentalities by which God will impart heaven's light to the world and thus, through divine discipline and training, [536] fit men and women for the society of heaven.[12]

Reward at the Last Great Day—In your work for your children take hold of the mighty power of God. Commit your children to the Lord in prayer. Work earnestly and untiringly for them. God will hear your prayers and will draw them to Himself. Then, at the last great day, you can bring them to God, saying, "Here am I, and the children whom Thou hast given me."[13]

When Samuel shall receive the crown of glory, he will wave it in honor before the throne and gladly acknowledge that the faithful lessons of his mother, through the merits of Christ, have crowned him with immortal glory.[14]

The work of wise parents will never be appreciated by the world, but when the judgment shall sit and the books shall be opened, their work will appear as God views it and will be rewarded before men and angels. It will be seen that one child who has been brought up in a faithful way has been a light in the world. It cost tears and anxiety and sleepless nights to oversee the character building of this child, but the work was done wisely, and the parents hear the "Well done" of the Master.[15]

Title to Admission to the King's Palace—Let the youth and the little children be taught to choose for themselves that royal robe woven in heaven's loom, the "fine linen, clean and white" which all the holy ones of earth will wear. This robe, Christ's own spotless character, is freely offered to every human being. But all who receive it will receive and wear it here.

Let the children be taught that as they open their minds to pure, loving thoughts and do loving and helpful deeds, they are clothing themselves with His beautiful garment of character. This apparel [537] will make them beautiful and beloved here and will hereafter be their title of admission to the palace of the King. His promise is:

"They shall walk with Me in white: for they are worthy."[16]

A Divine Welcome to the Redeemed—I saw a very great number of angels bring from the city glorious crowns—a crown for every saint, with his name written thereon. As Jesus called for the crowns, angels presented them to Him, and with His own right hand the lovely Jesus placed the crowns on the heads of the saints. In the same manner the angels brought the harps, and Jesus presented them also to the saints. The commanding angels first struck the note, and then every voice was raised in grateful, happy praise; and every hand skillfully swept over the strings of the harp, sending forth melodious music in rich and perfect strains.

Then I saw Jesus lead the redeemed company to the gate of the city. He laid hold of the gate and swung it back on its glittering hinges and bade the nations that had kept the truth enter in. Within the city there was everything to feast the eye. Rich glory they beheld everywhere. Then Jesus looked upon His redeemed saints; their countenances were radiant with glory; and as He fixed His loving eyes upon them, He said, with His rich, musical voice, "I behold the travail of My soul, and am satisfied. This rich glory is yours to enjoy eternally. Your sorrows are ended. There shall be no more death, neither sorrow nor crying, neither shall there be any more pain." I saw the redeemed host bow and cast their glittering crowns at the feet of Jesus; and then, as His lovely hand raised them up, they touched their golden harps and filled all heaven with their rich music and songs to the Lamb.... [538]

Language is altogether too feeble to attempt a description of heaven. As the scene rises before me, I am lost in amazement. Carried away with the surpassing splendor and excellent glory, I lay down the pen and exclaim, "Oh, what love! what wondrous love!" The most exalted language fails to describe the glory of heaven or the matchless depths of a Saviour's love.[17] [539]

[1]The Review and Herald, November 17, 1896.

[2]Testimonies For The Church 1, 403.

[3]Counsels to Teachers, Parents, and Students, 144.

[4]The Review and Herald, August 30, 1881.

[5]Counsels to Teachers, Parents, and Students, 131.

[6]The Health Reformer, December, 1877.

[7]The Signs of the Times, November 29, 1877.

[8]Testimonies For The Church 3, 566.

[9]The Desire of Ages, 48.

[10]Education, 307.

[11]The Desire of Ages, 312.

[12]Testimonies For The Church 8, 140.

[13]Manuscript 114, 1903.

[14]Good Health, March 1, 1880, par. 7.

[15]The Signs of the Times, July 13, 1888.

[16]Education, 249.

[17]Early Writings, 288, 289.

Chapter 86—Life In the Eden Home

Eden to Be Restored—The Garden of Eden remained upon the earth long after man had become an outcast from its pleasant paths. The fallen race were long permitted to gaze upon the home of innocence, their entrance barred only by the watching angels. At the cherubim-guarded gate of Paradise the divine glory was revealed. Hither came Adam and his sons to worship God. Here they renewed their vows of obedience to that law the transgression of which had banished them from Eden. When the tide of iniquity overspread the world, and the wickedness of men determined their destruction by a flood of waters, the hand that had planted Eden withdrew it from the earth. But in the final restitution, when there shall be "a new heaven and a new earth," it is to be restored more gloriously adorned than at the beginning.

Then they that have kept God's commandments shall breathe in immortal vigor beneath the tree of life; and through unending ages the inhabitants of sinless worlds shall behold, in that garden of delight, a sample of the perfect work of God's creation, untouched by the curse of sin—a sample of what the whole earth would have become had man but fulfilled the Creator's glorious plan.[1]

The great plan of redemption results in fully bringing back the world into God's favor. All that was lost by sin is restored. Not only man but the earth is redeemed, to be the eternal abode of the obedient. For six thousand years Satan has struggled to maintain possession of the earth. Now God's original purpose in its creation is accomplished. "The saints of the Most High shall take the kingdom, and possess the kingdom for ever, even for ever and ever."[2] [540]

"The Redemption of the Purchased Possession."—God's original purpose in the creation of the earth is fulfilled as it is made the eternal abode of the redeemed. "The righteous shall inherit the land, and dwell therein for ever." The time has come to which holy men have looked with longing since the flaming sword barred the first pair from Eden—the time for "the redemption of the purchased possession." The earth originally given to man as his kingdom, betrayed by him into the hands of Satan, and so long held by the mighty foe, has been brought back by the great plan of redemption.[3]

All that was lost by the first Adam will be restored by the second. The prophet says, "O Tower of the flock, the strong hold of the daughter of Zion, unto Thee shall it come, even the first dominion." And Paul points forward to the "redemption of the purchased possession."

God created the earth to be the abode of holy, happy beings. That purpose will be fulfilled when, renewed by the power of God and freed from sin and sorrow, it shall become the eternal home of the redeemed.[4]

Adam Restored to His Eden Home—After his expulsion from Eden Adam's life on earth was filled with sorrow. Every dying leaf, every victim of sacrifice, every blight upon the fair face of nature, every stain upon man's purity, were fresh reminders of his sin. Terrible was the agony of remorse as he beheld iniquity abounding and, in answer to his warnings, met the reproaches cast upon himself as the cause of sin. With patient humility he bore for nearly a thousand years the penalty of transgression. Faithfully did he repent of his sin and trust in the merits of the promised Saviour, and he died in the hope of a resurrection. The Son of God redeemed man's failure and fall; and now, through the work of the atonement, Adam is reinstated in his first dominion.

[541]

Transported with joy, he beholds the trees that were once his delight—the very trees whose fruit he himself had gathered in the days of his innocence and joy. He sees the vines that his own hands have trained, the very flowers that he once loved to care for. His mind grasps the reality of the scene; he comprehends that this is indeed Eden restored, more lovely now than when he was banished from it. The Saviour leads him to the tree of life and plucks the glorious fruit and bids him eat. He looks about him and beholds a multitude of his family redeemed, standing in the Paradise of God. Then he casts his glittering crown at the feet of Jesus and, falling upon His breast, embraces the Redeemer. He touches the golden harp, and the vaults of heaven echo the triumphant song, "Worthy, worthy, worthy is the Lamb that was slain, and lives again!" The family of Adam take up the strain and cast their crowns at the Saviour's feet as they bow before Him in adoration.

This reunion is witnessed by the angels who wept at the fall of Adam and rejoiced when Jesus, after His resurrection, ascended to heaven, having opened the grave for all who should believe on His name. Now they behold the work of redemption accomplished, and they unite their voices in the song of praise.[5]

Mansions Prepared for Earth's Pilgrims—A fear of making the future inheritance seem too material has led many to spiritualize away the very truths which lead us to look upon it as our home. Christ assured His disciples that He went to prepare mansions for them in the Father's house. Those who accept the teachings of God's word will not be wholly ignorant concerning the heavenly abode.... Human language is inadequate to describe the reward of the righteous. It will be known only to those who behold it. No finite mind can comprehend the glory of the Paradise of God.

[542]

In the Bible the inheritance of the saved is called a country. There the heavenly Shepherd leads His flock to fountains of living waters. The tree of life yields its fruit every month, and the leaves of the tree are for the service of the nations. There are ever-flowing streams, clear as crystal, and beside them waving trees cast their shadows upon the paths prepared for the ransomed of the Lord. There the widespreading plains swell into hills of beauty, and the mountains of God rear their lofty summits. On those peaceful plains, beside those living streams, God's people, so long pilgrims and wanderers, shall find a home.[6]

There are homes for the pilgrims of earth. There are robes for the righteous, with crowns of glory and palms of victory. All that has perplexed us in the providences of God will in the world to come be made plain. The things hard to be understood will then find explanation. The mysteries of grace will unfold before us. Where our finite minds discovered only confusion and broken promises, we shall see the most perfect and beautiful harmony. We shall know that infinite love ordered the experiences that seemed most trying. As we realize the tender care of Him who makes all things work together for our good, we shall rejoice with joy unspeakable and full of glory....

We are homeward bound. He who loved us so much as to die for us hath builded for us a city. The New Jerusalem is our place of rest. There will be no sadness in the City of God. No wail of sorrow, no dirge of crushed hopes and buried affections, will evermore be heard. Soon the garments of heaviness will be changed for the wedding garment. Soon we shall witness the coronation of our King. Those whose lives have been hidden with Christ, those who on this earth have fought the good fight of faith, will shine forth with the Redeemer's glory in the kingdom of God.[7]

Privileges of the Redeemed—Heaven is a good place. I long to be there and behold my lovely Jesus, who gave His life for me, and be changed into His glorious image. Oh, for language to express the glory of the bright world to come! I thirst for the living streams that make glad the city of our God.

The Lord has given me a view of other worlds. Wings were given me, and an angel attended me from the city to a place that was bright and glorious. The grass of the place was living green, and the birds there warbled a sweet song. The inhabitants of the place were of all sizes; they were noble, majestic, and lovely. They bore the express image of Jesus, and their countenances beamed with holy joy, expressive of the freedom and happiness of the place. I asked one of them why they were so much more lovely than those on the earth. The reply was, "We have lived in strict obedience to the commandments of God, and have not fallen by disobedience, like those on the earth." ... I begged of my attending angel to let me remain in that place. I could not bear the thought of coming back to this dark world again. Then the angel said, "You must go back, and if you are faithful, you, with the 144,000, shall have the privilege of visiting all the worlds and viewing the handiwork of God."[8]

The United Family of Heaven and Earth—There the redeemed shall "know, even as also they are known." The loves and sympathies which God Himself has planted in the soul shall there find truest and sweetest exercise. The pure communion with holy beings, the harmonious social life with the blessed angels and with the faithful ones of all ages who have washed their robes and made them white in the blood of the Lamb, the sacred ties that bind together "the whole family in heaven and earth"—these help to constitute the happiness of the redeemed.[9]

The nations of the saved will know no other law than the law of heaven. All will be a happy, united family, clothed with the garments of praise and thanksgiving. Over the scene the morning stars will sing together, and the sons of God will shout for joy, while God and Christ will unite in proclaiming, "There shall be no more sin, neither shall there be any more death."[10]

From that scene of heavenly joy [the ascension of Christ] there comes back to us on earth the echo of Christ's own wonderful words, "I ascend unto My Father, and your Father; and to My God, and your God." The family of heaven and the family of earth are one. For us our Lord ascended, and for us He lives. "Wherefore He is able also to save them to the uttermost that come unto God by Him, seeing He ever liveth to make intercession for them."[11]

Though Delayed, the Promise Is Sure—Long have we waited for our Saviour's return. But none the less sure is the promise. Soon we shall be in our promised home. There Jesus will lead us beside the living stream flowing from the throne of God and will explain to us the dark providences through which on this earth He brought us in order to perfect our characters. There we shall behold with undimmed vision the beauties of Eden restored. Casting at the feet of the Redeemer the crowns that He has placed on our heads and touching our golden harps, we shall fill all heaven with praise to Him that sitteth on the throne.[12]

[545]

Let all that is beautiful in our earthly home remind us of the crystal river and green fields, the waving trees and the living fountains, the shining city and the white-robed singers, of our heavenly home—that world of beauty which no artist can picture, no mortal tongue describe. "Eye hath not seen, nor ear heard, neither have entered into the heart of man, the things which God hath prepared for them that love Him."[13]

[546]

---

[1] Patriarchs and Prophets, 62.

[2] Ibid., 342.

[3] The Signs of the Times, December 29, 1909.

[4] The Review and Herald, October 22, 1908.

[5] The Great Controversy, 647, 648.

[6] The Review and Herald, October 22, 1908.

[7] Testimonies For The Church 9, 286, 287.

[8] Early Writings, 39, 40.

[9]The Great Controversy, 677.

[10]Prophets and Kings, 732, 733.

[11]The Desire of Ages, 832.

[12]Testimonies For The Church 8, 245.

[13]The Review and Herald, July 11, 1882.

Chapter 87—Pen Pictures of the New Earth

Visions of Future Glory—With Jesus at our head we all descended from the city down to this earth, on a great and mighty mountain, which could not bear Jesus up, and it parted asunder, and there was a mighty plain. Then we looked up and saw the great city, with twelve foundations and twelve gates, three on each side, and an angel at each gate. We all cried out, "The city, the great city, it's coming, it's coming down from God out of heaven!" And it came and settled on the place where we stood. Then we began to look at the glorious things outside of the city. There I saw most glorious houses, that had the appearance of silver, supported by four pillars set with pearls most glorious to behold. These were to be inhabited by the saints. In each was a golden shelf. I saw many of the saints go into the houses, take off their glittering crowns and lay them on the shelf, then go out into the field by the houses to do something with the earth; not as we have to do with the earth here—no, no. A glorious light shone all about their heads, and they were continually shouting and offering praises to God.

I saw another field full of all kinds of flowers, and as I plucked them, I cried out, "They will never fade!" Next I saw a field of tall grass, most glorious to behold; it was living green and had a reflection of silver and gold as it waved proudly to the glory of King Jesus. Then we entered a field full of all kinds of beasts—the lion, the lamb, the leopard, and the wolf, all together in perfect union. We passed through the midst of them, and they followed on peaceably after.

[547]

Then we entered a wood, not like the dark woods we have here—no, no; but light, and all over glorious; the branches of the trees moved to and fro, and we all cried out, "We will dwell safely in the wilderness and sleep in the woods."[1]

Graduate Work in the Hereafter—Do you think we shall not learn anything there? We have not the slightest idea of what will then be opened before us. With Christ we shall walk beside the living

429

waters. He will unfold to us the beauty and glory of nature. He will reveal what He is to us and what we are to Him. Truth we cannot know now because of finite limitations, we shall know hereafter.[2]

The Christian family is to be a training school from which children are to graduate to a higher school in the mansions of God.[3]

Heaven is a school; its field of study, the universe; its teacher, the Infinite One. A branch of this school was established in Eden; and, the plan of redemption accomplished, education will again be taken up in the Eden school....

Between the school established in Eden at the beginning and the school of the hereafter there lies the whole compass of this world's history—the history of human transgression and suffering, of divine sacrifice, and of victory over death and sin.... Restored to His presence, man will again, as at the beginning, be taught of God: "My people shall know My name: ... they shall know in that day that I am He that doth speak: behold, it is I." ...

[548] There, when the veil that darkens our vision shall be removed and our eyes shall behold that world of beauty of which we now catch glimpses through the microscope; when we look on the glories of the heavens, now scanned afar through the telescope; when, the blight of sin removed, the whole earth shall appear "in the beauty of the Lord our God," what a field will be open to our study![4]

Heavenly Knowledge Will Be Progressive—All the treasures of the universe will be open to the study of God's redeemed. Unfettered by mortality, they wing their tireless flight to worlds afar—worlds that thrilled with sorrow at the spectacle of human woe and rang with songs of gladness at the tidings of a ransomed soul. With unutterable delight the children of earth enter into the joy and the wisdom of unfallen beings. They share the treasures of knowledge and understanding gained through the ages upon ages in contemplation of God's handiwork. With undimmed vision they gaze upon the glory of creation—suns and stars and systems, all in their appointed order circling the throne of Deity. Upon all things, from the least to the greatest, the Creator's name is written, and in all are the riches of His power displayed.

And the years of eternity, as they roll, will bring richer and still more glorious revelations of God and of Christ. As knowledge is progressive, so will love, reverence, and happiness increase. The more men learn of God, the greater will be their admiration of His character.[5]

Social Life—There we shall know even as also we are known. There the loves and sympathies that God has planted in the soul will find truest and sweetest exercise. The pure communion with holy beings, the harmonious social life with the blessed angels and with the faithful ones of all ages, the sacred fellowship that binds together "the whole family in heaven and earth"—all are among the experiences of the hereafter.[6] [549]

Occupations in the New Earth—In the earth made new the redeemed will engage in the occupations and pleasures that brought happiness to Adam and Eve in the beginning. The Eden life will be lived, the life in garden and field. "They shall build houses, and inhabit them; and they shall plant vineyards, and eat the fruit of them. They shall not build, and another inhabit; they shall not plant, and another eat: for as the days of a tree are the days of My people, and Mine elect shall long enjoy the work of their hands."[7]

There every power will be developed, every capability increased. The grandest enterprises will be carried forward, the loftiest aspirations will be reached, the highest ambitions realized. And still there will arise new heights to surmount, new wonders to admire, new truths to comprehend, fresh objects to call forth the powers of body and mind and soul.[8]

On the Verge of Fulfillment—We are living in a most solemn period of this earth's history. There is never time to sin; it is always perilous to continue in transgression, but in a special sense is this true at the present time. We are now upon the very borders of the eternal world and stand in a more solemn relation to time and to eternity than ever before. Now let every person search his own heart and plead for the bright beams of the Sun of Righteousness to expel all spiritual darkness and cleanse from defilement.[9]

To us who are standing on the very verge of their fulfillment, of what deep moment, what living interest, are these delineations of the things to come—events for which, since our first parents turned their steps from Eden, God's children have watched and waited, longed and prayed! [550]

Fellow pilgrim, we are still amid the shadows and turmoil of earthly activities, but soon our Saviour is to appear to bring deliverance and rest. Let us by faith behold the blessed hereafter, as pictured by the hand of God.[10]

An Appeal for Personal Preparation—I urge you to prepare for the coming of Christ in the clouds of heaven. Day by day cast the love of the world out of your hearts. Understand by experience what it means to have fellowship with Christ. Prepare for the judgment, that when Christ shall come to be admired in all them that believe, you may be among those who will meet Him in peace. In that day the redeemed will shine forth in the glory of the Father and the Son. The angels, touching their golden harps, will welcome the King and His trophies of victory—those who have been washed and made white in the blood of the Lamb. A song of triumph shall peal forth, filling all heaven. Christ has conquered. He enters the heavenly courts, accompanied by His redeemed ones, the witnesses that His mission of suffering and sacrifice has not been in vain.[11]

---

[1] Early Writings, 17, 18.

[2] Counsels to Teachers, Parents, and Students, 162.

[3] The Review and Herald, March 30, 1897.

[4] Education, 301-303.

[5] The Great Controversy, 677, 678.

[6] Education, 306.

[7] Prophets and Kings, 730, 731.

[8] Education, 307.

[9] Testimonies to Ministers and Gospel Workers, 147.

[10] Prophets and Kings, 731, 732.

[11] Testimonies For The Church 9, 285, 286.